D0002106

THE GROWTH
OF
PRESIDENTIAL
POWER

THE GROWTH
OF
PRESIDENTIAL
POWER

A DOCUMENTED HISTORY

★★★★★★★★★★★★★★★★★★★★★★★★★

by
WILLIAM M. GOLDSMITH
Brandeis University

with an Introductory Essay by
Arthur M. Schlesinger, jr.

Volume II
Decline and Resurgence

CHELSEA HOUSE
NEW YORK 1983

Project Editor: Deborah Weiss
Managing Editor: Roberta Morgan
Assistant Editor: Kathryn Hammell
Editorial Consultant: Leon Freidman

This edition is an edited reprint of the 1974 edition
by Chelsea House Publishers

Library of Congress Cataloging in Publication Data

Goldsmith, William M.
    The growth of Presidential power.
    Includes bibliographies.
    CONTENTS: v. 1. The formative years.—v. 2. Decline and resurgence.—
v. 3. Triumph and reappraisal.
    1. Executive power—United States—History.
2. Presidents—United States—History. I. Title.
JK511.G64   353.03'2   74-9623
ISBN 0-87754-125-6

THE GROWTH
OF
PRESIDENTIAL POWER

Volume I
The Formative Years
Volume II
Decline and Resurgence
Volume III
Triumph and Reappraisal

I. The Whig Attack on the Presidency

THE WHIG ATTACK
ON THE PRESIDENCY

The Ambivalence of the Concept
Of Party in American History

The fate and character of presidential power have always been closely linked with
the history and function of political parties. How, indeed, could it be otherwise?
George Washington was the first and also the last American President to be elected
without the supportive role of a political party. James Monroe received all but one
of the electoral votes cast in 1820, but he, of course, was strongly supported by the
Republican party. None of the other 36 Presidents was that fortunate; none could
afford to ignore this critical engine or political accomplishment. Many Presidents
have had to help build or rebuild their own political parties in order to be elected or
maintain themselves in office. The history of the growth of presidential power leads
inevitably to the study of the growth and development of American political parties.

Political parties played a significant role in both creating and stabilizing
political institutions and the political process in the early American republic. In the
beginning, however, there was a deep prejudice against the idea of *party*, which most
Americans used interchangeably with the pejorative term *faction*. Washington, in his
Farewell Address (see Volume I of this series), denounced the spirit of party in no
uncertain terms, and warned his countrymen to avoid its evil effects at all costs:

> It serves always to distract the public councils and enfeeble the public
> administration. It agitates the community with ill-founded jealousies and
> false alarms; kindles the animosity of one part against another; foments
> occasionally riot and insurrection. It opens the door to foreign influence
> and corruption, which find a facilitated access to the government itself
> through the channels of party passion. Thus the policy and will of one
> country are subjected to the policy and will of another.[1]

Washington was not alone in sounding the alarm at the prospect of the
appearance of party or faction in the American political firmament. In 1789
Thomas Jefferson wrote concerning party spirit:

> Such addiction is the last degradation of a free and moral agent. If I could
> not go to heaven but with a party, I would not go there at all.[2]

Even Andrew Jackson, who later became a great party leader, joined the hue and
cry against the dangers of parties as late as 1815, calling for the extermination of the
"monster called party spirit."[3]

Richard Hofstadter accurately expressed the general attitude of the early American political leaders when he wrote:

> [T]he creators of the first American party system on both sides, Federalists and Republicans, were men who looked upon parties as sores on the body politic.[4]

This widespread fear of and antipathy to the determination of policy through organized groups or interests were rooted in the writings of the seventeenth and eighteenth century political philosophers, Hobbes, Hume and Rousseau. They argued persuasively that the spirit of party undermined the unity and stability of the political community. They, too, used the terms *party* and *faction* almost interchangeably, and stressed the selfish and irresponsible nature of their impact upon the state. Hobbes denounced them as "contrary to the peace and safety of the people"; and Hume criticized the "founders of parties," arguing that "factions subvert government, render the laws impotent, and beget the fiercest animosities among men of the same nation, who ought to give mutual assistance and protection to each other."[5] Rousseau viewed the rise of "partial associations . . . at the expense of the great association (the state)"[6] a distinct obstacle to the achievement of the central force for community among men—the general will.

James Madison, certainly the most brilliant and most original thinker of the early American era, was obviously influenced by these political philosophers, and in Federalist No. 10, his most comprehensive analysis of the objectives of representative government under the new Constitution, he defined faction, indicated its sources and argued emphatically for its control if the political community was going to be protected from its destructive consequences. The definition of faction which Madison spelled out in Federalist No. 10 is useful as a starting point in understanding the early American resistance to political parties:

> By a faction I understand a number of citizens, whether amounting to a majority or a minority of the whole, who are united and actuated by some common impulse of passion, or of interest, adverse to the rights of other citizens, or to the permanent and aggregate interests of the community.[7]

In this definition, Madison clearly revealed the reasons for his misgivings about the existence of factions or parties in the American system; they frequently came into conflict with the rights of other citizens or the interests of the community. Since he believed that these conflicts were rooted in the nature of man, and that differences in opinion, in religion, and most significantly in the inequality of the distribution of property made conflict inevitable, it followed that it was in the interest of the political community either to remove the causes or to control the effects of such conflicts. Madison argued that the cost of curing the "mischiefs of faction" was too high to pay, for such surgery would either involve the destruction of liberty or "giving to every citizen the same opinions, the same passions, the same interests," obviously an impossible and undesirable fantasy.

The father of the Constitution thus concluded that the only realistic alternative was to control the effects of faction, if it could not be eliminated, and he proceeded to carefully outline a blueprint for a political structure designed to achieve some approximation of the common good by blunting the forces of passionate self-interest. "Pure democracy" was rejected as a solution because it "can admit of no cure for the mischiefs of faction," but a republic "promises the cure for which we are seeking."[8] Madison attempted to show how this representative form of government would refine the destructive and selfish thrust of parties, by sifting their demands through the elaborate procedures of representative assemblies. The negative or destructive forces of faction would be blunted or modified in the course of these events and hopefully reshaped in the interests of stability and justice in the society, and in the preservation of liberty.

Regardless of its brilliance as an analytical treatise on the virtues of representative government, Federalist No. 10 presented essentially a very cautious and almost cynical argument regarding the function of parties and governments. It assumed the worst about the general mass of citizens—that "men were not angels,"—and attempted to create safeguards to protect them from their own vices. As individuals they represented no problem to the state, but when they organized into parties or factions to pursue their collective interests, they constituted a danger to the community which the political process had to attempt to restrain.

Certainly this is one of the more important functions of government, because the unrestrained pursuit of narrow self-interest, particularly when it assumes the character of a majority, can be destructive and intolerant to the interests and rights of the minority. A very legitimate function of government is to prevent this from happening. But surely the function of government includes more than this protective role. The Declaration of Independence inspires us to the pursuit of happiness and the Constitution includes in its litany of objectives, the establishment of justice, the promotion of the general welfare and the blessings of liberty as among the legitimate ends of government. How are these goals to be implemented by the state if it is not possible for men to come together into groups or parties to pursue them within the framework of the political process? The state must provide for the common defense and insure domestic tranquility; it must also protect minority rights and prevent selfish interests from pursuing their ends at the expense of the general good. But in order to accomplish these necessary and essential objectives, and also to go beyond them to strive towards justice and the common welfare, citizens must find a way of working through the system, of initiating goals, communicating their intentions, promoting their consideration, drafting legislation and monitoring its implementation. How will they assume these burdens?

There is another eighteenth century concept of party which provides an answer to this question. It was advanced by the great British parliamentarian, Edmund Burke, who was as equally gifted in his analysis of political theory as he was on the floor of the House of Commons. Burke argued for the existence of political parties as necessary and even desirable elements of the political process. His broad experience convinced him that regardless of what the seventeenth and eighteenth century political philosophers had believed, representative government could not exist without the support and the creative energy of organized political parties. "Party divisions," he wrote, "whether on the whole operating for good or for evil, are things inseparable from free government."[9]

Understanding the essential role of parties in the functional process of politics in a free society, Burke viewed their existence as not only something one accepted because it was necessary, but also as a dynamic force which possessed the potential for serving the public interest. He recognized the fact that parties frequently degenerated into the disfunctional role claimed by the classic philosophers, but he felt that they were also the only hope of preventing such decay:

> When bad men combine, the good must associate; else they will fall, one by one, an unpitied sacrifice in a contemptible struggle.[10]

Burke defined party as "a body of men united for promoting by their joint endeavors the national interest upon some particular principle in which they are all agreed."[11] This definition avoided the negative connotations advanced by the political philosophers and Madison, and emphasized instead the creative and dynamic role such a party could play in society. It comprehended the necessity of men as political animals joining with one another to achieve worthwhile common objectives.

Burke followed Aristotle's reasoning that "the man who lives wholly detached from others must be either an *angel* or a *devil*."[12] He understood that the political community was not simply a defensive arrangement to protect its members from outside forces and from internal anarchy, but it was also a dynamic socializing force which could achieve civilizing goals if it could act in a responsible and effective manner. Burke argued that individual men desiring to assert their "general principles in terms of the public interest, would have no real difficulty in finding other men with whom they could align into an effective group or party."

> Men thinking freely will, in particular instances, think differently. But still as the greater part of the measures which arise in the course of public business are related to, or dependent on, some great, *leading, general principles in Government*, a man must be peculiarly unfortunate in the choice of his political company, if he does not agree with them at least nine times out of ten. If he does not concur in these general principles upon which the party is founded, and which necessarily draw on a concurrence in their application, he ought from the beginning to have chosen some other, more conformable to his opinions.[13]

Granted that there are some important distinctions between what Madison defined as faction and what the American experience has come to consider as the proper role of political parties,[14] this unwillingness at the beginning, this stubborn resistance to consider the Burkean, more enlightened view of the role of political parties has presented certain theoretical and practical problems which later experience has had great difficulty with, or even found impossible to overcome. It makes all the difference in the world whether one accepts the existence of political parties as a necessary evil rather than as a potentially dynamic engine for achieving the public interest. The very structure and process of government is significantly affected by this important distinction. On the one hand, in Madisonian terms, government is seen as an intricate arrangement or obstacle course to deflect and dilute the harmful effects of combinations in search of their own narrow interests; on the other hand, Burke's concept views government as a potentially powerful and constructive instrument for achieving the common good.

There were certainly elements of both of these points of view in the early development of American political parties; but, the intellectual resistance to accept the broader concept tended to shroud its existence in practice and to blunt its impact, eventually impairing its growth at later stages in the history of the republic. But all of this is somewhat premature, for the reality of the evolution of American political parties was always closer to the Burkean model in practice than it was in theory, and the means whereby the growth of parties took place in the early experience of the republic contributed immeasurably to the survival and development of this new political system.

Arthur Schlesinger, jr., has carefully assessed the overall development of the early parties, which he has termed vital "to the establishment of nationhood":

> As national associations, they began to overcome the provincial loyalties of the thirteen colonies. As agencies of representation, they gave salient interests a voice in national decisions and thus a stake in the national political order. As agencies of recruitment, they brought men into national service and leadership. As agencies of mobilization, they involved the plain people in the national process. As vehicles for ideas, they advanced the nation's political education, both defining a framework of national consensus and debating national issues within that framework. As instruments of government, they met the problems created by the constitutional separation of powers, providing coherence within the executive and legislative branches and bridges between them. As agencies of compromise, they developed means, both within and between the parties, for the containment and mediation of national differences. In 1794-1799 the parties legitimized the ideal of political opposition in America—itself a startling development for a world in which that idea had very little legitimacy (indeed, it has little enough for much of the world today). In 1800-1801 the parties showed they could solve the most tense of all problems in new nations, the transfer of power from a governing party to its opposition.

> What political scientists have agreed to call the first American party system was thus both the creation and the creator of national political order. As the first of its sort in the world, it was a remarkable invention.[15]

Yet Schlesinger also observed that the "system had marked limitations."[16] He was referring to the patrician ethos which characterized the early years of both parties, the Federalists and the Republicans, and which resulted in the control of national politics by an elite drawn primarily from the social and economic leadership of the country. In the rapidly shifting winds of what Gaetano Mosca called "social forces," this proved to be more of a liability to the Federalists than it did to Republicans, the latter being more politically responsible and more ideologically inclined to respond to the growing interest on the part of the ordinary citizens in the affairs of government. The Republicans came to power at the turn of the century precisely because they were more conscious of and responsive to the basic needs and priorities of the people than were the Federalists, and because they were ideologically more attuned to the rumbling "social forces" of change.

This same demand—to be politically sensitive and effectively responsive to the underlying pressures for change and leadership—has continued to haunt American political parties throughout the past two centuries, and today it is every bit as real a problem as it was in the age of Jefferson and Jackson. At the root of this dilemma is the carryover of a characteristic American ambivalence with respect to the Madisonian and Burkean concepts of the role of party, inherited from the previous century. It is an ambivalence which is reflected in the difference existing between theory and practice, between the self-assured cynical concept of politics and the more idealistic and creative point of view. It is also mirrored in the gap between myth and reality—the myth of a series of gloriously successful political achievements and the reality of many missed opportunities for greatness.

The history of the Whig attack on the presidency in the 1830s and 1840s will illuminate a few of the darker shadows of this dilemma. In the remaining pages of this introduction I will attempt to fulfill this promise.

The concept of ambivalence is a recurring theme in American history and politics. Robert McCloskey defines it as a "characteristic of the American mind to hold contradictory ideas simultaneously without bothering to resolve the potential conflict between them."[17] There is evidence that Americans continued to hold ambivalent concepts about the role of parties in the political process long after they had demonstrated their value in practice. But perhaps there was only an apparent ambivalence, only an apparent contradiction, because American political parties do perform both Madisonian and Burkean roles in reality. They are both factions actuated by some common interest, adverse to the rights of other citizens, or to the permanent and aggregate interests of the community, and at the same time, a body of men united for promoting by their joint endeavors the national interest upon some particular principle on which they are all agreed.

But although American political parties have performed both of these functions at one time or another, to vacillate constantly between them and not to consciously reconcile both concepts into a dual purpose, can very well produce half-hearted irresolution in either direction. Or it can produce diametrically contradictory behavior at different times, which can be equally confusing and frustrating. Perhaps the most serious criticism that can be levelled at American political parties is that they have labored under this ambivalent concept of their role and function for 185 years, and as a result they have failed to carry out their full responsibilities in a continually developing and changing society. It is a conceptual as well as a functional problem.

Richard Hofstadter has introduced a valuable distinction which may prove illuminating in our continuing analysis of this problem and of the important relationship between Presidents, power and political parties. In analyzing the role of an opposition party, Hofstadter distinguished between the concepts of *responsibility* and *effectiveness*. He explained

When we speak of an opposition being *responsible*, we mean that it contains within itself the potential of an actual alternative government—that is, its critique of existing policies is not simply a wild attempt to outbid the existing regime in promises, but a sober attempt to formulate alternative policies which it believes to be capable of execution within the existing historical and economic framework, and to offer its executors a competent alternative personnel that can actually govern.[18]

He then went on to define the quality which characterizes a successful opposition party:

When we speak of an opposition as being *effective*, we mean not merely that its programs are expected to be capable of execution, that its alternative policy is real, but that its capability of winning office is also real, that it has the institutional structure and the public force which makes it possible for us to expect that sooner or later it will in fact take office and bring to power an alternative personnel. If opposition, no matter how constitutional its methods and realistic its program, is too minuscule or too fragmented to offer this alternative, it hardly qualifies on the grounds of effectiveness. It might then be an education force, but it is not a political one.[19]

It is clear that in their confusion about their role and function in the political process, their identity crisis, so to speak, American political parties have pursued first one and then the other of these goals; the successful party must reconcile the contradictions, and achieve both simultaneously. A party which concentrates exclusively upon its responsibility towards the quality of its leadership and the principles it espouses and neglects its organizational structure and the problem of appealing to its potential constituencies, will obviously be in trouble come the next election. On the other hand, a party which virtually ignores the quality and preparation of its leaders for high office and compromises one principle after another in its quest to improve its effective vote-getting ability, is not going to be able to govern even it if is supported by an overwhelming majority of the people.

This confusion of role and function, the ambivalence reflected by parties with respect to their real identity, has frequently crippled their growth and usefulness in American history, and has led to even more disastrous results when they fail to produce either the quality of leadership and/or policies necessary to achieve the high aspirations and goals set by the Founding Fathers.

The Formative Period

The Whig party became a major force in American politics in the immediate post-Jackson period, and its development of a significant attack upon the presidency and various aspects of presidential power in particular, make it a fitting subject for the beginning of Volume II of *The Growth of Presidential Power*. This attack was not simply a rhetorical bombast or a theoretical analysis; it found its way into the "woof and warf" of everyday political life in this country, brought on a major constitutional crisis during the first Whig administration, and left its mark on the struggle for presidential power during the rest of the century.

Andrew Jackson had greatly influenced the practice of American politics for several years before he entered the White House, and certainly during his two dynamic terms in office. After he left Washington, politics took on a new complexion. The issues he raised, the policies he set in motion, the men who either supported or opposed him, even the style and definition of the office he occupied, dominated the political atmosphere for some time to come. It was not just his overpowering personality, his charisma, which he stamped indelibly upon the major questions he tackled, the legislation he initiated or the measures he vetoed. Jackson was also a symbolic figure who heralded a new era in American politics, where almost every aspect of the system was in the process of change. It was, of course, not just Jackson who was responsible for this revolution. "Old Hickory" rode the crest of the waves of historical forces already set in motion during the age in which he came to power, and these forces influenced him as much as he gave them his unique *imprimatur*.

This Jacksonian revolution was described in greater detail in Volume I of *The Growth of Presidential Power* and need only be mentioned briefly here to set the stage for the discussion of the rise of the Whig party and its influence on the presidency. The Whigs were fundamentally the counterrevolutionary progeny of the age of Jackson. The party generated its major issues, its outstanding leaders and even its constituency primarily in reaction to Jacksonianism. At the time of Jackson's election in 1828 the old, or what recent students of political parties have begun to call the "first party system," had already disappeared, and the sentiments which supported it and the leaders who gave it character were either dead or dying.

The old parties had contributed substantially to their own downfall, because they had tended to encourage forces in the society which weakened the sense of deference upon which the first party system, or at least its leadership, had been based. The growth and diversity of the population contributed significantly to this development, fostering tension in the social structure which initially stimulated competition, but later undermined the elitist leadership which dominated both the old Federalist and Jeffersonian Republican parties. The parties had thrived in the early atmosphere of struggle over principles, but their leaders were incapable of catering to these new groups and their narrower interests. As one student of the early political parties has put it:

> [T]he first party system withered away because most of its builders did not regard themselves as professional party politicians. Such leaders as Washington, Jefferson and Hamilton had seen themselves as disinterested statesmen, not as political brokers among competing interests or as election managers, even when necessity forced them to behave as though they were. Confidence in their rectitude and the wisdom of the policies made Federalists insensitive and indifferent to the political dangers their rhetoric entailed. In a social order where habits of deference still persisted,

a statesman was accustomed to doing what he thought right regardless of personal risk, whereas a professional politician typically calculates risks and maneuvers accordingly within the mainstream of popular currents.[20]

Jefferson succeeded in calming the anxieties of the Federalists concerned that the advent of Republicanism would lead to the destruction of the foundations of property and the social order; but gradually the force of Federalism waned as its leaders proved to be incapable of sustaining their early support, much of which was based substantially upon fear and ignorance. The remaining Federalists were virtually isolated on a regional basis in New England and it soon became apparent that they could not hope to compete with the Republicans on a national basis.

[T]he failure of the Federalists to extend, or even maintain, the bases of support they held in 1800 brought about a condition of extreme party imbalance. At this point the Federalists confronted the alternatives of rebelling against the system or withdrawing from it. After experiencing failure with the first alternative, they adopted the second in most states.[21]

The Federalists passed the point of being an active competitive party sometime during the second term of the Madison administration, and the so-called "Era of Good Feeling" was characterized by a basically one-party system, with local factions and cliques vying for power. Up until 1824 the Republican caucus named the presidential slate which was duly elected, but the forces of a rapidly expanding population, much of it moving west, was increasingly critical of what it considered elitist politics. Thus, the 1824 caucus candidate (William H. Crawford) was summarily rejected by the voters in a four-cornered race which was ultimately decided in the House of Representatives.

Jackson, who had the largest number of popular votes in this election, charged that the voting results in the House had been determined by a deal between two of his opponents—both of whom had received less votes than he—and was consummated by the election of John Quincy Adams as President and his subsequent appointment of Henry Clay, the other opponent in question, as secretary of state. Jackson vowed to get even with the two alleged architects of the "deal," and left to organize his supporters to sweep the election of 1828. This is covered in much greater detail in Volume I of this series.

The organization which supported Jackson in 1828 could not be called a political party, because at that time it was an *ad hoc* group, put together specifically for the purpose of this national election. Jackson was opposed by Adams, who gathered what votes he could from his regional supporters in New England and the more conservative elements of the Republican and Federalist parties. There was little support for Jackson in the New England states in 1828 and Adams triumphed by three to one or better in four of those six states. On the other hand, in the South where Jackson was the sectional candidate there was little or no Adams support. In the contest in the middle states, however, the vote was extremely close (except in Pennsylvania), and the leading scholar of this period, Richard P. McCormick, indicated that the faction which chose sides and supported either Jackson or Adams tended to be more durable alignments, not based simply upon the sectional origin of the candidate, but rather upon economic and/or social motives of a more pervasive and lasting duration. The contest in these states appeared to take on the character of a two-party system.

The support Jackson received in the West, however, except for Clay's influence in Kentucky, really accounted for the margin of his substantial victory. These were the new states which had experienced marked population growth, and Jackson's candidacy struck a responsive chord in their increasing frustrations with the old system and its hierarchy of values and leadership. Not only was "Old Hickory" one of their own—a man of the frontier—but he emphasized and supported policies which seemed to respond to their interests. The struggle over the Bank and the ready availability of credit in particular reflected their concerns.

The rising opposition to Jackson and his policies slowly took form among the groups and individuals which had the most to lose from the direction in which "Old Hickory" and his followers were moving. They were composed, first of all, of those who were directly opposed to his policies and whose interests were damaged by his rise to power. This would include his old political opponents like Adams and Clay and their close supporters, as well as champions of the Bank like Nicholas Biddle and Daniel Webster (who received an annual retainer for legal services to the Bank and also borrowed extensively from it).

Clustered around these stalwart opponents were others affected by Jackson's war on the Bank, his stand against federal government support for national improvements, those who sought high tariff protection or no tariff at all, and those who opposed his efforts (unsuccessful) to annex Texas (a slave area) to the growing boundaries of the republic. They called themselves National Republicans, claiming to represent the real traditions of the Jeffersonian Republican party.

Friends of Henry Clay in New York City set the plans for the 1832 campaign in motion, and a demand for a national convention was issued at a Republican state convention in Kentucky in December 1830. The convention met in Baltimore on the second Monday of December, 1831, and unanimously nominated Clay and John Sergeant of Pennsylvania as their national ticket. The official convention address indicated that the National Republicans had been acting "together in political affairs for some years past," and had gathered at a national convention because "a careful and deliberate survey of the political condition of the country," and the conduct of the Jackson administration indicated that the "public good imperiously" required "a change."[22] The address charged that the President had failed to keep his pledge to suppress party strife and make removals only for reasons of incapacity and corruption. He had also conducted foreign affairs in a manner "derogatory to the honor of the country, and the dignity of the Government."[23]

Moreover, the document charged that the Jackson administration had been ambiguous with regard to internal improvements, hostile to the Bank of the United States, and had been characterized by its flagrant public subsidies to the press and its conduct of a venal spoils system. Even his cabinet had collapsed because of its internal bickering and lack of recognizable standards of morality. The final outrage was Jackson's decision to seek a second term in violation of his earlier pledge not to do so.

As an alternative, the National Republicans offered Henry Clay and his program for national development, which he called the American System. It incorporated a policy of internal developments (roads, canals, etc.), a reasonably high protective tariff to encourage the growth of domestic industry and support for the Bank of the United States. The National Republicans called upon the voters to defeat the Jackson administration which "had been justly discredited in public opinion," and assured its potential supporters that "nothing is wanted but zeal, activity and concert, to ensure success."[24]

Roy Nichols' description of the National Republican campaign captures the essence of its hopeless efforts:

> Clay and his associates did their best. They had learned some of the arts of organization. There was a flood of literature, political pamphlets, and press notices. There was a Clay campaign biography extolling his talents and achievements. There were Clay clubs, Clay balls, Clay barbecues, and Clay banquets with their unending toasts. Clay had, likewise, a campaign manager in the person of Josiah S. Johnston, a fellow Senator from Louisiana. Clay's campaign literature charged Jackson with being a dictator, a violator of pledges, and an extravagant spender of government money. He had corrupted the civil service, he was attacking the economy by his veto of the Bank bill. He had mishandled foreign affairs and lied about his acts. He had "encouraged a set of bullies to infest the halls of Congress and overawe members in discharge of their legislative duties," committing disgraceful assaults "with clubs and pistols" on members. He was even putting the Supreme Court to defiance.[25]

These "heroic" efforts never seriously threatened Jackson and Van Buren's well-oiled machine, and "Old Hickory" romped to an easy victory, carrying 16 out of 24 states. A third party, the Anti-Masons, also emerged during this period, but although they showed considerable strength in Massachusetts, New York and Pennsylvania, they carried only one state, Vermont. Jackson used the Bank veto message very skillfully as a campaign document, and although there was some antipathy to his new running mate, Martin Van Buren, in the South, he did much better in all the other sections than he had in 1828.

After the election of 1832 anti-Jackson activity increased in the Senate over the issue of the withdrawal of the government's funds from the Bank of the United States and the subsequent cashiering of Secretary of the Treasury William C. Duane. Jackson was finally censured by a Senate resolution, an unprecedented action which was spear-headed by Calhoun, Clay and Webster joining together to drive the motion through the upper house (see Volume I of this series). The omens for a better showing in 1836 on the part of the anti-Jackson coalition, however, were clear to all. First, Andrew Jackson would not be running again, and the probable candidate would be Martin Van Buren, who possessed none of Jackson's charismatic power, to say nothing of his impressive military and popular-hero credentials. Van Buren was also a northerner and a crafty politician at that, and there were clear indications, even in the election of 1832 when anti-Van Buren sentiment was recognizable in the South, that the "little Magician" would not be the automatic recipient of all Jackson's personal support.

Jackson's policies had not generated popular support only; they had also created significant enemies, and individuals of divergent views began to coalesce in opposition to the party and candidacy of his successor. There was little or no support for retaining the label of National Republicanism, for Clay and his followers had not really succeeded in convincing enough voters that they were the true descendents of Thomas Jefferson and the Republican tradition. A new name and a more vigorous public image was necessary. The opposition groups began calling themselves "Whigs" as early as the nullification crisis in South Carolina, and by 1836 the name had been adopted by all groups who banded together in the anti-Jackson-Van Buren coalition. The historical roots of the English Whigs, who stood for legislative opposition to the Crown, were clearly in their minds when they adopted this new party identity, for it was essentially a legislative challenge to executive power which brought the divergent elements of the American Whigs together.

The new coalition continued to claim the mantle of Jeffersonian Republican virtue, but the leaders sought and gained new recruits on a much broader ideological basis. After the election of William Seward as governor of New York on the Anti-Mason party ticket, Seward and his political advisor, Albany editor, Thurlow Weed, went over to the Whig party, lock, stock and barrel and eventually succeeded in bringing most of the Anti-Masons with them. A second large block of supporters were the nullifiers from South Carolina and elsewhere, who were embittered by Jackson's decisive action in that crisis (see Volume I of this series) and could no longer support the party of his successor.

In many ways it was a strange coalition, and some wondered how such a heterogeneous mixture could find a comfortable common denominator. Thurlow Weed mulled over this question when it was raised by one of his western lieutenants, Millard T. Fillmore:

> Into what crucible can we throw this heterogeneous mass of old national republicans, and revolting Jackson men; Masons and anti-Masons; Abolitionists and pro-slavery men; Bank men and anti-Bank men with all the lesser fragments that have been, from time to time, thrown off from the great political wheel in its violent revolutions, so as to melt them down into one mass of pure Whigs of undoubted good mettle?[26]

But could they be melted down into "one mass of pure Whigs of undoubted mettle?" Some had joined the coalition only temporarily, and on their own terms, and would leave it just as quickly as they had arrived, once they perceived that those terms would be compromised. John C. Calhoun was this kind of temporary Whig; he would not even allow himself to be called by that name. His biographer uses the term "united front" to better approximate the relationship which the coalition represented; a Leninist concept, the term defines a temporary relationship between parties of different ideological commitment, both of which find it to be in their interest to unite temporarily to work for the achievement of a common goal.[27]

> [O]n May 6, speaking against the reception of Jackson's Protest, he [Calhoun] took note of Clay's earlier use of the term Whig and dissociated himself from it. He agreed with the Senator from Kentucky that the revival of the party names of the Revolution was a happy indication "of a return to those principles that lie at the foundation of liberty," but as for himself, he wished "no change of party designations." "I am content," he

explained, "with that which designates those with whom I act. It is, I admit, not very popular, but is at least an honest and patriotic name. It is synonymous with resistance to usurpation—usurpation, come from what quarter and under what shape it may; whether it be from this Government on the rights of the States, or the Executive on the Legislative department." He was, in short, a Nullifier and intended to remain so.[28]

Another group of recruits within the Whig coalition who clung tenaciously to their independent identity were the states' rights men like John Tyler of Virginia. His son, editor of his letters and papers, argues very bitterly that the Whig party was not simply National Republicanism under a new name, but associates its genesis with the old revolutionary-Jeffersonian states' rights tradition:

> The National Republican party did indeed lose its identity, but instead of coalescing with the Federal Democrats, they joined with the State-rights men,—the lesser wing of the old Jackson party,—and together formed a *new* party, called the "Whigs."
>
> The National Republicans afterwards set up an exclusive title to the term "Whig," and reputable writers[29] have been betrayed into using the terms "Whig" and "National Republican" as synonymous; but nothing could be further from historical accuracy. The National Republican party fought for high tariff, internal improvements, and national bank; but with the rise of the Whig Party in 1834, in which year the name was first used, the admission went forth that all these questions had become "obsolete." Indeed, there was everything in the past to recommend the name "Whig" to the State-rights men. The old Jeffersonians had, in the stirring times of 1798-9, often applied the name to themselves in contradistinction to the Tories, who composed, in part, the Federal party.[30]

In fact, Tyler points out that Jefferson used the term as early as 1823, when in a letter to Lafayette he identified the position of Adams as "Toryism," as compared with the states' rights candidate, Crawford, whom he classified as a "Whig." It is an interesting passage by Jefferson and I shall quote it in full to underscore the truism (to paraphrase General MacArthur) that "Idealogues never die; they simply pass away."

> Who is to be the next President is the topic here of every conversation. My opinion on that subject is what I expressed to you in my last letter. The question will be ultimately reduced to the northernmost candidate (Adams) and southernmost (Crawford). The former will get every Federal vote in the Union, and many Republicans; the latter, all those denominated of the *Old School*; for you are not to believe that these two parties are amalgamated,—that the lion and the lamb are lying down together. . . . On the eclipse of Federalism with us, although not its extinction, its leaders got up the Missouri question, under the false front of lessening the measure of slavery, but with the real view of producing a geographical division of parties, which might ensure them the next president.

The line of division now is the preservation of State-rights as reserved in the Constitution, or by strained constructions of that instrument to merge all into a consolidated government. The *Tories* are for strengthening the executive and general government. The *Whigs* cherish the representative branch and the rights reserved by the States as the bulwark against consolidation, which must immediately generate monarchy. And although this division excites as yet no warmth, yet it exists, is well understood, and will be a principle of voting at the ensuing election with the reflecting men of both parties.[31]

This is a brilliant, if not a typical example of the ideological approach to history. In this passage, Jefferson is imposing his ideology upon a matrix of events which do not quite yield to these views. The ideology is based upon a philosophical concept of the historical forces in conflict with one another, and not upon the realities of that moment in history. This is not to say that this point of view did not contain any truth. For it did, and southerners like Calhoun and Tyler would demonstrate its validity in the 1830s. But it misses so much that it does not fit into the ideological perspective from which Jefferson viewed all events, and it tells us little useful information about what was going on at that moment in history.

For example, neither Adams nor Crawford was the more significant candidate in 1824, but rather it was Andrew Jackson who received the greatest number of popular votes, but failed to be elected. Jackson was the charismatic figure, the magnetic force who represented the rising tide of democracy in the country at that time, and this had little to do with states' rights or Federalism.[32] As a matter of fact, the traditional-historical forces of conservatism, which had in Jefferson's period concentrated in the Federalist party and tended to support the concentration of power in the Executive at the expense of the legislature, and the national government at the expense of the states, were about to make a significant historical about-face. Based upon the realities of power, they were to favor the legislature against the Executive, and the states against the national government. But Jefferson's ideological view of history and the alignment of political forces which he thought he saw prevented him from sensing these developments.

The role of the idealogue in politics is a particularly frustrating and agonizing one, because he is continually caught between the realities of power and his personal values derived from the perspective of historical principle (as he sees it). Politics by definition requires the continuous adjustment of different men's views and interests. But the last thing in the world that the idealogue wants to do is to compromise his principles based upon his perspective of history. Jefferson was constantly faced with this dilemma, and although he played the game of politics superbly and functioned as one of the most successful executive and administrative leaders ever to serve in the White House, he must have agonized terribly every time he was forced to suppress his ideological principles to decide an issue on the basis of the realities of power, as he was certainly forced to do in the purchase of Louisiana and the embargo crisis, to name just two instances.

In contrast, an essentially political man like Henry Clay was able to adapt himself very easily to such conflicts, because politics was so much a part of his nature that he never really stood above it or agonized about its necessary compromises. In fact, Clay adjusted himself so quickly and easily to the framework of compromise that it was frequently impossible to determine if he really did have any principles or objectives important enough to him that he could not compromise them.

Thomas Jefferson and John Caldwell Calhoun, on the other hand, were constantly caught up in this quandry. For Calhoun it might well have been more difficult than it was for Jefferson, because while his ideological fires burned just as intensely as the Virginian's, his political skills and fortunes were nowhere near as bright. This was partially because of the very different periods in which both men operated as leaders. Jefferson, happily, came to his maturity during a period when his views were gaining ascendancy in the nation; the reverse was true for Calhoun. This lonely, driven and brilliant man was fighting a losing battle most of his life and he must have known this, for it increased his bitterness while at the same time invigorated his tenacity in the struggle.

Calhoun was ultimately forced to compromise at least temporarily, and while such compromises were not happy experiences for him, they were always entered into with a larger objective in mind. He saw the Whig coalition in its early phase as a necessary alliance against the hated enemies, Jackson, and the concentration of national power, and he was willing to bed down with the likes of Clay and Webster to obtain what a medieval theologian would characterize as "proximate ends." But he, and probably they, too, knew there would come a breaking point when he would once again be in opposition, because his goals were not theirs, and in the final analysis, were fixed and not to be compromised even if they were unattainable.

The idealogue uses politics and attempts to exploit its resources for his own purposes, and as a result he abuses its institutions (like parties) and suffers the indignities of compromise only in the light of his higher purposes. The political man, on the other hand, plays the game of politics because it is in his blood, and it provides him with the only sustenance—power—capable of making life worth living. The ideal President and even the prospective candidate for President must incorporate characteristics of both; but rarely are they found in the most desirable proportions. The emphasis is either too ideological, as in Calhoun's case, where his contempt for politics frequently rendered his position absurd; or too pragmatically political, as in the case of Clay, where almost all issues and values were reduced to the negotiable currency of political compromise.

John Tyler and most of his states' rights colleagues were idealogues of a sort and their concept of the Whig party (or coalition) was one in which they too entertained their own private objectives. Even their definition of the origin and basis of the party's objectives was colored by their own ideological perspective, tinged with the self-serving asset of historical hindsight:

> The Whig Party, in its origins, was, therefore, properly a State-rights party,—formed out of a hotchpot of opposition. There were first the old National Republicans, at first barely concealing their nakedness under a few fig-leaves, and then lustily donning the straight jacket of strict construction only to throw it aside at a more distant day to shame the daylight with their harlot dress of many colors. Next, there were the nullifiers, opposed to Jackson since the election of 1832; then the Tyler class of

State-rights men, who condemned nullification, but saw too clearly the clovenfoot in the proclamation of Andrew Jackson; then the Democrats, who considered the removal of the deposits unconstitutional procedure, and fell off from the administration in 1834; and finally we notice the anti-Mason zealots, unscrupulous, vindictive, and unbending, but now, with a wry face, dealing in the arts of compromise, and affecting a reverential regard for the Constitution.[33]

These varying descriptions of the Whig party begin to take on something of the old parable of the three blind men and the elephant; each defined the whole on the basis of his special (and limited) perspective. In reality, the Whigs were a political coalition of men and groups brought together on the basis of their common opposition to Andrew Jackson and to some or all of his policies—seeking political power for different and even conflicting objectives. Most, or should I say all, parties are based upon reasonably similar circumstances involving some compromises, but the test of their historical significance and in fact of their durability, is whether their common purposes remain preeminently stronger than their real and potential differences.

But irrespective of their past and potentially future differences, the various groups began to work together with increasing effectiveness in practical politics, on the floor of Congress, and in local and state elections. Not only did they censure the President for his transfer of the funds and the dismissal of Secretary of the Treasury Duane, but the Senate failed to confirm a number of Jackson's nominations for appointment (including four governors of the Bank up for reappointment) and they even outgeneraled the administration forces by defeating Jackson's candidate (James Polk) for Speaker of the House. The Whigs suffered some electoral defeats in the middle states in the 1834 elections and in the South in 1835, but they won impressive victories in Indiana, Illinois and Louisiana where they elected Whig governors, and in Ohio where they won command of the legislature.

Every historian of the era stresses the significance of the Whig's opposition to "executive usurpation" as the common bond which held such dissonant groups together. One biographer of Clay has written:

It covered in a single phrase Jackson's proscription of office-holders, his defiance of the Supreme Court, his repeated vetoes, his assertion of the "unit principle" of the Cabinet, his dismissal of Duane, his removal of the deposits, his protest to Congress, his advancement of Van Buren, his reliance on the Kitchen Cabinet. It centered the attack on Jackson's whole theory and practice of personal leadership and authority. The influence of the Executive in the government having been suddenly and, perhaps, for the period, unduly expanded, the inevitable reaction, the reassertion of influence by the Legislature, was under way. It was therefore for the exploitation of that reaction that the Whig Party drew together.[34]

Calhoun, Clay and Webster first opened up the attack on Jackson's concept of presidential power when confronted with his veto of the Bank Bill, and again later during the floor debate on the censure motion in the winter of 1833-34. All three were outraged at Jackson's expanding definition of his presidential role as "immediate representative of the people." Calhoun scolded: "What effrontery! What boldness of assertion!"[35] He went on to warn that Jackson's objective was to wage war against the Senate and to enlist the people in such a struggle. Clay, if anything, was even more alarmed.

> We are in the midst of a revolution, but rapidly tending toward a total change of the pure republican character of the government, and to the concentration of all power in the hands of one man. The powers of Congress are paralyzed, except when exerted in conformity with his will, by frequent and extraordinary exercise of the executive veto, not anticipated by the founders of our Constitution, and not practiced by any predecessors of the present chief magistrate.[36]

Webster, in his most eloquent and incisive manner, sounded the note of "executive usurpation" in a different key:

> [T]he contest for ages has been to rescue liberty from the grasp of executive power. . . . Throughout all this history of the contest for liberty, executive power has been regarded as a lion which must be caged. . . . The President carries on the government; all the rest are but sub-contractors. Sir, whatever *name* we give him we have but one executive officer. A Briareus sits in the center of our system, and with his hundred hands, touches everything, moves everything, controls everything. I ask, Sir, is this republicanism? Is this legal responsibility?[37]

But these were, after all, just words. The real character of the Whig attack on presidential power would come only when the opposition party was in a position to do something about that power. For the time being, Jackson continued to overwhelm the Whigs, and even Van Buren overcame them. They would have to await further political and economic developments before they could truly test their mettle and their "theory" of executive subservience to the legislature in the White House itself. But that opportunity did not come in 1836.

The Whigs lost the election of 1836 simply because they were not prepared to win a national election. They could not settle upon a single candidate for either the presidency or the vice presidency; consequently they ran three candidates for President and as many for Vice President. The voters in various states selected different tandems of Whig candidates, and under these conditions it was difficult to amass any maximum strength behind any particular ticket. The strategy which finally emerged was to try to duplicate the election of 1824, when the divided strength of the field of candidates forced the election into the House.

Clay showed no interest in offering himself up as a sacrificial lamb once again, and left the field wide-open for other ambitious men. General William Henry Harrison, the old Indian fighter of the battle of Tippecanoe, and a disgruntled civil servant who had been removed from his diplomatic mission to Colombia by Jackson, was proposed initially by a newspaper in Pennsylvania, and later endorsed by the Whig convention in that state; he was subsequently nominated by state conventions in Ohio and New York. In Massachusetts a convention named Daniel Webster and Frances Granger, Harrison's vice presidential running mate on the

New York ballot, after negotiations, broke down for a Webster-Harrison ticket. In Tennessee, the anti-Jacksonites who joined the Whig party nominated Senator Hugh L. White.

Failing to come to any agreement on a single one of these candidates, the Whigs finally developed the strategy (a desperate afterthought) of attempting to beat Van Buren with all three candidates, by accumulating enough votes to throw the election into the House of Representatives. This was more of a rationalization for failure to agree than a winning strategy to obtain the presidency, however; the Whigs went down to defeat, although their combined candidates polled only 30,000 fewer popular votes than Van Buren. Massachusetts gave its votes to its senior senator, while New Jersey, Delaware, Kentucky, Ohio and Indiana voted for Harrison and Granger. White, running with John Tyler of Virginia, won in Tennessee and Georgia, and Harrison and Tyler took Maryland. South Carolina cast its votes for Willie P. Magnum of North Carolina and John Tyler for Vice President. This irregular voting pattern reflects the chaotic character of the campaign. It appears that the Whigs were not beaten by Martin Van Buren in 1836, but rather by themselves.

The 1836 campaign demonstrated several basic political truisms. The multiplicity of candidates led to a division of resources and planning which is fatal in a presidential campaign. The various Whig candidates had strong regional support, but the lack of unified leadership and central campaign direction and organization was extremely costly. There was no national convention and no real national organization, and under these circumstances it is no wonder that the Whigs failed to attract their maximum potential support.

The Democrats, on the other hand, capitalized on all of these deficiencies and organized their campaign as effectively as the Whigs proved ineffective. Since Van Buren had Jackson's unequivocal approval, he was the acknowledged candidate; the Democrats met in convention in Baltimore to give him their unanimous support and to name a vice presidential candidate—the popular Colonel Richard Mentor Johnson, who believed he slew Tecumseh in the War of 1812. Johnson provided strength to the ticket in the West, but he was no asset in the South where he lost votes because he lived with a mulatto woman and added to his woes by seeking to introduce the daughters of this union into proper society.

But Van Buren and the Democratic organization plied their political trade effectively, unified the party and held enough of the Jackson supporters in line to secure a marginal victory. They pleaded with those who had left the party to return and "let bygones be bygones." They wanted the recent differences to be considered "a misunderstanding rather than a schism," pleaded with the defectors to "promote a spirit of union among ourselves, without which democracy can never triumph."[38]

In Search of Victory

Looking ahead to the presidential election of 1840, the problem that the Whigs faced was to put their divided house in order and to demonstrate their ability to respond dynamically to the developing social forces appearing on the American landscape. Something very significant was happening to American life and politics during this Jacksonian period, and the future belonged to the political party which could identify these social forces at work and direct them towards their own national interests and goals. This was a very different function from that performed by the older political parties and leaders, and soon it would be made clear by the new political professionals that a new party image and a new type of candidate were essential ingredients for the "new politics" of the nineteenth century.

The social forces which began to emerge during the Jackson campaign in 1828 had by this time developed into a major groundswell in the American political environment. They were determined by the growth in population, the regional shifts in its concentration, and the demands these new centers of population made upon the political institutions of the period. The center of gravity of the country was moving west, and for the next 50 years or more, the geographical frontier, as Frederick Jackson Turner has demonstrated, was to be a decisive factor in shaping American political institutions, as well as influencing other aspects of our social and cultural development. At that particular moment in history, the frontier social forces were raising political and economic demands with which any serious political party wishing to capture national power would have to deal. There was also the question of frontier or western leadership, for part of the magic formula of the successful 1828 campaign was the symbolic as well as the real leadership of Andrew Jackson. The Whigs began to realize that they could not expect to make inroads among Democratic supporters in the West until they too responded to these very real social and political pressures.

Jackson had responded to the frontier demand for a greater role in the affairs of government by attacking the traditional elites (with the exception of Jefferson who was untouchable) and by introducing his "theory" of rotation in office. He was also sympathetic to their demand for expanded and more flexible credit resources, and he attempted to solve this problem by attacking the Bank of the United States and the centralized control of banking credit it explicitly or implicitly maintained, and destroying the Bank by transferring the government's deposits to so-called state or private banks. Emboldened by these moves, the state banks quickly reacted by making expanded credit available to western development, particularly entrepreneurial development. This would have serious consequences in the future.

One of the Whig party's highest priorities was to weaken the Democratic party's grip on these frontier issues in order to strengthen its own position at the ballot box. The growing interest and active participation in national politics was phenomenal during this period. During the pre-Jackson "Age of Deference," there was far greater interest in local politics than in presidential elections. William Nisbet

Chambers has collated voting data collected by Pole, McCormick and Burnham, which indicates that in elections in five selected states (Massachusetts, New Hampshire, Pennsylvania, Virginia and North Carolina) the vote for governor far exceeded the vote for presidential electors from 1789 to 1839 in every one of the five states except Pennsylvania. In 1840 this was reversed for the first time in 50 years.[39] Furthermore the overall turnout was increasing at an extraordinary rate. I have already indicated in Volume I that there was a greater than 300 percent increase in the number of voters participating in the 1828 election than had voted in 1824, and the level of voter participation continued to climb phenomenally with every election during the next decade. In 1824, 26.9 percent of all eligible white males voted in the presidential election; in 1828, 57.6 percent and in 1840 a fantastic 80.2 percent, or just over four-fifths of the total white male population of the country cast their votes for President.[40]

To grasp the full impact of these figures one should examine them with comparable voting behavior in Britain in the aftermath of the much-heralded "revolutionary" Reform Bill of 1832. After the enactment of this piece of voting reform legislation, which was sponsored by the British Whigs, approximately 650,000 persons took part in Parliamentary elections in Britain out of a total population of 16,000,000; in the United States, 1,153,350 voters went to the polls in 1828 in a population of approximately 12,000,000, while in 1840, 2,409,474 out of a total population of approximately 17 million were counted. The Reform Bill of 1832 increased the British voting population from approximately 10 to 14 percent of the eligible voters, while during the same period of time the changes that were taking place in America increased the voting population here from approximately a quarter of the eligible voters in 1824 to four-fifths in 1840.[41] The practical elimination of almost all forms of voting restrictions in the various states enhanced this development, but in no way accounted for the excitement and interest in politics among the common people during this period.

Such a significant and striking development is bound to require a multiple-cause explanation, several of which have already been mentioned. The growth in population and the westward movement were related developments, some immigrants immediately moving West after barely stopping to catch their breath on the eastern seaboard and other older northeastern settlers moving West to better provide for growing families. Expectations were high among all elements of the society—expectations of growth, expansion, personal gain and individual development. These demographic changes led very logically to increased political interest and activity in national affairs because the men and women who made up the westward migration rapidly developed needs and attitudes which required representation at the national level of government.

They required expanded credit for purchasing land as well as equipment for developing farms and businesses; they were concerned about better transportation, protection from the Indians and possible hostile foreigners (particularly Mexicans and Canadians); they wanted a strong national government which would recognize their existence, develop policies supportive of their newly established circumstances, and recognize their recently acquired status. They wanted leaders and representatives who understood their problems and responded to their growing needs.

The growing competition between the emerging parties also attracted large numbers of new voters to the polls. There was little point in voting when there were no real choices available and when the critical decisions were all unashamedly made at the Washington level by an elite group of national leaders. Following the rejection of the oligarchical procedure of the congressional caucus by the voters in 1824 (already described in Volume I), concern for politics, and particularly presidential politics, began to revive, and the impact of this renewed interest was felt in both the legislative and executive branches of the government. In fact it was not a distinctly new phenomenon, since competition in the early history of the republic had also called forth large numbers of voters in an electorate admittedly much smaller and more constricted by some forms of eligibility. But where there were no serious forms of voting restrictions and competition was very much alive, voter turnout was high:

> In Massachusetts, Maine, New Hampshire and Vermont, where there were no substantial restrictions on the suffrage, from three-fifths to as many as four-fifths of the adult white males might go to the polls. Indeed, the peaks of voter participation in those states before 1815 were to be exceeded slightly, if at all, after 1828. In every state, however, as party competition declined and Federalists retired, voter participation fell, and in the early 1820's only about a quarter of those eligible to vote were stimulated to cast their ballots.[42]

At the same time that large numbers of Americans were moving West, there were increasing numbers who were concentrating in cities essentially along the eastern seaboard, but also in other parts of the country, and a rising political party would also have to be concerned with their problems. The hard core of the earlier National Republicans, and later Whig coalition, was essentially commercially oriented, and represented at rock bottom, wealthy plantation owners in the South who were tied in with banking and commercial interests in the North, and bankers, industrialists, shipowners, and other business interests in the northeast who tended to be more conservative in their politics and were alarmed by Jackson's appeal to agrarian radicalism. They were most likely centered in

> the older, well established, commercially active, more prosperous, lowland communities, connected to the larger world by good roads, access to the sea, or major river routes tended to be Whig. On the other hand, the poorer, more sparsely populated, and more isolated areas tended to be Democratic. Other variables were involved, at least in New Hampshire: whether a town had a Congregational (Whig) or a Baptist (Democratic) church, whether it had a lively newspaper (probably Whig), or whether it was growing fast (probably Democratic). By and large well-established centers took on a Whig coloration: areas that were out of the mainstream were likely to be Democratic. The pattern, with variations, seems to hold for a number of other states . . . [including] much of the South, where complexes of town bankers, merchants, and lawyers, linked with planters or "cotton capitalists," provided vital leadership for the powerful southern Whig party. Virginia and North Carolina were exceptions, however, and South Carolina was always a special case.[43]

William Nisbet Chambers, in his comprehensive summary of the literature dealing with the economic and class origins of the Whigs, has examined some of the difficulties in attempting to pinpoint their social and economic origins:

If there was a Jacksonian persuasion, there was a general Whig persuasion also: the two parties were not cut from identical cloth. Men like Jackson, Nicholas Biddle of the Bank of the United States, Clay, Webster, Van Buren, Benton, Silas Wright of New York, Calhoun, and an array of lesser figures had defined a series of issues and given them partisan raiment. . . .
However, it has proved difficult for scholars to determine just who wore what party colors, and why. Brahmin historians of the nineteenth century thought they knew the answer: all respectable men voted Whig, and Democrats were rabble. More carefully researched studies by progressive historians from Charles A. Beard to Arthur Schlesinger, Jr. believed the distinction emerged from economic group interests or social class; and many of the issues of era did involve different ideas of social and economic arrangements. More recent studies have tended to focus on broad outlooks or perspectives—on the nostalgia for Arcadia or the prospect of enterprise, or on ethnic, religious, and cultural identifications. There is yet no scholarly consensus, and more research and analysis is needed. The problem is made more intricate by the different political positions men of similar economic interest or social status apparently took in different states or localities.
Even so, some patterns may be discerned. Nearly everywhere by the late 1830's at least, the wealthiest men appear to have been Whigs. Frank O. Gantell has shown that the thousand richest citizens of New York City were overwhelmingly of that persuasion, particularly after the controvery over the national Bank and the currency issue had shown where most leaders of either party stood.[44]

This was not a winning combination, however, as the elections of 1828 and 1832 demonstrated, and these groups realized that they would have to adapt methods and policies which would be more attractive to the general population if they were to win an election. Clay had always sensed this, and his American plan was essentially a policy designed for a broad national constituency. It offered tariff protection to the commercial and industrial interests of the eastern seaboard, transportation and other national improvements to his own constituency in the West (the Maysville Road), and financial stability to those like the southern planters who were dependent upon large-scale credit and banking resources. Clay had to modify his tariff position in order to hold on to southern support during this period.

But it was still not a program which could, under normal conditions, attract a majority of an increasingly restive, demanding and growing national electorate. The Whigs still had to reach down deeper into the bowels of the population if they were to become the majority party in national elections. They needed the workers in the growing industrial centers, the shopkeepers, the artisans, the developing middle classes in all sections of the country. They had to ride the crest of the growing interest in politics, and dramatize their ability to provide better solutions and more dynamic leadership than that provided by the Jackson party. In short, to win they had to become a "people's party" in addition to serving the high-income groups which made up their hard core constituency. There was an important element of levelling, a sense of an egalitarian revolt which was very much a part of the Jacksonian revolution. A political party which seriously hungered for national leadership needed also to appeal to this growing revolt against deference and in favor of equality. This was what Hofstadter defined as the *effective* function of the development of a political party.

Issues, Politicians and Candidates

The potential for a larger Whig constituency base in a growing population was closely related to the unprecedented economic and industrial development of the country during these years. During this period the United States passed through what the economic historian, Walt Rostow, has termed the pre-condition period for the "take-off" stage of a nations's economic growth. What he means by this is that the economy reached a point of development where it was in the process of overcoming the last vestiges of the obstacles imposed by the traditional society to economic growth. It was a period characterized by a gradual transition from a basically agricultural society, where property and property alone was valuable, to a society where the rudimentary sinews of later economic development—roads, ports, canals and railways—were beginning to appear and where capital in the form of money rather than land accumulated, or was attracted, in large enough amounts to support the barest beginnings of industry.

The entrepreneur appeared at this stage of development and replaced the landowner as the central focus of economic activity. It was a period of early capital investment, risk capital which was not characterized by the cautious and limited vision of the traditional society, but which anticipated the economic and social opportunities that could be realized once the country overcame its static inhibitions and resistance to change and began to mobilize its resources for the next stage in the transition—the so-called "take-off" stage of economic growth. Rostow estimates that the "take-off" stage period in the United States was considerably later than in Europe—that is northern Europe—and took place during the two decades that preceded the Civil War.[45]

Population in this country increased during these years at an unprecedented rate, not only because of the fertility of its citizens, but because the rate of immigration continued to hold up. In 1790 there were 3,929,214 people living in the United States, and 50 years later, in 1840, that figure had multiplied by over 400 percent (17,069,453). That meant that the decennial rate of growth over that period averaged 34.12 percent. The center of population was shifting westward and transportation was a critical problem. Canals and turnpikes were the two earliest means of long distance travel and shipping and those systems multiplied rapidly during that period. Roads were built connecting the recently settled cities on the western frontier with the eastern seaboard, and by 1840 they stretched as far west as Minnesota, Kansas and Oklahoma, as far north as Sault Saint Marie and as far south as Tampa Bay, Florida. The construction of canals followed, the biggest by far being the main artery to the midwest—the Erie Canal in upstate New York. Other canals joined Easton and Coalport, Pennsylvania; Easton and Jersey City; Toledo, Ohio and Evansville, Illinois; Cleveland and Portsmouth; and Toledo and Cincinnati. By a combination of canals, rivers and lakes, agricultural products could move east from the banks of the Ohio River to New York and other eastern port cities, and manufactured products could be transported west. The first railroads were added to this transportation network in 1830—the Baltimore and Ohio, the Mohawk and Hudson, the Charleston and Hamburg—and they were joined shortly by the Erie in New York, the Western in Massachusetts and a score of others which were under construction during the decade.

Trade, finance and manufacturing developed at a comparable pace. Investments in American factories rose from $50,000,000 in 1820 to $250,000,000 in 1840, a 500 percent increase. Exports never quite caught up with imports (although capital investment has to be recorded in that category), but certainly the ratio of the balance of trade improved tremendously. In 1784 the ratio of imports to exports was better than 4 to 1 ($18,000,000 to $4,000,000), but by 1835 the total trade figures had increased by over 1100 percent and the balance of trade had been reduced to a 5 to 4 margin ($126,000,000 to $104,000,000). All of this added up to a gigantic boom, subsidized by extraordinarily high levels of British investment, producing a great deal of dynamic activity and development, eventually followed by a significant inflation of values.

The historical convergence of all these social and economic forces transformed the character and leadership of the Whig party during this period as the Whigs progressed from a humiliating defeat in the election of 1836 until they finally came to power in 1840. During the early period of the republic, in the "Age of Deference," the party leadership was centered in the nation's capital in both the houses of Congress and the Executive office. There, presidential candidates were selected by Presidents in office or party legislative caucuses; but when the new men of politics emerged, individuals who were not necessarily legislators, Presidents, nor even presidential candidates, but who were first and foremost professional politicians, drawing their strength from their local political supporters and their ability to manipulate large blocs of votes at the developing national political conventions, rose to assume party leadership. These men out-maneuvered the old legislative Whig leaders like Webster and Clay and fashioned a party organization, a new image and a carefully selected presidential candidate, whose political profile was drawn deliberately to appeal to the forces described above. Gaetano Mosca, in his brilliant sociological study, *The Ruling Class*, speaks of the concept of the "political formula," which is a very close approximation to what was being generated in Whig politics during the latter half of the 1830s.[46] The Whig professional politicians had discovered the "political formula" through which they could capture the American presidency, and they developed it with consummate skill in the years and months preceding the 1840 presidential election.

According to Mosca, all societies can be divided into two classes, the rulers and the ruled. The ruling class emerges from the continuing struggle, not for existence but, more significantly, for preeminence. At any given time the character and makeup of a particular ruling class is dependent upon the preeminent social forces in that society. By social forces, Mosca refers simply to any human activity which has significant social and political influence. For example, in various primitive societies the chief social forces were usually war and religion, and so it followed that the principal warriors and the religious priests were the rulers of those particular societies. Social forces obviously change in time and place by virtue of many other factors—cultural, economic, physical, geographic, even scientific and technological. "As civilization grows," Mosca writes, "the number of the moral and material influences which are capable of becoming social forces increases."[47] Property is transformed into money; scientific knowledge gains in importance; basic skills in elementary mechanics which started great industrialists like Ford and Chrysler on their careers, have now been advanced to higher levels of computer technology which are in critical demand today.[48]

A ruling class emerges from the society in which it has won power by controlling those major forces which are dominant in the society. These forces are themselves frequently engaged in a life and death struggle, e.g. the military and the leaders of corporate wealth. The growth of new social forces and the decline of the old characterizes the constant process of change and dislocation within the ruling class and the society itself. The ruling class expresses its role and position through what Mosca then calls—"a political formula"—which is, in effect, a myth which currently prevails in the society. This "political formula" rationalizes and justifies the position of the ruling class and its possession of political power within the structure of the society which it dominates. It can be a racial myth, as in Nazi Germany; the myth of "the divine right of kings"; or perhaps even "the dictatorship of the proletariat." Such a myth is frequently referred to as an ideology today, but what it amounts to is an acceptable argument or rationalization for the domination of one group over another.

The new men of the Whig party thought they understood what the social forces were which were gaining strength and power in the post-Jacksonian world, and they moved to manipulate those forces and create the myth structure which would bring them to power. It involved the search for a certain type of leader, the development of a certain type of campaign, the rallying of elements of the population by the use of selective arguments and symbols. It was a perceptive if somewhat frightening forerunner of the politics of the modern world.

The challenge which existed for the embattled and power-hungry Whigs was to convince a majority of the increasingly large national electorate that their party and its leadership could provide the best solutions to their problems and the kind of dynamic policies that would best advance their interests. In order to achieve this objective, the Whigs had to find "gut" issues which responded to the everyday needs and frustrations of the voters rather than long-range policies involving theoretical principles and ultimate goals. Leaders like Calhoun, Webster and Clay could articulate such party principles and goals, but what was needed was some way of translating these principles and objectives into the everyday lives of the voters.

The Whigs accomplished this objective by simplifying the existing national problems, identifying their causes with the Democrats in power and promising to eliminate them when provided with the opportunity to govern. They concentrated their fire on Van Buren, because Jackson had retired from the fray undefeated and invulnerable, while "little Van" made a much easier target. Two months after Van Buren had been inaugurated, a serious economic depression rocked the country and caused many to lose faith in some of their unexamined emotional political commitments. Hundreds of banks closed, businesses failed and thousands were unemployed. The Panic of 1837 was a shattering social experience, but it made an effective campaign issue for the Whigs.

Of course such a serious economic collapse had multiple causes, and they cannot all be analyzed here in the detail which they require; but some of the most critical aspects should be considered because they bear heavily on questions of presidential power. Perhaps the most significant factor relevant to this period and to much of the rest of American history was the incredible optimism most Americans entertained with regard to the possibilities of increasing their personal fortunes. Alexis de Tocqueville, travelling in the United States early in the 1830s, observed:

> I know of no country, indeed, where the love of money has taken stronger hold on the affections of men and where a profounder contempt is expressed for the theory of the permanent equality of property. But wealth circulates with inconceivable rapidity. . . .[49]
>
> In the United States a man builds a house in which to spend his old age, and he sells it before the roof is on; he plants a garden and lets it just as the trees are coming into bearing; he brings a field into tillage and leaves other men to gather the crops; he embraces a profession and gives it up; he settles in a place, which he soon afterwards leaves to carry on his changeable longings elsewhere. . . .[50]

The engine of ambition keeps churning, but the goal is never reached:

> Among democratic nations, men easily attain a certain equality of condition, but they can never attain as much as they desire. It perpetually retires from before them, yet without hiding itself from their sight, and in retiring draws them on. At every moment they think they are about to grasp it; it escapes at every moment from their hold. They are near enough to see its charms, but too far off to enjoy them; and before they have fully tasted its delights, they die.[51]

Another shrewd foreign observer, the Russian, Moisei Ostrogorski, later wrote, "The haste to get rich was infecting the whole nation with intensity."[52]

In responding to the leveling demands of the common man, Jackson attacked the power and status of the Bank of the United States and broke its influence over the credit and financial structure of the country; yet, he had not thought through, nor were he or his associates capable of thinking through, the full dimensions of the implications of that action upon the economy of the country. His political feelers and understandings were far more sensitive and comprehensive than his economic perspective, and whereas the stroke against Biddle and the Bank proved to be a political coup of significant proportions, Jackson was hardly aware of what its economic impact would be.

Jackson dealt with all complaints to him on financial questions in his typical preemptory fashion. When informed that the aforementioned concurrent events had produced a dangerous tightness in the money market, he dismissed the complaint, saying:

> There is no real general distress. It is only with those who live by borrowing, trade on loans, and the gamblers in stocks. It would be a godsend to society if all such were put down.[53]

Later when a delegation came to him and pleaded for him to intervene to relieve the credit stringency, Jackson admitted that there was distress among "brokers and stock speculators and all who are doing business on a borrowed capital," and that they would suffer severely; but he declared that "all such people ought to break."[54] He told another committee that urged him to take steps to relieve the situation:

> Relief, sir! . . . Come not to me, sir! Go to the monster. . . . It is folly, sir, to talk to Andrew Jackson. The government will not bow to the monster. . . . You would have us, like the people of Ireland, paying tribute to London. . . . The failures that are now taking place are amongst the stockjobbers, brokers, and gamblers, and would to God they were all swept from the land! It would be a happy thing for the country. . . . Andrew Jackson yet lives to put his foot upon the head of the monster and crush him to the dust.[55]

When the spokesman for the group protested that his committee represented honest citizens and not gamblers and stockjobbers, the President was not deterred. "The mammoth, sir, has bled you." He asserted that he would "rather undergo the tortures of ten Spanish inquisitions" than to see the deposits be restored or the Bank rechartered.[56]

When still another committee informed the President that Nicholas Biddle had told them that he was simply following the recommendations of the Executive in curtailing the credit, they reported his rage increased beyond any level of description, and he responded:

> Did I advise him to interfere with elections and to corrupt the morals of the people? . . . I tell you I am opposed to all banks and banking operations from the South Sea Bubble to the present time. The Israelites during the absence of Moses to the mount made a golden calf and fell down and worshipped it; and they sorely suffered for their idolatry. Let the United States Bank relieve the community by issuing their notes, and I pledge myself that the state banks shall not oppress it.[57]

The last remark is particularly revealing, for after having condemned the Bank and attempting to doom its future existence, the President was desperately appealing to it to continue its operations. No effective policy was forthcoming from the administration, and Biddle finally did yield in time to avoid an immediate depression. But the tempo of expansion and inflation continued to undermine the financial foundations of the country, and in time the bubble burst.

Two developments which appeared to aggravate the problem were the law passed by Congress to distribute all surplus revenues over $5,000,000 after 1837, and Jackson's desperate and defiant Specie Circular. In the former case the Congress decided, probably for political purposes and also because of the constitutional controversy over national improvement programs, that the Treasury surpluses that had been piling up since the national debt was retired would be loaned to the states (but, in effect, permanently transferred to them)[58] in order that they could finance their own improvements or determine in what ways the funds should be otherwise dispersed. It was a measure that was pushed by the administration, but in the final analysis not opposed by anti-Jacksonites.

The second measure was the Specie Circular, issued independently by Jackson. By 1836 the President and his advisors had become thoroughly alarmed by the degree of land speculation that was taking place in the country. Up until 1834 the sale of public lands had never exceeded $4,000,000 annually, and for the previous five years had averaged $2,000,000. In 1834 for the first time the sale went over the $4,000,000 level and the next year, this figure was tripled, rising to $14,757,000. When the total sales figure reached $24,900,000 the following year, the administration recommended to the Congress that all further purchases of public land be restricted to payment in specie. Congress rejected his proposal and passed legislation which would have outlawed such a policy, but Jackson pocket-vetoed the bill on the advice of his attorney general, and put the policy into effect as an executive order after the Congress had gone home, thus avoiding the possibility of their overriding his veto. The administration floor leader in the Senate, Thomas Hart Benton, admitted that Jackson feared such action, and delayed issuing his order to avoid such a possibility.

Until very recently the most knowledgeable historians of the period were convinced that Jackson's attack upon the Bank and Biddle's harsh response were major causes of the economic chaos which developed soon after the United States funds were withdrawn from the Philadelphia Bank and deposited by Jackson in a number of state (and private commercial) banks. The period was marked by a considerable expansion of credit, a land-buying spree of gigantic proportions, increased prices and inflation, followed by the inevitable day of reckoning, a significant economic depression, unemployment and temporary economic stagnation. The Whigs quickly jumped into the fray and identified both Jackson and Van Buren with the policies that led to the economic decline. Later scholars have tended to bear out these charges, which were, at the time, largely politically motivated. Such eminent historians of the Jacksonian period as Richard Hofstadter, Arthur M. Schlesinger, jr., Bray Hammond and Marvin Meyers [See Richard Hofstadter, *The American Political Tradition* (New York, 1948); Arthur M. Schlesinger, jr., *The Age of Jackson* (Boston, 1945); Bray Hammond, *Banks and Politics in America* (Princeton, 1957); and Marvin Meyers, *The Jacksonian Persuasion* (Stanford, 1963).] all more or less supported this thesis, and provided various levels of evidence to substantiate its credibility.

An outstanding American economic historian of this period, Bray Hammond, has dismissed the Jackson policy contemptuously as too little and too late:

This document was notable for being the only administrative act of President Jackson that was consistent with the hard-money doctrine absorbed from his agrarian background and always professed by him. It was a step toward blessing America, the most progressive and dynamic of economies, with an exclusively metallic circulation such as Europe had in the Middle Ages; but its immediate purpose was to prevent "frauds, speculations, and monopolies in the purchase of public lands and the aid of which is said to be given to effect these objects by excessive bank credits." This purpose was laudable. But the measure itself was unconscionably clumsy and taken too late to do anything but harm. It was intended to protect poor settlers and to curb the land speculators, whom, however, it largely spared because they were better able to get control of specie than the poor settlers were; and, by permitting less public land to come on the market, it gave the speculators who had land in their possession already a further advantage.[59]

A more recent impressive study of this period challenges most of these basic premises. Based in some cases on newly acquired data, but more fundamentally upon a more sophisticated monetary and banking conceptual framework, Peter Temin argues quite persuasively:

The inflation and crises of the 1830's had their origin in events largely beyond Jackson's control and probably would have taken place whether or not he had acted as he did. The economy was not the victim of Jacksonian politics; Jackson's politics were the victims of economic fluctuations.[60]

To support this abrasive thesis, Temin presents evidence that the state banks did not expand their credit during this period by dangerously extending their notes beyond the previously accepted ratio to their specie reserves, but rather "bank reserves increased rapidly in the 1830's and . . . banks did not increase the volume of their obligations faster than they received new [specie] reserves." He carefully explains that this situation was not really caused by any significant domestic initiatives, but rather it came about as a result of "a combination of large capital imports from England and a change in the Chinese desire for silver which together produced a rapid increase in the quantity of silver in the United States."

Banks did not expand their operations because they were treating the government deposits as reserves, to finance speculation, or because the Bank of the United States was no longer restraining them; they expanded because their true—that is, specie—reserves had risen. . . . The Panic of 1837 was not caused by President Jackson's actions. The destruction of the Bank of the United States did not produce the crisis because it did not produce the boom.[61]

Temin goes on to demonstrate that neither the Specie Circular nor the distribution of the surplus had the effects attributed to them by the Whig politicians and in the analysis of later historians. He asserts that the depression of 1837 was "neither as serious as historians assume nor the fault of Nicholas Biddle. It was primarily a deflation, as opposed to a decline in production, and it was produced by events over which Biddle had little control."

Economists and historians will continue to discuss the "revisionist" attack upon the heretofore accepted conventional analysis of the problems of this period. Temin's arguments demand serious consideration which they have not yet received, but the data supporting them also requires the same withering analysis to which he has subjected previous evidence and explanations. Revisionist challenges frequently stimulate a dialectical analysis which ultimately produces new insights and understandings which go beyond not only the theories which are the initial targets for the critiques, but also considerably beyond the assertions advanced by the initial critics. It would do well for revisionists to bear this in mind when they stridently assert their sometimes inflated claims, often failing to recognize the major contributions of the objects of their attacks.

During these years expansion was also fostered by the availability of capital investment for internal improvements, both from the state government and from European investors, primarily British. "Between 1820 and 1838, eighteen states had authorized advances of credit of $60,000,000 for canals, $43,000,000 for railroads, $4,500,000 for turnpikes."[62] They also subscribed $52,500,000 in state bank stocks. British investment in the United States was slightly over $170,000,000, much of which was lent to states and municipalities. After the depression of 1837, many of these defaulted on interest payments or repudiated the loans outright.

Land values on the eastern seaboard went through the ceiling. A lot on William Street, near Wall Street in New York's financial section, was sold for $51,000. A country estate on the Hudson was cut into 125 city lots and sold for $200,000. Three estates in Hallets Cove brought $1,500 an acre. A purchaser paid $1,000 an acre for an 8-acre farm on Long Island—2 miles from Brooklyn. Fifteen acres of land near Hellgate were purchased for $15,000 and resold for $120,000. In Philadelphia, Lemon Hill on the Schuylkill brought $180,000, and the old prison site on Walnut Street sold for $219,000. In Chicago, lakefront lots, 45x200 sq. ft. brought $7,000 apiece.[63] These prices represented increases ranging from 100 to 1000 percent over previous valuations, and there seemed to be no limitations in sight.

Flour, which had sold at $5.62 a barrel in March, 1835, rose to $7.75 in March, 1836, and $12 in March, 1837. Pork climbed from $10 in March, 1835, to $16.25 a year later and to $18.25 in March, 1837. The wholesale price of coal mounted from $6.00 a ton in January, 1835 to $10.50 in January, 1837, and rents increased proportionately.[64]

The expansion of credit by the so-called state or private banks contributed significantly to the problem. These banks, as Henry Clay quite accurately put it, "were chartered without necessity, and multiplied beyond example."[65] They flourished during this period, increasing in number from 329 in 1829 to 788 by 1837. Their circulation increased even more rapidly, from $48,000,000 to $149,000,000, and their loans by almost 400 percent—growing from $137,000,000 to $525,000,000.[66]

The requirements of the specie circular, aggravated by the distribution, produced absurd disorder. It caused, in Mr. Gallatin's words, "a drain of specie on the banks of New York at a time when it was important that that point should be strengthened. It transferred specie from the place where it was most wanted, in order to sustain the general currency of the country, to places where it was not wanted at all.[67]

Another contemporary wrote:

The monetary affairs of the whole country were convulsed—millions upon millions of coin were *in transitu* in every direction and consequently withdrawn from useful employment. Specie was going up and down the same river to and from the South and North and the East and West at the same time.[68]

Two months after Van Buren was inaugurated the dam burst and the Whigs were handed their major "gut issue" for the 1840 Presidential campaign—a Democratic depression of major proportions.

One of the more significant causes of the Panic of 1837 was the comparable contraction of British trade and investment in the United States. British investors had poured millions of dollars into expanding American enterprises, and the southern economy was dependent upon the British cotton market. In fact, the two economies were very much dependent upon each other, for America provided a major outlet for British manufactured goods, a source for much needed raw materials and a happy hunting ground for investment capital. Consequently, the irregularities of American finances produced sensitive reactions in London. The Specie Circular came at a time when British specie reserves were falling away rapidly, and produced considerable concern on Threadneedle Street. The Bank of England twice raised its discount rate as a remedy to the crisis, and, alarmed by events in the United States, the Bank also instructed its agents in Liverpool to reject payments in paper by certain houses with heavy American interests. The result was a contraction of the demand for cotton and an immediate fall in prices. One of the first victims was an important New Orleans firm which was not able to realize enough on its cotton sales to meet its financial obligations. A number of similar failures developed rapidly in New Orleans and New York, and the chain reaction by which panics and depressions are created was well underway. As Bray Hammond succinctly put it:

The British had stopped buying, had stopped lending [because the higher discount rate attracted British investment at home], and expected payment of what was due them. The Americans found themselves unable to sell, unable to buy, unable to borrow, unable to pay.[69]

The impact of these events on American life was disastrous. In May 1837 all banks in New York City were forced to suspend payments and over 300 firms failed. By January of the following year, 618 banks had closed down. During this depressed economic period—which carried over in some respects until the election year of 1840—there were 33,000 insolvencies in the country with a total loss of 440 million dollars. And of course the situation was not limited to financial losses. The depressed state of the economy created hardships for large segments of the American people in every walk of life. In New York City, for example, the *Times* estimated the number of unemployed persons to be close to 50,000. As many as 6,000 were unemployed in the building trades alone. In one city ward, 9,500 applied for relief. Approximately one third of the working population of the city was out of work.

The working classes were not the only ones to feel the impact of this economic crisis:

> The propertied classes felt the immediate pinch of the general depression of values, and were especially articulate in voicing their grievances. Their plight is recorded poignantly, year after year, in the diary of a man like Philip Hone, merchant, mayor and *bon vivant* of New York. During 1838 he wrote that half of his friends were, like himself, deeply in debt, with no prospect of getting out. A year later Hone reported that he was now out of debt, but at the cost of two thirds of his fortune. Living was high, and Hone wondered "how the poor man manages to get dinner for his family."[70]

Nor was unemployment confined to New York City. All of the shoe factories in Haverhill, Massachusetts were closed down. New Bedford, Lowell and other New England industrial centers were plagued by unemployment and drastic reductions in wages for the "lucky" few who were able to hold on to their jobs. The decline in wages varied from 30 to 50 percent. For example, joiners who earned $2 a day in 1836, earned $1.25 a day in 1840; bricklayers' wages dropped from $2 to $1.50; stonecutters' from $2.50 to $1.50; plasterers' from $2 to $1.38; and common laborers saw their earnings decrease from $1 to $.68 a day. These figures were triumphantly published in Whig editor Thurlow Weed's *Albany Evening Journal*, confident that the frustration over these conditions would enable his party to wean many workers away from the Democrats and into the Whig fold.[71]

The Whigs were not slow nor at all reticent in exploiting the depressed conditions of 1837 to their party's advantage. They were in a good position to blame the Democratic party in power for the dramatic deterioration of economic conditions and for the frustration and paralysis which gripped the land. Moreover, it was not a critique aimed at a political party as such, but rather an attack directed at the leaders, Andrew Jackson, who had initiated the policies which led to these conditions, and even more so at his advisor and successor, Martin Van Buren. The Whigs reviled him as "little Van, a used up man," "Martin Van Ruin," "King Mat," the "Red Fox," the "little Magician," and "Sweet Sandy Whiskers." Thus, the attack upon presidential power that prior to this had been expressed in perhaps too abstract terms was transformed into a clearly personal attack on the President himself. Jackson's power could be assailed, and Calhoun, Clay and Webster did their best in this respect, but his prestige was such that he certainly could not be denigrated in the eyes of most Americans. Van Buren was a different matter, however, and in the atmosphere of the disastrous economic conditions of 1837 and the period immediately following, the man in the White House was fair game for the barbs of the opposition party.

But a political campaign for the presidency is not constructed entirely out of slogans and epithets, nor are the bitterness and frustration experienced through an economic depression automatically transferred into support for the opposition party. The Whigs had already found out in the previous election (when, badly divided, they presented three rather than a single alternative candidate), that unity and organizational support behind one strong candidate were essential to win a national presidential election. And even if the candidate is relatively unknown, one has to make him known in the public's mind in order to capture its imagination and support. The Whigs also learned that an essential aspect of the new American politics was theater, and they rapidly became one of the most theatrical political parties in American history.

But the drama could not unfold until they cast the leading character of the pageant they were to produce, and this rapidly became the important business of the day. Henry Clay was, of course, the most obvious candidate for the role, and yet his earlier performances had failed to excite the national electorate. Clay was a man of tremendous ability, an eloquent speaker and a brilliant debator. He had fashioned the program to oppose Jackson, and he was the real founder of the Whig coalition. By all the traditional claims of politics he was the logical candidate for this campaign, which appeared so promising for the Whig party. Yet he was a statesman of the old school who had twice before been badly beaten in presidential campaigns.

But the emerging political values were not dominated by either tradition or logic. The new leaders of the Whig party wanted to win the election of 1840, and they subordinated every other consideration to that goal. Clay did not shape up as the strongest possible candidate the Whigs could nominate, and that sealed his doom. They were not moved by appeals to the justice of his claims, but were influenced rather by what they considered were the prevailing political currents.

The "political formula" called for a candidate who was not shopworn, who had not collected political enemies as well as supporters; its most necessary ingredient was a new man, a military hero, if possible, a candidate who could be glamorized in the way that Jackson had been, a man of the people who perhaps, like Jackson, could be identified with the frontier. It could be easily forgotten that although Andrew Jackson had, indeed, risen from extremely humble origins, had little formal education and had great difficulty writing and spelling in his own language, he was, at the time he became President, the owner of one of the most stately homes in Tennessee (ironically called the Hermitage), possessed 100 slaves and one of the finest stables of thoroughbred race horses in the South. He was no longer a poor frontier yeoman, but he retained something of his identity in the minds of the public. Clay, on the other hand, was never thought of as the frontier type, although he came from a southwestern state as well. He too owned a great estate, possessed slaves, and certainly lived like a gentleman; the difference was that he had been always regarded as such. Perhaps it was his sophisticated and urbane manner, his eloquence, and, to a certain extent, the policies he fought for. He never repudiated the common man, but his major supporters were usually pillars of the community and well-established men of industry and commerce.

Calhoun rapidly took himself out of the running by returning to the womb of the Democratic party, which he had never really left. He gave lukewarm support to

Van Buren, because he decided to support him on his sub-Treasury proposal. Daniel Webster also longed for the presidential office, but he possessed even greater liabilities than Clay. He lacked Clay's charm and wit, presented a stern and granite-like New England visage, and never developed the loyal followers and supporters outside of his region that Clay had been able to attract. Both Clay and Webster, however, were potential candidates; in fact, Clay's supporters went to the Whig convention confident that he would be named, for he possessed the largest number of pledged delegates and he had the broadest support of the country. Webster never did have a real chance and remained in the running only in order to be able to influence the final outcome.

What defeated Clay at the convention was the skill and the power of the new leaders of the Whig party—men like Thurlow Weed of New York and Thaddeus Stevens of Pennsylvania. Weed was the major influence in the pre-convention jockeying for position in the selection of the candidate, and he had also been instrumental in building the Whig party both in his own state and nationally during the previous five years. On the eve of the 1840 elections, the Whigs were not only in serious contention for the presidency, but also bid fare to become the majority party in the country at large.

Thurlow Weed emerged in the 1830s as a central figure in New York state politics. As a leader of the Anti-Mason party at the turn of the decade, he had helped build it into a strong enough force to capture a substantial number of seats in the state legislature. But Weed became disillusioned with the Anti-Masons after their failure to develop significant national growth and support in the elections of the early 1830s, and he voted along with the other leaders to dissolve the party in the winter of 1834. From that point on, he joined with other anti-Jackson and Van Buren forces in the state to form the Whig party that same year. By that time he had also become the editor of a thriving politically oriented newspaper—the *Albany Evening Journal*—and had established a rather imposing reputation as not only a skilled political organizer and legislative leader, but also as a fiery and acid-pen journalist who was now able to transform his Albany paper into the foremost Whig journal in the state and one of the most widely read political newspapers in the country. Weed was merciless with his opponents in the rhetorical bombast of political journalism, but he was also a man of cheerful disposition, who made many friends, was admired by many more, and was somehow able to retain good relationships with even some of those who he had attacked most bitterly.

The story of Thurlow Weed's career is reminiscent of the familiar American saga—from rags to riches. He started out in a log cabin built in the shadows of the Catskill Mountains, the son of a ne'er-do-well drayman who was frequently out of work, and spent time in a debtors' prison. Young Thurlow shipped out as a cabin boy on a passenger boat which plied between Albany and New York on the Hudson River at the age of nine, and received very little formal education after that. At 14 he worked as printers' devil and apprentice to the editor of a small town newspaper in the western part of the state, and later became a journeyman printers' apprentice. By the age of 19 he was a regular journeyman printer and worked in various printing establishments upstate and in New York City. He later moved back up the Hudson when offered a position as the foreman of a print shop and newpaper in Albany, and there he began to pay more attention to politics, to write articles and editorials in the paper, and to develop a powerful style of political journalism.

By the time Weed was married the opportunity presented itself to move on to Norwich, New York where he could put out his own paper. He jumped at the chance, and his career as a newspaper part-owner and editor was launched. All during this period he was making friends and participating more and more in the political activity in the state, and when the murder of a former Mason—William Morgan—by the Masons was alleged because of a threatened exposé by him of the secret Masonic rites, Weed took up the Anti-Mason crusade in his newspaper. His was a particularly good voice to lead the press in such a campaign, because he soon became one of the founders of the Anti-Mason party. First elected to the state legislature in 1825, his career as a legislator and a political organizer, as well as an outspoken newspaper editor, developed rapidly. Both Weed and William Seward quickly tired of the limited Anti-Mason party, and with great skill, they maneuvered most of their Anti-Mason colleagues into the Whig party. The Anti-Masons were a typically ephemeral third party, arising overnight from almost nowhere, and disappearing almost as quickly after "stinging" the body politic in several critical elections.

In 1838 Thurlow Weed was the most powerful anti-administration politician in New York State and perhaps the nation. He harbored no secret ambitions for high office himself, but had been decisive in masterminding the election of William H. Seward as the first Whig governor of New York, and ran both the Whig party in the legislature and the party organization throughout the state. His career was based upon his sure-handed political organizational strength and his influence as a powerful and popular journalist. These were very different political skills and values than those possessed by the old Virginian and New England aristocracy and "President-makers"; the new party was dominated by state leaders like Weed, as well as national figures like Clay and Webster, but among the state leaders, Thurlow Weed was preeminent.

Thaddeus Stevens' career in Pennsylvania followed along some of the same lines as Weed's had. He too was the son of a poor, and in his case, indigent and drunken father, who deserted the family in his early childhood. His mother worked as a servant to keep her bright and club-footed son in school, and Stevens eventually went on to Dartmouth College, where he earned high honors. He apparently was a very competitive undergraduate and harbored a certain amount of sensitive bitterness about his deformity. The family moved on to Pennsylvania in the early years, and when Stevens graduated from Dartmouth, after delivering a graduation address in which he argued that the unequal distribution of wealth was necessary to progress, he went back to Pennsylvania where he taught school and read law.

His rise in the legal profession was meteoric, and ten years after he settled in Gettysburg he was the largest property owner in the county and had established a fine reputation as one of the top-ranking lawyers in the state of Pennsylvania. He too became one of the early leaders of the Anti-Masonic party in his state. He was first elected to the state legislature in 1833, and was reelected six times thereafter. In the course of this turbulent period, Stevens helped the Anti-Masons combine with the Whigs to win control of the lower house of the legislature and to elect an Anti-

Masonic governor. He stayed with the Anti-Masons longer than did Weed, but finally turned to the new Whig coalition in the last 1830s. By that time he was a powerful figure in state politics, a celebrated orator, as well as a consummate organizational politician who was credited with much of the success of the anti-Democratic party forces in the state.

Neither Weed nor Stevens was a typical representative of the earlier Whig leadership which had been drawn to the anti-Jackson coalition on the basis of principle and strong political differences. Both initially had been Anti-Masons, and Stevens clung to that persuasion almost up until the eve of the Whig convention in 1839. He and his Anti-Mason colleagues, who constituted a minority in the Pennsylvania Whig constituency, used their close alliance to prevent the Pennsylvania Whigs from endorsing Clay before the Harrisburg meeting. Both Weed and Stevens were by this time powerful forces in the politics of their own states, and their pre-convention maneuvers to knock Clay out of the race were the major factor in his defeat. In Weed's case he attempted first to persuade Clay to drop his candidacy, basing his opposition on his judgment that Clay brought too many disadvantages to the presidential race in 1840. Weed argued that the Kentuckian's indefinite position on slavery would alienate the powerful abolitionist forces in the party, and his Masonic background would not endear him to the Anti-Masons. On top of this, he had run for the presidency twice before and suffered humiliating defeats. The New Yorker gave no real consideration to the fact that Clay was unquestionably the major intellectual and political force in the Whig party, and by all odds its ablest statesman. Weed was interested in putting together the most powerful anti-Democratic coalition possible, and matters of intellectual and political preeminence and long-standing party obligation were pushed aside for this objective.

Stevens had no use for Clay either. He and his Anti-Mason supporters were opposed to the Kentuckian because of his Masonic background, but Stevens was even more hostile to Clay because of the slavery issue. Thaddeus Stevens was a zealous opponent of slavery and everything that it stood for, and he would have nothing to do with anyone who was even lukewarm on the issue. He played the game of politics skillfully and ruthlessly, using his influence as head of a large bloc of potentially Whig votes in Pennsylvania first to block the endorsement of Clay as the party's candidate by the state delegation, and then to cooperate with Weed to defeat Clay at the convention.

The story of Weed's subtle campaign against Clay in New York and his later manipulations on the national scene has been told many times and need not be rehashed in detail here. Failing to convince Clay to drop out of the race, Weed went about the task of engineering the selection of what he considered to be a stronger candidate. There is every reason to believe that William Henry Harrison was the candidate he ultimately wanted, but since there was veritably no Harrison support among New York Whigs, where Clay's stock was high, he adopted a very Machiavellian campaign to undermine the Kentuckian's support. Weed and his close allies dispatched numerous letters to Clay supporters, reassuring them of their loyalty to their candidate, but indicating their concern for his lack of support in their area. This was so-called "triangular correspondence." Through such efforts they were able to shake the confidence of Clay's supporters, and to build interest in another candidate, General Winfield Scott, a hero of the War of 1812 and somewhat of a "half way house," as Nathan Sargent, a Clay loyalist, put it. Using Scott as a decoy, Weed weakened Clay's support in New York State and later abandoned Scott's candidacy at the convention in favor of Harrison.

This was a very different type of politics from that conducted in the Virginia of Thomas Jefferson, James Madison and Patrick Henry, or the Massachusetts of the Adamses and the Cabots. It reflected much of the shifting values and power vectors of the period, emphasizing the role of the professional politician and his sensitivity to the mood and interests of the voter in selecting issues and candidates, rather than the influence of men of status and principle who operated independently of the general public and considered themselves the representatives of the public interest.[72] Ironically, Van Buren himself had been the first great practitioner of the new politics now to be turned so effectively against him.

In the weeks before the convention at Harrisburg, Clay was clearly the front runner, having been endorsed in all of the southern and southwestern states and also claiming majority strength in Illinois, Connecticut and Rhode Island. But states like New York and Pennsylvania, with their large voting populations were crucial, and although Clay had determined supporters in both these states, he also had both Weed and Stevens working against him. This was unfortunate. Weed, probably with the support of Webster, neutralized New York by supporting General Scott, while Stevens prevented Pennsylvania from going over to Harrison by his astute maneuvering. Still, on the first informal convention canvas, Clay out-polled his other opponents. But this was not to last. Michigan had not voted in the initial canvas, and Weed was already in a position to switch Scott's votes to Harrison when the time was right.

Before the voting even began, however, Weed and Stevens engineered a convention rule which clinched the ultimate victory for Harrison. They succeeded in passing a measure which provided for each state delegation the opportunity to caucus among themselves and then vote as a weighted unit for the candidate with the most delegates in their state. Such an arrangement obviously worked against Clay, who had solid support in a number of the larger states (New York, Pennsylvania, Ohio), but who lacked a majority in these critical industrial and urban areas. By the unit voting arrangement, Clay lost all of his votes in these states, and when Weed succeeded in switching his delegation to Harrison, it was all over. Clay felt that he had been betrayed by the stupidity and naiveté of his supporters, and even Weed admitted that "the mode of proceeding occasioned much solicitude."[73] Senator Thomas Hart Benton put a mathematical interpretation upon the affair:

> Algebra and alchemy must have been laid under contribution to work out
> a quotient from such a combination of signs and symbols. But it was done.
> Those who set the sum could work it; and the quotient was political death
> to Mr. Clay.[74]

The selection by the convention of John Tyler as the vice presidential candidate is still something of a mystery. Various claims of pre-convention agreements and commitments do not really appear to have much substance. It is clear that the victorious Weed-Stevens faction wanted to make some amends to the outraged Clay supporters, and they offered the vice presidential nomination to several of his more prominent allies before turning to Tyler. In fact, Weed had earlier offered it to Webster. When none of them would accept the nomination, the convention turned to an active candidate, John Tyler of Virginia, a solid states' rights man, who appeared to be quite upset by his fellow Virginian's defeat, and was reputed to have shed tears at the outcome. With the characteristic modesty which seems to run in the family, Tyler's son accounted for his father's selection by saying, "Everything pointed to the nomination of a Southern man, and to Mr. Tyler as that man."[75] He quoted a member of the convention as reporting that "Mr. Tyler was from the start the choice of a large majority of the convention. The fact is, that the defeat of Clay rendered Tyler's nomination all the more urgent as a concession to State-rights."[76]

> Mr. Tyler employed neither intrigue nor solicitation in obtaining the nomination; was faithful in his support of Mr. Clay, and neither gave nor asked pledges of any kind. To the last he was nothing but an honest State-rights man.[77]

The all-observing Philip Hone, commenting in his diary upon the "Tippecanoe and Tyler too" ticket, remarked: "There was rhyme but no reason in it."[78]

The really scandalous aspect of the convention was its silence on the issues of the day. The Whigs had established their credentials on the basis of their forthright struggle with the Jacksonians on the tariff, the National Bank, support for national internal improvements, a sound currency and the attack upon "executive usurpation." The convention wound up in Harrisburg without any platform or address to the people reiterating the Whig stand on these issues. When a delegate indiscretely reminded the convention chairman of this oversight, he was abruptly informed by another delegate that he should forget such a foolish suggestion and "Leave the nomination to its own weight."[79] This was apparently not an oversight, but a conscious effort to stress what Hofstadter defined as the *effective* role of the party in a national election. As one Yankee strategist warned in advising the Whigs not to pledge themselves "to any particular set of measures":

> To correct the abuses of the Administration is a sufficient motive to vigorous and effective effort, and in politics as well as in Philosophy—it is unwise to give more reasons than are necessary.[80]

Apparently the Whig leaders cooperated, for the most part, in this conspiracy of silence and emphasized their attack upon Van Buren and "executive usurpation" to the practical exclusion of positive programs of economic and social reform. The Democrats responded to this silence and noncommitalism by calling Harrison "General Mum." The failure to clarify the issues and reinforce the Whig program at this time would come back to haunt the party once power was acquired.

Martin Van Buren and Colonel Richard "Rumpsey Dumpsey" Johnson received the endorsement of the Democratic convention. With strong support from Jackson, Van Buren had no difficulty in obtaining the Democratic presidential nomination, but the convention balked at naming Johnson—probably because of his open flaunting of the conventions of traditional society, particularly as regarded segregation and the sanctity of marriage. But Johnson was finally named again by a state referendum, and the fight was on.

The Campaign and Election of 1840

Apart from the silence on issues, the 1840 campaign was certainly one of the most interesting and bizarre in American history. The Whigs were determined not to be out-hollered by the Democrats, out-spent or out-dramatized. They had discovered through adversity what results could be expected from waging a colorless campaign, and they did everything in their power to "go to the people" and pound on their doors. In short, they adopted the successful techniques of the Jackson campaigns. They bought up newspapers for party propaganda, held great mass rallies, utilized popular party spokesmen for speechmaking tours, and concentrated on mobilizing the largest possible number of voters. Slogans, songs and symbols were exploited most effectively as the Whig managers attempted to simplify the conflict by contrasting good and evil, simple homespun virtues versus the polished splendor of Van Buren's White House, and the corruption attendant upon all of that, as opposed to the simple qualities of honesty, frugality and efficiency. It was not only "Tippecanoe and Tyler too" that caught on, but also some rabble-rousing speeches that accused the administration of spending the country poor, and creating an opulent political dynasty which lived off the people's wealth.

The campaign was something like a long hiatus from reason, where every bizarre notion and attention-attracting gimmick was pressed into the service of the candidates, particularly the Whig candidates, to win votes. The log cabin and hard cider became the symbols of the revolution taking place, and Harrison's military achievements were inflated beyond credibility. The central operating principle was to tell the electorate what they wanted to hear in the manner in which they would most appreciate it:

> The log-cabin plain folks, "Old-Tip" appeal was always central, but special bids were concocted for almost every conceivable block of voters. To the devout and conservative: such Locofoco intellectuals as Orestes A. Brownson and Robert Dale Owen were labeled infidels and revolutionaries. To old soldiers, or the "veteran vote": the Hero of Tippecanoe was one of their own. To those who feared the enlargement of military forces in the face of border tensions with Canada: a plan by Van Buren was exposed to "take the crown and sceptre and announce to the world the high sounding title of Martin the 1st King of North America." To German immigrants: campaign biographies of Harrison were printed in their own language. To other avid readers: scurrilous campaign biographies were published of "Sweet Sandy Whiskers," the allegedly perfumed and corseted occupant of the White House, who had opposed the war and escaped military service. To working-men: Matty's policy, 12-½ cts. a day and French soup. Our policy, 2 Dolls a day and Roast Beef." To faithful Harrison farmers: an invitation was issued to name their

horses *Tip* and *Ty*, which many did. To anyone else, or the voter about to climb on the bandwagon:

> Without a why or wherefore
> We'll go for Harrison therefore.[81]

An unprecedented number of newspapers carried the story of the campaign to an incredibly growing electorate. In 1830 there were close to 900 newspapers throughout the country, 100 being dailies; ten years later that number had increased to almost 1600 with slightly over 200 dailies. In addition to this the parties put out their own newspapers, the most popular being the *Log Cabin*, edited by Horace Greeley and which ran off 80,000 copies a week. Henry Raymond of the *Times* called it the "most effective campaign paper ever written," and it circulated widely throughout the country, where many of its features were picked up and reprinted in other papers. The rhetoric of touring speakers and doggerel featured by the campaign was unbelievable. The Whigs dispatched a corps of speakers to cities and towns throughout the country to beef up the local efforts—among them a rabble-rousing blacksmith who made more than 300 speeches.

Truth, of course, was one of the first victims in such an encounter, and vile lies and slander were commonplace from the beginning to the end of the campaign. Van Buren, in particular, was a victim of attack; none was more brilliant than the three-day speech offered in the well of the House by Representative Charles Ogle, a protegé of Thad Stevens'. Ogle took for his text a statement of White House expenditures, and embellished it royally, item by item, in the most demagogic fashion. Describing the White House as a *"palace as splendid as that of the Caesars, and as richly adorned as the proudest Asiatic mansion,"* Ogle went on to itemize the adornments, much to the amusement of his colleagues and to the fury of his opponents who fumed as he droned on for three days.[82] Fist fights broke out on the House floor and general bedlam prevailed. Ogle continued, feeling constrained to enlighten his countrymen on "the pompous ceremonials that 'hold sway' at his [Van Buren's] republican court," and recorded all expenditures down to the last *chamber pot*. He conjured up a clearly distorted picture of "Sweet Sandy Whiskers" ensconced in all of this splendor, not eating "hog, hominy, fried meat and gravy, schnitz, knep and sourcrout (for the ethnic appeal)," but rather enjoying gourmet delicacies prepared by his "French cooks," served up on "massive gold plate and French sterling silver services."[83] On and on it went, and of course it was repeated in hundreds of dailies and weeklies throughout the land. Its patent distortions of fact never caught up with its demagogic procreator. The aristocratic Whig, Philip Hone, reflected that:

> Men's minds are wrought up to a pitch of frenzy and like tinder a spark of opposition sets them on fire. Riot and violence stalk unchecked through the streets, and lying is no longer considered a crime.[84]

By the time of the election he despaired that " 'universal suffrage' would not do 'for large communities' " with a "heterogeneous mass of vile humanity."[85]

Running through the bombast and hoopla of this first great theatrical Presidential campaign was the central issue which had been the initial basis for bringing together the divergent elements that made up the Whig party—the struggle against "executive usurpation" of power. It was, indeed, the resonant theme of the election. The keynote speaker at the Whig convention in Harrisburg in December 1839 raised the standard in unmistakable language:

> We are indeed in the midst of a revolution. Those walls of partition which our Fathers constructed between the different departments of the government, and which, judging from their own patriotic hearts, they thought would be impassable, have been insolently and audaciously broken down by Executive aggression, and he has assumed to himself a mass of power utterly incompatible with that equilibrium which all experience testifies is indispensible to the existence of free institutions. The forms of the Constitution are retained, but the spirit is gone— your President is a monarch almost absolute.[86]

The candidate selected at the convention had previously put himself on record on this subject. Writing to Whig Congressman Harmar Denny in 1838 while campaigning for the nomination, General Harrison outlined the reasons why he thought the remnants of the Anti-Masonic party, which was then meeting in convention, should support him. Among other points which he advanced was his strong opposition to "executive usurpation," and he outlined a seven-point program through which he argued he would "restore the Administration to its original simplicity and purity."[87] The seven points included his pledge to confine his service as President to a single term; to disclaim all right of control over the public treasury; to restrict himself from attempting to influence either state or federal elections, and also to restrain the influence of all federal employees in such elections; to restrict his exercise of the veto power to certain specified circumstances; to restrict the use of the office for partisan purposes; to submit the reasons for removal to all dismissed executive appointments and also to the Senate if he requests it; and finally to relieve the President of all responsibilities in the preparation of legislation for consideration by the Congress. This was the first, and quite formidable, blueprint for the Whig attack upon the presidency, and although others like Clay would refine and pursue some of its objectives with greater intensity than General Harrison, it provided the first comprehensive outline of what the Whigs intended to do with the office once they gained power.

General William Henry Harrison
Letter to Representative Harmar Denny
December 2, 1838

Arthur M. Schlesinger, jr., ed., *History of U.S. Political Parties* (New York, 1973) I, 695-99.

Dear Sir: As it is probable that you have by this time returned to Pittsburg, I do myself the honor to acknowledge the receipt of your letter from Philadelphia, containing the proceedings of the National Democratic Anti-Masonic Convention which lately convened in that city. With feelings of the deepest gratitude I read the resolution, unanimously adopted, nominating me as a candidate for the Presidency of the United States. This is the second time that I have received from that patriotic party, of which you yourself are a distinguished member, the highest evidence of confidence that can be given to a citizen of our Republic. I would attempt to describe my sense of the obligations I owe them, if I were not convinced that any language which I could command would fall far short of what I really feel. If, however, the wishes of the convention should be realized, and I should be the choice of those who are opposed to the present Administration, and success should attend their efforts, I shall have it in my power to manifest my gratitude in a manner more acceptable to those whom you represent than by any professions of it which I could at this time make. I mean, by exerting my utmost efforts to carry out the principles set forth in their resolutions, by arresting the progress of those measures "destructive to the prosperity of the People," and substituting for them those sound democratic republican doctrines upon which the Administrations of Jefferson and Madison were conducted.

Among the principles proper to be adopted by an Executive sincerely desirous to restore the Administration to its original simplicity and purity, I deem the following to be of prominent importance:

I. To confine his service to a single term.

II. To disclaim all right of control over the public treasure, with the exception of such part of it as may be appropriated by law, to carry out the public service, and that to be applied precisely as the law may direct, and drawn from the Treasury agreeably to the long established forms of that Department.

III. That he should never attempt to influence the elections, either by the People or the State Legislature, nor suffer the Federal officers under his control to take any other part in them, than by giving their own votes when they possess the right of voting.

IV. That, in the exercise of the veto power, he should limit his rejection of bills to, 1st. Such as are in his opinion unconstitutional. 2nd. Such as tend to encroach on the rights of the States, or of individuals. 3d. Such as, involving deep interests, may in his opinion require more mature deliberation, or reference to the will of the People, to be ascertained at the succeeding elections.

V. That he should never suffer the influence of his office to be used for purposes of a purely party character.

VI. That in removals from office of those who hold their appointments during the pleasure of the Executive, the cause of such removal should always be communicated to the person removed, and, if he request it, to the Senate, at the time that the nomination of a successor is made.

And last but not least in importance,

VII. *That he should not suffer the Executive Department of the Government to become the source of legislation, but leave the whole business of making the laws for the Union to be done by the department to which the Constitution has exclusively assigned it, until they have assumed that perfected shape where and when alone the opinions of the Executive may be heard.* [My emphasis.] A community of power in the preparation of the laws between the Legislative and the Executive Departments must necessarily lead to dangerous commutations and greatly to the advantage of a President desirous of extending his power. Such a construction of the Constitution could never have been contemplated by those who framed it, as they well knew that those who propose the bills will always take care of themselves, or the interests of their constituents; and hence the provision in the Constitution, borrowed from that of England, restricting the originating of revenue bills to the immediate Representatives of the People. So far from agreeing in opinion with the distinguished character who lately retired from the Presidency, that Congress should have applied to him for the project of a banking system, I think that such an application would have manifested not only great subserviency upon the part of that body, but an unpardonable ignorance of the chief danger to be apprehended from such an institution. That danger unquestionably consists in a union of interests between the Executive and the Bank. Would an ambitious incumbent of the Executive chair neglect so favorable an opportunity as the preparing of the law would give him to insert in it a provision to secure his influence over it? *In the authority given to the President by the Constitution, "to recommend to Congress such measures as he shall judge necessary and expedient," it was certainly never intended that the measures he recommended should be presented in a shape suited for the immediate decision of the Legislature.* [My emphasis.] The sages who made the Constitution too well knew the advantages which the Crown of England derived from the exercise of its power by its Ministers to have intended it to be used by our Chief Magistrate, or the Heads of Departments under his control. The boasted principle of the English Constitution, that the consent of the democratic branch of the Government was not only necessary to receive money from the People, but that it was its inviolable prerogative also to originate all the bills for that purpose, is true in theory as in the letter, but rendered utterly false and nugatory in effect by the participation of the Ministers of the Crown in the details of legislation. Indeed, the influence they derive from sitting as members of the House of Commons, and from wielding the immense patronage of the Crown, (constitutional or usurped,) gives them a power over that body that renders plausible at least the base flattery, or, as it is more probable, that intended sarcasm of Sir Walter Raleigh, in an address to James the First, that the demand of the Sovereign upon the Commons for pecuniary aid was intended only "that the tax might seem to come from themselves;" whereas, the inference is, it was really laid by the Sovereign himself.

Having thus given you my opinion of some things which might be done, and others which should not be done, by a President coming into power by the support of those of the People who are opposed to the principles upon which the present Administration is conducted, you will see that I have omitted one which is deemed by many of as much importance as any other. I allude to the appointment of members of Congress to office by the President. The Constitution contains no prohibition of such appointments, no doubt because its authors could not believe in its necessity, from the purity of character which was manifested by those who possessed the confidence of the People at that period. It is, however, an opinion very generally entertained by the Opposition party, that the country would have escaped much of the evil under which it has suffered some years past, if the Constitution had contained a provision of that kind. Having had no opportunity of personal observation on the conduct of the Administration for the last ten years, I am unable to decide upon the truth or error of this opinion. And I should be very willing that the known subserviency of the Legislature to the Executive, in several memorable instances, should be accounted for in a way somewhat less injurious to the character of our country and republicanism itself, than by the admission that the Fathers of the land, the trusted servants of a virtuous People, could be seduced from the path of duty and honor by the paltry trappings and emoluments of dependent offices. But if the evil really exists, and if there be good reason to believe that its source is to be found in the corruptibility of the members of the Legislature, an effectual remedy cannot be too soon applied. And it happens, in this case, that there is a choice of remedies. One of these, however, is, in my opinion, free from the objections which might be offered to the other. The one to which I object is, that which the late President has been so loudly called upon to adopt, in consequence of a promise made at the commencement of his Administration, viz. that the Executive, under no circumstance, should appoint to office a member of either branch of the Legislature. There are, in my mind, several weighty reasons against the adoption of this principle. I will detain you with a mention of two of them, because I believe you will agree with me that the alternative I shall present, while it would be equally effectual, contains no feature to which a reasonable objection could be made.

As the Constitution contains no provision to prevent the appointment of members of Congress to office by the Executive, could the Executive, with a due regard to delicacy and justice, without usurping power from the people, declare a disqualification which they had not thought necessary? And where is the American citizen, who regards the honor of his country, the character of its people, or who believes in the superiority of a republican form of government, who would be willing to proclaim to the world that the youthful nation which has attracted so much of its attention, which it has so much admired for its gigantic strength, its undaunted courage, its high attainments in literature and the arts, and the external beauty of its institutions, was, within, a mass of meanness and corruption? That even the chosen servants of the People were ever ready, for a paltry consideration, to abandon their allegiance to their lawful sovereigns, and to become the servants of a servant? The alternative to this degrading course is to be found in depriving the Executive of all motive for acquiring an improper influence over the Legislature. To effect this, nothing, in my opinion, is necessary but to re-establish the principles upon which the Administration was once conducted, with the single addition of limiting the service of the President to one term. A condensed enumeration of what I conceive these principles to have been is given above. And I think no one can doubt that, if faithfully carried out, they would be effectual in securing the independence of the Legislature, and confining the connexion between it and the Executive to that alone which is warranted by a fair construction of the Constitution.

I can conceive of but two motives which could induce a President of the United States to endeavor to perpetuate his power, by passing laws to increase his patronage, or gratify his vanity by obtaining their sanction to his schemes and projects for the government of the country, and thus assimilating his situation to that of the limited monarchs of Europe. The principles above suggested would effectually destroy any disposition of the person elected, by the combined votes of the Opposition, to place himself in either attitude. Retiring, at the end of four years, to private life, with no wish or prospect of "any son of his succeeding," legitimate or adopted, he would leave the Government as prosperous and pure in its administration as when it passed from the hands ·of the great "Apostle of Democracy" to those of the Father of our Constitution.

To the duties which I have enumerated as proper, in my opinion, to be performed by a President elected by the opposition to the present Administration, (and which are, as I believe, of constitutional obligation,) I will mention another, which I believe also to be of much importance; I mean the observance of the most conciliatory course of conduct towards our political opponents. After the censure which our friends have so freely and so justly bestowed upon the present Chief Magistrate, for having, in no inconsiderable degree, disfranchised the whole body of his political opponents, I am certain that no oppositionist, true to the principles he professes, would approve a similar course of conduct in the person whom his vote has contributed to elect. In a Republic, one of the surest tests of a healthy state of its institutions is the immunity with which every citizen may, upon all occasions, express his political opinions, and particularly his prejudices, in the discharge of his duty as an elector.

The question may perhaps be asked of me, what security I have in my power to offer, if the majority of the American People should select me for their Chief Magistrate, that I would adopt the principles which I have herein laid down as those upon which the Administration would be conducted. I could only answer, by referring to my conduct, and the disposition manifested in the discharge of the duties of several important offices which have heretofore been conferred upon me. If the power placed in my hands has, on even a single occasion, been used for any purpose other than that for which it was given, or retained longer than was necessary to accomplish the objects designated by those from whom the trusts were received, I will acknowledge that either will constitute a sufficient reason for discrediting any promise that I may make, under the circumstances in which I am now placed.

Clay took up the burden of refining the Whig assault on presidential power in an 1840 campaign appeal to Whig voters in Hanover County, Virginia. Like Harrison, the Kentuckian argued for a single term for the President and a divorce between "the purse and the sword," a complete separation of the power of the President to direct the affairs of the Treasury. Clay's legislative and legal background was reflected in his more precise command of language and his clearer conception of how these limitations would actually work. In the case of the Treasury, for example, Harrison employed enough ambiguous wording that his position could be interpreted very freely, while Clay specified that he believed the President should be prohibited from dismissing the secretary of the treasury (as Jackson had done in the case of Duane) "or other persons having immediate charge of it. . . ."[88]

But the argument was even more significant in the case of the veto power of the President and the power of removal. Again Harrison's language on the restriction of the veto power was vague enough to mean almost anything, while Clay clearly stated that Congress should be empowered to override the veto by a simple majority vote. In the case of the President's removal power, even Clay's language was not as precise as it could have been, but he did convey the impression that he thought the President should be limited in this responsibility, or as he put it, made responsible to the Senate for appointments originally approved by the Senate; Harrison's proposal however merely suggested that the reasons for the dismissal be reported to the Senate if the official in question requested it. None of these specific proposals found their way immediately into law or policy, but their long-range impact upon the power of the President would be significant.

Senator Henry Clay
The Whig Attack on the Presidency
Address (Extract) at Hanover County, Virginia
June 27, 1840

Calvin Colton, ed., *The Works of Henry Clay* (New York, 1904) V, 208-10.

. . . Whatever is the work of man necessarily partakes of his imperfections and it was not to be expected, that, with all the acknowledged wisdom and virtues of the framers of our Constitution, they could have sent forth a plan of government, so free from all defect, and so full of guaranties, that it should not, in the conflict of embittered parties and of excited passions, be perverted and misinterpreted. Misconceptions or erroneous constructions of the powers granted in the Constitution, would probably have occurred, after the lapse of many years, in seasons of entire calm, and with a regular and temperate administration of the government; but, during the last twelve years, the machine, driven by a reckless charioteer, with frightful impetuosity, has been greatly jarred and jolted, and it needs careful examination and a thorough repair.

With the view, therefore, to the fundamental character of the government itself, and especially of the executive branch, it seems to me that, either by amendments of the Constitution, when they are necessary, or by remedial legislation, when the object falls within the scope of the powers of Congress, there should be:

First, a provision to render a person ineligible to the office of President of the United States, after a service of one term.

Much observation and deliberate reflection have satisfied me that too much of the time, the thoughts, and the exertions of the incumbent, are occupied, during his first term, in securing his re-election. The public business, consequently, suffers; and measures are proposed or executed with less regard to the general prosperity than to their influence upon the approaching election. If the limitation to one term existed, the president would be exclusively devoted to the discharge of his public duties; and he would endeavor to signalize his administration by the beneficence and wisdom of its measures.

Secondly, the veto power should be more precisely defined, and be subjected to further limitations and qualifications. Although a large, perhaps the largest, proportion of all the acts of Congress, passed at the short session of Congress since the commencement of the government, were passed within the three last days of the session, and when, of course, the president for the time being had not the ten days for consideration, allowed by the Constitution, President Jackson, availing himself of that allowance, has failed to return important bills. When not returned by the president, within the ten days, it is questionable whether they are laws or not. It is very certain that the next Congress can not act upon them by deciding whether or not they shall become laws, the president's objections notwithstanding. All this ought to be provided for.

At present, a bill, returned by the president, can only become a law by the concurrence of two thirds of the members of each House. I think if Congress passes a bill after discussion and consideration, and, after weighing the objections of the president, still believes it ought to pass, it should become a law provided a majority of *all* the members of each House concur in its passage. If the weight of his argument, and the weight of his influence conjointly, can not prevail on a majority, against their previous convictions, in my opinion, the bill ought not to be arrested. Such is the provision of the Constitutions of several of the States, and that of Kentucky among them.

Thirdly, the power of dismission from office, should be restricted, and the exercise of it be rendered responsible.

The constitutional concurrence of the Senate is necessary to the confirmation of all important appointments; but, without consulting the Senate, without any other motive than resentment or caprice, the president may dismiss, at his sole pleasure, an officer created by the joint action of himself and the Senate. The practical effect is, to nullify the agency of the Senate. There may be, occasionally, cases in which the public interest requires an immediate dismission without waiting for the assembling of the Senate; but, in all such cases, the president should be bound to communicate fully the grounds and motives of the dismission. The power would be thus rendered responsible. Without it, the exercise of the power is utterly repugnant to free institutions, the basis of which is perfect responsibility, and dangerous to the public liberty, as has been already shown.

Fourthly, the control over the treasury of the United States should be confided and confined exclusively to Congress; and all authority of the president over it, by means of dismissing the Secretary of the Treasury, or other persons having the immediate charge of it, be rigorously precluded.

You have heard much, fellow-citizens, of the divorce of banks and government. After crippling them and impairing their utility, the executive and its partisans have systematically denounced them. The executive and the country were warned again and again of the fatal course that has been pursued; but the executive nevertheless persevered, commencing by praising, and ending by decrying, the State banks. Under cover of the smoke which has been raised, the real object all along has been, and yet is, to obtain the possession of the money power of the Union. That accomplished and sanctioned by the people—the union of the sword and the purse in the hands of the president effectually secured—and farewell to American liberty.

The sub-treasury is the scheme for effecting that union; and, I am told, that of all the days in the year, that which gave birth to our national existence and freedom, is the selected day to be disgraced by ushering into existence a measure imminently perilous to the liberty, which, on that anniversary, we commemorate in joyous festivals. Thus, in the spirit of destruction which animates our rulers, would they convert a day of gladness and of glory, into a day of sadness and mourning. Fellow-citizens, there is one divorce urgently demanded by the safety and the highest interests of the country—a divorce of the president from the treasury of the United States. . . .

These are the subjects, in relation to the permanent character of the government itself, which, it seems to me, are worthy of the serious attention of the people, and of a new administration.

During the campaign, General Harrison modified his corrective therapy for the presidency somewhat as he toured the countryside seeking votes. His speeches were designed more to stimulate enthusiasm among potential voters than to deal analytically with questions like presidential power. But he did continue to attack the power of the presidency and to promise to return to the purity and balance of government which he maintained was the intent of the Founding Fathers. Chambers has characterized some of these efforts of campaign oratory as dealing "in careful ambiguities and some sheer buncombe."[89] But the unremitting attack upon presidential power which characterized the Whigs' efforts continued, and apparently the substantial number of voters who turned out to hear him loved every minute of it. The following document is a section from one of these campaign speeches which Harrison delivered to a Dayton, Ohio, audience in mid-September, 1840. It is quite typical of his remarks on the presidency during the campaign.

General William Henry Harrison
Campaign Speech (Extract) at Dayton, Ohio
September 10, 1840

Arthur M. Schlesinger, jr., and Fred L. Israel, eds., *History of American Presidential Elections, 1789-1968* (New York, 1971) I, 738-40.

. . . It has been charged against me, fellow citizens, that I am a Federalist. While I acknowledge that the original Federal party of this country was actuated in its course by no improper motives, I deny that I ever belonged to that class of politicians. [Tremendous cheering.] How could I belong to that party? I educated in the school of anti-federalism, and though too young to take an active part in the politics of the country, when at the erection of the Constitution, the nation was divided into two great parties, my honored father has inducted me into the principles of Constitutional Democracy, and my teachers were the Henrys and the Masons of that period. He who declared that the seeds of monarchy were sown in the soil of the Constitution, was a leader in my school of politics. He, who said that "if this government be not a monarchy, it has an awful squinting towards a monarchy," was my Mentor. [Immense applause. Some time elapsed before order could be restored, at hearing these emphatic declarations of the General.] If I know my own feelings, if I know my own judgment, I believe now, as I did then, with the patriarchs of the Jeffersonian school, that the seeds of monarchy were indeed sown in the fertile soil of our Federal Constitution; and that though for nearly fifty years they lay dormant, they at last sprouted and shot forth into strong and thriving plants, bearing blossoms and producing ripe fruit. The Government is now a practical monarchy! [Loud and long cheering indicating that the people felt the full force of his declaration.] Power is power, it matters not by what name it is called. The head of the Government exercising monarchial power, may be named King, Emperor, President, or Imaum, [great laughter] still he is a monarch. But this is not all. The President of these United States exercises a power superior to that vested in the hands of nearly all the European Kings. It is a power far greater than that ever dreamed of by the old Federal party.

It is an ultra federal power, it is despotism! [Cheering.] And I may here advert to an objection that has been made against me. It has been said, that if I ever should arrive at the dignified station occupied by my opponent, I would be glad and eager to retain the power enjoyed by the President of the United States. Never, never. [Tremendous cheering.] Though averse from pledges of every sort, I here openly and before the world declare that I will use all the power and influence vested in the office of President of the Union to abridge the power and influence of the National Executive! [It is impossible to describe the sensation produced by this declaration.] Is this federalism? [Cries of no, no, for several seconds.] In the Constitution, that glorious charter of our liberties, there is a defect, and that defect is, the term of service of the President,—not limited. This omission is the source of all the evil under which the country is laboring. If the privilege of being President of the United States had been limited to one term, the incumbent would devote all his time to the public interest, and there would be no cause to misrule the country. I shall not animadvert on the conduct of the present administration, lest you may in that case, conceive that I am aiming for the Presidency, to use it for selfish purposes. I should be an interested witness, if I entered into the subject. But I pledge myself before Heaven and earth, if elected President of these United States, to lay down at the end of the term faithfully that high trust at the feet of the people! [Here the multitude was so excited as to defy description.]

I go farther. I here declare before this vast assembly of the Miami Tribe (great laughter) that if I am elected, no human being shall ever know upon whom I would prefer to see the people's mantle fall; but I shall surrender this glorious badge of their authority into their own hands to bestow it as they please!—(nine cheers.) Is this federalism? (No, no, no.) Again in relation to the charge of being a federalist, I can refer to the doings previous to, and during the late war. The federal party took ground against that war, and as a party, there never existed a purer band of patriots, for when the note of strife was sounded, they rallied under the banner of their country. But patriotic as they were, I do know that I was not one of them! [Cheering.] I was denounced in unmeasured terms as one of the authors of that war, and was held up by the federal papers of the day as the marked object of the party. I could here name the man who came to me, and a more worthy man never lived, to say that he was mistaken in his views of my policy, as Governor of Indiana, when I was charged by the federalists as uselessly involving the country in an Indian war. He told me that I acted rightly in that matter, and that the war was brought on by me as a matter of necessity. [Cries of name him, name him.] It was Mr. Gaston of North Carolina. [Three cheers.] Is this a proof that I was a federalist? [No, no, no.]

Before 1840 it was almost unheard of for a presidential candidate to conduct an active election campaign (including speaking tours up and down the country). But the Whigs of 1840 broke ground in many respects, and General Harrison and many of his outstanding supporters were out in the hustings, kicking up the dust and engaging in one of the most active political campaigns in American history. The general spoke 23 different times during the campaign to crowds estimated at from 1,000 to 100,000 at the Dayton meeting, other Whig leaders such as Clay and Webster joining him in some of these efforts. The stump speeches and the turnouts were unprecedented in American political history and contributed substantially to the groundswell of enthusiasm which finally produced the victory. Former President John Quincy Adams did not take too kindly to this sure sign of erosion of the "Age of Deference":

Electioneering for the Presidency has spread its contagion to the President himself, to his now only competitor, to his immediate predecessor, to one at least of his Cabinet councillors, the Secretary of War, to the ex-candidates Henry Clay and Daniel Webster, and to many of the most distinguished members of both houses of Congress. Immense assemblages of the people are held—of twenty, thirty, fifty thousand souls—where the first orators of the nation address the multitude, not one in ten of whom can hear them, on the most exciting topics of the day.[90]

Adams refused to appear on any such occasions, and was concerned as to where they would lead:

I received earnest invitations to attend these meetings . . . all of which I declined, both from general principles and from considerations specially and peculiarly applicable to myself. . . . Here is a revolution in the habits and manners of the people. Where will it end? These are party movements, and must in the natural progress of things become antagonistical. These meetings cannot be multiplied in numbers and frequency without resulting in yet deeper tragedies. Their manifest tendency is civil war.[91]

The Whigs in Power:
The Brief Tenure of William Henry Harrison

On election day, Harrison and Tyler won by a respectable margin (52.9 percent of the votes to 46.8 for Van Buren and Johnson) in the largest voter turnout for any presidential election up to that time. The 2,412,698 voters who cast their ballots represented 80.2 percent of the eligible voters in the country, and this percentage has only been exceeded twice in the presidential elections occurring in the 132 years since that time. The Whigs did considerably better in the electoral college where Harrison and Tyler won 19 states with 234 electoral votes to Van Buren's and Johnson's 7 states and 60 electoral votes.

Despite the fact that the Democrats were the majority party in the country, and remained so after the election, it was clear that the Whigs' aggressive campaign had developed the kind of enthusiasm that, coupled with the tremendous organizational efforts of leaders like Stevens and Weed,[92] resulted in the substantial turnout and the respectable margin of victory. The Democrats were able to carry only New Hampshire in New England, Virginia and South Carolina in the South and four states in the northwest and southwest. The Whigs carried all of the middle states, every large state in the Union except Virginia and piled up impressive victories in traditional Democratic strongholds like Tennessee, Georgia and North Carolina.[93]

The results of the congressional elections were especially gratifying to the party which constantly attacked "executive usurpation" and was struggling to reassert the legislative role, if not legislative supremacy, in government. In the Senate the Whigs were able to reverse a Democratic majority of 28 to 22, transforming it into the exact reverse: 28 Whigs to 22 Democrats. A similar reversal was achieved in the House where a previous Democratic margin of 124 to 118 was overturned, and 133 Whigs confronted 102 Democrats. This meant that the incoming Harrison administration would have a majority in both houses of Congress, which would seem almost to guarantee the initial success of its policies. This must have been heady wine for Clay and Webster who had been in the minority opposition for so long that they had probably forgotten what it was like to be in the majority. Even when they had commanded majority support in the Senate, they were forced to contend with the opposition party in control of the White House and frequently the House of Representatives.

Contemplating the victory from his idyllic retreat in Kentucky, however, Henry Clay must have had mixed feelings about these events. He certainly had to have felt a trace of bitterness over the fact that now that the Whigs had become powerful enough to win a national election, Harrison and not he was the victorious candidate for President. On the other hand, as the ideological and legislative leader of a party which espoused a return to legislative leadership, he could look forward to a session of Congress in which for the first time in years, he could develop real policy leadership and count upon active *support* from the White House. And Henry Clay was superbly qualified to pursue this role.

It is difficult to assess how important this opportunity was to a political man like Clay. Politics, and essentially national politics, had been his life's work, and he had been more successful at it than anyone in his era except Andrew Jackson.

Webster had defined the nature of the constitutional struggle in the nullification crisis and made a number of other noteworthy speeches on the floor of the Senate, and Calhoun had defended his region's interests against the power and logic of the national will; but Clay was the political figure in Congress who commanded the greatest respect and following, and who played the game of politics with such style and effectiveness that in the heat of battle both these other giants were child's play for "Harry of the West." Neither of these outsized figures had mastered the art of politics as Clay had; neither could generate the enthusiastic national or legislative following that he could. Clay lived and breathed politics, and everything that he did was fundamentally political in nature. To be transformed from the constantly losing opposition leader to the mainspring of a national party which had just achieved dominance in both the legislative and executive branches of the government was an historical moment of great importance. The question then became, would Clay be able to live with victory as brilliantly and as heroically as he had borne defeat for all these years?

There is no question that President-elect Harrison was concerned about this problem, and also in doubt as to how he would handle Clay and the other preeminent figure in his victorious party—the oft-described "godlike" Daniel Webster. He knew that they were bound to play significant roles in the new administration, but how best to utilize their indisputable talents and influence, and at the same time to control their ambitions, their personal jealousy and their frequently arrogant and dominating personalities was a problem of significant proportions.

Harrison was circumspect about publicly consulting with Clay, particularly before he announced his cabinet, for he was apprehensive about charges that he was under the Kentuckian's influence. In a pre-inaugural trip to Kentucky the old general tried to avoid a meeting with Clay, but he did not succeed in eluding the experienced old war horse of American politics. Harrison was in Frankfort, Kentucky, conferring with local enemies of Clay with regard to future appointments, when the senator appeared in the capital city with a group of his supporters. Clay literally abducted the President-elect, brought him to his estate in Ashland and conversed with him for some hours. It was not a particularly successful meeting however, and their future relationship was not improved by any understandings reached at that time. The President-elect offered Senator Clay the office of secretary of state, the most esteemed position in the cabinet, but Clay refused and did not even press Harrison at that time to influence other cabinet appointments. The President-elect was then free to offer Webster the State Department (instead of the Treasury) and mollified Clay by appointing his close colleague and friend, John Crittenden, attorney general. Subsequently, Clay pushed hard for only one cabinet appointment—that of John Clayton as secretary of the navy—but in a stormy session with the senator, the President turned him down. During the heat of the argument, Harrison was overheard to say: "Mr. Clay, you forget that I am the President."[94]

Clay's decision to stay out of Harrison's cabinet was probably prompted by his judgment that he could be far more influential in the role of the party's legislative leader in a Whig administration pledged to end "executive usurpation." If the Whigs proceeded to enact their program of reform, then the leader of the party in Congress would loom largest on the horizon as the Whig heir to the presidency in 1844, particularly if the infirm and elderly incumbent was willing to step down at the age of 81. After all, the Whig program would have to be fought for and won on the floor of Congress, and in addition, Clay already had significant influence among a majority of the President's cabinet, which again, under the Whig conception of the function of the executive branch, would be expected to play a more prominent role than it ever had before within the new administration. In theory it appeared to be a successful formula for enacting the Whig program, and accomplishing that, it would be a stepping-stone to the White House. For Clay this was important, for it was the only goal he had yet to achieve and it would crown his extraordinary career in American politics.

But there were difficulties with this "formula." Harrison was suspicious of Clay, and sensitive about the Kentuckian's efforts to manipulate him and to reduce his status as President. It was one thing to denounce "executive usurpation" on the campaign hustings, but quite another to abdicate and invite the congressional leaders of the party to dominate the presidential office once in power. President Harrison was not opposed to seeing Whig policies enacted; he just did not want them shoved down his throat by Henry Clay and a Whig majority in Congress. On the occasion of his inauguration, he reaffirmed his commitment to Whig doctrines, but gave no indication of the difficulties and consequences to his office that implementing this theory into practice would present.

The inaugural address of President William Henry Harrison was the longest in the history of the office. He was apparently assisted by both Clay and Webster in preparing the speech, and at least one-half of it is devoted to a denunciation of "executive usurpation." He embellished upon the Whig litany of presidential limitations offered during the campaign, defining, in effect, an office which would have become a mere cipher if his proposals had been put into practice. The address reflected no political understanding of the office, no recognition of the difficulties encountered by a Chief Executive defending himself against a naturally aggressive and jealous legislature, and did not even offer any realistic guidelines as to how his principled proposals would be administered. For example, he lamented the fact that the framers of the Constitution did not make the secretary of the treasury a position "independent of the Executive. He should at least have been removable only upon the demand of the popular branch of the Legislature," General Harrison argued.[95] Did that mean that the Chief Executive should not have the power to remove the secretary of the treasury, as the Whig campaign oratory had indicated? In the very next sentence, he promised "never to remove a Secretary of the Treasury without communicating all the circumstances attending such removal to both Houses of Congress."[96] Where did that leave the power of removal? Did Harrison relinquish it or not? And what did the verb "communicate" imply? Did it mean simply to inform, or was there the implication that the information before the Congress could be approved or disapproved?

All these questions later became very critical to the problem of presidential power, but Harrison revealed little or nothing about how the powers he denounced would actually be curtailed. As one reads the address, the impression grows that this man sensed very little about performing the actual role of the President of the United States. There is no sensitivity for the office reflected in his remarks, nor any informed recognition of executive responsibility. If he had lived to serve out his full term in office, it could have been a disaster from which the presidential office might not have recovered.

This is meaningless speculation, of course, because William Henry Harrison died in office a month after he delivered his inaugural address. Already he and Clay had clashed on critical matters too often, and the President had decided to terminate further verbal communication with the able leader of the Whig party and only to correspond with him in writing. Webster's growing influence with Harrison might have been partially responsible for this abrasive tension which developed between the Chief Executive and the leader of the Whig party in Congress; but more important, there was a gap that was becoming apparent between the Whig campaign rhetoric which Harrison piously reiterated time and time again before the election and in his inaugural, and the realities of power which these policies implied for a President confronted by a powerful party and a legislative leader with the stature of Clay.

Clay was a serious and perhaps the quintessential Whig. His attack upon "executive usurpation" had developed organically from the reality of his escalating conflicts with the powerful opposition party leader and President, Andrew Jackson. In fact the emergence of the Whig opposition to growing presidential power was an historical enigma, because many of the old National Republicans, the "birthright" Whigs, if you please, were closer social and economic heirs to the Hamiltonian tradition than to Jeffersonian Republicanism, regardless of their rhetoric. On economic and social questions they tended to agree with Hamilton, but repudiated his views on presidential power because the realities of their situation as the *outs* dictated a policy of strong opposition to the *ins* who advocated strong presidential power. As Leonard White has put it: "The Whigs were driven into an incongruous position on the nature and extent of executive power because they had to offer political opposition to the bold exercise of executive authority by Jackson."[97] But Henry Clay had as much to do with the evolution of Whig thinking and policy as any man in the party, and despite his presidential ambitions, he was totally committed to the attack upon "executive usurpation." What his attitude on the subject might have been had he been elected President rather than Harrison is a matter of speculation, but as the legislative leader of the party which had campaigned and been elected on a program designed to restore legislative initiative and lost legislative prerogatives, he was determined to press for implementing such policy.

As the last few months of the old Congress were still dominated by the Democratic majority, which was able to block Clay's leadership, the senator from Kentucky pushed for a special session to be held as quickly as possible in order to get the Whig program underway. However, Harrison and his secretary of state, Daniel Webster, favored a delay. If the organization of the Whig Congress could be postponed another eight months until Harrison and Webster had their administration well underway and the patronage all dispensed, etc., Clay with all his power in both the Senate and the House would have had a difficult time bending the President's policies to his purposes. This was the reality of political power, and Clay well understood what was at stake in this decision. That was why he pushed so hard for an extra session to be convened almost immediately. It was also the reason why Harrison, who was probably greatly influenced by Clay's old rival, Webster, realized the advantage of slowing the Clay steamroller down, so that it would not run right over the White House.

This clash between Clay, the real leader of the Whig party, and Harrison, its titular head and President, was inevitable regardless of all the Whig campaign oratory on the subject, but that it came so early in the new administration's tenure was indeed surprising. It was not triggered by any falling out on policy questions, but rather on the basis of pre-policy planning and essentially the timing of the special session of Congress. Clay was pushing hard for an immediate decision on an early call by the President, and Harrison was looking for reasons to delay.

The Chief Executive finally found a reason for delay in the complex case of the senatorial delegation from Tennessee, which was then in dispute in the state legislature. An early special session would probably bring two more Democrats to the Senate from Tennessee, for the Democrats maintained a slim majority in the legislature in that state. On the other hand, if the session were to be held after August, when a new election was scheduled, the Whigs were confident of sweeping the election and sending two Whigs from Tenessee to the Senate. This was a rather telling argument, since the Whig majority in the Senate was paper thin, and there had been poor attendance and some defections in the regular session. Nevertheless Clay pushed ahead, to the consternation of some of his most loyal followers. He held victory in sight, and he was unwilling to let up. When the President continued to delay his decision on the special session, the Whig legislative leader sent an imperious and somewhat demanding "confidential" letter to the President.[08]

Senator Henry Clay
Letter to President William Henry Harrison
March 13, 1841

George Rawlings Poage, *Henry Clay and the Whig Party* (Chapel Hill, North Carolina, 1936), 30.

Will you excuse me, for suggesting the propriety of a definite decision about an Extra Session, and of announcing the fact? There is much speculation and uncertainty about it, in circles [sic] and among members of Congress. Time is rapidly passing away, and members of your Cabinet have, it is alleged, added to the uncertainty.

After all that has occurred; after what you have said at Richmond and elsewhere, if the purpose of calling one should be abandoned, there is danger of the implication of vacillating counsels.

I have never doubted for a moment about it since Novr. In my deliberate opinion, the good of the Country and the honor and interest of the party demand it.

By way of stating the grounds for the convocation, I have sketched the rough draft of a proclamation which I respectfully submit for your perusal, as best indicating what strikes me as expedient.

I think your election should occupy the front and most prominent ground. The financial difficulties of the Gov't. alone form too narrow a basis to put the call upon; but the draft now enclosed covers that and all other grounds.

Altho' not well, I shall have the honor of dining with you today, when I should be most happy to learn your final decision.

Although America is not a country of titled monarchs, and despite the fact that the Whigs came to power in a campaign which downgraded the office of the Chief Executive, even as powerful a personality as Clay was walking on thin ice in addressing the President in this manner. Harrison clearly was offended by his "impetuous" demand, and sat down that very afternoon and answered Clay's letter in his own hand, "carrying its sting," as Poage puts it, "in its tail like a scorpion."[99]

President William Henry Harrison
Reply to Senator Henry Clay
March 13, 1841

Poage, 30-31.

My dear friend, You use the privilege of a friend to lecture me and I take the same liberty with you.

You are too impetuous. Much as I rely upon your judgment there are others whom I must consult and in many cases to determine [sic] adversely to your suggestion. In the matter to which your communication of this morning refers there is no difference of opinion as to the manner and there would be none as to the time but for the situation of Tennessee to whom we owe so much. Her feelings and interest must not be sacrificed if it can be avoided. The question will be finally settled on Monday having been adjourned over from a discussion which took place this morning.

I prefer for many reasons this mode of answering your note to a conversation in the presence of others.

Apparently Clay was enraged at the President's reply and correctly understood it as an explicit indication that his influence with the President in the future would be minimal. He exploded to a newspaper correspondent who happened to be calling on him at the time of its reception. While pacing the floor and crumbling the note in his hands, he said:

And it has come to this! I am civilly but virtually requested not to visit the White House,—not to see the President personally, but hereafter only communicate with him in writing. The prediction I made to him at Ashland last fall has been verified. [Clay had told Harrison then that others might come between them and sow dissention in the party.] Here is my table loaded with letters from my friends in every part of the Union, applying to me to obtain offices for them, when I have not one to give, nor influence enough to secure the appointment of a friend to the most humble position![100]

Clay saw Harrison that evening at a state dinner at the White House, but they never had another private conversation. Before leaving for Ashland, however, the Kentuckian wrote a final note to the President which terminated the discussion.

Senator Henry Clay
Final Note to President William Henry Harrison
March 15, 1841

Colton, V, 452-53.

My Dear Sir,—Your incessant engagements preclude the probability of my having any opportunity of a private conversation with you, prior to my departure from this city. I therefore adopt this mode of saying a few words before I go.

I was mortified by the suggestion you made to me on Saturday, that I had been represented as dictating to you, or to the new Administration—mortified, because it is unfounded in fact, and because there is danger of the fears, that I intimated to you at Frankfort, of my enemies poisoning your mind toward me.

In what, in truth, can they allege a dictation, or even interference, on my part? In the formation of your Cabinet? You can contradict them. In the administration of the public patronage? The whole Cabinet as well as yourself can say that. I have recommended nobody for any office. I have sought none for myself, or my friends. I desire none. A thousand times have my feelings been wounded, by communicating to those who have applied to me, that I am obliged to abstain inflexibly from all interference in official appointments.

I learned to-day, with infinite surprise, that I had been represented as saying that Mr. Curtis should not be appointed Collector of New York. It is utterly unfounded. I never uttered such expressions in relation to that or any other office, of the humblest grade, within your gift. I have never gone beyond expressing the opinion that he is faithless and perfidious, and, in my judgment, unworthy of the place. It is one of the artifices by which he expects to succeed.

If to express freely my opinion, as a citizen and as a Senator, in regard to public matters, be dictation, then I have dictated, and not otherwise. There is but one alternative which I could embrace, to prevent the exercise of this common right of freedom of opinion, and that is retirement to private life. That I am most desirous of, and if I do not promptly indulge the feeling, it is because I entertain the hope—perhaps vain hope—that by remaining a little longer in the Senate, I may possibly render some service to a country to whose interests my life has been dedicated.

I do not wish to trouble you with answering this note. I could not reconcile it to my feelings to abstain from writing it. Your heart, in which I have the greatest confidence, will justly appreciate the motives of, whatever others may say or insinuate, your true and faithful friend.

Clay's efforts to promote a special session of Congress were finally successful, despite his difficulties in convincing President Harrison. Apparently his strong influence with members of Harrison's cabinet had something to do with this, for the cabinet actually made the decision to reconvene Congress on May 31 of that year. When the leader of the Whig party in Congress returned to Washington to attend the special session, President Harrison was dead and Clay was confronted with a new, and as it turned out, an even more stubborn defender of executive prerogatives, and also a President who was extraordinarily sensitive to the slightest hint of legislative interference or efforts to influence his independent opinions and actions.

John Tyler in Office

John Tyler was the first Vice President of the United States to succeed to the presidency. The event caused something of a constitutional flurry since some were in doubt as to whether he remained as the Vice President acting in the office of the President or whether he actually succeeded to the office and title of the President of the United States. Fortunately Tyler himself had no doubts on this score and insisted upon the latter definition, despite some grumbling in Congress. He must be credited with having made a sound contribution to constitutional practice by his interpretation of this procedure. Any other view would have left the country without a real Chief Executive for a period too long and too dangerous even to contemplate it seriously.

Tyler was notified of Harrison's death soon after the event by a courier dispatched by the cabinet to his home in Williamsburg, Virginia. He hurried to Washington to take the oath of office and moved into the White House in the course of the next ten days. The new Chief Executive at once asked President Harrison's cabinet to remain in office and they complied with his request. But the trimmings of power were easier to come by than its actuality and before many days had passed, Tyler too would confront the leader of the Whig party and the Whig battle cry of "executive usurpation."

President Tyler soon delivered his own inaugural address. It was a very different expression of policy than Harrison's speech of the previous month. There was no lengthy denunciation of presidential power, although he did genuflect once or twice in the direction of the Whig party principles. There were no promises to create an independent secretary of the treasury, or to relinquish the removing power or the veto, but he did promise to apply the latter with discretion and decried the Whig anathema—"the union of the purse and sword." He also created some hopes in the Clay camp that he would not frustrate their plans to reestablish a central banking institution, similar if not identical to the Bank of the United States, but the statement was enigmatic enough not to reassure them too much:

> I shall promptly give my sanction to any constitutional measure which, originating in Congress, shall have for its object the restoration of a sound circulating medium. . . . In deciding upon the adaptation of any such measure to the end proposed, as well as its conformity to the Constitution, I shall resort to the fathers of the great republican school for advice and instruction, to be drawn from their sage views of our system of government. . . .[101]

Of course this could mean anything. Washington approved Hamilton's plan for the establishment of the original bank, after studying Madison's attack on it in Congress and carefully analyzing Jefferson's and Randolph's disapproving opinions submitted to him in writing (see Volume I of this series). Madison allowed the Second Bank of the United States to be chartered, although he still disapproved of it in principle. Tyler had always been opposed to the Bank and had supported Jackson's veto of it while in the Senate, but had not approved of his removal of the government's funds. What he would do now as a President who had attained this high status through the activity of a political party which was committed to the establishment of such a bank remained to be seen. There were conjectures in both directions from the best-informed individuals closest to the President. Even his secretary of state and quite intimate advisor, Webster, guessed wrong at his decision.[102]

Of even greater significance than his enigmatic statement on the bank was another paragraph in Tyler's unprecedented "inaugural" address, which was more specific about what his future attitudes would be. Parenthetically, one does not ordinarily think of John Tyler as a birthright Whig. He was fundamentally a states' rights Democrat who had left the fold when Jackson introduced the Force Bill in the nullification crisis. In fact he was the only senator to vote against it, the rest of the opposition taking the curious position of refusing to vote on the measure.

An indication of his strict sense of integrity was exhibited when he resigned his seat in the Senate rather than vote in compliance with instructions from the Virginia state legislature to expunge the Senate vote (which he supported) to censure the President on his removal of the funds and his firing of Secretary of the Treasury Duane. States' rights and southern institutions were the loadstones of John Tyler's political principles, and his adherence to the Whig party came only after he came to the conclusion (as had Calhoun at the time) that Andrew Jackson had abandoned both to advance his national and personal power. In a critical situation where any other principles or policies came into conflict with these fundamental points of view, he left no doubt in anybody's mind where he would stand. In his inaugural address, he stated:

> Those who are charged with its [the national government's] administration should carefully abstain from all attempts to enlarge the range of powers thus granted to the several departments of the Government other than by an appeal to the people for additional grants,

lest by so doing they disturb the balance which the patriots and statesmen who framed the Constitution designed to establish between the Federal Government and the States composing the Union. . . . . An opposite course could not fail to generate factions intent upon the gratification of the selfish ends, to give birth to local and sectional jealousies, and to ultimate either in breaking asunder the bonds of union or in building up a central system which would inevitably end in a bloody scepter and an iron crown.[103]

The states' rights position had generated from Jefferson's and Madison's day, when it was essentially a theory advocating local Democratic autonomy, but it had become an undisguised defense of the institution of slavery, which by Tyler's time was almost entirely restricted to the southern states. Southerners feared the growing power of the federal government, which could be used as an instrument of outlawing slavery and otherwise interfering with their way of life. They fought tenaciously against every new increment of federal power, seeing in each such step a potential weapon against their interests. While the doctrine of strict construction of the Constitution was for Madison and Jefferson a principle which would protect the liberties of a free people from the encroachment of oppressive government, for the states' rights sectionalists, although they wrapped themselves in the mantle of Jeffersonian Republicanism, their interpretation of strict construction was narrowly conceived to protect their minority and sectional interests in slavery from the intrusion of the gathering disfavor by the will of the national majority. The logic of their position induced them to define the Constitution as a compact between equal and sovereign entities, rather than as the voice of a sovereign nation, a national federal union of equal but not sovereign (except in the specific manner in which the Constitution defined that sovereignty) states.

The states' rights men, like the idealogues, used politics and political parties as a means to achieving their ends, and their commitment to both was only as strong and lasted only as long as both served these interests. They were ready and willing to cut away from either when it appeared to them that these institutions were failing to perform their required functions. They did not differ from any other serious group in demanding that political parties or the political process respond to their needs and interests. Such is the nature of politics. The difference was in the manner in which these interests were approached.

Aristotle defined man as a political and rational animal, and by that he meant that the state and political institutions are necessary and essential to man's survival and development. No two men have precisely the same interests, and a city or a nation, in some sense, contains as many interests as it does citizens. It follows then that compromise is the essence of this process of politics, for all of these various interests have to be reconciled before parties and political policies can function and perform their creative and constructive roles. The political man, albeit pursuing his own interests, recognizes this and adjusts his conduct accordingly.

The idealogue and the states' rights advocate, however, cannot accept the political process in quite the same sense. They must impose upon political parties and the political process rigid and uncompromising demands to which these institutions frequently cannot respond. At this point there is a stand-off, perhaps a defection from a political party, and in the case of the political process, sometimes a paralysis of government, a total withdrawal from politics and the assertion of claims through other means, even in the ultimate case, resorting to a civil war. One has to consider the logical consequences of these positions in evaluating their justification and their role in the historical process.

Perhaps both Clay and President Tyler sensed the inevitability of their personal conflict from the beginning, but the President's earliest actions and words belied this and even indicated that he wanted to avoid it. His relations with Clay in the past had been good; in fact it was generally thought that Clay had been responsible for Tyler's elevation to the vice presidential candidacy. Their initial correspondence after Tyler was sworn in was extremely cordial, and the President seemed to be attempting to convince the Kentuckian that he intended to defer to his views on patronage and other personnel matters in the administration. But soon after Clay began to press forward with the Whig legislative program, in apparent disregard for Tyler's well-established opposition to the Bank, the cordiality began to disappear and was replaced by a reserved and contemptuous attitude. Perhaps in the cold light of the dawn over the White House, the new President did not take too kindly to the Whig design for the executive office, inferior to and responsive to the demands and policies of the legislature. Perhaps too, he realized the implications of this position as it related to the core of the states' rights interests.

Clay's strategy was to drive ahead with a fully developed Whig economic program emerging from Congress, and he assumed that the Whig President would cooperate. In his capacity as majority leader in the Senate he submitted a series of resolutions which outlined the contours of the Whig program. They indicated that Congress should confine itself to the consideration of urgent questions; that it ought to deal first, if not exclusively, with problems of an economic and social nature which were troubling the people, and paramount among these were:

> The repeal of the sub-Treasury; the incorporation of a bank adapted to the wants of the people, and of the government; the provision of an adequate revenue for the Government by the imposition of duties, and including an authority to contract a temporary loan to cover the public debt created by the last Administration; the prospective distribution of the proceeds of the public lands; the passage of necessary appropriations bills, and some modification of the banking system of the District of Columbia, for the benefit of the people of the District.[104]

Finally, the Clay resolutions urged a division of labor between the two houses in preparing these measures.

Despite the importance of all the measures mentioned in the resolutions, Clay and the Whigs were particularly intent upon eliminating the sub-Treasury system established by Van Buren, and to move ahead in creating a national bank. The opposition of the new President was certainly anticipated in this case, despite the well-known support of the Bank by most leading Whigs, and the effort was made to arrive at some understanding with him before they reached an impasse. Both men were apprehensive about the possibility of obtaining such an agreement, however. Clay wrote his friend, Francis Brooke:

I repair to my post in the Senate with strong hopes, not, however, unmixed with fears. If the Executive will cordially cooperate in carrying out the Whig measures, all will be well. Otherwise everything is at hazard. . . .[105]

Tyler was also concerned. Writing to Judge Tucker, he revealed that

my fear now is that nothing short of a National Bank, similar in all its features to that which has recently passed out of existence, will meet the views of the prominent men in the Whig Party.[106]

Five days later, the President wrote to Clay, hoping to obtain his agreement to delay consideration of the Bank Bill:

Considering the brief time allowed me and the extreme pressure on my time, it will not be expected that I shall come before Congress with matured plans of public policy connected with deeply interesting and intricate subjects. . . As to a Bank, I design to be perfectly frank with you— I would not have it urged too prematurely. The public mind is in a state of great disquietude in regard to it . . . I have no intention to submit anything to Congress on this subject to be acted on, but shall leave it to its own action, and in the end shall resolve my doubt by the character of the measure proposed, should any be entertained by me.[107]

The President sent his first message to Congress at the beginning of the special session which began in June 1841. He began with a plea to the Congress to make provisions to cover the losses incurred by his predecessor in moving out of his private home and taking up residence in Washington, and suggested that the Congress reimburse the former President's family of the expenses incurred by this sudden change which developed late in life. The message then went on to describe the condition of the country, to cite the rising population growth, and also to examine in some detail the growing fiscal deficit in government income.

All of this underscored the necessity of coming to grips with the problems the country faced in attempting to recover its economic equilibrium. The President had no answers here, but he reviewed the three previous efforts at establishing "a suitable fiscal agent, capable of adding increased facilities in the collection and disbursement of the public revenues, rendering more secure their custody, and consulting a true economy in the great, multiplied and delicate operations of the Treasury Department."[108] He indicated that all three efforts—the Bank of the United States, the dispersion of government funds and depositing them in various "state banks" and finally the sub-Treasury scheme masterminded by Van Buren, had not only failed to demonstrate their value in the public interest but had been rejected by the people.

This more than hinted that he would not respond favorably to a proposal to establish another national bank. Yet in the end, he threw the gauntlet back to the Congress, inviting their attention to the problem and making no specific suggestions concerning in which direction they should move:

To you then, who have come more directly from the body of our common constituents, I submit the entire question, as best qualified to give a full exposition of their wishes and opinions. I shall be ready to concur with you in the adoption of such a system as you may propose, reserving to myself the ultimate power of rejecting any measure which may, in my view of it, conflict with the Constitution or otherwise jeopardize the prosperity of the country—a power which I could not part with even if I would, but which I will not believe any act of yours will call into requisition.[109]

There was certainly a different emphasis in Tyler's description of the veto power here from former President Harrison's discussion of it in his inaugural address. Coupled with the knowledge of the President's long history of opposition on constitutional grounds to the establishment of a national bank, and his unique and quite courageous record of sticking to his principles under fire, there was cause for some concern about a future confrontation with the senator from Kentucky on this issue.

Events moved ahead rapidly in the Senate where the policy initiative now rested with Clay. After introducing the outline of the Whig legislative program, the majority leader acted immediately to implement these policies. His major concern was the bank question because it was the most controversial and because this was the issue which threatened to divide the Whig President from his party in Congress. Before any parliamentary moves were made, however, Senator Clay and President Tyler had a face-to-face confrontation. It was a significant meeting, for in truth, the future of the Whig party, and actually the power of the presidential office for some time to come, hung in the balance of the resolution of this issue.

Tyler had been exploring several alternative ideas to the establishment of a national bank; he searched for some kind of fiscal instrument which could fulfill the essential functions of a bank, but at the same time avoid the constitutional problems which were bothering him. The President finally decided to sound out reactions to an old proposal advanced earlier by Hugh Lawson White—to establish a bank in the District of Columbia which could in turn establish branches in the several states if they agreed to such an arrangement. Tyler won the reluctant approval of his cabinet for this proposal, and later discussed it with Clay. The President tried hard to interest Clay in the idea, but he would have none of it. Then Tyler, according to a report by his son, lost his temper and exploded:

> Then, Sir, I wish you to understand this—that you and I were born in the same district; that we have fed upon the same food, and have breathed the same natal air. Go you now, then Mr. Clay, to your end of the avenue, where stands the Capitol and there perform your duty to the country as you think proper. So help me God, I shall do mine at this end of it as I think proper.[110]

Clay did just that. He had himself appointed chairman of a select committee to work on fiscal matters raised by the President's report, and he quickly rammed through the Senate a bill to repeal the Van Buren sub-Treasury law. Following closely upon that, the Whig majority leader introduced a resolution directing the secretary of the treasury to introduce a plan for a national bank best adopted to the public service, but his colleagues convinced him to modify this request by adding the phrase "or fiscal agent," and suggested that it be free from constitutional objections.

This set the stage for Secretary of the Treasury Ewing to introduce a bill incorporating Senator White's plan, which already had the approval of the President and his cabinet.

The later speeches by the Senate Whig majority leader clearly indicate that he was annoyed by the conditions first imposed by his colleagues and which now appeared in the Ewing bill. In effect the Whigs were contradicting their basic principles by this type of bargaining with the Chief Executive. The *raison d'etre* of the Whig party was its resentment against "executive usurpation," but here the Whigs were in power in the Congress, and yet even before the Senate considered the question in committee, they were bending to conditions imposed by the Whig President. On the other hand, Clay was a practical politician and he did not want to permanently impair the party or its future. He probably went along with the compromises because he was primarily interested in getting a law establishing some kind of national bank, and although he later indicated he thought talk of a "fiscal agent" was both stupid and hypocritical, as a political man he put his political objectives first and finally accepted this euphemism.

It should be noted this point that Henry Clay and the "birthright" Whigs, as distinguished from those recently attracted in the national canvas and other groups like the states' rights champions who attached themselves to the party for their own purposes, nurtured a concept of the role of government and party which was closer to the parliamentary model than it was to the strong presidential system which developed with Jefferson and Jackson. The essential element of the developing parliamentary system (so described because it was still in its formative stage in Britain) was the principle of the supremacy of the legislature, set forth in John Locke's *Second Essay on Civil Government*, and fought for and won during the Glorious Revolution of the seventeenth century. The monarch, or Executive, became somewhat of a shadowy figure under parliamentary government and gradually more and more power was concentrated, not only in Parliament, but in the ruling party or faction in parliament, and more particularly among the King's Ministers who represented the leadership of the majority party or faction.

Out of this group of Ministers or advisors to the King grew the concept of the cabinet and of the Prime Minister, who was in essence the parliamentary leader of the majority party, faction or coalition in power. Only in the nineteenth century did this so-called Prime Minister or *primus inter pares* become not only the leader of Parliament, but also Chief Executive of the government. All of these parliamentary developments were by no means fixed or firmly established at the mid-point of the nineteenth century, but they were operative in a functional way, and known and admired by many of the "birthright" Whigs who had become exasperated during the Jackson era with what they termed the "executive usurpation" of the President. Henry Clay was certainly *primus inter pares* among these Whigs, and as the leader of the Whig party in Congress and in the country, he more or less began to assume the role of a prime minister, constituting a real challenge to the man everyone considered an "accidental" President.

To go one step further, the Whigs had developed a somewhat parliamentary or more elevated concept of the President's cabinet than that with which their recent predecessors had functioned. This concept, as was the case of most of their principles, arose primarily in the years of opposition to Jackson, and was based upon those aspects of his administration of which they were most critical. The Whigs were not only alarmed at what they considered to be the extreme degree of "executive usurpation" which they felt characterized the Jackson and Van Buren regimes, but they were also opposed to the downgrading of the President's official cabinet, his constitutional advisors (as they referred to cabinet members), and to Jackson's reliance on an informal group of advisors and ghost writers who hovered around him continuously, held various sinecures in the executive branch and really exercised a considerable degree of influence in the affairs of state.

The Whigs considered this so-called "Kitchen Cabinet" of Jackson's to be unconstitutional and destructive to the ends of representative government. The members of the Kitchen Cabinet were shadowy figures who usually did not hold any elective office and who were not responsible to the public at large in the same sense in which a cabinet member and head of an executive department was. The emergence of such a cabal, as the Kitchen Cabinet was sometimes called, and its meteoric rise in the corridors of power was yet another Whig argument against the unconstitutional drift of policy and practice of which the Jacksonian Democrats were guilty.

The remedy for this evil, in the opinion of Clay and the congressional Whig leaders, was the restoration of the truly constitutional role and the prestige the Congress and the President's official family, his appointed cabinet. They believed that this cabinet, like its parliamentary model, should be made up primarily of outstanding members of the President's party, hopefully in most instances drawn from the Congress. It ought to play a key role in the decision-making process of the executive branch, serving as a link, or a "buckle" as Bagehot put it, between the legislative and executive branches, and also representing the interests of the party in power and the public at large, as well as those of the individual occupying the White House.[111]

There is no formal document setting forth the Whig concept of cabinet government in its full grandeur, nor do I want to convey the impression that all of this was clearly defined in the minds of the leading Whigs. But there are various hints of it revealed in a number of different ways. Whig documents frequently referred to cabinet members as "ministers" or "constitutional advisors" of the President. President Harrison appeared to select his cabinet quite consciously with this concept in mind, and, according to Webster, they functioned very much along the procedural lines of a parliamentary cabinet. Their appointment by the duly elected President also gave them something of a better claim to the continuity of party leadership than even their present head had. One close student of the period argued

> When it became apparent that there was a serious difference of opinion between the President and the party leaders in Congress on some of the cardinal measures of the Whig program, there was a tendency on the part of the latter to exalt the Cabinet appointed by Harrison as holding a better popular title than did the new President, and to seek the use by the "ministers" to coerce him into compliance with their wishes.[112]

A story told by Tyler's son bears out the concept of the cabinet's own exalted self-image and also contains an accurate description of their role under the Whig President who preceded Tyler:

[W]hen the President confronted the Cabinet at the first meeting following Harrison's death the Secretary of State, Webster, said, "Mr. President, I suppose you intend to carry out the ideas and customs of your predecessor, and that this Administration, inaugurated by President Harrison, will continue in the same line of policy." Seeing that Tyler assented, Mr. Webster continued, "Mr. President, it was the custom of our cabinet meetings of President Harrison that he should preside over them. All measures relating to the Administration were to be brought before the Cabinet and their settlement was to be decided by the majority of votes, each member of the Cabinet and the President having but one vote."[113]

Tyler was apparently amazed at what his son termed such an "exhibition of adamantine cheek," and responded sharply to this suggestion:

I beg your pardon, gentlemen; I am very glad to have in my Cabinet such able statesmen as you have proved yourselves to be. And I shall be pleased to avail myself of your counsel and advice. But I can never consent to being dictated to as to what I shall or shall not do. I, as President, shall be responsible for my administration. I hope to have your hearty cooperation in carrying out its measures. So long as you see fit to do this, I shall be glad to have you with me. When you think otherwise, your resignations will be accepted.[114]

This statement of the President's was reported by his son who acted as his private secretary and who was probably present at the time. He volunteered this recollection in an interview almost 50 years later, but there was undoubtedly some basis for the reconstruction of the incident and it probably reflects Tyler's attitude with respect to the vague assertion of a Whig concept of cabinet government. However, it was also probably influenced by hindsight, viewed in the light of the subsequent conduct of the President and his cabinet in the crisis which was to erupt over his veto of the Second Bank Bill. At any rate there was no further talk of this principle of the operation of the cabinet during Tyler's administration, and it was another source of irritation between John Tyler and the so-called "birthright" Whigs.

Another constant source of contention with respect to Tyler's cabinet was that it was understood that many of its members were much closer to Clay than to the President. This was a reasonable assumption since Clay was a very outgoing and personable party leader, who inspired great loyalty among his friends and supporters—and every member of the cabinet had served in the Congress except the secretary of the navy. All had some previous contact or friendship with the majority leader of the Senate. There is some evidence in Secretary Ewing's diary and elsewhere, however, that all of the members of the cabinet were not uniformly in awe of Clay, and some were quite critical of his tactics and demeanor during this crisis.

A description of the senator from Kentucky in action at the Whig party caucus indicates something of the exciting and forceful influence Clay had on his colleagues:

> Clay was particularly effective in the party caucus. . . . William Gilmore Simms, the Southern novelist, in a letter to Senator James H. Hammond in 1858 described such a caucus held by the Whigs during Harrison's brief administration. Simms' account belongs to the realm of oral history, for it was based on a description given him probably by a South Carolina congressman. The question before the caucus was whether to recommend to the President the summoning of an extra session of Congress, a proposal strongly favored by Clay. At this caucus, according to Simms, all members except two were opposed to the calling of an extra session. But Clay "entered the assembly, passed down its lines, speaking as he went, in triumphant manner, with bold fearless eloquence, breast open, and, at length, confronting Webster, he seemed to concentrate the whole weight of what he had to say upon him. And so powerful was his eloquence, so keen his shafts, so personal their aim, that Webster actually crouched under him, and slid down in his seat, so that his head was almost on a level with his belly. And Clay triumphed. There were but *two* after he was done, who voted in opposition to the measure."[115]

Under these tenuous and ambiguous circumstances the bank struggle was launched. Clay was impatient to get on with the Whig program, pleased and confident with his new role as a leader of the majority party in the Senate and anxious to rack up a brilliant record of achievement which would carry him into the White House in 1844. Tyler, on the other hand, was increasingly suspicious of the Whig leaders in the legislature, jealous of Clay's influence in what he now considered was his administration, and determined not to yield any of his states' rights principles. He too was interested in the presidential race in 1844, and had probably decided to succeed himself. It was not a happy or auspicious moment to predict a bright future for this new majority party, and its approaching doom could be feared but could not be entirely unanticipated.

Clay was in full command in the Senate and he marshalled the first bank bill through in rapid order. He had first introduced his own bill, which did not contain all of the desired concessions to the President, but through the intervention of several other Whig members of Congress, he finally accepted a compromise, the Ewing bill. It incorporated all of the modifications (including the title "fiscal bank") except one into the measure which cleared the Senate. The one exception was the clause granting the "fiscal bank" the power of branching out into the respective states. This was a critical issue with Tyler because he believed it yielded the principle of states' rights to the federal government. If the Congress of the United States had the power to create a national bank which could establish branches in the several states without first obtaining their authorization, then the same Congress could impose upon the states any law requiring their compliance, including the outlawing of slavery. This was the rub and the reason why the states' rightists fought the national bank issue so tenaciously.

But Clay was again willing to compromise, although he did not go as far as the Ewing bill in incorporating Senator White's plan. The Ewing-White proposal, which purportedly had the prior approval of President Tyler and his cabinet, conditioned the branching power of the "fiscal bank" on the approval of the state legislatures. Clay was willing to go half way, and finally accepted an amendment to his bill which authorized the branching power of the bank, subject only to the veto of the state legislature. The language of the amendment stated that after the "fiscal bank" proposal had become law, the legislature should "unconditionally assent or dissent to the establishment" of the branch in that state. Of course whether the legislature assented or dissented, there was no distinction between the Clay compromise and the Ewing-White proposal approved by the President. But the amendment further stated that in the event that the state legislature neither assented or dissented, approval would be "thereafter presumed." Once established, branch offices could only be withdrawn with the approval of Congress.[116]

This compromise provoked an interesting response. Some dyed-in-the-wool "Bank men," including the congressman from Clay's own district, voted against the bill when this compromise was incorporated in it because they believed that it yielded too much in principle to the opposition. On the other hand, determined opponents of federal power like Calhoun opposed it as a sham. "How can you compromise between assent and dissent?" the South Carolinian asked. "You might as well attempt to compromise between a negative and a positive, between virtue and vice, between truth and falsehood, between right and wrong."[117]

> That the sovereign power of any State shall be presumed to be surrendered because it does not answer a demand which it does not recognize the right of being asked. It is a proposition to authorize the Congress to say to any State, "You have declined giving your assent and therefore we take it."[118]

Of course Senator Calhoun and the rest of the Democrats voted against the measure, but it passed both houses after long and furious debate. Clay and his stronger Whig supporters probably honestly felt that they had accommodated the President's constitutional objections to the bill, but the debate and maneuvering were accompanied by so much gossip and back-biting that it was difficult to decide whether Tyler's increasing alienation from his own party was based upon principle, or animosity growing out of a power struggle with Clay. The President resented the innuendos passed around Washington that he had broken faith with his party, that he was playing up to the anti-bank Democrats, that he was rejecting the advice of his cabinet and listening to the voices of a "cabal" of spoilers—some Whigs and some Democrats—who sought to separate him from the Whig party and form a new party which would ride to victory with him in 1844.

Clay and the "birthright" Whigs on the other hand, could not conceive that the President was blocking their efforts to respond to the country's economic crisis solely on the basis of long held but, in their opinion, totally erroneous constitutional views. They resented his growing alienation from their party, his reliance on the advice of those they considered enemies, and his failure to recognize his responsibility to the party which had put him in the White House. It was a war of charge and counter-charge, rumor and counter-rumor, and it rapidly undermined the fragile unity of the new majority party.

There is substantial evidence that Tyler's constitutional advisors urged him to sign the "fiscal bank" bill, but he apparently felt under no obligation to accept their advice, nor did he believe that his presence on the Whig ticket obligated him to support a national bank.[119] Quite the contrary, he maintained that his position on the bank had been well-known when he was selected by the Whigs to run as their vice presidential candidate at Harrisburg, and that he had never wavered in his opposition to a bank before, during, or after the Whig campaign of 1840.

This has been disputed by some and affirmed by others. There is no point in pursuing the argument. The more significant question is: How could such politically sophisticated and experienced men allow their rigidity on this question to destroy a newly achieved national and regional unity, forged in the process of almost a decade's opposition to a despised foe and the noxious policies implemented by his administration? The Whig party was formed to rid the country of the traces of Jacksonianism and to bring to power a party of interests in many ways fundamentally opposed to those supporting Andrew Jackson. Having achieved victory having acquired the power and initiative not only to destroy much that their predecessors had erected in terms of policies and practices, but also to initiate or restore other policies which the Jacksonians had ignored, why did the Whigs fall apart just at the historical moment when they were about to fulfill the objectives for which they had initially come into existence?

The answer is not simple, but if probed deeply enough, it will reveal some of the most serious weaknesses in both the theory and practice of American politics. This was a critical turning point in the history of this country and certainly in the history of the presidency and the diminution of its powers. I would argue that these events set in motion certain long-range developments in the process of the emasculation of presidential power which it took over 25 years to develop and over half a century to overcome. But before outlining such arguments and suggesting inferences which may be drawn from them, there is some further narrative detail which must be covered.

Presidential Vetoes and a Cabinet Crisis

A series of interlocking and unfortunate events followed almost sequentially from the President's veto of the first bank bill. But even before the event took place, rumors were plentiful all over Washington that the President would veto the bill. His son denounced the measure as being unconstitutional and was overheard to have said that "to suppose that [my] father would be gulled by such a humbug compromise as the bill contained, was to suppose that he was an ass."[120] Several days later, ignoring his cabinet's advice, Tyler vetoed the bill.

There was nothing particularly distinguished in the veto message. He reviewed his long established opposition to the theory successfully invoked by Hamilton that the government of the United States has the power to establish a bank (see Volume I of this series) and argued that he could not sanction such a bill "without surrendering all claim to the respect of honorable men, all confidence on the part of the people, all self-respect, all regard for moral and religious obligations, without an observance of which no government can be prosperous and no people can be happy."[121]

It would be to commit a crime which I would not willfully commit to gain any earthly reward, and would justly subject me to the ridicule and scorn of all virtuous men.[122]

After such a hyperbolic invocation, anything else would be anticlimactic. It was. The President indicated why the Whig compromise on the branching power failed to relieve him of his high obligation to veto the bill. The tricky language devised by the Whig caucus did not conceal the fact, he argued, that the bill invaded the sacred rights of the states to determine their own destiny by empowering the Congress to establish offices of discount in a state

not only with its assent, but against its dissent. . . . On general principles the right in Congress to prescribe terms to any State implies a superiority of power and control, deprives the transaction of all pretense to compact between them, and terminates, as we have seen, in the total abrogation of freedom of action on the part of the States.[123]

And that was the heart of the matter—states' rights. A potential threat to the doctrine so jealously defended by the slave states received priority consideration from the President over any Whig claims to doctrine, loyalty or party unity. The only real Whig defections in the Senate were two committed states' rightists who also drew the line on this issue when confronted with appeals to party unity. A party, and particularly the Whig party, could never hope to command the commitment that states' rights invoked, and this Whig President was willing to see the party which had brought him to the presidency destroyed rather than endanger the principle which slave state representatives considered their first line of defense.

Clay delayed his denunciation of the veto message until negotiations were already underway between leading Whigs, the President and his cabinet to frame another bank measure acceptable to the Chief Executive. If Clay had been willing (and also able) to hold his tongue on this occasion and pass over what he considered was a traitorous act on the part of Tyler, the second compromise bank bill might have eventually won the day. But the man they called "The Great Pacificator" could no more hold his tongue at that time than he could fail to use it to good effect once it was in motion. His denunciation of Tyler's veto was as masterful a demonstration of prowess at parliamentary polemics as ever graced the United States Senate floor. Clay used wit, ridicule and invective to drill the veto message and its author full of holes and to rebuke the action of a Whig President who had killed the key Whig proposal to restore fiscal responsibility to the country.

The senator from Kentucky began his speech with the admission that there was no chance of the Senate overturning the President's veto since the measure was a party issue and had been opposed by the entire Democratic delegation along with the two defecting Whigs from Virginia, William S. Archer and William C. Rives. Clay indicated that in recognition of this fact he would have refrained from speaking on the issue had not the President's message violated the "friendly spirit of concession and compromise"[124] which had animated the severely amended Whig bill in the first place.

He has commented, I think, with undeserved severity on that part of the bill; he has used, I am sure unintentionally, harsh if not reproachful language; and he has made the very concession, which was prompted as a peace-offering and from friendly considerations, the cause of stronger and more decided disapprobation of the bill. Standing in the relation to that bill, which I do, and especially to the exceptionable clause, the duty which I owe to the Senate and to the country, and self-respect, impose upon me the obligation of at least attempting the vindication of a measure which has met a fate so unmerited, and so unexpected.[125]

Clay first referred to Tyler's inaugural address and repeated the President's solemn promise to sanction " 'any constitutional measure, which, originating in Congress, shall have certain defined objects in view.'. . . for its object the restoration of a sound circulating medium, so essentially necessary to give confidence in all the transactions of life, to secure to industry its just and adequate rewards, and to re-establish the public prosperity."[126] The Whigs in Congress had welcomed this assurance and were convinced that despite his previous position as a representative of a slave state advocating states' rights, as the Whig President of all 26 states Tyler would certainly approve a measure designed by his party colleagues in the Senate to implement just these goals which he had enunciated. The President had also referred in his inaugural to the guidance he wished to invoke from the "fathers of the great republican school" in respect to determining the constitutionality of the measure proposed.[127]

Clay now reminded him of that promise and detailed an irrefutable review of the letter of the law on this subject. Five different acts of five different Republican Congresses had authorized or implemented the principle of the authority of the Congress to establish a bank, called by its rightful name and not shrouded by what Clay considered an appellation "revolting to my ears."[128] Even though Thomas Jefferson and James Madison had initially opposed the establishment of a bank and raised constitutional arguments against its creation, they later agreed to sanction its existence, while Washington and Monroe, on the other hand, never had any serious reservations on the question in the first place. Despite his doubts, when Madison was confronted with the bill authorizing the establishment of the Second Bank of the United States, he did not veto it but signed the measure into law. Clay asked:

Did James Madison surrender "all claim to the respect of honorable men, all confidence on the part of the people, all self-respect, all regard for moral and religious obligations?" Did the pure, the virtuous, the gifted James Madison, by his sanction and signature to the charter of the late bank of the United States, commit a crime, which justly subjected him "to the ridicule and scorn of all virtuous men?"[129]

This was the tenor and the thrust of the speech. It was delivered in the Senate to a gallery packed with visitors who had waited in line to be admitted to hear Clay in promised top form. They were not disappointed. One description of the speech indicated that Clay extorted "expressions of rapturous applause from his most bitter enemies, . . ." and was also able to "thrill his friends with delight."[130] But the far from impartial reader of this address, sitting in the White House, was not so enthusiastic about Clay's performance. A number of observers have reported Tyler's extreme dissatisfaction and anger with the attack.

At the conclusion of his stirring speech, Clay alluded to several alternatives which had been available to President Tyler and which Clay implied would have been more satisfactory than a veto. If the President had recognized the right of Congress to legislate in this area but preferred to remove himself from the embarrassment or even guilt of concurring, he could have allowed the bill to become a law without signing it. Clay also suggested that the President might have considered the option he took advantage of when his state legislature instructed him to vote against his will to expunge the censure resolution against President Jackson. Rather than either ignore or comply with this directive, Tyler had resigned from the Senate. Of course Clay was implying that such an alternative was again available to him. This probably was not a serious suggestion, and Clay later indicated he had no intention of urging upon Tyler such an action, yet it is interesting in relation to the comparisons made above with the model of parliamentary government, that the Prime Minister or leader of the party is expected to resign if defeated in the Parliament in a decisive vote on a major issue.

Whatever its intention, Clay's speech ruptured every possibility of further close cooperation and communication between the majority leader and the President. The chasm was widened and deepened and the fate of the Whig party and the future of the presidency hung in the balance. Both of the leading actors in this drama exhibited monumental egos and little long-range vision in allowing their personal conflict to get as far out of hand as it did. Political personalities, even heroes, do not exist as if they were in a vacuum in pure space, but are, at least in part, the creatures of the roles they perform and the institutions of which they are part. Insofar as their actions reflected positively or negatively with respect to the institutions upon which they were dependent, they also contributed positively or negatively to their own futures. Neither Clay nor Tyler had any future whatsoever without a strong Whig party.

Clay had given almost ten years of his life at the peak of his career to build this party and he should have realized at this moment in history that an irreparable break between the Whig President and the Whig leader of Congress would shake the public's confidence in the ability of the party to govern and would jeopardize its future. One can sympathize with his impatience with Tyler and his anger at the President's betrayal of his obligations to the party that elected him. It was a cruel thrust, but there was a ring of truth when Clay pointed out in his attack upon the veto:

—if at Harrisburg, or at the polls, it had been foreseen, that General Harrison would die in one short month after the commencement of his administration; that Vice-President Tyler would be elevated to the presidential chair; that a bill, passed by decisive majorities of the first whig Congress, chartering a national bank, would be presented for his sanction, and that he would veto the bill, do I hazard any thing, when I express the conviction, that he would not have received a solitary vote in the nominating convention, nor one solitary electoral vote in any State of the Union?[131]

But the party had assumed responsibilities to the public in seeking its support in the election of 1840, and as the real leader of that party, Clay had an obligation to do everything in his power, including restraining his personal pique, to see that the commitment was met.

On the other hand, Tyler was a fool if he believed that he had any future in American politics independent of the fate of the Whig party. Despite a distinguished record in his own state, John Tyler had been plucked from relative national obscurity when he was placed on the ballot with Harrison, and he would return to that obscurity once he lost the support of the Whig party. But beyond that obligation to self he also should have felt an obligation to the party which had elected him to be a representative, if nothing else, of a point of view in which the establishment of a national bank was an integral element. The Whigs had been preaching its necessity for years. Tyler need not have necessarily made the office of the presidency subject to the dictates of the Whig congressional caucus and its leader, Clay, in order to establish that rapport and cooperation which would have contributed to the strength of the party. But on this particular issue, especially in the light of its long constitutional history, which Clay eagerly recited, it was suicidal to buck the overwhelming consensus of the Whigs in Congress and probably in the nation and face the destruction of the party because of this division.

Yet neither Clay nor Tyler had this kind of loyalty and commitment to the party at this point, nor could they even clearly see that their own futures were intimately tied up with its success or failure. Clay, with more justification than Tyler, was bulling ahead with the Whig legislative program, knowing full well that without the President's support it had no chance of passing. It would appear that his devotion to his own interests and career were paramount at this point, for he probably thought that even if the fiscal program did fail, he would not be blamed and would be able to emerge in 1844 as the successful Whig candidate for President. That scenario, of course, turned out to be accurate with one critical element absent—success.

Tyler was apparently caught up in a more complex matrix of self-delusions. His commitment to the Whigs and their principles was minimal in the first place. He was a states' rights man first, and had entered the Whig party only because of antagonism to the strong nationalistic policies of Jackson. He was also very vain, and his pride was injured by Clay's status as a party leader and the Whigs loyalty and deference to him rather than to their new President. He resented the gossip and slurs he heard whispered about Washington concerning Clay's dictatorship within the party, and he foolishly relied upon a group of unofficial advisors who shared the same states' rights prejudices as he and who urged him on to defy Clay and the Whig leadership. There was clearly no early organized effort on his part to establish a new party or to attract members of the opposition party, but these possibilities always remained somewhere in the background as a potential threat, and, when no other options were possible, were pursued half-heartedly in what must have been one of the monumental political failures in history.

In all of this there was much of the characteristic ambivalence with regard to political parties themselves discussed earlier in the section. Clay was far less of a victim to this paralyzing disease than Tyler, for he was more of a party man and defined his ambitions within the framework of party structure and policies. Tyler, on the other hand, reflected a typically American indifference to party and party interests, and one can easily see him substituting the term "faction" for party because its policies and objectives happened to run counter to his own interests at the moment. When the party afforded a means of advancing his own ideological and personal interests it was convenient to be a party man and to support it, but the moment these interests came into conflict with party policies, it was the party which came out second best.

In the final analysis Clay, too, failed to suppress his own ego and personal ambitions to the welfare of the party and its policies. He could have modified his behavior, suppressed his justifiable anger and contempt for the President and pursued the objective of party unity much more effectively than he did. What interceded in his case was his resentment at not being in the White House himself and his further ambition to become President, contrary to the remark for which he is famous,—"I had rather be right than be President."[132] In the clutch he demonstrated quite the opposite and probably failed in his pursuit of the presidency just because of this.

The drama was now rushing toward a climax. The President resented Clay's attack upon him in the Senate, but he still appeared willing to negotiate with representatives of the Whig caucus who were attempting to work out a second compromise bank measure which would overcome his objections. Before Clay's speech, which was delayed for three days in order that the negotiations to reach a settlement could proceed, Tyler was visited by Representative Alexander Stuart of Virginia, who offered a revised version of the bank bill to the President for his consideration. In brief, it eliminated the complicated language of the previous Clay amendment, conditioning the branching power simply upon the right of the states to reject the establishment of such a "fiscal agent" if they saw fit. This compromise both preserved the energy and initiative of the "fiscal agent," but also protected the principle of states' rights by giving the state veto power over the right of the central "fiscal agent" to establish a branch in that state.

Benton reports that after studying the revised section of the proposed bill, the President told Stuart that "it would do. [Tyler made] no objection whatever to the clause in regard to the establishment of agencies in the several States without their assent."[133] Several other minor modifications were included by both Stuart and the President, and he finally grasped Stuart's hand and exclaimed with much feeling:

> Stuart! if you can be instrumental in passing this bill through Congress, I will esteem you the best friend I have on earth.[134]

The original paper containing the draft of this amendment to the bill, with President Tyler's handwriting inscribed upon it, was seen by enough senators (including the leading Democratic opponent of the bank, Senator Benton) to authenticate the meeting and indicate the probable veracity of Stuart's description of it.

Testimony of Tyler's cabinet members further corraborates Congressman Stuart's report of the President's enthusiastic approval of this compromise measure at that time. The secretary of war, John Bell, discussed the matter with the President and the secretary of the treasury the day after Representative Stuart's visit to the

President, and both confirmed his interest in a new compromise bill which removed the features he found so obnoxious in the first bill:

> I called on the President on official business on the morning of Monday the 16th of August, before the first veto message was sent in. I found him reading the message to the Secretary of the Treasury. He did me the honor to read the material passages to me. Upon reading that part of it which treats of the superior importance and value of the business done by the late Bank of the United States in furnishing exchanges between different States and sections of the Union, I was so strongly impressed with the idea that he meant to intimate that he would have no objection to a bank which should be restricted to dealing in exchanges, that I interrupted him in the reading and asked if I was to understand (by what he had just read) that he was prepared to give his assent to a bank in the District of Columbia, with offices in the States, having the privilege, without their assent, to deal in exchanges between them and in foreign bills. He promptly replied that he thought experience had shown the necessity of such a power in the government. And (after some further remarks favorable to such a bill) expressed the opinion that nothing could be more easy than to pass a bill which would answer all necessary purposes—that it could be done in three days.[135]

Ewing's report records almost identical statements on the part of the President.[136]

Discussions on this matter proceeded between the President and members of his cabinet over the next few days, and every record of these conversations seems to confirm these facts. First, the President met with three members of the Whig caucus—Senator Berrien and Representative Seargent and Representative Stuart—and after meeting with members of his cabinet, he came to an agreement on the principles of a second bank bill which would be submitted by Berrien and Seargent and would have the President's unofficial approval. Second, Webster and Ewing were assigned to draw up such a bill in consultation with Berrien and Seargent. Finally, the bill was drafted; Berrien, Seargent, Webster and Ewing agreed on its provisions; and the two Whig legislators agreed to introduce it into both houses if it received the approval of the Whig caucus, which it did.

Evidence suggests that the President began to sour on the compromise immediately after Clay's attack upon him in the Senate, the day his first veto was transmitted to that body. This was not based upon the terms of the prior agreement, the provisions of the bill, or constitutional reservations, but upon a state of mind in which the President felt alienated from the Whigs and reluctant to do anything that strengthened the hand of their leader in Congress. On several occasions he asked various members of the cabinet to do everything in their power to delay the passage of the bill, but by that time it was out of their hands, and they were helpless to carry out such instructions.

Contrary to general impressions, members of the President's cabinet were not uncritical Clay loyalists, and Ewing indicates that some of them were also opposed to his tactics and timing in this crisis:

The events of the day caused me much reflection. On the one hand, Mr. Clay was evidently hurrying matters to a catastrophe, intending to hasten the new Bank bill upon My. Tyler; force him to approve or Veto—drive Tyler into the Democratic party—denounce the Administration and make himself as the head of the Whig Party an opposition candidate for the Presidency. . . .

On the whole I became satisfied that Mr. Clay was impatient, and uphappy in his then present position. He had been the undisputed leader of the Whig Party for many years while they were in the minority and he could not well endure now they were in power, that his supremacy (sic) should be questioned or the power of the Party divided. He wished submission from the Cabinet—this so far as I and some others were concerned was impossible. I would not even consult with him, after a breach between him and the President took place until after I presented my letter of resignation.[137]

The members of the cabinet felt themselves caught in an impossible position. They saw their roles as constitutional advisors to the President violated by the Whig concept of party government, and yet on the other hand, Tyler demonstrated precious little respect for their advice, betrayed their confidential discussions and repudiated cabinet decisions which were made in good faith. During this crisis they were concerned as to whether or not they should resign if the President vetoed both the "fiscal corporation" and the land bills, two important Whig measures.

At this point further misunderstandings developed. The President received even more shocking accounts of plans by the Whig leaders to "head him," when a rather prominent Whig representative from the House, who had formerly been a close colleague of Tyler's from Virginia, denounced the President in a letter which accidentally reached his hands, and spoke in even more unfortunate terms of Whig plans to do the President in.[138] Clearly these rumors and reports of Whig maneuvers against the President badly upset him, further alienated him from the Whig leadership and gave him cause to think again about frustrating their efforts to betray him.

In the tense atmosphere of the Capitol at that moment in history, it was difficult to factor out myth from reality, truth from fiction. The leading Whigs later argued that they had very honestly and sincerely attempted to reach a workable compromise with the President, a compromise that would hold the party together; at the same time they sought to establish what they considered to be a much needed fiscal instrument to stabilize the monetary exchange of the country. They finally received confirmation of the President's agreement to such a compromise from three different members of Congress and from members of his cabinet, as well. They too were under the impression that Tyler had approved the compromise bill, and that there would be no further question of a veto. Given this version of the situation, the onus for the final rupture fell solely upon the President, for he had convinced the Whigs that a compromise settlement had been reached; when they served him up with the agreed upon legislation, he betrayed them again by vetoing the bill.

There are, however, conflicting reports as to whether the President saw the final versions of the bills after they had been drawn up by Ewing and Webster in consultation with Berrien and Seargent. Webster, who had no motive to testify otherwise and whose word should be relied upon here, recorded in a private memorandum written some time later that the President had indeed seen this final version of the bill before it was submitted to both houses and had suggested several minor changes but no basic alterations. Tyler flatly denied this, declaring "under all the solemnities that can attend such a declaration, that my assent to that bill was never attained."[139]

As always, the truth probably lies somewhere in the middle of both interpretations of the same events. Certain basic facts are, however, clear and uncontradictable. At least a preliminary agreement between representatives of the Whig caucus and the President was reached. All the members of his cabinet who were knowledgeable of these events confirm that much. Bills incorporating the major aspects of this agreement were introduced and passed in both houses of the Congress, where many members were under the impression that the President had given prior approval to the measure. But it is also evident that Tyler began hedging his bets shortly after he gave the impression to Stuart that he was going along with the compromise, and later he did attempt to get his cabinet to postpone consideration of the bills before they were voted upon. One can only surmise that either the President had read the draft proposal too hastily and changed his mind when he considered its language more carefully, or that he became bitter and less reconcilable after reports and rumors reached him indicating that Clay and the Whig leadership were out to undermine his standing both in office and in the Whig party.

There is a third possibility, which has never seemed quite as likely; that is, that Tyler was merely playing the Whigs along, had fully decided to bolt the party, and was laying the groundwork with these vetoes for a new coalition of states' rights and anti-bank forces which would maintain him in power.

What is more important and certainly more feasible than determining the truth of these complex motives and events, is a correct appraisal of the result or cost of these developments with respect to the future of the Whig party and the office of the presidency. Both were severely damaged by this disastrous experience. In the case of the Whig party, it began its rather rapid national decline almost before it had reached its first pinnacle of success. The President's power and influence were greatly emasculated, with the exception of the terms of the wartime leaders, from this point on until the end of the century. What reasons can be adduced for such unfortunate and really tragic developments?

In order to answer that question it is necessary to return to the narrative of these events. The compromise Fiscal Corporation Bill (a revised name insisted upon by the President) quickly passed both houses of Congress and was eventually vetoed by him. The measure received the full support of the Whig party, only one member in the Senate refusing to go along with the caucus decision to support the bill. This would indicate something of the good faith of the Whigs in attempting to breach the gap between the legislative and executive members of their party, hoping to restore confidence in its ability to govern. But already too many divisive elements had intruded upon the situation to expect a happy ending.

Clay was not happy with the bill, and he expressed his feeling of dissatisfaction to the Senate, stating that in his opinion it fell far short of establishing the kind of bank

> he thought the interest of the country required, the Constitution authorized, and the people expected. It was short, far short of that; but nevertheless the bill proposed the establishment of a bank which would accomplish two of the great objects, which any bank could effect; the regulation of the exchanges of the country, and the other, the supply of a currency possessing a uniform value throughout the Union.[140]

After stating these reservations, however, Clay honored the Whig caucus decision and indicated that in balance the bill deserved his support and that he would vote for it

> although it did not all the good which might be effected from an institution of this kind, it did much—a great deal.[141]

President Tyler vetoed the second Whig bank bill on the grounds of its fundamental conflict with the Constitution. Once again he argued that there was no constitutional provision empowering Congress to establish a bank whose powers would supercede those of the states in which its branches would be established. In the veto message he reviewed the familiar ground he had been over before, but surprisingly even singled out for attack those aspects of the bill to which his earlier agreement had been sought and attained. The name "Fiscal Corporation of the United States," for example, which members of his cabinet and the Congress attest he demanded be attached to the bill, was subjected to the criticism that it implied an institution which was national in character. The President was again pointing out that the character of the local "fiscal institution" which was to be established in the District of Columbia was a fiction, and that, in effect, this so-called "fiscal institution" was to perform all the functions of a national bank. This of course was true, but it was a fiction adopted by the Whigs at the request of the President and designed to appease his rigid states' rights principles. For the President to "expose" this action and to imply that it was a circumlocution of constitutional restriction only convicted him and his artificial constitutional rigidity rather than the duplicity of the Whig members of Congress, most of whom wanted a straight forward national bank to be called by its rightful name from the very beginning. Two days after the President's veto message a letter appeared in the *New York Herald*, a newspaper favored by and favorable to the Tyler administration, which must have emanated from the President or someone very close to him, for it revealed accurate knowledge of the substance of confidential cabinet discussions. In the course of such revelations, members of the President's cabinet were maligned, as they had been regularly in the columns of that newspaper:

> The Cabinet, one and all, are hard at work to allay all open evidences of a rupture, and counseling their friends to go home and raise the standard of revolt there, while their own efforts are directed to undermine and circumvent the President here. This is their game. Who would have believed that high-minded and honorable men (for such members of the

Cabinet ought to be) would thus concert a system of party movement, by which to destroy the very man at whose will they hold their offices, and who is constitutionally responsible for all their official acts? What treachery! What ingratitude! Why do they not act like men, and at once give in their resignations, and suffer the President to bring to his aid such men as he has confidence in?[142]

These two breaches of faith, the veto of the Fiscal Corporation Bill, and the revelation of confidential discussions in the cabinet, constituted the straw that broke the cabinet's back. Two days after the veto message, four of the six members of the cabinet resigned and condemned the President for his betrayals of their trust in him, and several days later a fifth member of the cabinet, Francis Granger, also resigned. Webster alone decided to stay on, his decision based upon a somewhat more sympathetic attitude toward the President, not to mention a strong antipathy towards Clay, and also his involvement in negotiations with the British regarding the Canadian border, which he was loathe to abandon in midstream. In his letter of resignation, Secretary of the Navy George Badger confirmed the reports of Stuart and Ewing that the President had approved the bill submitted to the Congress:

At the Cabinet meeting held on the 18th of August, last, . . . the subject of an exchange bank, or institution, was brought forward by the President himself, and was fully considered. . . . It will be sufficient to say that it was then distinctly stated and understood that such an institution met the approbation of the President, and was deemed by him free of constitutional objections; that he desired (if Congress should deem it necessary to act upon the subject during the session) that such an institution should be adopted by that body, and that members of his cabinet would aid in bringing about that result; and Messrs. Webster and Ewing were specially requested by the President to have communication upon the subject with certain members of Congress. In consequence of what passed at this meeting, I saw such friends in Congress as I deemed it proper to approach, and urged upon them the passage of a bill to establish such an institution, assuring them that I did not doubt it would receive the approbation of the President.[143]

Badger, as did the others, made it clear that the basis for his resignation was not simply a disagreement with the President on a policy matter, which would not necessarily have been grounds for his action, but rather the manner in which he believed that Tyler had betrayed his confidence:

It is scarcely necessary to say that I have not supposed, and do not now suppose, that a difference merely between the President and his cabinet, either as to the constitutionality or the expediency of a bank, necessarily interposes any obstacles to a full and cordial cooperation between them in the general conduct of his Administration; and therefore deeply as I regretted the veto of the first bill, I did not feel myself at liberty to retire on that account from my situation. But the facts attending the initiation and disapproval of the last bill made a case totally different from that—one it is believed without parallel in the history of our cabinets; presenting, to say nothing more, a measure embraced and then repudiated—efforts prompted and then disowned—services rendered and then treated with scorn and neglect. Such a case required, in my judgment, upon considerations, private and public, that the official relations subsisting between the President and myself should be immediately dissolved.[144]

Ewing was equally displeased with the conduct of the President, characterizing Tyler's actions as an affront to his personal honor:

This bill, framed and fashioned according to your own suggestions, in the initiation of which I and another member of your Cabinet were made by you the agents and negotiators, was passed by large majorities through the two Houses of Congress, and sent to you, and you rejected it. Important as was the part which I had taken, at your request, in the origination of this bill, and deeply as I was committed for your action upon it, you never consulted me on the subject of the veto message. You did not even refer to it in conversation, and the first notice I had of its contents was derived from rumor. And to me, at least, you have done nothing to wipe away the personal indignity arising out of the act. I gathered, it is true, from your conversation, shortly after the bill had passed the House, that you had a strong purpose to reject it; but nothing was said like softening or apology to me, either in reference to myself or to those with whom I had communicated at your request, and who had acted themselves and induced the two Houses to act upon the faith of that communication. And strange as it may seem, the veto message attacks in an especial manner the very provisions which were inserted at your request; and even the name of the corporation, which was not only agreed to by you, but especially changed to meet your expressed wishes, is made the subject of your criticism. Different men might view this transaction in different points of light, but under these circumstances as a matter of personal honor, it would be hard for me to remain of your counsel, to seal my lips and leave unexplained and undisclosed where lies in this transaction the departure from straightforwardness and candor. . . .[145]

Daniel Webster was the only member of Tyler's cabinet not to resign in this crisis. He had long favored a strong national bank, and like the other members of the President's official family, he had urged Tyler to sign both of the banking bills passed by Congress. As a Clay enemy of many years, however, he was not too enthusiastic about contributing to the Kentuckian's elevation to the presidency, and he might well have reasoned that if he withdrew from the cabinet, the Tyler administration would come apart at the seams, signaling the demise of the Whig party. Webster was also more sympathetic to Tyler, feeling that pressure from Clay and the Whig caucus vying for a leadership role which rightfully belonged to the Chief Executive, was pushing the President's hand too rapidly. In all fairness, it should also be noted, as Webster's very sympathetic biographer has done, that the secretary of state had recently bought and furnished a new home in Washington, and as a man who cherished the material aspects of existence and who was not indifferent to the role of the secretary of state as the center of diplomatic and social life in Washington, Webster was not exactly enthusiastic about returning to a cold winter in Marshfield or Boston.

In the few letters which Webster wrote during this period, he appeared to be alarmed at the storm brewing within the Whig party, but was more of an observer than a participant. When the members of the cabinet met for dinner at Badger's home right after the President's veto message was sent to the Congress, Webster withdrew because he became aware that Clay would be present and that the resignation of the cabinet would be discussed. Those present agreed to resign that evening. When they informed Webster of their decision the following morning, he wrote that he thought "they were acting rashly and that he would consider his own course."[146]

I shall not act suddenly; it will look too much like a combination between a Whig cabinet and a Whig Senate to bother the President. It will not be expected of me to countenance such a proceeding.

Then again I will not throw the great foreign concerns of the country into disorder or danger, by any abrupt party proceeding.

How long I may stay, I know not, but I mean to take time to consider.[147]

Webster met with the President at the White House on the afternoon in which the formal resignations from the other cabinet members were received; apparently Tyler said nothing to his secretary of state to convince him to stay on in his position. Tyler's son indicated that the President respected the reasons Webster outlined in his public statement explaining why he decided to remain in the cabinet, particularly his concern over ongoing foreign policy negotiations, and his criticism of his colleagues for disrupting the first Whig administration. But in addition to these reasons, the President was reported to have said:

Webster had too much sagacity not to see that the rule sought to be established was Clay rule, and nothing more.[148]

Whatever his motives, Daniel Webster did not resign. On this same afternoon he was reported to have asked Tyler:

Where am I to go, Mr. President?
The President's reply was only in these words, *You must decide that for yourself, Mr. Webster.*
At this Mr. Webster instantly caught, and said, *If you leave it to me, Mr. President, I will stay where I am.*
Whereupon, President Tyler, rising from his seat and extending his hand to Mr. Webster, warmly rejoined, *Give me your hand on that, and now I will say to you that Henry Clay is a doomed man from this hour.*[149]

Webster's failure to join his other Whig colleagues was not a popular decision in the party, although he convinced his own state delegation that he ought to stay on. John Quincy Adams described the meeting with Webster in his diary, indicating that Webster stated that the President had never treated him with disrespect and probably desired that he remain as secretary of state. Adams characterized Webster as attempting to convey the impression (and perhaps believing it) that he was indifferent to the office itself, an assessment which Adams granted the secretary of state might have believed or thought he believed, but was transparently not accurate. The former President relied upon Shakespeare's Sir John Falstaff's recruit "Bullcalf" to drive home the point:

> In very truth, sir, I had as lief be hanged, sir, as go; and yet, for mine own part, sir, I do not care; but rather because I am unwilling, and for mine own part have a desire to stay with my friends; else, sir, I did not care for mine own part so much.[150]

Webster's action, or perhaps inaction, probably kept the nearly dead presidency of John Tyler alive, psychologically if not formally, for there were certain constitutional complications in the existence of a President without any constitutional advisors and a Congress poised to adjourn the following day. Several days later the secretary of state issued a formal statement of explanation:

> Lest any misapprehension should exist, as to the reasons which have led me to differ from the course of my late colleagues, I wish to say that I remain in my place, first, because I see no sufficient reasons for the dissolution of the late Cabinet, by the voluntary act of its own members. I am perfectly persuaded of the absolute necessity of an institution, under the authority of Congress, to aid revenue and financial operations, and to give the country the blessings of a good currency and cheap exchanges. Notwithstanding what has passed, I have confidence that the President will cooperate with the legislature in overcoming all difficulties in the attainment of these objects; and it is the union of the Whig Party—by which I mean the whole Party, the Whig President, the Whig Congress, and the Whig people—that I look for the realization of our wishes. I can look nowhere else. In the second place, if I had seen reasons to resign my office, I should not have done so, without giving the President reasonable notice, and affording him time to select the hands to which he should confide the delicate and important affairs now pending in this department.[151]

Webster's Whig colleagues in the Congress were not so tolerant of their President's conduct as the secretary of state. The same day that the cabinet resignations were sent to the President, a caucus of Whig members of the Senate and House met to consider the veto and to plan any steps they might take to counteract it. Great formality was adhered to as the caucus appointed officers, passed two formal resolutions and named a committee of two members from the Senate and five from the House to implement the decisions of the body. That committee was instructed to return to the full caucus in two days with a draft of a public address to the nation from the Whig party in Congress, reviewing its accomplishments and failures during the extra session of Congress, explaining the causes for the failures, "together with such other matters as may exhibit truly the condition of the Whig Party and Whig prospects."[152]

The committee returned with one of the most fascinating documents in the history of the American presidency—a statement by the leading members of the

Whig party, virtually expelling John Tyler, a Whig President in office, from the party. In its opening paragraphs the address reviewed the events which had led up to the impasse. It referred to the almost 12 years of effort and struggle the Whigs had gone through to build a party and to mount a serious and effective opposition force to Jackson's Democratic party. It pointed out that throughout this period the Whigs were forthright in announcing their program of reform which had emphasized:

1. the restraint of executive power and patronage;
2. the wholesome regulation of the currency and the advancement of interests of industry; and
3. the establishment of an economical administration of the finances.[153]

The document went on to outline the policies the Whigs had designed to implement these general objectives, and the establishment of a national bank was a critical focal point of this program. Leading Whigs like Clay and Webster had fought Jackson on this issue even before the existence of the party, and now their opportunity to fulfill such a long delayed goal had been denied by them by one of their own, using an instrument of presidential power—the veto—which the Whigs had also denounced. It was an incredible state of affairs.

The document was not simply an idle piece of political rhetoric. On the contrary, it was the real intention of the Whig members of Congress who participated in the caucus to expel the President from their ranks. They charged that he "has permitted himself to be beguiled into an opinion that, by an exhibition of his prerogative, he might be able to divert the policy of his Administration into a channel which would lead to new political combinations, and accomplish results which must overthrow the present divisions of the party in the country. . . ."[154] They believed that this had been brought about by Tyler's receptiveness to the advice of those "who have been busy to prostrate our purposes. . . ."[155] In short, the President was a traitor who first abandoned his own party, defeated one of its major policy reforms and was now attempting to shift the present balance of political power, which was in favor of the Whigs, into one more favorable to his states' rights views, in order presumably to draw support from the existing ranks of both of the two major parties.

The Whigs also condemned the President for ignoring the advice of his constitutional advisors, outstanding members of the party, all of whom, with the exception of Webster, had, or were in the process of resigning; they repudiated responsibility or blame for "the administration of the Executive branch of the Government."[156] Finally, they reaffirmed their support for traditional Whig policies, going beyond earlier statements to urge the "further limitation of the veto."[157]

The publication of this "address" to the people was an unprecedented action taken by a party seeking to expel a sitting President from its ranks. Nothing remotely like it had ever happened before, or would probably ever happen again. It reinforced an irreparable breach between most of the Whig members of Congress and the Whig President, and the party never fully recovered from this rupture. Not only did it further exacerbate and divide its two major ideological wings, but it took

84

its toll upon the office of the presidency itself, which after the Tyler administration (with the exception of the two war Presidents, Polk and Lincoln) never quite recovered either its prestige or its power for the remainder of the century.

Minutes of the Congressional Whig Caucus Meeting
September 11, 1841

Niles Register, September 18, 1841, 35.

At a meeting of the Whig members of the Senate and House of Representatives of the 27th congress of the United States, held in the city of Washington, on the 11th of September, 1841—
The hon. Nathan F. Dixon, of Rhode Island, on the part of the senate, and the hon. Jeremiah Morrow, of Ohio, on the part of the house, were called to the chair, and Kenneth Rayner, of North Carolina, Christopher Morgan, of New York, and Richard W. Thompson, of Indiana, were appointed secretaries.
Mr. Mangum, of North Carolina, offered the following resolutions:
Resolved, That it is expedient for the whigs of the senate and house of representatives of the United States to publish an address to the people of the U. States, containing a succinct exposition of the prominent proceedings of the extra session of congress, of the measures that have been adopted, and those in which they have failed, and the causes of such failure; together with such other matters as may exhibit truly the condition of the whig party and whig prospects.
Resolved, That a committee of three on the part of the senate, and five on the part of the house, be appointed to prepare such address, and submit it to a meeting of the whigs on Monday morning next, the 13th inst. at half past 8 o'clock.
And the question being taken on said resolutions, they were *unanimously* adopted.
Whereupon the following gentleman were appointed said committee: Messrs. Berrien, of Georgia, Tallmadge, of New York, and Smith, of Indiana, on the part of the senate; and Messrs. Everett, of Vermont, Mason, of Ohio, Kennedy, of Maryland, John C. Clark, of New York, and Rayner, of N. Carolina, on the part of the house.
When, on motion, the meeting adjourned, to meet again on Monday morning.

Address to the Country By the Congressional Whig Caucus
September 13, 1841

Niles Register, September 18, 1841, 35-36.

Fellow-Citizens:—The extra session of congress has, at length, been brought to a close. The incidents which belong to the history of this session, and especially those which have marked its termination, are of a nature to make so strong an impression upon the country, and to excite so much interest in the future action and relations of the whig party, that the whig representatives in both houses of congress have thought it their duty, before separating, to address their constituents with a brief exposition of the circumstances in which they conceive themselves to be placed by the events which have recently transpired.

This session of congress was called as almost the first measure of that illustrious and lamented citizen whose election to the presidency was no less significant of the general sentiment of condemnation of the acts of the preceeding administration, than it was expressive of a wish for an immediate and radical change in the public policy. The improvidence of those who had just been expelled from power had rendered it inevitable; and the country hailed the meeting of a new congress as the sure pledge of relief from all those evils which the disastrous incompetency of the men at the head of affairs had brought upon it.

The people desired the early adoption of the policy which had been promised them by the whig party. That policy had been brought to the consideration of the country throughout a contest of nearly twelve years' duration, maintained with unexampled devotion; and its principles were illustrated by the precepts and practice of the most eminent and patriotic of our citizens in every form by which they were able to address themselves to the intelligence of the people. No one misapprehended these principles; they were identified with the labors of that great party whose unparalled success was both the token and the reward of the general confidence of the nation. They promised reform

1st. In the restraint of executive power and patronage;

2d. In the wholesome regulation of the currency and the advancement of the interests of industry; and

3d. In the establishment of an economical administration of the finances.

They proposed to accomplish the first of these objects by limiting the service of the president to a single term; by forbidding all officers of the government from interfering in elections; and by a voluntary self-denial, on the part of the chief magistrate, in that excessive use of the veto power which had recently become so offensive to the country as an instrument of party supremacy.

They hoped to achieve their next object by the establishment of a national bank; by the adjustment of the system of duties upon a moderate and permanent scale, adopted as nearly as practicable to the interest, and conformable with the views of every portion of the union; by the establishment of a uniform system of bankruptcy; and by the distribution of the proceeds of the public lands amongst the states—a measure recommended not only by considerations of justice to the states themselves, but also by a sad experience of the embarrassment produced in the currency resulting from the administration of a fund of such variable amount as an item in the ordinary revenue of the government. The establishment of an economical administration of the finances they expected to attain by putting down all useless offices; by enforcing a strict accountability of the public agents; and more conspicuously, by making exact and adequate provision for the ascertainment and eventual liquidation of that public debt which the past administration had created by permitting their expenditures to overrun their receipts, and which they had concealed from public observation by the easy device of repeated issues of government notes.

These were the prominent points to which the policy of the whig party had been directed, and which constituted the great issues before the country in the recent presidential election. We are aware that our adversaries in that contest now deny these issues, founding their denial chiefly upon the fact that no formal manifesto was put forth to declare the terms upon which we insisted. We chose rather to appeal to the widely diffused knowledge of our principles which had been impressed upon every man's mind in that long struggle of years gone by; with which one party had been identified, and of which its very name was an exponant.

It need not be said that, in a representation spread over a territory of such extent as that comprehended by our union, and exhibiting interests so diversified, what might be called the characteristic principles of the whig party, throughout this wide sphere, should be subject to occasional modifications, dependent upon local influences; and that it was incumbent, therefore, upon the party to move together in a spirit of mutual concession and accommodation of sectional difference of opinion. It need not be told that, in the system of measures which we have enumerated, conflicting views might naturally exist between the representatives of distant portions of our republic, and that only by the yielding of minor interests to the establishment of the general good, entire harmony was to be obtained in the action of congress. This was natural, and to be expected. But we felt a proud consciousness that in the patriotism of the party all such difficulties would vanish, and that the demands of an enlarged welfare would be met and fulfilled, through the virtue of that spirit of compromise and forbearance, that liberal and comprehensive sentiment of self-denial and concession, which rests at the heart of our confederacy, and which constitutes the living principle of our union. Before the appointed day arrived for the meeting of congress, and that at the expiration of but one short month from the date of his inauguration, our beloved president was snatched from us by the grasp of death: too soon for the happiness of his country, but not too soon to awaken in our bosoms a deep and awful sense of the irreparable loss which we have sustained in the deprivation of a great and good man—not too soon to convince us how long and how bitterly our country is doomed to deplore this heavy misfortune. In this our calamity, we hoped to find consolation in the character and principles of him whom the constitution had designated to fill the office of the departed chief. It is true, that towards that individual, even at the moment of the selection for the vice presidency, no very earnest public attention had been directed; and it is equally true that but a passing regard was bestowed upon the current of his previous life and opinions. We only knew him as one professing to be a member of the whig party, and as seeking to identify himself with those great leaders of that party whose opinions and principles were deeply engraved in the most conspicuous acts of our political history, and were read and understood by every citizen in the land. In this connection, where he had sought to be prominent, we discerned what we conceived, and what doubtless he meant, to be a pledge of faithful adherence to the cardinal doctrines for which we struggled, and with which the hopes of the country were indissolubly bound up. We hoped to find consolation also in the fact that his accession to the presidency brought him into communion and intimate political fellowship with the chosen vanguard of the whig party—the first selection made by general Harrison of a cabinet, distinguished for its paramount ability, integrity and fidelity to the glorious cause in which we had conquered—a cabinet eminently crowned with the public confidence, in whom all men trusted as in the very embodiment of the principles of the party to which they belonged: who were inseparably associated with its glory, and in whose generous and honorable relation to the president we had the security of wise and prosperous councils, and he the pledge of a co-operation which should enable him to accomplish all that the nation desired. These hopes were still further enlivened by the encouraging tone in which the president referred, in his first address to the nation, to the "ever glorious example" afforded him by the fathers of the great republican school, and the declaration of his determination to walk in the path which they pointed out.

In the indulgence of these hopes, congress entered upon its labors. By adopting rules for the despatch of business conformable to the emergency of an extra session, and in view of the great amount of legislation which the times required, we have been enabled to achieve all, and even more than all, that our constituents could have demanded at our hands. The leading and great measures of this session, have been under discussion, in congress and out of it, for many years past, and little remained to be said beyond a repetition of former debates. There was nothing in the circumstances or position of either party in congress to require, or even to justify, protracted discussions; and the majority, therefore, felt themselves entitled to give to the extra session the character of a congress of action and decision, rather than one of debate; and we feel assured that in this effort we have done no more than respond to the just expectations of the people.

First in urgency amongst the bills passed during the session, and that to which the public command most imperatively drew the notice of congress, was the repeal of the sub-treasury law. Our next care was the enactment of the land bill. This was followed by an act converting the debt which the preceding administration had entailed upon the country into a loan of twelve million of dollars, which is limited for its redemption to a period of three years. Associated with this measure was the revenue bill, rendered necessary not only as a provision towards the extinguishment of the loan, but also as indispensable for the supply of means to meet the ordinary and necessary appropriations of the year. The bankrupt act, so earnestly and so long solicited by a large and meritorious class of our citizens, has been passed under circumstances which cannot but reflect the highest honor upon the representatives of many sections of the country. As a measure standing alone, it might perhaps have been destined to a further delay, but being brought, as it was, into that series of measures which were supposed to embrace the scheme of relief which the nation at large required, it met from a whig congress that support of which the chief argument and highest value are driven from the respect which every one felt to be due to a comprehensive policy, whose scope should include every interest in the nation. It is a trial for the benefit of the country, and remains to be altered or improved as the public wants may hereafter be found to require. The importance, in the present posture of our affairs, of attending to the national defences, suggested the measures of establishing a home squadron, of repairing and arming the fortifications, of providing for the defence of the lakes; and of bringing the nation at large into a state of readiness against hostile aggression—in regard to which measures, as great unanimity prevailed in congress, we may safely assure ourselves they will meet the undivided approbation of our constituents throughout the whole union.

This rapid review, fellow citizens, will exhibit what we have done. What we have failed to do remains to be told.

It is with profound and poignant regret that we find ourselves called upon to invoke your attention to this point. Upon the great and leading measure touching this question, our anxious endeavors to respond to the earnest prayer of the nation have been frustrated by an act as unlooked for as it is to be lamented. We grieve to say to you that by the exercise of that power in the constitution which has ever been regarded with suspicion, and often with odium, by the people—a power which we had hoped was never to be exhibited, on this subject, by a whig president—we have been defeated in two attempts to create a fiscal agent, which the wants of the country had demonstrated to us, in the most absolute form of proof, to be eminently necessary and proper in the present emergency. Twice have we, with the utmost diligence and deliberation, matured a plan for the collection, safe-keeping and disbursing of the public moneys through the agency of a corporation adapted to that end, and twice has it been our fate to encounter the opposition of the president, through the application of the veto power. The character of that veto in each case, the circumstances in which it was administered, and the grounds upon which it has met the decided disapprobation of your friends in congress, are sufficiently apparent in the public documents and the debates relating to it. This subject has acquired a painful interest with us, and will doubtless acquire it with you, from the unhappy developments with which it is accompanied. We are constrained to say, that we find no ground to justify us in the conviction that the veto of the president has been interposed on this question solely upon conscientious and well considered opinions of constitutional scruple as to his duty in the case presented. On the contrary, too many proofs have been forced upon our observation to leave us free from the apprehension, that the president has permitted himself to be beguiled into an opinion that, by this exhibition of his prerogative, he might be able to divert the policy of his administration into a channel which should lead to new political combinations, and accomplish results which must overthrow the present divisions of party in the country, and finally produced a state of things which those who elected him, at least have never contemplated. We have seen from an early period of the session, that the whig party did not enjoy the confidence of the president. With mortification we have observed that his associations more sedulously aimed at a free communion with those who have been busy to prostrate our purposes, rather than those whose principles seemed to be most identified with the power by which he was elected. We have reason to believe that he has permitted himself to be approached, counselled and influenced by those who have manifested least interest in the success of whig measures. What were represented to be his opinions and designs have been freely and even insolently put forth in certain portions, and those not the most reputable, of the public press, in a manner that ought to be deemed offensive to his honor, as it certainly was to the feelings of those who were believed to be his friends. In the earnest endeavor manifested by the members of the whig party in congress to ascertain specifically the president's notions in reference to the details of such a bill relating to a fiscal agent as would be likely to meet his approbation, the frequent changes of his opinion, and the singular want of consistency in his views, have baffled his best friends, and rendered the hope of adjustment with him impossible.

Congress, early in the session, called upon the secretary of the treasury for the plan of a fiscal agent: the result of this call was a bill which was reported in detail, with an argument in its favor, and it was, as we had a right to regard it, received by all as the bill of the president. In fact, it was known to contain provisions, in reference to the assent of the states, which corresponded with the private opinion of no member of the cabinet. This bill the president had even informed more than one member of the house he would be willing to sign if passed by congress—yet it contained provision for *local discounting*, in regard to which his veto message affirms his objection to be altogether insuperable. The president has subsequently declared that this was not his measure, and that when he said he would sign this bill he had not read it. The plan of an exchange bank, such as was reported after the first veto, the president is understood by more than one member of congress to whom he expressed his opinion, to have regarded as a favorite measure. It was in view of this opinion, suggested as it is in his first veto, and after using every proper effort to ascertain his precise views upon it, that the committee of the house of representatives reported their second bill. It made provision for a bank without the privilege of local discounting, and was adapted as closely as possible, to that class of mercantile operations which the first veto message describes with approbation, and which that paper specifically illustrates by reference to the "dealings in the exchanges" of the Bank of the United States in 1833, which the president affirms "amounted to upwards of one hundred millions of dollars." Yet this plan, when it was submitted to him, was objected to on a new ground. The last veto has narrowed the question of a bank down to the basis of the sub-treasury scheme, and it is obvious from the opinions of that message that the country is not to expect any thing better than the exploded sub-treasury, or some measure of the same character, from Mr. Tyler.

In the midst of all these varities of opinion, an impenetrable mystery seemed to hang over the whole question. There was no such frank interchange of sentiment as ought to characterize the intercourse of a president and his friends, and the last persons in the government who would seem to have been intrusted with his confidence on those embarrassing topics were the constitutional advisers which the laws had provided for him.

In this review of the position into which the late events have thrown the whig party, it is with profound sorrow we look to the course pursued by the president. He has wrested from us one of the best fruits of a long and painful struggle, and the consummation of a glorious victory: he has even perhaps thrown us once more upon the field of political strife, not weakened in numbers, nor shorn of the support of the country, but stripped of the arms which success had placed in our hands, and left again to rely upon that high patriotism which for twelve years sustained us in a conflict of unequalled asperity, and which finally brought us to the fulfillment of those brilliant hopes which he has done so much to destroy.

In this state of things, the whigs will naturally look with anxiety to the future, and inquire what are the actual relations between the president and those who brought him into power; and what, in the opinion of their friends in congress, should be their course hereafter. On both of these questions we feel it to be our duty to address you in perfect frankness and without reserve, but, at the same time, with due respect to others.

In regard to the first, we are constrained to say, that the president, by the course he has adopted in respect to the application of the veto power to two successive bank charters, each of which there was just reason to believe would meet his approbation; by his withdrawal of confidence from his real friends in congress and from the members of his cabinet; by his bestowal of it upon others notwithstanding their notorious opposition to leading measures of his administration, has voluntarily separated himself from those by whose exertions and suffrages he was elevated to that office through which he reached his present exalted station. The existence of this unnatural relation is as extraordinary as the annunciation of it is painful and mortifying. What are the consequences and duties which grow out of it?

The first consequence is, that those who brought the president into power can be no longer, in any manner or degree, justly held responsible or blamed for the administration of the executive branch of the government; and that the president and his advisers should be exclusively hereafter deemed accountable. But, as by the joint acts of Providence and the people he is constitutionally invested with the powers of chief magistrate, whilst he remains in office he should be treated with perfect respect by all. And it will be the duty of the whigs, in and out of congress, to give to his official acts and measures fair and full consideration, approving them and co-operating in their support where they can, and differing from and opposing any of them only from a high sense of public duty.

The more important question remains to be touched. What ought to be the future line of conduct of the whig party in the extraordinary emergency which now exists?

They came into power to accomplish great and patriotic objects. By the zeal and perseverance of the majorities in congress, some of the most important of those objects have been carried at the extra session. Others yet remain to be effected. The conduct of the president has occasioned bitter mortification and deep regret. Shall the party, therefore, yielding to sentiments of dispair, abandon its duty, and submit to defeat and disgrace? Far from suffering such dishonorable consequences, the very disappointment which it has unfortunately experienced should serve only to redouble its exertions, and to inspire it with fresh courage to persevere with a spirit unsubdued and a resolution unshaken, until the prosperity of the country is fully re-established, and its liberties firmly secured against all danger from the abuses, encroachments or usurpations of the executive department of the government.

At the head of the duties which remain for the whigs to perform towards their country stands conspicuously and pre-eminently above all others—

First. A reduction of the executive power, by a further limitation of the veto, so as to secure obedience to the public will, as that shall be expressed by the immediate representatives of the people and the states, with no other control than that which is indispensable to avert hasty or unconstitutional legislation.

By the adoption of a single term for the incumbent of the presidential office.

By a separation of the purse from the sword, and with that view to place the appointment of the head of the treasury in congress; and

By subjecting the power of dismissal from office to just restrictions, so as to render the president amenable for its exercise.

Second. The establishment by congress of a fiscal agent, competent to collect, safely keep, and disburse the public moneys, to restore the currency and to equalize the exchanges of the currency; and

Third. The introduction of economy in the administration of the government, and the discontinuance of all sinecures and useless offices.

To the effectuation of these objects ought the exertions of the whigs hereafter to be directed. Those only should be chosen members of congress who are willing cordially to co-operate in the accomplishment of them. Instead of striking our flag, let it be reared still higher, with a firmer hand, bearing upon its folds in conspicuous letters, *The will of the nation uncontrolled by the will of one man, one presidential term, a frugal government, and no sub-treasury, open or covert, in substance or in fact: no government bank, but an institution capable of guarding the people's treasure and administering to the people's wants.*

Rallying under that banner, let us appeal to that people whose patriotic exertions led to victory in the late glorious struggle. Let us invoke the action of the legislative councils of the sovereign states of this union. Instructed by their immediate constituents let them ascertain and express the public will in relation to these great questions; and especially let them within their respective constitutional spheres, exert themselves to give it effect.

Animated by these principles, and guided by Providence, defeat is impossible, and triumphant success inevitable. We may confidently hope that vast numbers of our fellow citizens, who have been hitherto separated from us, will unite with us under such glorious a standard; and that majorities in both houses of congress sufficiently large may be secured to carry any measure demanded by the welfare of the nation, in spite of the interposition of the power with which any one man may have been accidentally invested. Disappointed in that if such should be our lot, there will remain the hope of an amendment of the constitution curtailing the executive power. And if that should fail, we have only to recur to the noble example of our ancestors, to recollect the duty we owe to ourselves and posterity, and to bear with manly fortitude three years longer the sufferings inflicted during the last twelve years by the mal-administration of the executive department of the government. We shall have the consolation of reflecting that, in the mean time, if the president can prevent the attainment of all the good which congress is desirous to accomplish, congress may check or prevent some of the mischiefs which, under a different state of majorities in the body, he might have the power to impose.

Committee of the Senate

J. MacPherson Berrien
N. P. Tallmadge
O. H. Smith

Committee of the
House of Representatives

J. P. Kennedy
S. Mason
Horace Everett
J. C. Clark
K. Rayner

Whereupon the question was taken upon the adoption of said address, and it was *unanimously* adopted.

Ordered, That twenty thousand copies of said address be printed, and circulated among the people of the United States.

Ordered, That said address be signed by the members of the committee appointed to prepare the same and that the proceedings of this meeting be signed by the presidents, and countersigned by the secretaries.

On motion, the meeting then adjourned *sine die.*

Nathan F. Dixon ⎱ presidents
Jeremiah Morrow ⎰

K. Rayner ⎱
Christopher Morgan ⎬ secretaries
R. W. Thompson ⎰

Only a handful of Whigs like Webster and Caleb Cushing, a congressman from Massachusetts, publicly took issue with the Whig manifesto. Cushing denounced the "caucus dictatorship" that had been set up in Congress

which, not satisfied with ruling that body to the extinguishment of individual freedom of opinion, seeks to control the President in his proper sphere of duty, denounces him before you for refusing to surrender his independence and his conscience to its decree, and proposes through subversion of the fundamental provisions and principles of the constitution, to usurp the command of the government. It is a question, therefore, in fact, not of legislative measures, but of revolution.[158]

He quickly retreated to a more practical question, however, and asked:

Is it wise for the Whig Party to throw away the actuality of power for the current four years? If so, for what object? . . . Is the contingent possibility of advancing to power four years hence any one particular man in its ranks, whoever he may be, and however eminently deserving, a sufficient object to induce the Whig Party to abdicate the power which itself as a body possesses now?[159]

Daniel Webster was the one major figure in the Whig party not provoked by the President's actions, and he continued to plead for unity in the party and understanding of the President's position. His letter to the two Massachusetts senators, Isaac Bates and Rufus Choate, stated the argument for delaying consideration of the second bank bill and preventing further disruption of the party as succinctly as it was made by anyone. But it should be noted that Webster did not succeed in influencing many, if any, of his Whig colleagues, even those two Massachusetts senators who were closest to him. The fact that Webster wanted to remain as secretary of state and had been hostile to Clay for some time were two additional reasons for his attempt to reconcile a breach in the Whig party's ranks at that moment in history.

Secretary of State Daniel Webster
Letter to Isaac Bates and Rufus Choate,
Senators from Massachusetts
August 25, 1841

George Ticknor Curtis, *Life of Daniel Webster* (New York, 1870) II, 79-80.

Gentlemen: As you spoke last evening of the general policy of the Whigs, under the present posture of affairs, relative to the Bank Bill, I am willing to place you in full possession of my opinion on that subject.

It is not necessary to go further back into the history of the past than the introduction of the present measure into the House of Representatives.

That introduction took place within two or three days after the President's disapproval of the former bill; and I have not the slightest doubt that it was honestly and fairly intended as a measure likely to meet the President's approbation. I do not believe that one in fifty of the Whigs had any sinister design whatever, if there was an individual who had such design.

But I know that the President had been greatly troubled in regard to the former bill, being desirous, on the one hand, to meet the wishes of his friends if he could; and, on the other, to do justice to his own opinions.

Having returned this first bill with his objections, a new one was presented in the House, and appeared to be making rapid progress.

I know the President regretted this, and wished the whole subject might have been postponed.

At the same time, I believe he was disposed to consider, calmly and conscientiously, whatever other measure might be presented to him.

But, in the mean time, Mr. Botts's very extraordinary letter made its appearance. Mr. Botts is a Whig of eminence and influence in our ranks. I need not recall to your minds the contents of the letter. It is enough to say that it purported that the Whigs designed to circumvent their own President; to "head him," as the expression was, and to place him in a condition of embarrassment.

From that moment I felt that it was the duty of the Whigs to forbear from pressing the Bank Bill further at the present time.

I thought it was but just in them to give decisive proof that they entertained no such purpose as seemed to be imputed to them. And, since there was reason to believe that the President would be glad of time for information and reflection before being called upon to form an opinion on another plan for a bank—a plan somewhat new to the country—I thought his known wishes ought to be complied with.

I think so still. I think this is a course just to the President, and wise on behalf of the Whig party.

A decisive rebuke ought, in my judgment, to be given to the intimation, from whatever quarter, of a disposition among the Whigs to embarrass the President.

This is the main ground of my opinion; and such a rebuke, I think, would be found in the general resolution of the party to postpone further proceedings on the subject to the next session, now only a little more than three months off.

The session has been fruitful of important acts. The wants of the Treasury have been supplied; provisions have been made for fortifications and for the navy; the repeal of the Sub-Treasury has passed; the Bankrupt Bill, that great measure of justice and benevolence, has been carried through; and the Land Bill seems about to receive the sanction of Congress.

In all these measures, forming a mass of legislation more important, I will venture to say, that all the proceedings of Congress for many years past, the President has cordially concurred.

I agree that the currency question is, nevertheless, the great question before the country; but, considering what has already been accomplished in regard to other things—considering the difference of opinion which exists upon this remaining one—and considering, especially, that it is the duty of the Whigs effectually to repel and put down any supposition that they are endeavoring to put the President in a condition in which he must act under restraint or embarrassment, I am fully and entirely persuaded that the bank subject should be postponed to the next session.

I am, gentlemen, your friend and obedient servant,

Daniel Webster

The overwhelming majority of the congressional Whigs saw the situation much differently. Their address to their Whig supporters throughout the country argued persuasively that the "actuality of power" was to no avail if the President continued to block the party's will with his veto. Some historians have sided with Caleb Cushing who described the Whig caucus address as the opening gun in Henry Clay's campaign for the presidency in 1844. What they fail to comprehend is that such an objective would not necessarily have been in conflict with the Whig's basic objectives, for at that time the congressional Whigs were of the opinion that the trappings of power and the control of the presidency were to no avail if the party's policies were unable to be put into effect. The "birthright" Whigs desired Clay's leadership in the presidency, because he was their recognized and ablest leader, and they began to feel that elevating him to the highest office was the only way they could accomplish their major objectives. But the realization came too late, for the failure of the party to enact its economic reforms after its first brilliant electoral victory in 1840, cost it the votes of many of its marginal supporters, who had the power to determine a national election.

The Congress adjourned the same day as the Whig address to the American people was approved by the party caucus, but not before it received from the President the nominations for cabinet positions vacated by the five departing members of Harrison's original cabinet (Postmaster General Francis Granger, the fifth member of the group, resigned the same day, Monday, September 13, after being instructed to do so by the New York Whig delegation). Obviously Tyler had anticipated the move, and there is every indication that he planned to make some changes in his cabinet anyway. But the mass resignations, coming as they did in conjunction with the party caucus denunciation of the President, widened an irreparable breach that would never be healed, and had a damaging impact upon the future of the Whig party.

Clay was the central figure in this high drama, for it was expected by all that he would run for the presidency in 1844; it was suggested by his enemies (including the President) that he had masterminded this crisis to alienate the Whigs from the nominally Whig inhabitant of the White House. The evidence that he met with the departing cabinet members at a dinner the night their decision to leave was apparently made, and that he purportedly stood to gain most by such a breach, were arguments advanced to support this thesis.

On the other hand, despite his impatience to accomplish the financial reform, which he hoped the establishment of a bank would lead to, Clay had been surprisingly forbearing during the Whig's negotiations to work out a suitable compromise with the President. Working through representatives of the caucus and members of the cabinet, the Whigs twice agreed to make substantial changes in their own initial plans for the bank, changes designed to ameliorate the President's objections. Certainly Clay was part of such an agreement on a compromise proposal, for he was the dominant figure in the Whig caucus at that time. If he had been simply attempting to manipulate Tyler into an impossible position, he would never have gone along with the compromise in the first place; if the President had agreed to sign either the first or second bank bills, regardless of personal feelings, there would not have been an irreparable breach within the Whig party.

But motives are always difficult to assign, and exploring Tyler's motives in this instance is no more verifiable than attempting to assess Clay's. The President's enemies pictured him as being irreconcilable to a compromise from the beginning, intent upon crushing Clay and either dominating the Whig party or leading most of its supporters into another party, which he planned to head. Such an interpretation suggests that he desired the breach, worked to foment it, and would have initiated it anyway at some later date if the opportunity had not presented itself in the bank vetoes cases. There is no doubt that Tyler wished to succeed himself, to graduate from an "accidental" to an elected presidency. When it became apparent that he could not successfully challenge Clay for the leadership of the party, which purportedly would lead to the next nomination, he might well have developed alternate plans for retaining possession of the first magistracy, plans that entailed encouraging a coterie of advisors other than his Whig cabinet, advisors some of whom were Whigs, and others Democrats, but all of whom were devoted to his own states' rights ideology.

Tyler's friends argued that he was the aggrieved party in the dispute, that he leaned over backwards to cooperate with Clay and the Whigs up to the point where his basic constitutional principles would be compromised by any further concessions. This account is hard to square with his behavior during the negotiation over the second bank bill, but be that as it may, this exploration of motives and intent is not a very useful one. The reality of the situation was that the first Whig President and the first Whig-dominated Congress were set on a collision course by these events and motives, whatever they were, and the end result was the ultimate destruction of the Whig party. I say this mindful of the fact that the Whigs continued to make a substantial showing in the next two national elections, losing the election of 1844 by a hair's breadth and winning in 1848 by a somewhat larger margin. These marginal elections were the result of a number of factors affecting specific situations, but do not detract from my substantive argument regarding the decline of the party. The Whigs were confronted with the challenge of becoming the majority party in 1840, a challenge to which they failed to respond by their inability to reconcile their internal differences and to exhibit to the country their ability to respond to its problems and needs; in short, they proved unable to govern. Whatever one's explanation of the struggle between Clay and Tyler during this period, the end result was a failure in national leadership at a moment in history when such leadership was desperately needed.

The Chief Executive who attempts to defend a strong presidency against a determined Congress needs the support of his own party in Congress to win his battle. He cannot go it alone, ignoring the reality of party existence in American political life, or conceiving of the government as a pure structure of separate and independent branches. First of all the branches are not separate, nor are they independent of each other. Their activities and responsibilities intersect at every step of the political process, and although some degree of independence and integrity is essential to each branch, it is impossible to conduct a viable government while one branch remains aloof from the other co-equal branches of government.

As devastating as this breach was to the future of the Whig party, it was perhaps even more so for the future integrity of the presidency in the remaining non-war years of the nineteenth century. The Whigs were locked into their metaphysical attack upon the presidency because of their years of opposition to Jackson, but they might well have been cured of their myopic view of the system if they had truly tasted power after their victory in 1840. Power is a sobering antidote to ideological politics. "Executive usurpation" was a good campaign slogan and battle cry during a period of confusion over a chaotic economic depression, which was linked in the public's mind to the fiscal policies of the Jackson administration. But when the dust settled, and the Whigs found themselves in control of both the White House and Congress, they could have forgotten about "executive usurpation" long enough to weld an efficient alliance between the two branches of government in order to implement Whig policy.

Tyler's rigid commitment to a different ideology—states' rights—and his vain and awkward alienation from most members of his own party widened the gap between these two essential elements of a party coalition in power and led to the irreconcilable breach between the Whig party in Congress and the Whig President in the executive mansion. As the separation expanded and soured over the years, the President was helpless to arrest his loss of prestige and power.

In the weeks and months following the events of the summer of 1841, relations between the congressional Whigs and the President regressed, if anything, from their nearly nonexistent level of trust and confidence at that time. In the spring of 1842, Henry Clay retired from the Senate and returned to Ashland, determined to pursue his quest for the presidency in 1844, although he denied such political ambition in his public statements. In a thrilling and emotional departure speech in the Senate, the veteran political leader indicated that he had originally intended to retire at the end of the special session and had only returned for a few months of the regular session in the vain hope that the damage done during the earlier meetings could be erased, and successful fiscal measures established. He pointed out that he had initially agreed to serve only because

> I felt desirous to co-operate with my political and personal friends in restoring, if it could be effected, the prosperity of the country, by the best measures which their united counsels might be able to devise; . . . [160]

In the pursuit of these objectives, Clay had been attacked as a "dictator," and yet he pointed out:

> The idea of a dictatorship is drawn from Roman institutions; and at the time the office was created, the person who wielded the tremendous weight of authority it conferred, concentrated in his own person an absolute power over the lives and property of all of his fellow-citizens; he could levy armies; he could build and man navies; he could raise any amount of revenue he might choose to demand; and life and death rested on his fiat. If I were a dictator, as I am said to be, where is the power with which I am clothed? Have I any army? any navy? any revenue? any patronage? in a word, any power whatever? [161]

He went on to argue that it is a strange "dictator" indeed who conducts no cruel executions, spills no blood and who voluntarily retires in a much shorter period than usually allotted to the dictators of the Roman Empire. But he added

> [If being a *dictator* meant] to have ardently desired to see a disordered currency regulated and restored, and irregular exchanges equalized and adjusted; if to have labored to replenish the empty coffers of the treasury by suitable duties; if to have endeavored to extend relief to the unfortunate bankrupts of the country, who have been ruined in a great measure by the erroneous policy, as we believed, of this government; to limit, circumscribe, and reduce executive authority; to retrench unnecessary expenditure and abolish useless offices and institutions; and the public honor to preserve untarnished by supplying a revenue adequate to meet the national engagements and incidental protection to the national industry; if to have entertained an anxious solicitude to redeem every pledge, and execute every promise fairly made by my political friends,

with a view to the acquisition of power from the hands of an honest and confiding people; if these constitute a man a *dictator*, why, then, I must be content to bear, although I still ought only to share with my friends, the odium or the honor of the epithet, as it may be considered on the one hand or the other.[162]

Having failed to achieve what he considered to be the most important of these objectives, Clay retired to re-think and re-plan his own final effort to achieve the presidency, an objective which had eluded him all of his life. But to charge a leader of Clay's ability with inordinate ambition because he continued to seek executive office after failing to move the government from his parliamentary cockpit, is, in my opinion, to misuse the term. Over the past decade Clay had helped to build a party which had established its right to national leadership on the basis of the claim to pursue just these objectives. The Kentucky statesman had played a much, much greater role in this effort than John Tyler could ever hope to claim. Tyler, although a distinguished Virginia politician, was a national cipher, and it was purely an accidental series of events which catapulted him into the White House. If anyone demonstrated arrogance and ambition in this crisis, it was Tyler, who owed a greater obligation and loyalty to the party and the leaders who had brought him to power through their efforts and influence, than he ever seemed to acknowledge or understand.

One does not emerge into the presidential office from nowhere. The presidency is fought for and won and lost by political parties which reflect different policies, attitudes, even philosophies about the manner in which the public business should be conducted. A successful candidate for the presidency, or a vice presidential successor to the office, theoretically carries with him a very special mandate from the people. The people normally see in him, albeit in a rather blurred and inexact image or profile, a fairly general set of expectations. Such expectations are more or less specific, more or less realistic, according to the nature of the political campaign which led to the electoral decision, the political party which shaped the platform of the candidate, and the character, the record, and the promises of the candidate himself. But the acceptance of such an obligation is, or should be, just as real and binding upon a new President or a newly installed vice presidential successor, as many of the binding obligations which the Chief Magistrate inherits from the precedents and traditions established by his predecessors.

There should be a sense of trust here that is honored, first, by an individual, who by standing for office and enunciating a program, asserts the first part of a contract with the public and is confirmed by his election to that office; secondly, once elected he has an obligation to the traditions, precedents and constitutional definition of the powers of the presidency. The newly inaugurated Chief Executive has an obligation to try to understand and respect his important history, not as a rigid and fully prescribed set of limits within which a President must totally confine himself, but as general guidelines to actions and decisions, some of which are bound to go beyond but not necessarily against this tradition and background. When this trust is not recognized and honored, the President and the citizens whom he represents are in deep trouble. Such a President cuts himself off from the past and from the men and traditions which made the office what it had become up to his time. He owes these men and their traditions not only a debt of gratitude, but the respect and dignity which their contributions deserve. At the same time, he also is obligated to the party which put him in power, and the citizens who responded to the party's call to arms. He should attempt to honor in practice the mutually agreed upon expectations of the campaign. Frequently this embodies not a set of specific policies, but rather a far more general, even vague set of objectives, which are best understood by understanding the party and its *raison d'etre*, rather than a particular speech or a convention platform.

Sometimes this is an unfortunate source of genuine and honest confusion, but a determined decision to avoid or circumscribe such a contract is nothing less than the betrayal of a high trust, and destructive to the interests of the political system itself. The quality of the system—its freedom and viability—are dependent upon its ability to present the citizen-voter with real alternatives, both in terms of personalities as well as with respect to policy. When a President ignores this contract and fails to understand the critical role trust plays in sustaining faith in the system, he contributes seriously to the impairment of the quality and viability of the system.

John Tyler frequently paraded arrogantly in the presidential office, as if he had inherited no obligations in his "accidental" ascendancy to the White House. In point of fact he had not emerged like Pallas Athene from the brain of the almighty Zeus, but at a Whig convention in Harrisburg, Pennsylvania, where he had been the third or fourth choice in an impossible selection process (which has not improved much to this day) and placed on the ticket to balance it regionally, and in some sense ideologically. Oddly enough, especially in regard to the outcome, he was placed on the ticket because of his publicly asserted friendship with Henry Clay, who the convention wanted to provide with a consolation prize for having lost the nomination for the presidency.

What of course compounded the problem in this case was the fact that the Whigs, in their effort to attract the maximum number of supporters among the electorate, refrained from enunciating a specific platform. Their reasoning for this was that their position on the major questions was well-enough known to the faithful, who were certainly not in the majority of the voting public nationally. The challenge to the Whigs in 1840, at least as the party leaders saw it, was to whip up enough enthusiasm among the uncommitted to overcome the existing advantage of the majority party, and to challenge the Democrats for that portion of the marginal vote which would spell the difference between victory and defeat.

The Whigs rose to this challenge admirably, responding to what Hofstadter defined as the effective role of the political party, but their success in this area was achieved at the expense of his other category—the responsible role—which they submerged for the duration of the 1840 campaign. The vice presidency of John Tyler was one of the by-products of that conscious decision to sacrifice responsibility to effectiveness, so Tyler himself cannot be blamed entirely for its tragic results. But as a sophisticated and experienced man of politics, he understood what the real Whigs stood for as well as Clay himself, and if he was intent upon clarifying and distinguishing his position from that of Harrison on the critical question of the establishment of some sort of a national bank to stabilize the money system of the country, he should have made this a condition of his willingness to accept the Whig nomination. As Clay cruelly pointed out in his attack upon the first veto, if Tyler had asserted this point at Harrisburg, he probably would not have received a single vote in the convention.

Here again is another reflection of the ambivalence with respect to party that has characterized American political history from the beginning. Clay and the congressional Whigs represented the positive emergence of the strong sense of party identification, party loyalty, party program and policies; Tyler, on the other hand, was the real defender of "factional" interest—states' rights—but at the same time a man who intended to remain totally independent of the discipline of the party. He was content to stand as a Whig when this was the only viable option in a national election campaign, but he asserted his independent conscience and commitment to the ideology of states' rights when it came to carrying out his executive role, a role bestowed upon him by virtue of his alleged commitment to the Whig party. The brilliant Whig victory in 1840 ran aground on the rocks of independent resistance to party discipline one year later, by a President who possessed no fundamental concept of the role of responsible parties in the democratic system nor the responsibility of their elected representatives to party interest and party policies when in office.

This is one of the most agonizing dilemmas of party politics in a representative democratic system. Without political parties of at least some degree of discipline and responsibility, the system takes on the character of anarchy, a bedlam of independent and irresponsible individuals and groups pressing their claims and advancing their selfish interests in a chaotic and confused state of dissonance. Representatives and responsible political parties are necessary to eliminate this chaos, to still the din of deafening voices and to clarify and offer viable alternatives to the voting citizen. Of course this becomes more and more difficult in larger and more complex societies, when the number and size of conflicting interests and problems provide substantial obstacles to such a politicizing process.

The cost of such a solution to the individual (whose allegiance to a political party is imperative) is often fairly high, too high for some to pay, and yet it is the only clear alternative to the pure chaos of a non-party system. The very nature of the political process immediately suggests the necessity of compromise, for it attempts to decide many problems for which there are many individual and frequently conflicting attitudes, needs and interests. Political parties have been described as "necessary evils," a phrase which itself reveals the inherent contradictions and ambivalence in their acceptance by the system. Yet without some degree of political responsibility in an open political system, the values and protections of constitutional democracy would be ineffective and unworkable.

Henry Clay appeared to understand this basic political truth. During the previous decade he had tried to make the system work by building an opposition party which challenged the group in power and offered a real alternative in leadership and policies to the voting citizens. Can anyone be surprised at his chagrin when he discovered that the elected representative of that political party, accidentally elevated to the White House, revealed no fundamental understanding of this basic principle of the system, nor of his obligation and the implied loyalty to it? Tyler's declaration of independence from the obligations assumed by membership in and acceptance of that party's support for public office rendered the Whig party impotent to respond to the nation's needs and problems once that office was obtained. His rigid and doctrinaire concept of the "separation of powers" and his insistence upon the exploitation of the veto power to protect this sterile myth of independence completely ignored the connecting links of party, which allow a written Constitution to become alive and functional. Obligation to the principle of a responsible party system does not entirely demand the sacrifice of all individuality and conscience, but it always balances these values against the equally important purposes of the party's role in the political system, and the necessity of maintaining a significant degree of internal discipline in order to protect and enhance those purposes.

In the summer of 1842 another serious disagreement between the President and the Congress developed. Clay had vacated the congressional scene, and it was the House of Representatives which became the center of this new political storm. Again the issue emerged in the form of a presidential veto—the veto of a Whig measure to reduce certain tariff schedules which had been provided for in the compromise Tariff of 1833, combined with the proposed continuation of the distribution of the proceeds from the sale of the public lands. The President objected to both aspects of the bill arguing on the grounds of strict policy disagreement, rather than any alleged unconstitutionality of the measure.

This was the first time a President had openly asserted this prerogative, although several previous presidential vetoes had been based on the same consideration (see Volume I of this series). The bill was returned to the House and passed in substantially the same form a second time by the Whig majority, but it was rejected by Tyler again. By this time the adrenalin was rising—the Speaker appointed a special committee of the House, to be chaired by John Quincy Adams, to review the President's veto message. Adam's committee reported back to the House several days later, severely censuring the President for his vetoes and asserting more strongly than ever the Whig theory of "executive usurpation." The report argued that "executive usurpation" was a transformation of the true theory of the Constitution, which not only separated the Executive from the legislative power but "made [it] dependent upon, and responsible to it."[163] The report went on to explain:

> Until a very recent period of our history, all reference, in either House of Congress, to the opinions or wishes of the President, relating to any subject in deliberation before them, was regarded as an outrage upon the rights of the deliberative body, among the first of whose duties it is to spurn the influence of the dispenser of patronage and power. Until very recently, it was sufficient to impair the influence of any member to be suspected of personal subservience to the Executive; and any allusion to his wishes, in a debate, was deemed a departure not less from decency than from order.[164]

The report then reviewed Tyler's recent use of the veto power, reflecting rather despondently upon the accommodations made by the Congress to the President's reservations on the initial bank bills, only to be nullified by "the weak and wavering obstinacy of one man, accidentally, and not by the will of the people, invested with the terrible power—as if prophetically described by one of his own ministers, at this day, as the right to deprive people of self government."[165]

Since the report was prepared by the hand of former President of the United States John Quincy Adams, and since it also involved the veto of a measure, part of whose objective was to return the proceeds of the sale of the public lands to the states for internal improvements, Adams reacted strongly to this reversal of what he considered to be a critical function of national government. The argument against what ten[166] of the thirteen-man committee considered an unconstitutional abuse of the veto power culminated in a denunciation of the President, the charge that he should be impeached and finally a call for a constitutional amendment to strip the President of the veto power.

Report of the Select Committee
Of the House of Representatives
On the Veto Message by President John Tyler
May 16, 1841

Congressional Globe, 27th Cong., 2d sess., August 16, 1842, XI, 894-96.

The select committee, to whom was referred the message of the President of the United States, returning to this House the act, which originated in it, "to provide revenue from imports, and to change and modify existing laws imposing duties on imports, and for other purposes," with his objections to it, with instructions to report thereon to the House, have attended to that service, and respectfully report:

The message is the last of a series of executive measures, the result of which has been to defeat and nullify the whole action of the legislative authority of this Union, upon the most important interests of the nation.

At the accession of the late President Harrison, by election of the people, to the executive chair, the finances, the revenue, and the credit of the country, were found in a condition so greatly disordered, and so languishing, that the first act of his administration was to call a special session of Congress, to provide a remedy for this distempered state of the great body politic. It was even then a disease of no sudden occurrence, and of no ordinary malignity. Four years before, the immediate predecessor of General Harrison had been constrained to resort to the same expedient—a special session of Congress; the result of which had only proved the first of a succession of palliatives, purchasing momentary relief at the expense of deeper-seated disease and aggravated symptoms, growing daily more intense through the whole four years of that administration. It had expended, from year to year, from $8,000,000 to $10,000,000 beyond its income; absorbing, in that period, nearly $10,000,000 pledged for deposits with the States, $8,000,000 of stock in the Bank of the United States, from $5,000,000 to $6,000,000 of trust funds, and as much treasury notes; and was sinking under the weight of its own improvidence and incompetency.

The sentence of a suffering people had commanded a change in the administration, and the contemporaneous elections throughout the Union had placed in both Houses of Congress majorities, the natural exponents of the principles which it was the will of the people should be substituted in the administration of their Government, instead of those which had brought the country to a condition of such wretchedness and shame. There was perfect harmony of principle between the chosen President of the people and this majority, thus constituted in both Houses of Congress; and the first act of his administration was, to call a special session of Congress, for their deliberation and action upon the measures indispensably necessary for relief to the public distress, and to retrieve the prosperity of the great community of the nation.

On the 31st day of May, 1841, within three months after the inauguration of President Harrison, the Congress assembled at his call. But the reins of the executive car were already in other hands. By an inscrutable decree of Providence, the chief of the people's choice, in harmony with whose principles the majorities of both Houses had been constituted, was laid low in death. The President who had called the meeting of Congress, was no longer the President when the Congress met. A successor to the office had assumed the title, with totally different principles, though professing the same at the time of his election, which, far from harmonizing, like those of his immediate predecessor, with the majority of both Houses of Congress, were soon disclosed in diametrical opposition to them.

The first development of this new and most unfortunate condition of the General Government was manifested, by the failure, once and again, of the first great measure intended by Congress to restore the credit of the country, by the establishment of a national bank—a failure caused exclusively by the operation of the veto power by the President. In the spirit of the Constitution of the United States, the executive is not only separated from the legislative power, but made dependent upon, and responsible to it. Until a very recent period of our history, all reference, in either House of Congress, to the opinions or wishes of the President, relating to any subject in deliberation before them, was regarded as an outrage upon the rights of the deliberative body, among the first of whose duties it is to spurn the influence of the dispenser of patronage and power. Until very recently, it was sufficient greatly to impair the influence of any member to be suspected of personal subserviency to the Executive; and any allusion to his wishes, in debate, was deemed a departure not less from decency than from order. An anxious desire to accommodate the action of Congress to the opinions and wishes of Mr. Tyler had led to modifications of the first bill for the establishment of a national bank, presented to him for his approval, widely differing from the opinions entertained of their expediency by the majority of both Houses of Congress; but which failed to obtain that approval for the sake of which they had been reluctantly adopted. A second attempt ensued, under a sense of the indispensable necessity of a fiscal corporation to the revenues and credit of the nation, to prepare an act to which an informal intercourse and communication between a member of the House, charged with the duty of preparing the bill, and the President of the United States himself, might secure, by compliance with his opinions, a pledge in advance of his approval of the bill, when it should be presented to him. That pledge was obtained. The bill was presented to him in the very terms which he had prescribed as necessary to obtain his sanction, and it met the same fate with its predecessor; and it is remarkable that the reasons assigned for the refusal to approve the second bill are in direct and immediate conflict with those which had been assigned for the refusal to sign the first.

Thus the measure first among those deemed by the Legislature of the Union indispensably necessary for the salvation of its highest interests, and for the restoration of its credit, its honor, its prosperity, was prostrated, defeated, annulled, by the weak and wavering obstinacy of one man, accidentally, and not by the will of the people, invested with that terrible power—as if prophetically described by one of his own chosen ministers, at this day, as "the right to deprive the people of self-government."

The first consequence of this executive legislation was not only to prostrate the efforts of the Legislature itself, to relieve the people from their distress, to replenish the exhausted treasury, and call forth the resources of the country, to redeem the public faith to the fulfilment of the national engagements, but to leave all the burdens and embarrassments of the public treasury, brought upon it by the improvidence of the preceding administration, bearing upon the people with aggravated pressure. The fatal error of the preceding administration had been an excess of expenditure beyond its income. That excess had been an average of eight millions of dollars a year, at least, during the four years of its existence. The practical system of its fiscal operations had been a continued increase of expenditures and diminution of revenues, and it left as a bequest to its successor, no effective reduction of expenses, but a double reduction of revenue to the amount of millions, to occur of course, by the mere lapse of time, unless averted, within fifteen months, by subsequent legislation.

By the double exercise of the Presidential interdict upon the two bills for establishing a national bank, this legislation was prevented. The excess of expenditures beyond the revenue continued and increased. The double reduction of revenue prescribed by the compromise of 1833, was suffered to take its full effect; no reduction of the expenditures had been prescribed; and in the course of eighteen months, since the inauguration of President Harrison, an addition of at least fifteen millions to the enormous deficit already existing in the treasury at the close of the last Administration, is now charged upon the prevailing party in Congress, by those who had made it the law; while the exercise of the veto power alone disabled the Legislature itself from the power of applying the only remedy which it was within the competency of legislation itself to provide.

The great purpose for which the special session of Congress had been called was thus defeated by the exercise of the veto power. At the meeting of Congress, at the regular annual session, the majorities of both Houses, not yielding to the discouragement of disappointed hopes and baffled energies, undertook the task of raising, by impost duties, a revenue adequate to the necessities of the treasury, and to the fulfilment of the national obligations.

By the assiduous and unremitting labors of the committees of both Houses charged with the duties of providing for the necessities of the revenue, and for the great manufacturing interest of the Northern, Central, and Western States, which must be so deeply affected by any adjustment of a tariff to raise exclusively a revenue adequate to the necessary expenses of the Government from duties on imports, a tariff bill, believed to be nearly, if not wholly, sufficient for that purpose, was elaborated and amply discussed, through a long series of weeks, in both branches of the Legislature. The process of gestation, through which alone such a complicated system could be organized, necessarily consumed many months of time; nor were the committees of the House exempted from severe reproach, which the purchased presses of the Executive Chief are even yet casting upon Congress, without rebuke or restraint from him. The delays were occasioned by the patient and unwearied investigation of the whole subject by the appropriate committees. As the period approached when the so-called compromise tariff was to be consummated, leaving the Government without any revenue tariff sanctioned by the law, the prudence of Congress, without precipitating their decision upon the permanent system which they fondly hoped to establish, provided and sent to the President a temporary expedient, limited in its operation to the space of one month; during which, to avoid, as they thought, the possibility of a collision with the apprehended antipathics of the President, they had suspended for the same month the distribution of the proceeds of the sales of public lands; which, by a previous law, was to take effect the day after the expiration of the compromise. Not only was this most conciliatory measure contemptuously rejected, but, in total disregard of the avowed opinions of his own Secretary of the Treasury, concurring with those nearly unanimous of all the most eminent lawyers of the land, in solitary reliance upon the hesitation opinion of the Attorney General, he has undertaken not only to levy taxes to the amount of millions upon the people, but to prescribe regulations for its collection, and for ascertaining the value of imported merchandise, which the law had, in express terms, reserved for the legislative action of Congress.

And now, to crown this system of continual and unrelenting exercise of executive legislation by the alternate gross abuse of constitutional power, and bold assumption of powers never vested in him by any law, we come to the veto message referred by the House to this committee.

A comparative review of the four several vetoes which, in the course of fifteen months, have suspended the legislation of this Union, combined with that amphibious production, the reasons for approving and signing a bill, and at the same time striking, by judicial construction, at its most important enactment, illustrated by contemporaneous effusions of temper and of sentiment divulged at convivial festivals, and obtruded upon the public eye by the fatal friendship of sycophant private correspondents, and stripped to its naked nature by the repeated and daring assumption both of legislative and of judicial power, would present anomalies of character and conduct rarely seen upon earth. Such an investigation, though strictly within the scope of the instructions embraced in the reference to this committee, would require a voluminous report, which the scantiness of time will not allow, and which may not be necessary for maturing the judgment of the House upon the document now before them.

The reasons assigned by the President for returning to the House of Representatives, with his objections, the bill to provide revenue from imports, and to change and modify existing laws imposing duties, and for other purposes, are preceded by a brief dissertation upon the painful sensations which *any individual* invested with the veto power must feel in exercising it upon important acts of the Legislature. The paragraph is worded with extreme caution, and with obvious intent to avoid the assertion, made in such broad and unqualified terms in the letter read at the Philadelphia Independence-day dinner party, that Congress can enact *no law* without the concurrence of the Executive. There is in this paper a studious effort to save *any individual* from the imputation of asserting the unqualified independence of the Executive upon the Legislature, and the impotence of Congress to enact any law without him. That assertion, made in so explicit and unqualified terms in the Philadelphia letter, is here virtually disclaimed and disavowed. The exercise of *some* independence of judgment, in regard to all acts of legislation, by any individual invested with the veto power, is here curtailed and narrowed down to the mere privilege of not yielding his well-considered, most deeply fixed, and repeatedly declared opinions on matters of great public concernment, to those of a co-ordinate department, without requesting that department seriously to re-examine the subject of their difference. The co-ordinate department *to* the Legislature is no longer the co-ordinate branch *of* the Legislature. The power of Congress to enact a law without the co-operation of any individual Executive, is conceded—not merely by unavoidable inference; for the closing paragraph of the message, recurring again to the same troublesome reminiscence, observes that, after all, the effect of what he does is substantially to call on Congress to *reconsider* the subject. If, on such reconsideration, a majority of two-thirds of both Houses should be in favor of this measure, it will become a law, notwithstanding his objections. The truism of this remark may, perhaps, be accounted for by the surmise that it was a new discovery, made since the writing of the Philadelphia dinner-party letter; and the modest presumption ascribed to the Constitution, that the Executive can commit no error of opinion unless two thirds of both branches of the Legislature are in conflict with him, is tempered by the amiable assurance that, in that event, he will cheerfully acquiesce in a result which would be precisely the same whether he should acquiesce in it or not. The aptitude of this hypothetical position may be estimated by the calculation of the chances that the contingency which it supposes is within the verge of possibility.

The reasons assigned by the President for his objections to this bill are further preceded by a narrative of his antecedent opinions and communications on the subject of distributing the proceeds of the sales of the public lands. He admits that, at the opening of the extra session, he recommended such a distribution, but he avers that this recommendation was expressly coupled with the condition that the duties on imports should not exceed the rate of twenty per cent., provided by the compromise act of 1833.

Who could imagine that, after this most emphatic *coupling* of the revenue from duties of impost, with revenue from the proceeds of the sales of the public lands, the first and paramount objection of the President to this bill should be, that it unites two subjects which, so far from having any affinity to one another, are wholly incongruous in their character; which two subjects are identically the same with those which he had coupled together in his recommendation to Congress at the extra session? If there was no affinity between the parties, why did he join them together? If the union was illegitimate, who was the administering priest of the unhallowed rites? It is objected to this bill, that it is both a revenue and an appropriation bill? What then? Is not the act of September 4, 1841, approved and signed by the President himself, both a revenue and an appropriation bill? Does it not enact that, in the event of an insufficiency of impost duties, not exceeding twenty per centum ad valorem, to defray the current expenses of the Government, the proceeds of the sales of the lands shall be levied as part of the same revenue, and appropriated to the same purposes? The appropriation of the proceeds of the sales of the public lands, to defray the ordinary expenditures of the Government, is believed to be a system of fiscal management unwise, impolitic, improvident, and unjust; and it is precisely for that reason that the bill now before the House provides that they shall not be so appropriated. The public lands are the noble and inappreciable inheritance of the whole nation. The sale of them to individuals is not a tax upon the purchaser, but an exchange of equivalents, scarcely more burdensome to the grantee than if he should receive it as a gratuitous donation. To appropriate the proceeds of the sales to defray the ordinary expenses of the Government, is to waste and destroy the property. This property is held by Congress in trust. Mr. Tyler speaks of the distribution as if it was giving away the property. It is precisely the reverse. It is restoring it to the owner. To appropriate the proceeds to defray the current expenditures, is to give it up to dilapidation and waste. It is, in political economy, precisely the same as if an individual landholder should sell off, year after year, parcels of his estate, and consume its proceeds in the payment of his household expenses. The first principle of political economy necessary for a nation is to raise, by *taxation*, within the year, the whole sum required for the expenditures of that year. Every departure from this principle is a step in the path of national bankruptcy and ruin. The daily demands of the treasury must be supplied by the income derived from taxation by the year, and not by the dissipation of the common property.

The second reason of the President for objecting to the passage of this bill, is not more ponderous than the first. It is the destitute and embarrassed state of the treasury, and the impolicy, if not unconstitutionality, of *giving away* a fruitful source of revenue, which, if retained, may be seized by the Government, and applied to meet its daily wants. But the President had just told us that this fruitful source of revenue was a subject wholly dissimilar in its character from that of revenue raised by duties of impost—so dissimilar, that the union of them formed in his mind an insurmountable objection to the passage of the bill. "I most respectfully submit (says the message) whether this is a time to *give away* the proceeds of the land sales, when the public lands constitute a fund which, of all others, may be made most useful in sustaining the public credit." And how could it be made thus useful? Precisely by *giving them away*. By giving them away forever! For, if the principle be once established, that the proceeds of the sales of the public lands shall be substituted in the place of revenue, by taxation, to defray the ordinary annual expenses of the National Government, never more will the people of any State in this Union have the benefit of one dollar from this richest of mines of inexhaustible wealth, bestowed upon them by their bountiful Creator, for the improvement of their own condition; but *given away*—yes, to the last cent, *given away* forever—to pamper the reckless extravagance of a Government forever preaching retrenchment and economy, and forever heaping million upon million of annual expenditures "to suckle armies and dry-nurse the land."

The committee submit to the House their unhesitating opinion, that the appropriation of any part of the proceeds of the sales of the public lands to the ordinary annual expenditures would be the only effectual and irretrievable *giving away* of that great and inestimable inheritance of the American people; that, if once that growing and inexhaustible fund shall be doomed to form the whole or any part of the *ways* and *means* for the annual estimates of the receipts and expenditures of the National Government, the people may bid farewell—a long farewell—to every hope of ever receiving a dollar's useful improvement from that gift of God to them, thus cruelly and perfidiously wrested from their hands.

Nineteen of the States of this Union, in the ardent—perhaps, in some cases, inconsiderately ardent—pursuit of this improvement of their own condition, have become involved—some of them heavily involved—in debt. The greatest portion of this debt has been contracted for the accomplishment of stupendous works, to expedite and facilitate the intercourse of travel and of trade between the remotest extremes of this great Republic, swarming, from year to year, with redoubling millions of population. It is no exaggerated estimate of the value of these works to say that, the saving of time, of labor, and of expense, to individual citizens of the Union, enjoying the benefit of these public works, more than repays, in every single year, the whole cost of their construction.

But, while these immense benefits have been thus secured to the people, as a community of individuals, the States which authorized them have contracted a burden of liabilities heavier than they are able to bear. They need the assistance of a friendly and powerful hand; and where should they find it but in the sympathies of the National Government?—in their fidelity to the trust committed to their charge in this immense and almost boundless public domain? The application of the proceeds of the public lands to alleviate the burden of these debts pressing upon the people of almost all the States, is, if not the only, the most unexceptionable mode of extending the mighty arm of the Union to relieve the people of the States from the pressure of the burden bearing upon them—a relief consisting only of the distribution among them of their own property—a relief furnishing them the means of paying to the United States themselves no inconsiderable portion of the debts due from the States to them; so that, by one and the same operation, the people of the States will be relieved from the intolerable pressure of their debt, and the common treasury of the Union will receive back in payment of debt no small part of the same sums allotted to the States as their respective portions of this distribution.

The committee regret that the shortness of the time which they have allowed themselves for the preparation of this report constrains them to pass over numerous other considerations, amounting to the clearest demonstration that the distribution among the States of the proceeds of the sales of the public lands will be infinitely more conducive to the ends of justice, and to the relief of the people from their embarrassments, than the devotion of the same funds to be swallowed up in the insatiate gulf of the ordinary annual expenses of the Federal Government; to perish, in the using, like the nine millions of the fourth instalment promised to the States, the seven or eight millions of stock in the Bank of the United States, and the five or six millions of Indian trust and navy pension funds—all sunk, during the Van Buren Administration, without leaving a wreck behind.

This review of the reasons of the President for objecting to the passage of the bill might be extended far more into detail, and all leading to the conclusion that they are feeble, inconsistent, and unsatisfactory. It remains only for the House to take, by yeas and nays, the question upon the final passage of the bill; and as the majority of the committee cannot indulge, even hypothetically, the absurd hope of a majority either in this or the other House of Congress competent to the enactment of the bill into a law, they leave the House to determine what further measure they may deem necessary and practicable, by the legislative authority, in the present calamitous condition of the country.

They perceive that the whole legislative power of the Union has been, for the last fifteen months, with regard to the action of Congress upon measures of vital importance, in a state of suspended animation, strangled by the *five* times repeated stricture of the executive cord. They observe that, under these unexampled obstructions to the exercise of their high and legitimate duties, they have hitherto preserved the most respectful forbearance towards the executive chief; that while he has, time after time, annulled, by the mere act of his will, their commission from the people to enact laws for the common welfare, they have forborne even the expression of their resentment for these multiplied insults and injuries. They believed they had a high destiny to fulfil, by administering to the people, in the form of law, remedies for the sufferings which they had too long endured. The will of one man has frustrated all their labors, and prostrated all their powers. The majority of the committee believe that the case has occurred, in the annals of our Union, contemplated by the founders of the Constitution by the grant to the House of Representatives of the power to impeach the President of the United States; but they are aware that the resort to that expedient might, in the present condition of public affairs, prove abortive. They see that the irreconcilable difference of opinion and of action between the legislative and executive departments of the Government is but sympathetic with the same discordant views and feelings among the people. To them alone the final issue of the struggle must be left. In the sorrow and mortification under the failure of all their labors to redeem the honor and prosperity of their country, it is a cheering consolation to them that the termination of their own official existence is at hand; that they are even now about to return to receive the sentence of their constituents upon themselves; that the legislative power of the Union, crippled and disabled as it may now be, is about to pass, renovated and revivified by the will of the people, into other hands, upon whom will devolve the task of providing that remedy for the public distempers which their own honest and agonizing energies have in vain endeavored to supply.

The power of the present Congress to enact laws essential to the welfare of the people has been struck with apoplexy by the Executive hand. Submission to his will, is the only condition upon which he will permit them to act. For the enactment of a measure earnestly recommended by himself, he forbids their action, unless *coupled* with a *condition* declared by himself to be on a subject so totally different that he will not suffer them to be coupled in the same law. With that condition, Congress cannot comply. In this state of things, he has assumed, as the committee fully believe, the exercise of the whole legislative power to himself, and is levying millions of money upon the people, without any authority of law. But the final decision of this question depends neither upon legislative nor executive, but upon judicial authority; nor can the final decision of the Supreme Court upon it be pronounced before the close of the present Congress. In the mean time, the abusive exercise of the constitutional power of the President to arrest the action of Congress upon measures vital to the welfare of the people, has wrought conviction upon the minds of a majority of the committee, that the veto power itself must be restrained and modified by an amendment of the Constitution itself: a resolution for which they accordingly herewith respectfully report.

John Quincy Adams	*Truman Smith*
John M. Botts	*F. Granger*
James Cooper	*H. S. Lane*
K. Rayner	*Jeremiah Morrow*
Thomas J. Campbell	*J. A. Pearce*

Resolved by the Senate and House of Representatives of the United States of America in Congress assembled, (two-thirds of both Houses concurring therein,) That the following amendment of the Constitution of the United States, in the seventh section of the first article, be recommended to the Legislatures of the several States, which, on the adoption of the same by three-fourths of the said Legislatures, shall become part and parcel of the Constitution:

Instead of the words "two-thirds," twice repeated in the second paragraph of the said seventh section, substitute, in both cases, the words "a majority of the whole number."

The President was so infuriated by this message of censure that he responded with a protest, on the model of Jackson's in 1834, but which was repudiated by the House and excluded from the official record. And also just like Jackson, Tyler challenged the House to impeach him if he had been guilty of any high crime or misdemeanor. He hoped to turn the censure message around and to condemn the House for its improper criticism of what he defended as a very legal and proper execution of duty. Neither statement had any concrete impact upon the attitude or policy of either branch, of course, but they were directed not to the opposite party, exclusively, but rather to the public in order to influence its thinking on the question.

President John Tyler
Protest Message to the
House of Representatives
August 30, 1842

James D. Richardson, ed., *Messages and Papers of the Presidents* (New York, 1897) V, 2043-46.

By the Constitution of the United States it is provided that "every bill which shall have passed the House of Representatives and the Senate shall before it become a law be presented to the President of the United States; *if he approve*, he *shall* sign it; but if *not*, he *shall* return it with his objections to that House in which it shall have originated, who shall enter the objections at large upon the Journal and proceed to reconsider it."

In strict compliance with the positive obligation thus imposed upon me by the Constitution, not having been able to bring myself to approve a bill which originated in the House of Representatives entitled "An act to provide revenue from imports, and to change and modify existing laws imposing duties on imports, and for other purposes," I returned the same to the House with my objections to its becoming a law. These objections, which had entirely satisfied my own mind of the great impolicy, if not unconstitutionality, of the measure, were presented in the most respectful and even deferential terms. I would not have been so far forgetful of what was due from one department of the Government to another as to have intentionally employed in my official intercourse with the House any language that could be in the slightest degree offensive to those to whom it was addressed. If in assigning my objections to the bill I had so far forgotten what was due to the House of Representatives as to impugn its motives in passing the bill, I should owe, not only to that House, but to the country, the most profound apology. Such departure from propriety is, however, not complained of in any proceeding which the House has adopted. It has, on the contrary, been expressly made a subject of remark, and almost of complaint, that the language in which my dissent was couched was studiously guarded and cautious.

Such being the character of the official communication in question, I confess I was wholly unprepared for the course which has been pursued in regard to it. In the exercise of its power to regulate its own proceedings the House for the first time, it is believed, in the history of the Government thought proper to refer the message to a select committee of its own body for the purpose, as my respect for the House would have compelled me to infer, of deliberately weighing the objections urged against the bill by the Executive with a view to its own judgment upon the question of the final adoption or rejection of the measure.

Of the temper and feelings in relation to myself of some of the members selected for the performance of this duty I have nothing to say. That was a matter entirely within the discretion of the House of Representatives. But that committee, taking a different view of its duty from that which I should have supposed had led to its creation, instead of confining itself to the objections urged against the bill availed itself of the occasion formally to arraign the motives of the President for others of his acts since his induction into office. In the absence of all proof and, as I am bound to declare, against all law or precedent in parliamentary proceedings, and at the same time in a manner which it would be difficult to reconcile with the comity hitherto sacredly observed in the intercourse between independent and coordinate departments of the Government, it has assailed my whole official conduct without the shadow of a pretext for such assault, and, stopping short of impeachment, has charged me, nevertheless, with offenses declared to deserve impeachment.

Had the extraordinary report which the committee thus made to the House been permitted to remain without the sanction of the latter, I should not have uttered a regret or complaint upon the subject. But unaccompanied as it is by any particle of testimony to support the charges it contains, without a deliberate examination, almost without any discussion, the House of Representatives has been pleased to adopt it as its own, and thereby to become my accuser before the country and before the world. The high character of such an accuser, the gravity of the charges which have been made, and the judgment pronounced against me by the adoption of the report upon a distinct and separate vote of the House leave me no alternative but to enter my solemn protest against this proceeding as unjust to myself as a man, as an invasion of my constitutional powers as Chief Magistrate of the American people, and as a violation in my person of rights secured to every citizen by the laws and the Constitution. That Constitution has intrusted to the House of Representatives the sole power of impeachment. Such impeachment is required to be tried before the most august tribunal known to our institutions. The Senate of the United States, composed of the representatives of the sovereignty of the States, is converted into a hall of justice, and in order to insure the strictest observance of the rules of evidence and of legal procedure the Chief Justice of the United States, the highest judicial functionary of the land, is required to preside over its deliberations. In the presence of such a judicatory the voice of faction is presumed to be silent, and the sentence of guilt or innocence is pronounced under the most solemn sanctions of religion, of honor, and of law. To such a tribunal does the Constitution authorize the House of Representatives to carry up its accusations against any chief of the executive department whom it may believe to be guilty of high crimes and misdemeanors. Before that tribunal the accused is confronted with his accusers, and may demand the privilege, which the justice of the common law secures to the humblest citizen, of a full, patient, and impartial inquiry into the facts, upon the testimony of witnesses rigidly cross-examined and deposing in the face of day. If such a proceeding had been adopted toward me, unjust as I should certainly have regarded it, I should, I trust, have met with a becoming constancy a trial as painful as it would have been undeserved. I would have manifested by a profound submission to the laws of my country my perfect faith in her justice, and, relying on the purity of my motives and the rectitude of my conduct, should have looked forward with confidence to a triumphant refutation in the presence of that country and by the solemn judgment of such a tribunal not only of whatever charges might have been formally preferred against me, but of all the calumnies of which I have hitherto been the unresisting victim. As it is, I have been accused without evidence and condemned without a hearing. As far as such proceedings can accomplish it, I am deprived of public confidence in the administration of the Government and denied even the boast of a good name—a name transmitted to me from a patriot father, prized as my proudest inheritance, and carefully preserved for those who are to come after me as the most precious of all earthly possessions. I am not only subjected to imputations affecting my character as an individual, but am charged with offenses against the country so grave and so heinous as to deserve public disgrace and disfranchisement. I am charged with violating pledges which I never gave, and, because I execute what I believe to be the law, with usurping powers not conferred by law, and, above all, with using the powers conferred upon the President by the Constitution from corrupt motives and for unwarrantable ends. And these charges are made without any particle of evidence to sustain them, and, as I solemnly affirm, without any foundation in truth.

Why is a proceeding of this sort adopted at this time? Is the occasion for it found in the fact that having been elected to the second office under the Constitution by the free and voluntary suffrages of the people, I have succeeded to the first according to the express provisions of the fundamental law of the same people? It is true that the succession of the Vice-President to the Chief Magistracy has never occurred before and that all prudent and patriotic minds have looked on this new trial of the wisdom and stability of our institutions with a somewhat anxious concern. I have been made to feel too sensibly the difficulties of my unprecedented position not to know all that is intended to be conveyed in the reproach cast upon a President without a party. But I found myself placed in this most responsible station by no usurpation or contrivance of my own. I was called to it, under Providence, by the supreme law of the land and the deliberately declared will of the people. It is by these that I have been clothed with the high powers which they have seen fit to confide to their Chief Executive and been charged with the solemn responsibility under which those powers are to be exercised. It is to them that I hold myself answerable as a moral agent for a free and conscientious discharge of the duties which they have imposed upon me. It is not as an individual merely that I am now called upon to resist the encroachments of unconstitutional power. I represent the executive authority of the people of the United States, and it is in their name, whose mere agent and servant I am, and whose will declared in their fundamental law I dare not, even were I inclined, to disobey, that I protest against every attempt to break down the undoubted constitutional power of this department without a solemn amendment of that fundamental law.

I am determined to uphold the Constitution in this as in other respects to the utmost of my ability and in defiance of all personal consequences. What may happen to an individual is of little importance, but the Constitution of the country, or any one of its great and clear principles and provisions, is too sacred to be surrendered under any circumstances whatever by those who are charged with its protection and defense. Least of all should he be held guiltless who, placed at the head of one of the great departments of the Government, should shrink from the exercise of its unquestionable authority on the most important occasions and should consent without a struggle to efface all the barriers so carefully erected by the people to control and circumscribe the powers confided to their various agents. It may be desirable, as the majority of the House of Representatives has declared it is, that no such checks upon the will of the Legislature should be suffered to continue. This is a matter for the people and States to decide, but until they shall have decided it I shall feel myself bound to execute, without fear or favor, the law as it has been written by our predecessors.

I protest against this whole proceeding of the House of Representatives as *ex parte* and extrajudicial. I protest against it as subversive of the common right of all citizens to be condemned only upon a fair and impartial trial, according to law and evidence, before the country. I protest against it as destructive of all the comity of intercourse between the departments of this Government, and destined sooner or later to lead to conflicts fatal to the peace of the country and the integrity of the Constitution. I protest against it in the name of that Constitution which is not only my own shield of protection and defense, but that of every American citizen. I protest against it in the name of the people, by whose will I stand where I do, by whose authority I exercised the power which I am charged with having usurped, and to whom I am responsible for a firm and faithful discharge according to my own convictions of duty of the high stewardship confided to me by them. I protest against it in the name of all regulated liberty and all limited government as a proceeding tending to the utter destruction of the checks and balances of the Constitution and the accumulating in the hands of the House of Representatives, or a bare majority of Congress for the time being, an uncontrolled and despotic power. And I respectfully ask that this my protest may be entered upon the Journal of the House of Representatives as a solemn and formal declaration for all time to come against the injustice and unconstitutionality of such a proceeding.

Relations between the Whig party members in Congress and the Whig President continued to deteriorate during the remaining years of Tyler's term. The Whigs were unable to command a two-thirds vote in the Congress to support the constitutional amendment on the veto power proposed by the Adams committee, and it died, as did a motion to impeach the President submitted by the controversial Representative Botts from Tyler's home state of Virginia. Before leaving the Senate, Clay had also sponsored a similar constitutional amendment to eliminate the two-thirds vote necessary to override the President's veto when a bill had passed through Congress the second time. The senator, as usual, presented a very cogent argument for his position, but neither the Congress nor the American people were ready at that time to inflict such a crippling blow on this formidable weapon of presidential power.

Nevertheless, presidential power suffered substantially at the hands of Clay and the Whigs, and the destructive battle that continued for the remainder of Tyler's single term further weakened the prestige and the power of the Chief Executive. It was an unfortunate by-product of this useless struggle. The Whigs had been drawn into the battle against "executive usurpation" because they had formed a coalition in the 1830s in opposition to the most powerful President who had yet come on the American scene. It was not enough for Webster, Clay and initially even Calhoun, to struggle against Andrew Jackson's policies. They were led by the logic of their rhetoric to accept the argument that Jackson had violated the balance of power envisaged by the Constitution, and had advanced the presidency to a level in the system where it threatened the independence and integrity of the other two branches of government. To what extent they actually believed this argument, as opposed to the consideration of its appeal to a constituency which revered the hallowed symbols of constitutional symmetry, is difficult to say. At any rate they were trapped by their own words, if indeed they ever did want to reject them, and Clay and his supporters continued to attack "executive usurpation" after they had achieved Whig domination over both branches in the 1840 election.

It is certainly conceivable that if William Henry Harrison had lived, the congressional Whigs might have gradually forgotten all about this argument, for certainly the aging general appeared to have no desire to continue a powerful and dominating presidency. In fact his inaugural speech seemed to indicate that he was naively intent upon emasculating the major prerogatives of the office during his own forthcoming term. Many of his comments reveal an ignorance of even minimal executive powers essential to protect the effective functions of the Chief Magistrate, and had he lived, he would have soon discovered this and been forced to retract his threats. But Harrison passed away almost before his term began, to be replaced by a Whig President who not only appeared to repudiate all of the Whig doctrines, including the attack upon "executive usurpation," but was a states' rights ideologue with a rigid and essentially sterile concept of the separation of powers and the independence of the President from the political events surrounding him.

Tyler could be characterized as a states' rights purist. His vetoes and State of the Union Messages reeked of a rigid and formal view of the separation of powers and the over-formal independence of the President. What this arid philosophy produced was the isolation of the President from the ongoing political process, alienating him from his potential supporters in Congress, and in so doing not only sowing the seeds of destruction for a potentially great American political party, but also actually weakening the office he was attempting to defend and making it more vulnerable to further crippling attacks in the future.

The election of 1844 demonstrated some political truths it would be useful to consider seriously. The Whigs had put together a winning combination in 1840 and swept the presidential and congressional elections. Harrison began his term with a strong majority in the House and marginal advantage in the Senate. He had captured a respectable 52.9 percent of the popular vote, and had done even better in the electoral college, where he won 19 states with 234 electoral votes to Van Buren's 7 states with 60 electoral votes. Harrison carried every one of the large states in the Union except Virginia, and built up impressive support in all sections of the country. But the Democrats were still a very formidable political party, probably still held a numerical majority, and it took a striking combination of unique developments in this election to account for the Whig victory.[167] The severe depression during the Democratic regime of Van Buren, coupled with the almost decade-long attack on financial policies which the Whigs argued had been responsible for the '37 depression, swung many marginal voters towards the Whigs. The hunger of the Whigs for office and their tireless efforts during the campaign (their strong organizational efforts begun several years before the election), the hoopla created over the public relations transformation of an old and not particularly brilliant military commander and public office-holder into the hero of the frontier conquest over the Indians, all added to the mood for a change from the Jacksonians who had ruled for 12 long years.

But this mood among the electorate, this momentary disillusionment with the Jacksonians and enthusiasm for change, would not necessarily crystallize into a permanent party realignment unless developments in the first Whig administration warranted such an historic shift. If the Whigs had been able to put their financial program into effect and the country had felt a positive impact from it, the possibility of consolidating the marginal shifts of 1840 into more permanent support for the Whig party would have been possible. Since the very opposite took place, namely the dismal failure to move forward in any substantial way, along with a disastrous rupture between the Whig dominated Congress and the Whig President, the Whigs approached the 1844 election with no advantages, in all probability as underdogs. The party had been badly beaten in the congressional elections of 1842 and had yielded its majority in the House to a much larger Democratic margin.[168] Most of the hard line states' rightists had gone along with Tyler and would follow him into ultimate obscurity, but this was still another marginal dropout from the winning coalition of 1840.

Henry Clay had retired from his seat in the Senate early in 1842 and returned to Ashland to make plans for running for the presidency in 1844. He stood stronger than ever in the party's affections, and the solid Whig vote in 1844 would be as reliable as it was in 1840. But it was still a minority party vote, and although it would hold up fairly well, a victory for the Whigs would have required the kind of performance in office that would have inspired confidence among more than the faithful (who might be expected to understand what prevented their implementing the party program during the previous four years). Clay was an extraordinary parliamentarian, but his political judgment was invariably wrong. To have expected the large number of uncommitted voters who were attracted to the Whigs in 1840 to continue to support the party in 1844, in the face of the debacle of the first Whig administration under Tyler, was an act of self-deception. Some political leaders underrate the average voter, and this frequently produces surprises. On the other hand, to overrate him and to expect him to delineate all of the reasons why the Whigs were not able to deliver their program, after being swept into power with control of both houses of Congress and the presidency, is simply poor political judgment. Could Clay expect the people to wait four long years while he was in exile and then to rally around him as he returned to the wars? The average voter simply did not act in this fashion then, or now. The Whigs lost their chance to become a major factor in American politics by their tragic failures in 1841, and in this sense neither the party nor Clay ever fully recovered, regardless of their victory in 1848, with another war hero.

Hamilton argued in the Federalist Papers that the essential quality in a President is energy, but Henry Steele Commager has pointed out that energy without essential prudence can be destructive to the ends of a free society.[169] A President must discover a way to assert his authority, but not in such a manner as to alienate him from his potential supporters and cut him adrift in the tempestuous seas of power politics. He has to persuade men that his policies are right for them and right for the country. He cannot barricade himself behind formal constitutional powers and hope to succeed. He has to convince, compromise and even inspire to win his points. He has to lead a party as well as a nation, for without an organized group of supporters in Congress and in the country at large he is powerless to act in anything but a negative manner; and in time he can be stripped even of the influence of this power. He has to initiate and propose, but both actions necessarily assume that his ideas, plans and proposals will be given a considerate hearing by those whose joint authority he needs to execute policy.

Tyler never allowed himself the chance to become such a President. His monumental ego and states' rights ideology prevented him from reasoning through to a solution of his early problems with his own party in the legislature. Nothing whatsoever could be achieved without its support. And that unfortunately is something of a summary of the first Whig administration in power. It achieved very little, and sowed the destructive seeds of division and despair, hurting not only the political party which brought it to power, but also the institution of the presidency, which it nominally had captured. A President without a party is like a man without a country. He has no ground to stand on and fight, and finds himself adrift in unfriendly seas, vulnerable to all forms of opposing elements, and he rapidly loses his way. But it was not only the first Whig administration and the Whig party which suffered from this tragic failure. The people were betrayed, because they had decided to be governed by this great conservative party, and they really never received any suitable recompense in return for their confidence and support.

Great national parties are not easy to come by; they do not appear overnight and disappear in a matter of weeks or months. This country has produced very few such parties in its 185-year history and perhaps the Whigs were not ordained to become one of them. Perhaps their potential internal divisions were greater than the common ground holding them together. Tyler may have been an accidental President, but the forces and strategies that selected him were assuredly no accident. This reminds us again that the effective role of political parties demands also the assertion of their responsible obligations.

The great parties in American history have always come into being to serve some great national purpose. The Jeffersonian Republicans challenged the deferent society of aristocratic elites, defended eroding civil liberties and opened up questions of foreign policy to public review. The Jacksonian Democrats enlarged the scope of democracy in America, encouraged the greater participation in government by the average citizen and fashioned a presidential model which forged new links between the office and the public interest. In a little over a decade, another new party would be born in the struggle to preserve the Union and it would survive the most severe trial by fire in the history of the republic.

Perhaps the real weakness of the Whigs was that they were not responsive enough to the real needs and problems which confronted the nation. They attempted to avoid and then compromise the question of slavery. They never provided the quality of national leadership which would inspire real confidence and bring the country together for great tasks. But political parties rise and fall, perhaps in direct relation to their ability to perceive change and to react positively and imaginatively to its demands. The central institutions of our government, however, although not immune to the process of change, require a certain stability in order to incorporate what is useful in the new and to discard what is obsolete in the old. This is not an easy task. These institutions are fragile and impressionable, and the delicate balance between them is quite as important as their individual claims of independence.

During the 1830s the cry was "executive usurpation." The argument was that the Jacksonian presidency had asserted its powers so aggressively that it had created a dangerous imbalance of power between the executive and legislative branches. The Whigs set out to redress this imbalance, but they faltered along the way. Had they succeeded in achieving all of their anti-Executive policies, they probably would have emasculated the presidency beyond recognition. As it was, their rhetoric set the tone for all peacetime presidencies for the rest of the century. As astute an historian as David Donald argues that even in wartime on non-military, domestic problems, Lincoln was still a Whig President. The anti-presidential rhetoric of the Whigs, however, coupled with the severe breach between the two branches which took place during the Tyler administration, led to the general weakening of presidential power, the increasing assertion of legislative hegemony and finally to a sustained period of what Woodrow Wilson called—congressional government— which dominated national affairs, in peacetime, for the next 60 years.

NOTES

1. James D. Richardson, ed., *Messages and Papers of the Presidents of the United States* (New York, 1897) I, 211.
2. Quoted in Arthur M. Schlesinger, jr., ed., *History of U.S. Political Parties* (New York, 1973) I, xxxiv.
3. Quoted in Schlesinger, I, xxxvi.
4. Richard Hofstadter, *The Idea of a Party System* (Berkeley, California, 1969), 2.
5. Quoted in Schlesinger, I, xxxiv.
6. Quoted in Schlesinger, I, xxxiv.
7. Jacob Cooke, ed., *The Federalist* (Cleveland, Ohio, 1961), 57.
8. Cooke, 61-62.
9. Quoted in Hofstadter, 30-31.
10. Quoted in Hofstadter, 32.
11. Quoted in Hofstadter, 32.
12. The words "angel or devil" are Burke's peculiarly eighteenth-century Christian rendering of the Greek words which are normally translated as "a God or a beast."
13. Quoted in Hofstadter, 32-33.
14. David Truman,—in *The Governmental Process* (New York, 1951)—and others have identified Madison's "factions" as interest groups and not political parties, and there is much in the language of his definition which incorporates the activity of such groups. On the other hand, since his contemporaries used party and faction interchangeably, and since there is no separate treatment of political parties in the Federalist Papers, one must conclude that Madison made no such distinction between the two and defined a functional area within which both somehow can fit, and indeed belong.
15. Schlesinger, I, xxxv.
16. Schlesinger, I, xxxv.

17. Robert G. McCloskey, "The American Ideology," in Michael Kammen, ed., *The Contrapuntal Civilization* (New York, 1971), 230.
18. Hofstadter, 4.
19. Hofstadter, 5.
20. Paul Goodman, "The First American Party System," in William Nisbet Chambers and Walter Dean Burnham, eds., *The American Party Systems: Stages of Political Development* (New York, 1967), 87.
21. Richard P. McCormick, "The Second American Party System," in Chambers and Burnham, 96.
22. Roy F. Nichols, *The Invention of American Political Parties* (New York, 1967), 309.
23. Nichols, 309.
24. Nichols, 309.
25. Nichols, 312.
26. Quoted in Robert Gray Gunderson, *The Log Cabin Campaign* (Lexington, Kentucky, 1957), 40.
27. For a discussion of the "united front," see Philip Selznick, *The Organizational Weapon: A Study of Bolshevik Strategy and Tactics* (New York, 1952), 126-44.
28. Charles M. Wiltse, *John C. Calhoun*, vol. II, *Nullifier, 1829-1839* (Indianapolis, Indiana, 1949), 231.
29. He was referring primarily to Professor H. Von Holst in his *Constitutional and Political History of the United States*, trans. John J. Lalor (Chicago, 1888).
30. Lyon G. Tyler, ed., *The Letters and Times of the Tylers* (New York, 1970) I, 477.
31. Tyler, I, 477-78.
32. But even if one goes along with Jefferson's concept of a states' rights-Federalism conflict, Jackson carried seven of the states' rights states to Crawford's two, and beat him in the popular vote in these states, 78,115 votes to 29,585. See voting table for 1824 election in Arthur M. Schlesinger, jr., ed., *The Coming to Power* (New York, 1972), 497.
33. Tyler, I, 478.
34. George Rawlings Poage, *Henry Clay and the Whig Party* (Chapel Hill, North Carolina, 1936), 10-11.
35. Richard K. Cralle, ed., *Speeches of John C. Calhoun* (New York, 1903) VII, 417.
36. Calvin Colton, ed., *The Works of Henry Clay* (New York, 1904) V, 576.
37. Quoted in Wilfred E. Binkley, *President and Congress* (New York, 1962), 100.
38. Nichols, 321.
39. William Nisbet Chambers, "Election of 1840" in Arthur M. Schlesinger, jr. and Fred L. Israel, eds., *History of American Presidential Elections* (New York, 1971) I, Table I.
40. Chambers, "Election of 1840," Table 2. Chambers indicates he has drawn his data from J. R. Pole, *Political Representation in England and the Origins of the American Republic* (London and New York, 1966), 544-64.
41. Richard P. McCormick, "New Perspectives on Jacksonian Politics," *American Historical Review*, LXV (January, 1960), 292. Turnout data compiled by Walter Dean Burnham, Washington University, St. Louis, Missouri. These comparative figures are taken from William Nisbet Chambers' introductory essay, "Party Development and the American Mainstream," in Chambers and Burnham, 11.
42. Richard P. McCormick, *The Second American Party System: Party Formation in the Jacksonian Era* (Chapel Hill, North Carolina, 1966), 88.
43. Chambers, "Election of 1840," 653.
44. Chambers, "Election of 1840," 652.
45. W. W. Rostow, *The Stages of Economic Growth* (Cambridge, England, 1960). Rostow covers the "pre-conditions" for "take-off" on pages 6-7 in Chapter 3. An interesting confirmation of the Rostow thesis can be found in the historical section of Robert Dahl's brilliant study of New Haven—*Who Governs* (New Haven, 1961)—where he discovered that every mayor elected in that city from 1784 (when the records of such elections begin) to 1842 came from the patrician class which dominated the traditional society. In 1842, New Haven elected its first mayor who was not drawn from that class, a carpet manufacturer and insurance agent, a man who had struggled upwards to economic preeminence from poor and humble social origins. From 1842 to almost the turn of the century all the successive mayors of the city were drawn from similar social and economic backgrounds—entrepreneurs is what Dahl calls them—and during that long half-century, there was never another patrician elected mayor of the city. At the turn of the century the entrepreneurs were replaced by the immigrant ethnics of Irish extraction in the early years and later on as their numbers increased, the Italians.
46. Gaetano Mosca, *The Ruling Class* (New York, 1939), 70-72.
47. Mosca, 144.

48. John Kenneth Galbraith makes use of this same argument in regard to his new potential ruling class—the technostructure—in *The New Industrial State* (New York, 1971).
49. Alexis de Tocqueville, *Democracy in America* (New York, 1962) I, 51.
50. Tocqueville, II, 136.
51. Tocqueville, II, 138-39.
52. Moisei Ostrogorski, *Democracy and the Organization of Political Parties*, ed. Seymour Martin Lipset, (Chicago, 1964) II, 34.
53. Quoted in Bray Hammond, *Banks and Politics in America: From the Revolution to the Civil War* (Princeton, New Jersey, 1957), 429-30.
54. Quoted in Hammond, 430.
55. Hammond, 430.
56. Quoted in Hammond, 430.
57. Quoted in Hammond, 431.
58. The initial idea was to have made these disbursements an outright gift, but this was frustrated by an amendment added to the legislation which prevented this and required each state to transmit to the secretary of the treasury certificates of indebtedness to the United States government covering the amount deposited. "These certificates were to be subject to sale or assignment by the secretary whenever the Treasury's funds from other sources were inadequate; to bear interest from the date of such sale or assignment; and to be redeemable by the states at their pleasure." But the states largely ignored this aspect of the legislation and utilized the money without regard for these reservations. (Frederick Jackson Turner, *The United States: 1830-1850* [New York, 1950], 436.)
59. Hammond, 455.
60. Peter Temin, *The Jacksonian Economy* (New York, 1969), 16-17.
61. Temin, 22-23.
62. Thomas C. Cochran and William Miller, *The Age of Enterprise* (New York, 1942), 42.
63. This data is taken from John Bach McMaster, *A History of the People of the United States* (New York, 1906) VI, 336-37.
64. Arthur M. Schlesinger, jr., *The Age of Jackson* (Boston, 1945), 218.
65. Colton, VI, 370.
66. Cochran and Miller, 43.
67. Hammond, 456.
68. Hammond, 456.
69. Hammond, 459.
70. Samuel Rezneck, "The Social History of an American Depression," in *American Historical Review*, XL (July 1935), 663.
71. All of these statistics are derived from Robert Gray Gunderson's comprehensive study of the 1840 election, *The Log Cabin Campaign* (Lexington, Kentucky, 1957), 13-16.
72. The Whig party no doubt contained the elite of the community the men of means and of intelligence, but here as well as in the rival camp the politicians held the outposts and directed the operations.
    . . . The Whig national convention which met, in 1839, at Harrisburg to nominate the candidates for the Presidency, supplied only too eloquent proof of it. The candidate was marked out beforehand by the whole history of the party which for the last fifteen years had been contending with the Jacksonian democracy; he was the great Whig leader, Henry Clay. But the politicians did not believe implicitly in his success; they were afraid that at the election he would not be able to rely with certainty on the support of various factions of the ill-assorted coalition formed against Van Buren. And Clay saw himself rejected by his own party in favor of General Harrison. In their justifiable exasperation Clay's friends shouted treason. In reality there was none whatever, from the standpoint occupied by the Organization of the Party. It was not its business to give expression to feeling or to affirm principles, but to carry an election; the Presidency was a prize to be won. If Clay, in spite of his glorious past, or on account of that past, did not offer satisfactory guarantees of success, did not the most elemental practical sense enjoin that he should be thrown over and another candidate adopted, were he ever so inferior to him. The rejection of Clay by the national convention was therefore quite in the logic of the system. . . . (Ostrogorski, II, 43-44).
73. Gunderson, 58.
74. Gunderson, 58-59.
75. Tyler, I, 595.
76. Tyler, I, 595.
77. Tyler, I, 595.
78. Gunderson, 64.
79. Gunderson, 65.

80. Gunderson, 65.
81. Chambers, "Election of 1840," 673.
82. Gunderson, 102-03.
83. Gunderson, 103.
84. Gunderson, 147.
85. Gunderson, 252.
86. Chambers, "Election of 1840," 702-03.
87. Chambers, "Election of 1840," 695.
88. Colton, V, 209.
89. Chambers, "Election of 1840," 682.
90. Charles Francis Adams, ed., *The Memoirs of John Quincy Adams* (Philadelphia, Pennsylvania, 1876) X, 352-53.
91. Adams, X, 352.
92. When he was still shopping for votes at the Harrisburg nominating convention, Harrison had written to Stevens and promised him a cabinet position as postmaster general if he could line up the Pennsylvania delegation to support the hero of Tippecanoe, but Harrison reneged, despite the fact that Stevens did produce the votes in the convention. Harrison wrote to Webster that "there is no consideration which would induce me to bring him into the Cabinet. We should have no peace with his intriguing, restless disposition. . . ." (Quoted in Fawn M. Brodie, *Thaddeus Stevens: Scourge of the South* [New York, 1959], 83.)
93. Chambers, "Election of 1840," 680-82, has a more thorough analysis of the election results.
94. Poage, 20.
95. Richardson, IV, 1868.
96. Richardson, IV, 1868.
97. Leonard D. White, *The Jacksonians: A Study in Administrative History* (New York, 1956), 564.
98. Neither this letter nor President Harrison's reply are printed in the ten-volume edition of *The Works of Henry Clay*. Poage has taken them from the Clay papers in the Library of Congress. According to the endorsement on the letters, Clay recovered them from Harrison's grandnephew in June 1841. Their publication at that time would have been injurious to Senator Clay's public position and to his party's objectives in Congress.
99. Poage, 31.
100. Nathan Sargent, *Public Men and Events* (Philadelphia, Pennsylvania, 1875) II, 116.
101. Richardson, IV, 1892.
102. Fletcher Webster, ed., *The Writings and Speeches of Daniel Webster* (Boston, 1903) VII, 108.
103. Richardson, IV, 1892.
104. Poage, 42.
105. Henry Clay to Francis Brooke, May 14, 1841, in Colton, IV, 453-54.
106. Tyler to Judge Tucker, April 25, 1841, in Tyler, II, 32.
107. Quoted in Robert J. Morgan, *A Whig Embattled: The Presidency Under John Tyler* (Lincoln, Nebraska, 1954), 29.
108. Richardson, IV, 1896.
109. Richardson, IV, 1899.
110. Tyler, II, 33-34.
111. Walter Bagehot, *The English Constitution* (London, 1955), 14-15.
112. Poage, 36.
113. Quoted in Binkley, 113.
114. Quoted in Oliver Perry Chitwood, *John Tyler, Champion of the Old South* (New York, 1964), 270.
115. Clemont Eaton, *Henry Clay and the Art of American Politics* (Boston, 1957), 93-94.
116. *Congressional Globe*, 27th Cong., 1st sess., X, 254.
117. *Congressional Globe*, 27th Cong., 1st sess., X, 254.
118. *Congressional Globe*, 27th Cong., 1st sess., X, 254.
119. Webster asserted as much in a memorandum found among his papers in the Library of Congress. Chitwood, 223-24.
120. Poage, 70.
121. Richardson, IV, 1917.
122. Richardson, IV, 1917.
123. Richardson, IV, 1920.
124. Colton, V, 276.
125. Colton, V, 276.
126. Colton, V, 277.
127. Colton, V, 277.

128. Colton, V, 278.
129. Colton, V, 281-82.
130. "Diary of Thomas Ewing, August and September, 1841," in *American Historical Review*, XVIII, No. 1 (October 1912), 103.
131. Colton, V, 283.
132. Clay is reported to have made this statement to a colleague in the Senate when he was urged not to make a speech condemning slavery, but recognizing its legal existence. (See Sargent, II, 74.)
133. Stuart's statement is contained in Thomas Hart Benton, *Thirty Years View* (New York, 1854) II, 344.
134. Benton, II, 344.
135. Benton, II, 343-44.
136. "Diary of Thomas Ewing," 99.
137. Ewing memorandum in "Diary of Thomas Ewing," 105-06.
138. Von Holst draws our attention to some of the more stinging passages in that letter:
     He has turned and twisted, and changed his ground so often in his conversations, that it is difficult to conjecture which of the absurdities he will rest his veto upon. . . . Our Captain Tyler is making a desperate effort to set himself up with the loco-focos, but he'll be headed yet, and I regret to say, it will end badly for him. He will be an object of execration with both parties; with the one, for vetoing our bill, which was bad enough—with the other, for signing a worse one; but he is hardly entitled to sympathy. . . . The veto will be received without a word, laid on the table, and ordered to be printed. . . . You'll get a bank bill, I think, but one that will serve only to fasten him, and to which no stock will be subscribed; and when he finds out that he is not wiser in banking than all the rest of the world, we may get a better. . . . (Von Holst, II, 432.)
139. Quoted in Chitwood, 259.
140. *Congressional Globe*, 27th Cong., 1st sess., Sept. 1, 1841, X.
141. *Congressional Globe*, X, 418.
142. Quoted in Sargent, II, 139. The author indicates that no doubt was entertained by members of the cabinet that this letter was inspired by the President, if not indicated by him to his son, in an effort to get them to resign. Adams, in his diary, indicates that Webster reported to the Massachusetts delegation that the letter was written by one of Tyler's sons.
143. Quoted in Benton, II, 354-55.
144. Quoted in Benton, II, 355.
145. Quoted in Benton, II, 354.
146. Webster, XVIII, 110.
147. Webster, XVIII, 110.
148. Quoted in Tyler, II, 119.
149. Tyler, II, 122.
150. Adams, XI, 13.
151. Benton, II, 356.
152. *Niles Register*, Sept. 18, 1841, 35.
153. *Niles Register*, Sept. 18, 1841, 35.
154. *Niles Register*, Sept. 18, 1841, 36.
155. *Niles Register*, Sept. 18, 1841, 36.
156. *Niles Register*, Sept. 18, 1841, 36.
157. *Niles Register*, Sept. 18, 1841, 36.
158. Benton, II, 359.
159. Benton, II, 360.
160. Colton, V, 354.
161. Colton, V, 356-57.
162. Colton, V, 357.
163. *Congressional Globe*, 27th Cong., 2d sess., 1842, XI, 894.
164. *Congressional Globe*, 27th Cong., 2d sess., Aug. 16, 1842, XI, 897.
165. *Congressional Globe*, 27th Cong., 2d sess., Aug. 16, 1842, XI, 897.
166. Two different minority reports were issued by three members of the committee, but space does not permit any analysis or comment on them.
167. In an interesting essay on the election of 1844, Charles Sellers argues that the developing "equilibrium of partisan attachments was obscured from contemporaries by the ephemeral electoral upheaval of 1840. . . ." (Charles Sellers, "Election of 1844," in Schlesinger and Israel, I, 747.)
168. The Whig majority in the House was over 30 in 1840, but the Democratic majority in 1842 climbed to 60 seats.
169. *New York Review of Books*, Col. XX, No. 16 (October 18, 1973), 50-51.

Bibliography

Adams, Charles Francis, ed. *The Memoirs of John Quincy Adams.* Philadelphia, Pennsylvania: J. B. Lippincott Company, 1876.

Bagehot, Walter. *The English Constitution.* London: Geoffrey Cumberledge, Oxford University Press, 1955.

Benton, Thomas Hart. *Thirty Years View.* New York: D. Appleton and Company, 1854.

Binkley, Wilfred E. *President and Congress.* Third revised ed. New York: Vintage Books, 1962.

Brodie, Fawn M. *Thaddeus Stevens: Scourge of the South.* New York: W. W. Norton and Company, 1959.

Chambers, William Nisbet, and Burnham, Walter Dean, eds. *The American Party Systems: Stages of Political Development.* New York: Oxford University Press, 1967.

Chitwood, Oliver Perry. *John Tyler, Champion of the Old South.* New York: Russell and Russell Publishers, 1964.

Cochran, Thomas C., and Miller, William. *The Age of Enterprise.* New York: Harper and Row, 1942.

Congressional Globe. 27th Cong., 1st sess., 1841, X.

        27th Cong., 2d sess., 1842, XI.

Colton, Calvin, ed. *The Works of Henry Clay.* New York: G. P. Putnam's Sons, 1904.

Cooke, Jacob, ed. *The Federalist.* Cleveland, Ohio: Wesleyan University Press, 1961.

Cralle, Richard K., ed. *The Speeches of John C. Calhoun.* New York: D. Appleton and Company, 1903.

"Diary of Thomas Ewing, August and September, 1941." *American Historical Review.* XVIII. No. 1 (October 1912).

Eaton, Clemont. *Henry Clay and the Art of American Politics.* Boston: The Library of American Biography, 1957.

Gunderson, Robert Gray. *The Log Cabin Campaign.* Lexington, Kentucky: University Press of Kentucky, 1957.

Hammond, Bray. *Banks and Politics in America: From the Revolution to the Civil War.* Princeton, New Jersey: Princeton University Press, 1957.

Hofstadter, Richard. *The Idea of a Party System.* Berkeley, California: University of California Press, 1969.

Kammen, Michael, ed. *The Contrapuntal Civilization.* New York: Thomas Y. Crowell Company, 1971.

McMaster, John Bach. *A History of the People of the United States.* New York: D. Appleton and Company, 1906.

McCormick, Richard P. *The Second American Party System: Party Formation in the Jacksonian Era.* Chapel Hill, North Carolina: Chapel Hill Books, 1966.

Mosca, Gaetano. *The Ruling Class.* New York: McGraw-Hill, 1939.

Nichols, Roy F. *The Invention of American Political Parties.* New York: The Macmillan Company, 1967.

Niles Register. September 18, 1841.

Ostrogorski, Moisei. *Democracy and the Organization of Political Parties.* Edited by Seymour Martin Lipset. Chicago: Quadrangle Books, 1964.

Poage, George Rawlings. *Henry Clay and the Whig Party.* Chapel Hill, North Carolina: University of North Carolina Press, 1936.

Richardson, James D., ed. *Messages and Papers of the Presidents of the United States.* Vols. I, IV, V. New York: Bureau of National Literature, 1897.

Sargent, Nathan. *Public Men and Events.* Vol. II. Philadelphia, Pennsylvania: J. B. Lippincott Company, 1875.

Schlesinger, Arthur M., jr. *The Age of Jackson.* Boston: Little, Brown and Company, 1945.

ed. *The Coming to Power.* New York: Chelsea House Publishers/ McGraw-Hill, 1972.

, ed. *History of U. S. Political Parties.* New York: Chelsea House Publishers/R. R. Bowker Company, 1973.

, eds. and Israel, Fred L., *History of American Presidential Elections, 1789-1968.* New York: Chelsea House Publishers/McGraw-Hill, 1971.

Selznick, Philip. *The Organizational Weapon: A Study of Bolshevik Strategy and Tactics.* New York: McGraw-Hill, 1952.

Temin, Peter. *The Jacksonian Economy.* New York: W. W. Norton and Company, 1969.

Tocqueville, Alexis de. *Democracy in America.* 2 vols. New York: Vintage Books, 1962.

Tyler, Lyon G., ed. *The Letters and Times of the Tylers.* New York: Da Capo Press, 1970.

Webster, Fletcher, ed. *The Writings and Speeches of Daniel Webster.* Boston: Little, Brown and Company, 1903.

White, Leonard D. *The Jacksonians: A Study in Administrative History.* New York: The Macmillan Company, 1956.

Wiltse, Charles M. *John C. Calhoun.* Vol. II, *Nullifier, 1824-1839.* Indianapolis, Indiana: The Bobbs-Merrill Company, 1949.

II. The President as Wartime Leader

THE PRESIDENT AS
WARTIME LEADER

For the first 50 years of the republic, the President's power as Commander in Chief was tested in one major war and in several quasi-wars or skirmishes, but this power did not emerge as a central focus of presidential activity until the middle of the nineteenth century in the wartime administrations of James Knox Polk and Abraham Lincoln. Both Presidents were actively engaged in the events leading to the wars in which each served as Commander in Chief of the Armed Forces, and as a result were also very much involved in the conduct of these wars. The activities of Polk's predecessor, John Tyler, and Polk himself led inexorably to the war between Mexico and the United States; and certainly crucial decisions made by Abraham Lincoln during his presidential campaign and after becoming President made war between the states inevitable.

The Constitution assigns to the Congress the responsibility of declaring war, but the President, in his various capacities as Chief Diplomat, Commander in Chief and Executive head of the government, has frequently engaged in activities which have aggravated situations and have made war more or less inevitable. This rather gray area of public policy-making needs far more careful examination and illumination than it has thus far received, for it has become a major source of controversy raging about the presidency in the second half of the twentieth century.

But there are other critical aspects of the President's responsibilities as Commander in Chief which demand careful study as well. The President's role as Commander in Chief of the Armed Forces is a very crucial function of his office which Madison hardly discharged at all, but which was decisive in the American victory in the Mexican War and in the ultimate success of the Union forces in the Civil War. The question of civilian supremacy over the military is deeply involved in the President's ability and opportunity to discharge this important duty. Perhaps it is because of the successful examples established by both Polk and Lincoln that this principle was not seriously challenged in the first 160 years of the republic.

Yet succeeding Presidents have been presented with a new problem of wartime leadership. This problem is the concept of "total war" which Edward S. Corwin has introduced to cover the modern total expansion of the functional aspects of warfare, and the involvement of the total community in their execution. Most earlier wars in history were fought by highly trained professional soldiers, drawn up in battle array under circumstances which usually limited the range and the impact of the struggle. Normally entire populations and their resources were not involved in these wars; they were confined to a limited number of members of the military caste. There were of course many exceptions, for cities were sacked and entire populations killed or enslaved before the modern period. But total war did away with the comfortable "nice little wars" that sometimes took place for territorial expansion (e.g., the Mexican War) or even defensive actions designed to prevent attacks upon the honor and rights of Americans on the high seas or to protect American territorial integrity (e.g., the War of 1812). It is a state of warfare which unfortunately has characterized the conflicts of the twentieth century, but which first emerged on this continent during the Civil War.

In his penetrating discussion of total war Corwin grants that there was some sense of totality in the more traditional concept of historical conflicts in situations in which the antagonists did not heed the rights of others and pursued their own ends with ruthless determination, but that is not the sense in which he has used the term. In his book, *Total War and the Constitution*, Corwin explains that the totality that he is concerned with is "a 'functional totality,' by which I mean the politically ordered participation in the war effort of all personal and social forces, the scientific, the mechanical, the commercial, the economic, the literary and artistic, and the psychological." He dates the origin of the concept to the proclamation of the Committee on Public Safety to the people of France at the beginning of the War of 1793. "The young men will go to battle; the married men will forge arms and transport food; the women will make tents, garments, and help in hospitals; the children will cut old rags into strips; the old men will place themselves in the public square to inflame the courage of the warriors, incite hatred against the Kings, and recommend the unity of the Republic."

My purpose for this section is to consider the powers of the President as Commander in Chief from these three perspectives. First the war-making powers of the President in the Tyler and Polk administrations will be analyzed. Similarly, under the very unusual circumstances of his career, Abraham Lincoln's actions, stemming from his careful constitutional definition of the minimal conditions for peace and national unity even before his election to the presidency, will be examined for their relevance to the final acts of secession and ultimately to the conflict between the states. In addition the sensitive relations between the President as Commander in Chief and his subordinate military commanders will be explored with respect to the Polk and Lincoln administrations. Finally the President's powers in total war will be analyzed from the perspective of Lincoln's experience in the Civil War.

The War-Making Power

Tyler's Secret "War Diplomacy"

In the twilight of his first and last term in the White House, John Tyler engaged in a desperate gamble to recoup his national prestige and to recover the ground he had lost in the first disastrous years of his administration, when he had almost transformed his "accidental" presidency into an abortive one. Tyler had been frustrated in all feeble attempts to make progress on the domestic front, where he usually met the bitter opposition of both national parties. When not opposed by both, it was usually because one party was merely using him as a weapon against the other. Such was the life of a President without a party. Nearing the end of his administration he gambled on a flamboyant diplomatic stroke which he hoped would gain for him the plaudits of the multitude and perhaps even make him a viable candidate for reelection in 1844. Even after this remote dream became totally implausible, Tyler persisted in his efforts to bring Texas into the Union because he hoped association with at least one successful policy might embellish his tattered reputation in history.

Tyler was a proud, if not an arrogant man, and he had been very deeply scarred by his unsuccessful encounter with Clay and his subsequent explusion from the Whig party. The prospect of obliterating these unhappy memories by a brilliant stroke of statesmanship which would at once strengthen and expand the scope of the republic and his own stature, was irresistible to the President, and he schemed and labored resolutely to achieve this goal. For many reasons, however, Tyler had to cover his tracks carefully, and he was forced to operate secretly most of the time, waiting until his plans had ripened before he outrightly produced a negotiated treaty with Texas, requiring only ratification by the Senate to bring the "Lone Star Republic" into the bosom of the federal Union.

There were other good reasons for the President's plans and his secrecy. Apart from the highly personal and subjective motives outlined above, Tyler was also very much a states' rights idealogue, and this point of view (or ideology) was at the foundation of his moves to bring Texas into the Union. States' rights ideology permeated most southerners' reasoning as they struggled to protect the institution of slavery. Slavery was secure as long as its institutional conduct was governed and protected by the states and not subject to national interference. But the possibility of congressional interventioи was an ominous and omnipresent threat, and the southern states never felt entirely secure, especially when they saw their power in the national government steadily eroding, as the number of northern and western states grew in number. Most Americans at this point in history were willing to tolerate slavery in the southern states, where it already existed, but were strongly opposed to its expansion into the newly settled territories, which would some day hopefully be admitted into the Union as non-slave states. As a result, most southerners felt uneasy and insecure, since the welfare of the basic social, institutional and economic framework of their society rested on the toleration of individuals who were more and more opposed to these social institutions and principles.

None of this should be interpreted as a claim that the population of the North was enlightened on the question of race and was in favor of full equality for Negroes. This was not so, except among vocal minorities like the abolitionists. But there was growing sentiment against the extension of slavery, and the South feared this attitude as an indication of its weakening power in Congress and its ultimate status as a greatly outnumbered minority voice. The acquisition of the vast territory of Texas, most of it lying below the Mason-Dixon line, suggested the possibility of an additional slave state or states, and the reversal of a trend against southern and slave power.

The circumstances surrounding the creation of the independent Republic of Texas were unique on the North American continent. The Mexican government, at the insistence of two trusted Americans, Moses Austin and Stephen F. Austin, adopted a colonization law in 1823 which invited immigrants of mixed nationality—American, European and native Mexicans—to settle in the Mexican territory now known as Texas. Settlers flocked into the area at a rate which alarmed the Mexican government, and in 1830 another law was passed, repealing the earlier statute, forbidding further American colonization, and imposing restrictions on the settlers.

By the mid-thirties there were upwards to 30,000 Americans in Texas, but the differences in language, culture, religion, etc. created mounting problems and friction between Mexican government officials and the settlers. When Mexico abolished slavery in 1829, for example, many of the settlers continued to hold slaves. The Mexican government tried in vain to enforce its authority by levying duties which were challenged or ignored, establishing military garrisons and finally by instituting martial law in an attempt to disarm the settlers. All of these measures only made already inflamed feelings worse. But despite the law and other difficulties, American settlers continued to pour into Texas, creating the kinds of friction which eventually led to a revolt. The subsequent battles through which Texas won its independence have been glamorized by Hollywood, but in reality do not make pleasant or even exciting reading. The Texas volunteers, largely recruited from outside of the area, underwent two savage massacres at Fort Alamo and Goliad before defeating the major Mexican army at San Jacinto, although outnumbered two to one.

The problems of incorporating Texas as a state or states, or even as a territory, could have been quite formidable, for there was no resolution of the dispute between Mexico and Texas with regard to their common border; the immediate incorporation of Texas as a state would have probably brought on immediate war between the United States and Mexico, if not interminable and irresolvable disputes. Furthermore, there was substantial apprehension among those who did not wish to see more slave states represented in the Congress. Andrew Jackson, who was an enthusiastic supporter of Texas independence and later a staunch advocate for statehood, was apprehensive about this opposition and was unwilling during his presidency to propose such an action. Even after Texas declared its independence from Mexico, and despite the interest shown by Sam Houston and his supporters in annexing Texas as a state(s) or a territory, at the very end of his second term the most Jackson was willing to grant was recognition of Texas as an independent republic. Van Buren, Harrison and even the early Tyler followed his lead.

But by 1843, President Tyler correctly sensed the developing groundswell in the country in support of "manifest destiny," and he jumped on the band wagon, substituting the imperatives of national expansion and ideological interest for the reasoned arguments of justice and international diplomacy. It was a question of "style" as well as of content, for the manner in which the United States went about taking, or better, seizing territory which had never historically been considered part of its sovereign domain, was as reprehensible as the fact of its undisguised aggression itself. As long as Daniel Webster remained secretary of state, however, the annexation of Texas appeared to be remote, if not impossible. But once Webster had successfully concluded his negotiations with Lord Ashburton over the disputed Canadian border and that agreement had been ratified as a treaty, President Tyler was ready to dispense with his services and replace him with a southern man, amenable to the aggressive pursuit of an agreement with Texas. Webster had opposed annexation as early as 1837, and considered such a move unconstitutional. He felt that San Francisco was "twenty times as valuable to us as all Texas."[1] The President did not hide his territorial objectives from his intimates. His son indicated that "it was necessary to have in the office of Secretary of State *one who would go the full length of the Texas Question.*"[2] But at the same time, Tyler wanted to stay on good terms with the New England statesman and neutralize Webster's impact on these policies. Accordingly he attempted to appoint Webster ambassador to Great Britain. But Edward Everett, who held that post at the time, refused to be transferred to the Far East for family reasons, and Webster finally had to return to private practice. Benton asserted that the New Englander was "frozen out" of the Tyler circle by well-calculated snubs and clear indications that he had overstayed his leave. Tyler's biographer denies these charges, but there is no doubt that Webster was forced to leave in order to make way for a new departure in executive policy-making, a departure that bordered on a serious violation of accepted constitutional principles. There is also no question that Tyler and his new secretary of state, Abel P. Upshur, were intent upon bringing Texas into the Union, but some diehard strict constitutionalists like John Quincy Adams and Webster would challenge the constitutionality of such an annexation. As chairman of the Committee on Foreign Affairs of the House, Adams submitted the following resolution:

> Resolved, That by the constitution of the United States no power is delegated to their congress, or to any department or departments of their government, to affix to this union any foreign state, or the people thereof. Resolved, That any attempt of the government of the United States, by an act of congress or by treaty, to annex to this union the republic of Texas, or the people thereof, would be a violation of the constitution of the United States, null and void, and to which the free states of this union and their people ought not to submit.[3]

This was not the first time Adams spoke out on this subject. He had conducted a filibuster against a move to bring about annexation through a joint resolution of both houses as early as 1838, and four years later he delivered a ringing condemnation of the proposal to his constituents in Braintree, Massachusetts, charging that annexation was nothing, more or less, than an effort to expand the slave-owning area of the country and to enhance the dwindling national political power of slave owners.[4]

Daniel Webster took a similar view, indicating that "if there were insuperable objections, even to entertaining any negotiations on the subject of [Texan] annexation" in an earlier period, "it seems to me that time and events have served only to strengthen such objections."[5] But the President and his new secretary of state gambled on the conjecture that the American people and the Congress would feel otherwise on this question, and they went all out to put this speculative assumption to the test.

While the administration was laying the groundwork for an approach to the Texans, the Lone Star Republic was not anxiously standing by in the role of an ardent suitor, but had tempered its initial passion for statehood considerably, and was exploring other means to insure the security of its borders and to protect its independence. The British for reasons of their own were extremely interested in persuading the Texans and the Mexicans to negotiate a stable peace and to settle outstanding differences. Of course this foreign influence and interference disturbed the American leaders.

Meanwhile, Tyler dispatched the notorious General Duff Green to Great Britain on a special mission to arrange, if possible, a meeting of American and British representatives in Washington to negotiate a reciprocal lowering of tariff barriers. Green was a successful newspaper owner and editor in New York, St. Louis and Washington and an inveterate political operator. During the first Jackson administration he had cornered the government printing contracts, but as a close friend of Calhoun's, he fell out with Jackson when the Calhoun break developed. His daughter later married Calhoun's son. Duff Green was a strong slavery man (Adams called him the ambassador of slavery) and an advocate of the southern cause. He found himself in financial straits in the early forties, and through his cultivation of Tyler, he actually utilized his mission to England to attempt to raise capital for his own enterprises. Green annoyed the American ambassador in London, Edward Everett, right from the point of his arrival, and he continued to be something of a hairshirt for the New Englander throughout his stay. He demanded introductions to all the men of power in the British government, and was totally insensitive to the impact that his role as special envoy had upon the position of the regularly posted diplomat in residence.

Very early in his stay in London, Duff Green picked up information regarding what he understood to be a British plot to recapture lost influence in North America and to deal a severe blow to the slave interests in the South. The British Parliament had earlier emancipated the slaves in the West Indies at a reputed cost of $100,000,000 to the British taxpayers, and it was Duff Green's opinion that because they faced bankruptcy as a result of this "catastrophic error," the British were attempting to undermine the highly competitive slave economy of the South. The British secretary of foreign affairs, Lord Aberdeen, was "alleged to have promised a government guarantee of interest on a loan to Texas on condition that the Texan government would abolish slavery."[6] Green contested that if the British succeeded with Texas, they would be well on their way towards this final goal.

Although General Green could present no hard evidence of the reality of the "plot" to the President and his faithful cohorts, the notion that such skullduggery was underway, masterminded by the hateful British, was enough to keep the Texas question quite open and at the top of the agenda of the pro-slavery government in Washington. The opening gun in the Tyler annexation campaign was a letter from Congressman Thomas W. Gilmer to the Tyler organ in the capital, the *Madisonian*, arguing that annexation would open up new markets for the non-slave states, through which to absorb their manufacturing and agricultural surpluses. The only section that would experience disadvantages would be the cotton and sugar producing slave states which would face competition from the new slave based economy. This is the way the proposal for annexation was argued by Gilmer and others who followed him. Why the one section which, according to the argument, stood to suffer most from its adoption was so active in pursuing this objective was never explained.

As the year progressed, the arguments for annexation became more frequent. Andrew Jackson supported the cause from the "Hermitage," going along with Gilmer's arguments, but adding his own concern over the danger of allowing Texas to drift away and come under the influence of the hated British:

> The present golden moment to obtain Texas must not be lost, or Texas must, from necessity, be thrown into the arms of England, and be forever lost to the United States. Need I call your attention to the situation in the United States—England in possession of Texas, or in strict alliance, offensive and defensive, and contending for California. How easy would it be for Great Britain to interpose a force sufficient to prevent emigration to California from the United States, and supply her garrison from Texas! Every *real American*, when they view this, with the danger to New Orleans from British arms from Texas, must unite, heart and hand, in the annexation of Texas to the United States. It will be a strong iron hoop around our Union, and a bulwark against all foreign invasion or aggression. I say again, let not this opportunity slip to regain Texas, or it may elude our grasp forever, or cost us oceans of blood and millions of money to free us from evils that may be brought upon us. . . .[7]

Of course, an appeal of this nature, written by a beloved national military and political hero would be bound to have a strong appeal. Editorial opinion was fostered by the *Madisonian*, and was reflected in other pro-annexation newspapers throughout the land. These early expansionist calls-to-arms touched very deep roots in the American psyche.

As the country and the population grew, the aspirations for more and more land also expanded. The boundaries which were accepted at the time of the American Revolution continued to advance, and where Americans had once been satisfied to settle no farther than the east bank of the Mississippi, they now moved well beyond that point to the Rockies and ultimately to the Pacific Ocean. In the South and the North they had been restricted by other sovereignties, but now even these claims were being challenged. God, nature and natural right were invoked to lay claim upon the land which the Americans were devouring.

Thomas Jefferson had justified American supremacy in the North Atlantic on the interesting geographical grounds that:

> We begin to broach the idea that we consider the whole gulph [sic] Stream as of our waters, in which hostilities and cruising are to be frowned on for the present, and prohibited as soon as either consent or force will permit us.[8]

A member of the House, Representative Widgry, affirmed that he felt the limits of American jurisdiction "on the Southeast should be the Gulf Stream, a line drawn by the god of nature."[9] More modest claims limited southern border designs to the Rio Grande; they were defended on the basis of the superiority of the white anglo-saxon race:

Another reason why this river seems to be marked out for a boundary is this:—On this side of the Rio Grande, the country is seasonable, fertile, and every way desirable to the people of the United States. On the other side the lands are unproductive, crops cannot be matured without irrigation; in short they are entirely calculated for a lazy, pastoral, mining people like the Mexicans.[10]

Even John Quincy Adams gave strong support to this policy of "manifest destiny" in principle:

[T]he world shall be familiarized with the idea of considering our proper dominion to the continent of North America. From the time when we became an independent people it was as much a law of nature that this should become our pretension as that the Mississippi should flow to the sea. . . .[11]

One of the more picturesque expressions of "manifest destiny" was contained in the remarks of a certain Major Devezac at the New Jersey State Convention in 1844:

Land enough—land enough! Make way, I say for the young American Buffalo—he has not yet got land enough; he wants more land as his cool shelter in summer—he wants more land for his beautiful pasture grounds. I tell you, we will give him Oregon for his summer shade, and the region of Texas as winter pasture. (Applause) Like all of his race, he wants salt, too. Well, he shall have the use of two oceans—the mighty Pacific and the turbulent Atlantic shall be his. . . . He shall not stop his career until he slakes his thirst in the frozen ocean. (Cheers).[12]

With Abel Upshur safely ensconced in the State Department, President Tyler was ready to move on Texas. The new secretary of state posed no problems when it came to the defense of states' rights and slavery. He considered servitude the normal state of the Black man, reflecting an ordinance of God. He recorded these views in an article in the *Southern Literary Messenger* in 1839. Any attempt at emancipation, Upshur reasoned, would interfere with the laws of nature. Slavery was essential to the agriculture of the South, but it also served as the true foundation for southern democracy, for by making southern whites, irrespective of how poor, superior to all Blacks, it provided the sense of equality, dignity and self-respect so essential to the operation of a democratic society.[13]

Not long after he was appointed to the cabinet position as chief foreign policy advisor to the President and administrative head of the country's diplomatic corps, Abel Upshur wrote to his friend and, to some extent, mentor, John C. Calhoun, and solicited his advice on major policy questions. Upshur presented an alarmist's view of England's determination to abolish slavery throughout the American continent, based upon the uncorroborated and misleading report made by Duff Green. Calhoun, who was Green's father-in-law and political intimate, was obviously already fully informed of this so-called "international plot," and since it coincided with his own objectives, needed little urging to accept it as fact. Upshur noted to Calhoun how apprehensive he was about slavery being barred in Texas and the impact that this would have with respect to the enforcement of the Fugitive Slave Law upon escapees fleeing into Texas from Louisiana and Arkansas.

But then he appealed to the aging South Carolinian for advice with regard to larger policy questions based upon his own erroneous and almost paranoid speculations.

Secretary of State Abel P. Upshur
Letter (Extract) to John C. Calhoun
August 14, 1843

Frederick Merk, *Slavery and the Annexation of Texas* (New York, 1972), 20. (See also Calhoun Papers, Clemson University Library, Clemson, South Carolina, November 8, 1843.)

What then ought we to do? Ought we not to move immediately for the admission of Texas into the Union as a slave holding State? Should not the South *demand* it, as indispensable to their security: In my opinion, we have no alternative. To admit Texas as a non-slave holding State, or to permit her to remain an independent and sovereign non-slave holding state, will be fatal to the Union, and ruinous to the whole country. I have no doubt that a proposition to admit her into the Union would be received, at first, with a burst of repugnance at the North; but the more the subject is reflected on, the more clearly will they see that the measure is absolutely necessary. To the South, it is a question of *safety;* to the North, it is one of interest. *We* should introduce rivals of our most productive industry [cotton growing], and should be, so far, losers; they [the North] would profit by that very rivalry. I have never known the North to refuse to do what their interest required, and I think it will not be difficult to convince them that their interest requires the admission of Texas into the Union as a slaveholding State.

Pray favor me with your views upon the subject as much at large as you deem proper. Would it not be well to break the subject to the people of the South through the public prints? Both parties may unite in that, for it is a *Southern* question, and not one of whiggism and democracy. The Southern people are far, far too lethargic upon this vital question. They ought to be roused and made of one mind. The history of the world does not present an example of such insult, contempt, and multiplied wrongs and outrages from one nation to another as we have received and are daily receiving from our Northern *brethren!!* It is a reproach to us that we bear it any longer. We are *twelve States,* and we have a right to be heard and regarded in a matter which concerns not only our rights, but our safety. The present is a proper occasion, and this is a proper subject on which to unite the South as one man. Can nothing be done to produce this result? Are there no idle pens in So. Carolina which would agree to be so employed? I trust that something will be done *among the people;* without their support, the Government is powerless.

The remarkable thing about this letter is that it was written by a member of the President's cabinet, the secretary of state of the United States. It raises a series of questions with respect to purely sectional concerns, and speculates, with respect to strategy and tactics, how the South could force its policies upon the rest of the

138

nation. And it was not simply idle speculation. The writer held perhaps the second most influential position in the government, and the recipient of the communication was the most powerful and influential political and ideological leader in the slave states.

Calhoun's answer was perhaps even more significant, because it laid out a blueprint for manipulating the public's attitude on the annexation question, and was aimed at achieving the end desired by the slave states in particular. One can note in this document a Machiavellian mastery of the cover-up, a very professional sense of timing and coordination of a campaign, where the sources of the propaganda would at first be concealed. Next, the step-by-step development of the plan would be controlled in order to cultivate a climate sufficiently receptive to each individual aspect; finally, the introduction of a *quid pro quo* proposition—the question of the simultaneous acquisition of Oregon—to appease sectional interests. This was brilliant sectional politics, but immoral and divisive policy for a free and democratic nation.

John C. Calhoun
Confidential Letter (Extract) to
Secretary of State Abel P. Upshur
August 27, 1843

Merk, 21-22.

You do not, in my opinion, attach too much importance to the designs of Great Britain in Texas. That she is using all her diplomatick arts and influence to abolish slavery there, with the intention of abolishing it in the United States, there can no longer be a doubt. The proceedings of the abolition meeting recently held in London, & the answer of Lord Aberdeen to the Committee, which, they appointed to call on him in reference to the subject, taken in connection, fully establishes the facts on both points.

That her object is power and monopoly, and abolition but the pretext, I hold to be not less clear. Her conduct affords the most conclusive proof. No nation, in ancient, or modern time, ever pursued dominion & commercial monopoly more perseveringly & vehemently than she has. She unites in herself the ambition of Rome and the avarice of Carthage.

If she can carry out her schemes in Texas, & through them her designs against the Southern States, it would prove the profoundest & most successful stroke of policy she ever made; and would go far towards giving her the exclusive control of the cotton trade, the greatest trade, by far, of modern Commerce. This she sees and is prepared to exert every nerve to accomplish it.

The danger is great & menacing, involving in its consequences the safety of the Union and the very existence of the South; and the question is, what is to be done? On that you desire my views, I shall give them freely and frankly.

In my opinion, the first step ought to be a demand on the British government for explination. There are sufficient facts to warrant it, before the publick, & I presume you have others unknown to it. The demand ought to be accompanied by a forcible statement, explanatory of the danger of the measure to our peace & security, and its certain tendency to involve the two countries in the most deadly conflict.

That ought to be followed by a suitable representation to the Texian government, tracing its hostile and dangerous character, both to them & us, accompanied by the expression of the most friendly feelings & disposition; and a communication to our Minister in Mexico apprizing him of the facts & the course adopted, with instructions to baffle, as far as it may be possible, the attempts of the British government to draw Mexico into her schemes. In addition, an able minister, completely identified with the South, and taken from South of the Potomack out [sic] to be sent to France, and be instructed to make suitable representations, explanatory of the ambitions & monopolizing sperit [sic] of Great Britain in this movement on Texas, and to show how far it would go to consummate her schemes of universal dominion & monopoly, should she succeed in her design. The like representation should be made to the Prussian Government, through our Minister at Berlin on the subject. The part of Germany under the control & influence of Prussia begins to be jealous of Great Britain, on the subject of commerce. All these papers should be drawn up with the utmost care, & so as to be calculated to make a deep impression on the publick mind generally, & to rouse the South should they be called for at the next Session, as they ought, if Great Britain should not explicitly disavow. In that event, the Message ought to take due notice of the subject.

In the meantime, I am of the impression, with you, that the attention of the people of the South ought to be turned to the subject, but not through the papers of this State. I have taken so prominent a stand on all subjects connected with abolition, that any movement, at this time, in this stte [sic] would be regarded as intended for electioneering & would do more harm, than good. I am decidedly of the opinion, that it ought to commence in Virginia, & through the Columns of the Enquirer, and that the opening & leading articles should be from your Department & pen. No one else, has the whole subject so fully before him, or can do it as full justice. You can have it communicated by some friend. They can be copied & followed up in the Southern papers.

I am of the impression, that the question of annexation ought not to be agitated till discussion has prepared the publick mind to realize the danger; but assurance ought to be given to the Texian government of the hearty cooperation of the Executive towards effecting it, when the proper time arrives.

Connected with this subject, Cuba deserves attention. Great Britain is at work there, as well as in Texas; and both are equally important to our safety. Much can be done in France in reference to each. Would it not be well for our govt. & that of France to enter into a guaranty of its possession to Spain, against the interference of any other power? The overthrow of the British influence there & the establishment of the French, would seem to be favourable to an arrangement of the kind. I throw it out for reflection. Would it not also be well if the West should push the Oregon question, to unite with it the annexation of Texas, in the shape of an amendment of the bill and make them go hand in hand.

While this correspondence was passing between Upshur and Calhoun, Lord Aberdeen, the British secretary for foreign affairs (the British counterpart to our secretary of state) allowed himself to be drawn into a discussion of British policy and objectives in North America, in reply to a question raised in the House of Lords by Lord Brougham, an active critic of slavery and the slave trade. To put this in proper perspective, however, it must be understood that his moral condemnation of slavery was of critical importance in Britain at that moment in history because the Parliament had so recently emancipated British slaves in the West Indies, at a tremendous cost to the British taxpayer. The British certainly favored the universal emancipation of all slaves and they used their influence throughout the world to achieve such an objective; on the other hand emancipation was a general moral goal, and was not to be confused with practical day-to-day policies. This distinction is important, because it differentiated between commitment to a long-range ideal and the implementation of this ideal by short-range active policies.

But aggressive sectionalists and defenders of slavery either did not understand or were not willing to admit or reveal this distinction, and in this instance they acted as if Lord Aberdeen's statement against slavery completely confirmed their most extreme speculations. Merk indicates that when President Tyler became aware of Lord Aberdeen's indiscreet reply "he was stimulated to decision on two fronts: the Texan and the British."[14] Upshur was given permission to offer a treaty of annexation to Texas, and the President later reflected upon how delighted his new secretary of state was upon receiving this news:

> I remember how highly gratified he (Upshur) was, when after receiving voluminous dispatches from abroad, mostly bearing on the matter, I announced to him my purpose to offer annexation to Texas in the form of a treaty, and authorized him at once, and without delay to communicate the fact to Mr. Van Zandt, the accomplished minister from that Republic.[15]

It should be carefully noted that Tyler's decision to offer the treaty was based almost entirely upon an unverified report of Britain's intentions with regard to Texas—a report he had received from Duff Green. When Upshur attempted to corroborate Green's charges regarding British policy by questioning Tyler's duly appointed ambassador to Great Britain, Edward Everett, he was clearly and unequivocally informed that Green was in error, to put it in its most polite form. Everett had been instructed by Upshur to demand an explanation of the British foreign minister's statement in the House of Lords. He was further directed to present "a forcible statement, explanatory of the [British] measure to our peace and security, and its certain tendency to involve the two countries in the most deadly conflict."[16] Everett was also told to obtain evidence of British hostility to American slavery so that the government could use it in its presentation to the Senate of the anticipated treaty of annexation with Texas.

The secretary for foreign affairs replied unequivocally to all the American ambassador's questions, and reviewed and certified Everett's reply before it was dispatched to Washington. Aberdeen assured the United States that his government had never proposed to Texas that the abolition of slavery be made part of a peace treaty with Mexico. He further stated that Great Britain had never considered a loan to Texas on the condition or consequence of the abolition of slavery. All that the British government had done with respect to the issue of slavery was to advise the Mexicans to sign a peace treaty with Texas and hope that the abolition of slavery might become part of such an agreement. This official statement completely contradicted Duff Green's charges, but the Tyler administration continued to use them as a means of frightening the Texans into agreeing to annexation.

Lord Aberdeen was supported in these denials by the Texas representative in Britain, who dismissed Duff Green as an alarmist, spreading false impressions in the American press. Many years later, this Texan, Ashbel Smith, in his *Reminiscences of the Texas Republic*, stated that "at no time, in no manner, did the British government attempt to exercise any political influence in the affairs of Texas...."[17] Smith charged Upshur with "inflaming the public mind [in the United States] still more by charging on the British government the machinations and plots of anti-slavery fanatics for interfering with Southern institutions. . . ."[18]

When informed by Everett that there were individuals in the United States who believed Duff Green's charges that the British were plotting to eliminate slavery first in Texas and then throughout the slave states of the South, Lord Aberdeen countered that it was "a notion too absurd and unfounded to need serious contradiction." He did promise, however, "that bearing in mind the sensibilities that existed on this subject," he would "endeavor hereafter to express himself with great caution, when it became necessary to speak of Slavery."[19]

Nevertheless the American secretary of state pressed on with his negotiations with Texas. Although most Texans had been enthusiastic about becoming part of the United States following their violent separation from Mexico, the interim years had considerably moderated that attitude, and their leaders resisted the early approaches of the United States to negotiate a treaty of annexation. The Texans continued to reject these proposals, saying that they were currently engaged in negotiations with Mexico aimed at protecting the security of their new borders. But Upshur was not deterred.

He opened up the question of negotiating a treaty of annexation with Texas in a discussion he had with Isaac Van Zandt, the minister from the Texas Republic, on September 18, 1843. Van Zandt reminded Upshur of previous statements he had made to both the secretary of state and the President of his government's official indifference to annexation, but he did suggest informally (and without authorization) that if the American government would make a definite proposal of annexation, together with strong assurances that the administration could obtain the necessary two-thirds approval of such a treaty in the Senate, Texas might agree to negotiations.

Van Zandt wrote to his own secretary of state that "annexation was the great measure of the administration here," and that he (Upshur) "was actively engaged under the instructions from the President in preparing the minds of the people for it, and in learning the views of Senators on the subject; and so soon as they conceived it safe, they would renew the proposition. . . ."[20] Upshur pressed the Texan to obtain from his government, by special courier, the full authority to enter into such negotiations, but Van Zandt resisted his pressures and advised the American secretary of state that such authority would not be granted without having first received a firm treaty proposal from the United States.

One month later Upshur opened up the question again. He was still not prepared to offer Texas any written or iron-clad assurances, but he was able to promise the Texas minister that the Tyler administration would support the plan with all of its power and energy. He reminded Van Zandt that pressures from abroad and from Mexico made annexation all the more advisable, but the Texas government still refused to authorize its representative to begin negotiations. In the meantime, the British representative in Texas convincingly assured the Republic's secretary of state, Anson Jones, that the British government had never had any intention of interfering with slavery in Texas.

In October 1843 Upshur finally convinced Van Zandt to send off a request by special messenger to his superiors in Texas, asking whether the leaders of the Lone Star Republic were ready to reverse their earlier position. The reply, which arrived in Washington on December 13, 1843, reaffirmed that the Texans were unwilling to negotiate the annexation question with the Americans, and that they considered it foolhardy to do so without first having received from the President and his secretary of state some assurance that the Senate would uphold the treaty.

Nevertheless, Secretary of State Upshur persisted in his courtship of the Texans, and after the beginning of the new year, he dispatched by special messenger detailed instructions to the American representative in Texas, William S. Murphy, directing him to approach the President of the Republic, General Sam Houston, with renewed arguments for annexation. Upshur wanted to assure Houston directly that the American people were now very enthusiastic about admitting the new state and that he could also assure the hero of the Texas war of independence "that a clear constitutional majority of two-thirds [of the Senate] are in favor of the measure."[21] Upshur's source for this extraordinary piece of misinformation was his pro-slavery, states' rights ally, Representative Thomas A. Gilmer, and later events proved without the trace of a doubt that this gentleman did not know what he was talking about.

Meanwhile back in Texas the situation was changing. Sam Houston reversed his position and secretly recommended to the Texas legislature that "annexation to the United States was very desirable."[22] Perhaps the failure of negotiations with Mexico to produce a satisfactory settlement was behind his decision, but at any rate he was extremely cautious, warning his fellow Texans not to appear too eager for the marriage, and counseling them of the uncertainty of Senate approval of a treaty. "The voice of supplication seldom commands respect," he told them.[23] While waiting for approval of his proposal to the congress, Houston sent new instructions to Van Zandt, authorizing him to proceed with negotiations if he was reasonably certain that the American Congress was ready to approve annexation. The major questions for negotiations were: (a) whether Texas would enter the union as a state(s) or a territory; (b) the status and determination of the Republic's debt, and (c) the resolution of the problem of the public domain.

As things finally began to move, the timetable jumped ahead. Even before his new instructions arrived in Washington, Van Zandt raised a very critical question (in writing) which put the rather vague and abstract American promises to test:

Would the United States agree to station army and navy forces at points along the Texas border to protect the Lone Star Republic against invasion during the interval between the signing of the annexation treaty and its ratification? The question raised serious constitutional issues, because the Texans were calling upon the President to make a commitment which the Constitution did not specifically authorize him to consummate. The Constitution clearly prescribes that only Congress can declare war, and yet the Texans were requesting a virtual declaration of war with Mexico. To fulfill such a commitment, the President as Commander in Chief (in peacetime) would have had to deploy American troops and American naval forces in territories and waters which were claimed by another sovereign nation. Texas and Mexico had never settled their boundary dispute, and the territory claimed by Texas between the Nueces and the Rio Grande Rivers was inhabited primarily by Mexicans and considered by the Mexican government to be part of their sovereign territory.

Among the cardinal principles adhered to by the states' rights political leaders were the strict interpretation and enforcement of the Constitution. In fact, strict constructionism was the foundation of the states' rights ideology. Tyler had made a *cause célèbre* of strict constructionism all of his political life and prided himself on his principled actions in its defense—actions undertaken at several critical points in his career when he had risked the rebuke of popular opinion and the sacrifice of personal interest in defense of his constitutional views. Upshur too was a zealot in this respect, and under the *nom de plume* of "A Virginian," he had recently written a biting attack upon Justice Story's broad interpretation of the Constitution.

To respond positively to Van Zandt's question, Upshur and President Tyler had to overstep a very thin line between constitutional and unconstitutional actions. The deployment of troops and naval forces into the sovereign territory and waters of another nation was a provocation to war which threatened to render the constitutional procedure for declaring war impotent. Nevertheless, Upshur gave Van Zandt verbal assent, but he did not commit these assurances to paper. A record of his verbal commitment is contained, however, in Van Zandt's dispatch to Texas' Secretary of State Jones. It read:

I am authorized by the [American] Secretary of State, who speaks by the authority of the President . . . to say that the moment a treaty of annexation shall be signed, a large naval force will be assembled in the Gulf of Mexico, upon the coast of Texas, and that a sufficient number of the Military force will be ordered to rendezvous upon the borders of Texas ready to act as circumstances may require; and that these assurances will be given preliminary to the signing of the treaty, if desired by the Government of Texas; and that this government will say to Mexico that she must in no wise disturb or molest Texas.[24]

Whether John Tyler and Abel P. Upshur were strict constructionists or not, this commitment went well beyond the limits of even the broadest possible interpretation of the President's constitutional power as Commander in Chief or principal agent of foreign relations. Despite the fact that the commitment clearly states that it would not be in force until a treaty between the United States and

Texas had been signed, such a treaty would have no binding force until ratified by the Congress, which is not mentioned in the commitment. But the circumstances of this situation go beyond even this constitutional violation. Texas at that time was at once an independent and sovereign nation, and, from another viewpoint, part of Mexico. The Mexicans did not recognize Texan independence (except under the duress of the capture of their leader) and certainly there had been no resolution of the conflict over boundaries if such recognition was ever to be forthcoming. In short, Mexico still claimed sovereign territory over large areas of Texas, which the President of the United States and his secretary of state were committing this country to defend. Tyler and Upshur were shrewd enough not to put such a commitment in writing, for they realized that it would probably be subject to later Senate inspection, so the pledge was made orally, but it was later recorded in Van Zandt's official dispatch to his secretary of state in Austin.

To expose fully Tyler and Upshur's duplicity in this situation, we must take note of chargé d'affaires in Texas, William S. Murphy's, additional commitment, in writing, on the question—this time to Texas secretary of state, Anson Jones. On February 14, 1844, more than three weeks after Upshur's oral assurance to Van Zandt, Murphy indicated to the leaders of the Texas government that he had no hesitation about promising, on the part of his government, that Mexico (or any other foreign government) would not be permitted to invade Texas because of the ongoing treaty negotiations:

> As far, therefore, as my power and authority may go, I will take care that my government is speedily apprized of your views and wishes, and that a sufficient naval force will be placed in the Gulf of Mexico, convenient for the defence of Texas, in case of any invasion which may threaten her seaboard pending such negotiation; also that measures shall be taken, as required by you, to repel any invasion by land of a like character.[25]

In addition to this, Murphy also assured President Houston that the United States naval force which was available in the Mexican Gulf would have no difficulty controlling a much smaller Mexican fleet, and although he had no figures with respect to the land forces available, he assured Houston that they would be adequate to the responsibility of protecting the border.[26]

The next day Murphy sent Upshur a report on his activities, noting at the end: "I took upon myself a great responsibility, but the cause required it, and you will, I hope, justify me to the President."[27] In addition to all of this, the American chargé d'affaires in Austin also attached to the report a hastily drawn personal note which was marked "confidential":

> The President of Texas begs me to request you, that no time be lost in sending sufficient fleet into the Gulf, subject to my order, to act in Defence of the Texan Coast in case of a naval descent by Mexico & that an active force of Mounted men, or Cavalry be held ready on the line of U.S. contiguous to Texas, to act in her defence by land—for says the President [Houston]: "I know the Treaty will be made & we must suffer for it if the U. States is not ready to defend us—" Do comply with his wishes immediately.[28]

Murphy went even further. At the suggestion of the President of Texas, he sent a secret message to Lieutenant J. A. Davis who commanded a U.S. schooner, the *Flirt*, "to proceed to Vera Cruz to ascertain whether hostile action by sea or land was meditated by Mexico."[29] Davis was also directed to convey to other American vessels he encountered in the area that it was desirable to cruise between Vera Cruz and Galveston while awaiting further orders.

Upshur met a tragic death before he received Murphy's message. A violent explosion on board the United States warship *Princeton* took the lives of a number of passengers, including the secretary of state, the secretary of the navy, Thomas Gilmer, and a number more who were injured. The *Princeton* was the pride of the United States Navy and had been taking the President and his wife along with a distinguished group of guests on a festive cruise down the Potomac. The President and his wife were below deck when the explosion occurred, but others like Senator Benton who were on deck were knocked unconscious, injured or, in a number of cases, killed.

Murphy's dispatch apparently shocked the President, for it revealed that his pledges to the Texas government were now on the record. Tyler was experienced enough to know that if a battle developed over the treaty in the Senate, the President might be required to produce any correspondence which promised military assistance to the Texans, and he acted quickly to cover his earlier indiscreet, but still officially unrecorded, commitments. At Tyler's instructions, acting Secretary of State Nelson wrote immediately to Murphy, countermanding his pledges to Anson Jones and Sam Houston, and contradicting his own promises made through Upshur to Van Zandt, as well.

Enter: John C. Calhoun

Tyler's denial of a commitment of military and naval assistance was not allowed to stand for long. Upshur was replaced in the State Department by John Caldwell Calhoun, and this gentleman was not about to reverse the drive for annexation nor to abandon the Texans from fear of future criticism from the Senate, a forum in which he had frequently received the most severe criticism, but which had never moved him to change his position once it was carefully established.

It was alleged that Calhoun's appointment was forced on Tyler by the clever machinations of his friend and advisor, Henry Wise of Virginia. Wise, himself, told the tale over 25 years later; he claimed that he conferred with the President shortly after the *Princeton* explosion and argued passionately for the appointment of Calhoun. Tyler was adamantly opposed to bringing the South Carolinian into his cabinet, perhaps because he saw Calhoun as a future rival for the presidency. At any rate he rejected Wise's entreaties until the Virginian told him that he had been so indiscreet as to tell Calhoun's close colleague, Senator McDuffie from South Carolina, that the President wanted McDuffie to prevail upon his fellow South Carolinian to accept the post, and that Calhoun had already agreed to serve. Wise pleaded that if the appointment was not immediately forthcoming "you will place me where you would be loath to place a foe, much less a friend. I can hardly be your friend any longer unless you sanction my unauthorized act for your sake, not my own."[30] The President was said to be dumbfounded by this revelation, but finally capitulated and appointed Calhoun secretary of state.

The story certainly may be false, but there were reasons for Tyler's lack of enthusiasm. First of all, Calhoun was a potential candidate for the presidency. He was also a difficult man and not particularly close to Tyler, and because of some of his inflexible views, he could become a burden to the administration. On the other hand, he was firmly committed to annexation, and would spare no effort in continuing Upshur's aggressive efforts to conclude a treaty. During the final stages of the negotiations, the Texas representatives again brought up the question of military and naval support for the Republic before the treaty was ratified by the U.S. Senate. Concerned over the prospect that negotiations might break down at that point, Tyler capitulated, and the secretary of state was authorized to provide the Texans with written assurances equally as strong as the original commitments by Upshur and Murphy:

> I am directed by the President to say that the Secretary of the Navy has been instructed to order a strong naval force to concentrate in the Gulf of Mexico, to meet any emergency; and that similar orders have been issued by the Secretary of War, to move the disposable military forces on our southwestern frontier for the same purpose. Should the exigency arise to which you refer in your note to Mr. Upshur [January 17, 1844], I am further directed by the President to say, that, during the pendency of the treaty of Annexation, he would deem it his duty to use all the means placed within his power by the constitution to protect Texas from all foreign invasion.[31]

As strong as these assurances were, the Texans perceived a general weakness which was contained in the final sentence of the statement. Knowing the Constitution, the Texans reasoned that in actuality the President possessed no power to protect Texas "from all foreign invasion," because the war powers could only be implemented after the Congress declared war.

But Calhoun was not fazed by any of this. He made additional detailed oral pledges to the Texans to ease their concerns. He promised that a powerful naval force of 10 or 12 ships would be ordered to the Gulf of Mexico to meet any emergency. The commander of this fleet was instructed to warn the Mexican commander that any serious indication of a naval attack against Texas would be considered a hostile act by the United States and that the President would feel bound to use every means to repel it.[32] In addition, the secretary of state promised the Texans that General Gaines, who was the commander of the western division of the regular United States Army, would be under orders to repel any Mexican attack by land. He also assured them that he and the chargé d'affaires would maintain contact with Texas officials, and should any threat to Texas territory be indicated, the President of the United States would be informed as quickly as possible, and he would immediately recommend to the Congress such measures as might be necessary for the defense of Texas. In the meantime he would consider it his responsibility to defend Texas against any attack.[33] These pledges were not recorded in the Department of State files on the negotiations, but they were thoroughly detailed in the correspondence of the Texas representatives to their government. In other words, the Republic of Texas was better informed on the extent of the commitment of the President and the secretary of state than were the United States Government or its Congress.

No mention of the boundaries of Texas was made in the draft treaty thus negotiated. The treaty simply stated that Texas would cede "all its territories" to the United States.[34] The Texans felt that the treaty represented a reasonable bargain, but they also indicated that if they had only dealt with the President and the secretary of state, they would have come off much better. The supporters of the treaty were confident that the treaty would be approved by the Senate, but the Texans were assured that if it was not, the President would quickly submit it as a resolution to both houses, a maneuver which eliminated the required two-thirds approval in the treaty procedure.

The treaty covering the annexation of Texas was signed by the two Texas representatives[35] and the President on April 12, 1844, and was submitted to the Senate ten days later. Presumably the delay in its submission to the Senate was due to the time required by the Department of State to prepare copies of documents to be presented along with the treaty as background material, illuminating some of the reasons for its urgency. All of this was to become the substance of the debate on the treaty which took place in the Senate over the next two months.

One of the documents submitted by the President was a reply by Secretary of State Calhoun to a letter from the British minister in Washington, Richard Packenham; it is one of the most incredible documents in American history. Packenham's letter was a cover note transmitting a dispatch which Lord Aberdeen wished to have recorded in the State Department files. The British foreign minister wanted to reiterate the British position on slavery and the annexation of Texas, which he quite rightly believed had been misrepresented by the expansionists in the United States (including the President and the secretary of state). Aberdeen affirmed Britain's opposition to slavery on moral grounds and expressed his country's desire to see it eliminated all over the world; but at the same time he asserted that his country would do nothing secret or underhanded to achieve this goal, in Texas or anywhere else. The British would have been delighted if a settlement between Mexico and Texas outlawed slavery in the Republic, but they would not resort to any measures, secret or open, to accomplish this objective in Texas or in the United States.

That statement should have settled the question once and for all, but Calhoun picked up his pen and wrote a reply, hoping to teach the British a lesson in sociology. Basing his argument on incredibly distorted statistics drawn from the most recent United States census, Calhoun attempted to persuade Packenham that regardless of the objectives or even the results of the emancipation of slaves in the British possessions, experience over a period of 50 years in the United States demonstrated that it would be neither humane nor wise to abandon the condition of servitude of "Africans" in the slave states. Calhoun based his argument on census data which indicated that the lot of the Negro had become much worse rather than better in the free states. The rate of Negroes who were recorded as being dumb, deaf, blind, idiots and insane was one out of every 96, the secretary of state argued, while their counterparts in states where slavery persisted was one out of every 672. Such a statistic is flabbergasting. When one adds to this list of Negroes who suffered from any of the above disorders others who were either in jail or who were paupers, the ratio diminished to one in every six in the so-called "free" states, as compared with one in 154 in the slave states.

Using the two extremes of North and South, the secretary of state cited the case of Maine, where census data indicated one Negro out of every 12 was either deaf and dumb, blind, insane or an idiot, as compared with one out of every 1105 in Florida. One cringes with shame to think that an American "statesman" could use such obviously fallacious figures to argue an equally fallacious point. But incredible as it now seems, it was not only written by the secretary of state in the Tyler administration, but the transmittal of the treaty to the Senate was held up for several days pending the completion of this document. Either the President or his secretary of state was under the absurd notion that its inclusion in the papers to be sent to the Senate would improve the case for annexation. It had just the opposite effect, for it made slavery the central issue of the debate.

Fortunately, a distinguished physician, Dr. Edward Jarvis, of Concord, Massachusetts, and a disciple of the distinguished pioneer in the field of vital statistics, Dr. Lemuel Shattuck of Massachusetts General Hospital, read this distorted argument and was shocked at its obvious inaccuracies. He decided to do something about it, and undertook his own survey, conducting an exhaustive study of every town and county in the free states listed as containing Negro insane. Jarvis filled page after page in the *American Journal of the Medical Sciences* with data citing the alarming number of errors in the census report. He found repeated cases where the number of insane Negroes listed in the census was much larger than the total Negro population of the community. In Worcester, Massachusetts, for example, he discovered that the 133 Negro insane reported were actually 133 insane whites who were confined to the state hospital in that city.

> This single mistake multiplies the coloured lunatics of this state threefold, and if this were corrected it would reduce the proportion of coloured insane from one in forty-three to one in one hundred and twenty-nine.[36]

Dr. Jarvis' research brought to the attention of the scientific community and later to the Congress itself the gross mishandling of data characteristic of the earlier census reports. The Concord physician was later to become head of the American Statistical Association and a consultant to the 1850 census, when a good many of the gross errors due to faulty conceptualization, analysis and data gathering were corrected. But Calhoun's letter containing the inaccurate information and even more inaccurate arguments remained on the diplomatic record. Furthermore it shrouded the annexation question in blatantly pro-slavery propaganda, which Calhoun apparently desired for his own reasons.

The President's message accompanying the transmittal of the treaty with Texas to the Senate contained no startling new arguments. Tyler outlined the tremendous resources which the Republic possessed and elaborated upon its great potential as a new state(s) within the federal Union. He also stressed its potential as a market for products coming from other sections of the country. His description of the background of the negotiations, however, was not revealing. He argued that:

> This course [annexation] has been adopted by her [Texas] without the employment of any sinister measures on the part of this Government. No intrigue has been set on foot to accomplish it. Texas herself wills it, and the Executive of the United States, concurring with her, has seen no sufficient reason to avoid the consummation of an act esteemed to be so desirable by both.[37]

This account hardly squared with the almost desperate efforts of both Upshur and Calhoun to persuade the Texans to accept annexation during the previous months. The President's references to Mexico were even less satisfactory. He expressed his intention to be conciliatory in his approach to the Mexican government, and yet he offered no explanations which Mexico might accept for ignoring its claims to the disputed land; for the President's failure to communicate with Mexico for many months or inform its officials of the ongoing direction of American policy; and finally for moving in troops and naval forces to protect the disputed border.

Towards the end of the message President Tyler raised the spectre of British intrigue:

> Least of all was it [the United States] ignorant of the anxiety of other powers to induce Mexico to enter into terms of reconciliation with Texas, which affecting the domestic institutions of Texas [read slavery], would operate most injuriously upon the United States and might seriously threaten the existence of this happy union. Nor could it be unacquainted with the fact that although foreign governments might disavow all design to disturb the relations which exist under the Constitution between these states, yet *that one, the most powerful amongst them, had not failed to declare its marked and decided hostility to the chief feature in those relations, and its purpose on all suitable occasions to urge upon Mexico the adoption of such a course in negotiating with Texas as to produce the obliteration of that feature from her domestic policy as one of the conditions of her recognition by Mexico as an independent state.*[38]

In this statement it would seem the President of the United States was not only affirming the notion that the protection of slavery in Texas and in the South was his principal objective in annexation, but that he was still repeating an unsubstantiated charge which had frequently and recently been totally denied by the British foreign minister.

Several events during the next few days contributed to the defeat of the treaty in the Senate. An anti-slavery senator, Benjamin Tappan of Ohio, was outraged that the Senate debate on the treaty, which took place in executive session, and all the papers and documents communicated to the Senate by the President would not be disclosed to the public. He therefore sent a copy of the treaty and its accompanying documents to his brother, Lewis, a leading abolitionist. Lewis Tappan consulted Albert Gallatin, secretary of the treasury under Jefferson and a veteran of the battle against the Sedition Act, who told him to go ahead and leak the materials to the press. The next day William Cullen Bryant of the *New York Evening Post* published an "extra," printing the text of the treaty and all of the accompanying documents. Tyler's secret diplomacy was exposed.[39]

On the same day letters on the subject of the annexation of Texas appeared in the press from Henry Clay and Martin Van Buren, the front runners for the presidency as candidates for the Whig and Democratic parties respectively. Both were trying desperately to hold on to their northern and western supporters now outraged at the blatant pro-slavery strategy of the administration. Many believed that the southerners had whipped up the annexation crisis for the sole purpose of bringing more slave states into the Union.

Finally there was an attack on the treaty by Senator Thomas Hart Benton, the leader of the old Jacksonian forces in the Senate. Benton was certainly not an abolitionist and he wanted Texas in the Union, but he was no hypocrite, and he was appalled by the machinations of Tyler and Calhoun on the annexation question. Apart from this, he hated both men with a passion. His defection was the decisive factor which defeated the treaty, but the margin was so ample that it might very well have lost without Benton's stirring denunciation of "secret diplomacy."

Benton spoke for three days against the treaty. It is impossible in a few sentences to capture the full flavor of his remarks. But his central point was that the President and his former and current secretaries of state were involving the country in an unjustified war with Mexico over the Texas question. Benton went pretty far afield when he came to the point of ascribing motives, however. At one point he suggested the whole scheme was concocted in order to reelect the President; it was an accusation which had real plausibility, but later he charged the ultimate goal was the secession of the slave states. But he hit the mark squarely when he described with fitting moral outrage the duplicity of the administration in pressing for a quick annexation, and the constitutional violations it was willing to incur in order to achieve that goal. He pointed out the shameful treatment of Mexico throughout, and castigated the imperious manner in which this country's representatives communicated with that government.

> Texas and Mexico were at war, and to annex the country was to adopt the war: far from hastening annexation, an event desirable in itself when it could be honestly done, a premature and ill-judged attempt, upon groundless pretexts, could only clog and delay it. . . .[40]
>
> The treaty, in all that relates to the boundary of the Rio Grande, is an act of unparalleled outrage on Mexico. It is the seizure of two thousand miles of her territory without a word of explanation with her, and by virtue of a treaty with Texas, to which she is no party. Our Secretary of State (Mr. Calhoun) in his letter to the United States chargé in Mexico, and seven days after the treaty was signed, and after the Mexican minister had withdrawn from our seat of government, shows full well that he was conscious of the enormity of this outrage; knew it was war; and proffered volunteer apologies to avert the consequences which he knew he had provoked.[41]

During the debate, Benton and others kept pressing the administration for all the information in their possession relative to any commitments the government had made to Texas with respect to military and naval assistance. The administration attempted to avoid detailed discussion of this matter, but a number of resolutions were introduced demanding such papers; on May 15, 1844, President Tyler informed the Senate that he had indeed instructed a squadron of warships to concentrate in the Gulf of Mexico and had alerted a sizeable military force to mobilize "on the borders of Texas." The President took pains to explain that these moves were initiated in response to Mexico's announcement that she would consider the ratification of a treaty of annexation "a declaration of war against her by the United States. . . ."[42]

President John Tyler
Special Message to the Senate in
Answer to their Resolution of May 13
May 15, 1844

Richardson, V, 2169-71.

In answer to the resolution of the Senate of the 13th instant, requesting to be informed "whether since the commencement of the negotiations which resulted in the treaty now before the Senate for the annexation of Texas to the United States, any military preparation has been made or ordered by the President for or in anticipation of war, and, if so, for what cause, and with whom was such war apprehended, and what are the preparations that have been made or ordered; has any movement or assemblage or disposition of any of the military or naval forces of the United States been made or ordered with a view to such hostilities; and to communicate to the Senate copies of all orders or directions given for any such preparation or for any such movement or disposition or for the future conduct of such military or naval forces," I have to inform the Senate that, in consequence of the declaration of Mexico communicated to this Government and by me laid before Congress at the opening of its present session, announcing the determination of Mexico to regard as a declaration of war against her by the United States the definitive ratification of any treaty with Texas annexing the territory of that Republic to the United States, and the hope and belief entertained by the Executive that the treaty with Texas for that purpose would be speedily approved and ratified by the Senate, it was regarded by the Executive to have become emphatically its duty to concentrate in the Gulf of Mexico and its vicinity, as a precautionary measure, as large a portion of the home squadron, under the command of Captain Conner, as could well be drawn together, and at the same time to assemble at Fort Jesup, on the borders of Texas, as large a military force as the demands of the service at other encampments would authorize to be detached. For the number of ships already in the Gulf and the waters contiguous thereto and such as are placed under orders for that destination, and of troops now assembled upon the frontier, I refer you to the accompanying reports from the Secretaries of the War and Navy Departments. It will also be perceived by the Senate, by referring to the orders of the Navy Department which are herewith transmitted, that the naval officer in command of the fleet is directed to cause his ships to perform all the duties of a fleet of observation and to apprise the Executive of any indication of a hostile design upon Texas on the part of any nation pending the deliberations of the Senate upon the treaty, with a view that the same should promptly be submitted to Congress for its mature deliberation. At the same time, it is due to myself that I should declare it as my opinion that the United States having by the treaty of annexation acquired a title to Texas which requires only the action of the Senate to perfect it, no other power could be permitted to invade and by force of arms to possess itself of any portion of the territory of Texas pending your deliberations upon the treaty without placing itself in an hostile attitude to the United States and justifying the employment of any military means at our disposal to drive back the invasion. At the same time, it is my opinion that Mexico or any other power will find in your approval of the treaty no just cause of war against the United States, nor do I believe that there is any serious hazard of war to be found in the fact of such approval. Nevertheless, every proper measure will be resorted to by the Executive to preserve upon an honorable and just basis the public peace by reconciling Mexico, through a liberal course of policy, to the treaty.

The difficulty with the President's explanation was that both he and his secretary of state had already made similar commitments to the Texas government before any such statement was made by the Mexican government. In fact such assurances, as we have seen, were the necessary pre-conditions for Texas entering into treaty negotiations with this country in the first place. This evidence was finally extracted from the State Department files by an insistent group of senators led by Benton. The President's compliance with this series of resolutions by the Senate was probably based upon his assessment that the treaty still had a chance of passing, but the Senate Whigs together with Benton's group of unhappy Democrats rejected it, and it failed to receive the necessary two-thirds majority by a fairly wide margin (35 opposed and 16 in favor). The Senate was so distressed with the President and his actions that it foolishly refused to remove the "secret" classification from some other documents the President had sent to the Senate, including the Jackson "golden moment" letter, which the Senate considered was simply propaganda in favor of the treaty.

Having already flaunted the Constitution in his secret military commitments to Texas, President Tyler compounded his unconstitutional behavior by directing a message to the House of Representatives in June 1844, after the defeat of the treaty in the Senate, defending his conduct in American relations with Mexico and suggesting to the House that he would look favorably upon "any other expedient compatible with the Constitution," as long as it served the end of getting Texas into the Union.[43] In short the end justified the means. Tyler also took advantage of this occasion to make public the communication from former President Jackson and other documents supporting annexation which the Senate would not divulge during the secret hearings on the treaty.

The First Dark Horse Candidate

While all of this was going on, a presidential campaign which had great bearing on the Texas question was well under way. Martin Van Buren was the strongest Democratic contender, but he had never been popular with the southern wing of the party, and his position on the annexation of Texas made him less popular in the South than ever. Still, he clearly held the lead over his most prominent challenger, General Lewis Cass of Michigan. Cass was a rather formidable figure in the West. He had served under Harrison in the Indian fighting days, put in a long stretch as governor of the Michigan Territory and had been appointed ambassador to France under Jackson.

Van Buren remained the odds-on favorite all during the winter and spring of 1843-44. The best-known Democrat aside from Jackson, he had greater strength within the party than any other candidate. He had nailed down the support of the "hard money" men, the former officeholders who hoped to return to their jobs, and many of the old Jackson supporters. By January 1844, 18 of the 26 states had held conventions and 12 of the 18 had endorsed Van Buren. Of even greater significance was that none of the other six had endorsed any single candidate except Kentucky, which chose the former Vice President, Colonel Richard Johnson. Calhoun finally withdrew from the race, denouncing the convention system; the road again looked clear for Van Buren. Yet there was strong sentiment in the party in opposition to Van Buren. Cass was still very much in the picture. Tyler was intent upon running under the banner of a third party, and there were some dark horses lurking in the Democratic party presidential barn.

One of them was James Knox Polk from Columbia, Tennessee. Polk had a worthy background in both national and state politics. He was elected to Congress in 1825 and reelected every two years until 1839 when he resigned. In 1833 he was appointed to the powerful Ways and Means Committee of the House and later elevated to the chairmanship of that committee, where he fought for Jackson's position on the Bank, and was such a loyal adherent to the administration that several anti-Jacksonians attempted to goad him into a duel. Polk was elected Speaker of the House and served in that office until 1839 when he returned to Tennessee in order to try to recapture state leadership from the anti-Jackson faction headed by Congressman John Bell and Senator Hugh L. White. He was elected governor of Tennessee in his first attempt, but Whig support was so strong in the state that he was swept out of office when he ran for reelection in 1841 and lost again in 1843.

In the face of two statewide defeats in recent elections, Polk did not loom upon the 1843 landscape as even a very strong candidate for the vice presidency, let alone the presidency. But history contains many surprises, and Polk was a determined and courageous man. He refused to let his narrow defeat in 1843 knock him out of either the state or the national political picture, and slowly but effectively he plotted his course towards national office—although he was aiming at the vice presidency until several surprising developments opened up the possibility of his obtaining the Democratic nomination for President. The spring of 1844 was dominated by the Texas question and the national political party conventions. President Tyler submitted the signed treaty with Texas to the Senate on April 22, 1844. Five days later the two leading candidates for the presidency from the two major parties, Henry Clay and Martin Van Buren, published letters in the Washington press condemning the immediate annexation of Texas, thereby creating the major issue in the election of 1844. Clay's objections to the treaty of annexation did not differ substantially from Van Buren's criticisms of Tyler's secret diplomacy and the threat of war:

> I consider the annexation of Texas, at this time, without the assent of Mexico, as a measure compromising the national character; involving us certainly in war with Mexico, probably with other foreign powers; dangerous to the integrity of the Union; inexpedient in the present financial condition of the country; and not called for by any general expression of public opinion.[44]

These two letters are printed in full below, not simply because they were critical documents in the presidential campaign of 1844, but because they were probably decisive in changing the direction of and certainly the cast of leading characters in this period of American history.

Henry Clay
Letter to the Washington *National Intelligencer*
April 17, 1844

Niles Register, May 4, 1844, 152-53.

Gentlemen: Subsequent to my departure from Ashland, in December last, I received various communications from popular assemblages and private individuals, requesting an expression of my opinion upon the question of the annexation of Texas to the United States. I have forborne to reply to them, because it was not very convenient, during the progress of my journey, to do so, and for other reasons, I did not think it proper, unnecessarily, to introduce at present a new element among the other exciting subjects which agitate and engross the public mind.—The rejection of the overture of Texas, some years ago, to become annexed to the United States, had met with general acquiescence. Nothing had since occurred materially to vary the question. I had seen no evidence of a desire being entertained, on the part of any considerable portion of the American people, that Texas should become an integral part of the United States. During my sojourn in New Orleans, I had, indeed, been greatly surprised, by information which I received from Texas, that, in the course of last fall, a voluntary overture had proceeded from the executive of the United States to the authorities of Texas to conclude a treaty of annexation; and that, in order to overcome the repugnance felt by any of them to a negotiation upon the subject, strong and, as I believed, erroneous representations had been made to them of a state of opinion in the Senate of the U. States favorable to the ratification of such a treaty. According to these representations, it had been ascertained that a number of senators, varying from thirty-five to forty-two, were ready to sanction such a treaty. I was aware, too, that holders of Texas lands and Texas scrip, and speculators in them, were actively engaged in promoting the object of annexation. Still, I did not believe that any executive of the United States would venture upon so grave and momentous a proceeding, not only without any general manifestation of public opinion in favor of it, but in direct opposition to strong and decided expressions of public disapprobation. But it appears that I was mistaken. To the astonishment of the whole nation, we are now informed that a treaty of annexation has been actually concluded, and is to be submitted to the senate for its consideration. The motives for my silence, therefore, no longer remain, and I feel it to be my duty to present an exposition of my views and opinions upon the question, for what they may be worth, to the public consideration. I adopt this method as being more convenient than several replies to the respective communications which I have received.

I regret that I have not the advantage of a view of the treaty itself, so as to enable me to adapt an expression of my opinion to the actual conditions and stipulations which it contains. Not possessing that opportunity, I am constrained to treat the question according to what I presume to be the terms of the treaty. If, without the loss of national character, without the hazard of foreign war, with the general concurrence of the nation, without any danger to the integrity of the Union, and without giving an unreasonable price for Texas, the question of annexation were presented, it would appear in quite a different light from that in which, I apprehend, it is now to be regarded.

The United States acquired a title to Texas, extending, as I believe, to the Rio del Norte, by the treaty of Louisiana. They ceded and relinquished that title to Spain by the treaty of 1819, by which the Sabine was substituted for the Rio del Norte as our western boundary. This treaty was negotiated under the administration of Mr. Monroe, and with the concurrence of his cabinet, of which Messrs. Crawford, Calhoun, and Wirt, being a majority, all southern gentlemen, composed a part. When the treaty was laid before the house of representatives, being a member of that body, I expressed the opinion, which I then entertained, and still hold, that Texas was sacrificed to the acquisition of Florida. We wanted Florida; but I thought it must, from its position, inevitably fall into our possession; that the point of a few years, sooner or later, was of no sort of consequence, and that in giving five millions of dollars and Texas for it, we gave more than a just equivalent. But, if we made a great sacrifice in the surrender of Texas, we ought to take care not to make too great a sacrifice in the attempt to re-acquire it.

My opinions of the inexpediency of the treaty of 1819 did not prevail. The country and congress were satisfied with it, appropriations were made to carry it into effect, the line of the Sabine was recognised by us as our boundary, in negotiations both with Spain and Mexico, after Mexico became independent, and measures have been in actual progress to mark the line, from the Sabine to Red river, and thence to the Pacific ocean. We have thus fairly alienated our title to

Texas, by solemn national compacts, to the fulfilment of which we stand bound by good faith and national honor. It is, therefore, perfectly idle and ridiculous, if not dishonorable, to talk of resuming our title to Texas, as if we had never parted with it. We can no more do that than Spain can resume Florida, France, Louisiana, or Great Britain the 13 colonies, now composing a part of the U. States.

During the administration of Mr. Adams, Mr. Poinsett, minister of the United States at Mexico, was instructed by me, with the president's authority, to propose a re-purchase of Texas; but he forbore even to make an overture for that purpose. Upon his return to the United States, he informed me, at New Orleans, that his reason for not making it was, that he knew the purchase was wholly impracticable, and that he was persuaded that, if he made the overture, it would have no other effect than to aggravate irritations, already existing, upon matters of difference between the two countries.

The events which have since transpired in Texas are well known. She revolted against the government of Mexico, flew to arms, and finally fought and won the memorable battle of San Jacinto, annihilating a Mexican army and making a captive of the Mexican president. The signal success of that revolution was greatly aided, if not wholly achieved, by citizens of the United States who had migrated to Texas. These succors, if they could not always be prevented by the government of the United States, were furnished in a manner and to an extent which brought upon us some national reproach in the eyes of an impartial world. And, in my opinion, they impose on us the obligation of scrupulously avoiding the imputation of having instigated and aided the revolution with the ultimate view of territorial aggrandizement. After the battle of San Jacinto, the U. States recognised the independence of Texas, in conformity with the principle and practice which have always prevailed in their councils of recognising the government "de facto," without regarding the question *de jure*. That recognition did not affect or impair the rights of Mexico, or change the relations which existed between her and Texas. She, on the contrary, has preserved all her rights, and has continued to assert, and so far as I know yet asserts, her right to reduce Texas to obedience, as a part of the republic of Mexico.—According to late intelligence, it is probable that she has agreed upon a temporary suspension of hostilities; but, if that has been done, I presume it is with the purpose, upon the termination of the armistice, of renewing the war and enforcing her rights, as she considers them.

This narrative shows the present actual condition of Texas, so far as I have information about it. If it be correct, Mexico has not abandoned, but perseveres in the assertion of her rights by actual force of arms, which, if suspended, are intended to be renewed.—Under these circumstances, if the government of the United States were to acquire Texas, it would acquire along with it all the incumbrances which Texas is under, and among them the actual or suspended war between Mexico and Texas. Of that consequence there cannot be a doubt. Annexation and war with Mexico are identical. Now, for one, I certainly am not willing to involve this country in a foreign war for the object of acquiring Texas. I know there are those who regard such a war with indifference and as a trifling affair, on account of the weakness of Mexico, and her inability to inflict serious injury upon this country. But I do not look upon it thus lightly. I regard all wars as great calamities, to be avoided, if possible, and honorable peace as the wisest and truest policy of this country. What the United States most need are union, peace, and patience. Nor do I think that the weakness of a power should form a motive, in any case, for inducing us to engage in or to depreciate the evils of war.—Honor and good faith and justice are equally due from this country towards the weak as towards the strong. And, if an act of injustice were to be perpetrated towards any power, it would be more compatible with the dignity of the nation, and, in my judgment, less dishonorable, to inflict it upon a powerful instead of a weak foreign nation. But are we perfectly sure that we should be free from injury in a state of war with Mexico? Have we any security that countless numbers of foreign vessels, under the authority and flag of Mexico, would not prey upon our defenceless commerce in the Mexican gulf, on the Pacific ocean, and on every other sea and ocean? What commerce, on the other hand, does Mexico offer, as an indemnity for our losses, to the gallantry and enterprise of our countrymen? This view of the subject supposes that the war would be confined to the United States and Mexico as the only belligerents. But have we any certain guaranty that Mexico would obtain no allies among the great European powers? Suppose any such powers, jealous of our increasing greatness, and disposed to check our growth and cripple us, were to take part in behalf of Mexico in the war, how would the different belligerents present themselves to Christendom and the enlightened world? We have been seriously charged with an inordinate spirit of territorial aggrandizement; and, without admitting the justice of the charge, it must be owned that we have made vast acquisitions of territory within the last forty years. Suppose Great Britain and France, or one of them, were to take part with Mexico, and, by a manifesto, were to proclaim that their objects were to assist a weak and helpless ally to check the spirit of encroachment and ambition of an already over-grown republic, seeking still further acquisitions of territory, to maintain the independence of Texas, disconnected with the United States and to prevent the further propagation of slavery from the United States, what would be the effect of such allegations upon the judgment of an impartial and enlightened world?

Assuming that the annexation of Texas is war with Mexico, is it competent to the treaty-making power to plunge this country into war, not only without the concurrence of, but without deigning to consult congress, to which, by the constitution, belongs exclusively the power of declaring war?

I have hitherto considered the question upon the supposition that the annexation is attempted without the assent of Mexico. If she yields her consent, that would materially affect the foreign aspect of the question, if it did not remove all foreign difficulties. On the assumption of that assent, the question would be confined to the domestic considerations which belong to it, embracing the terms and conditions upon which annexation is proposed. I do not think that Texas ought to be received into the Union, as an integral part of it, in decided opposition to the wishes of a considerable and respectable portion of the confederacy. I think it far more wise and important to compose and harmonize the present confederacy, as it now exists, than to introduce a new element of discord and distraction into it. In my humble opinion, it should be the constant and earnest endeavor of American statesmen to eradicate prejudices, to cultivate and foster concord, and to produce general contentment among all parts of our confederacy. And true wisdom, it seems to me, points to the duty of rendering its present members happy, prosperous, and satisfied with each other, rather than to attempt to introduce alien members, against the common consent and with the certainty of deep dissatisfaction.—Mr. Jefferson expressed the opinion, and others believed that it never was in the contemplation of the framers of the constitution to add foreign territory to the confederacy, out of which new states were to be formed. The acquisitions of Louisiana and Florida may be defended upon the peculiar ground of the relation in which they stood to the states of the Union. After they were admitted, we might well pause a while, people our vast wastes, develop our resources, prepare the means of defending what we possess, and augment our strength, power, and greatness. If hereafter further territory should be wanted for an increased population, we need entertain no apprehensions but that it will be acquired by means, it is to be hoped, fair, honorable, and constitutional.

It is useless to disguise that there are those who espouse and those who oppose the annexation of Texas upon the ground of the influence which it would exert, in the balance of political power, between two great sections of the Union. I conceive that the motive for the acquisition of foreign territory would be more unfortunate, or pregnant with more ill consequences, than that of obtaining it for the purpose of strengthening one part against another part of the common confederacy. Such a principle, put into practical operation, would menace the existence, if it did not certainly sow the seeds of a dissolution of the Union. It would be to proclaim to the world an insatiable and unquenchable thirst for foreign conquest or acquisition of territory. For if today Texas be acquired to strengthen one part of the Confederacy, to-morrow Canada may be required to restrength to another. And, after that might have been obtained, still other and further acquisitions would become necessary to equalize and adjust the balance of political power. Finally, in the progress of this spirit of universal dominion, the part of the Confederacy which is now weakest, would find itself weaker from the impossibility of securing new centres for those peculiar institutions which it is charged with being desirous to extend.

Would Texas, ultimately, really add strength to that which is now considered the weakest part of the confederacy? If my information be correct, it would not. According to that, the territory of Texas is susceptible of a division into five states of convenient size and form. Of these, two only would be adapted to those peculiar institutions to which I have referred, and the other three, lying west and north of San Antonio, being only adapted to farming and grazing purposes, from the nature of their soil, climate, and productions, would not admit of those institutions. In the end, therefore, there would be two slave and three free states probably added to the Union. If this view of the soil and geography of Texas be correct, it might serve to diminish the zeal both of those who oppose and those who are urging annexation.

Should Texas be annexed to the Union, the United States will assume and become responsible for the debt of Texas, be its amount what it may. What it is, I do not know certainly; but the least I have seen it stated at is thirteen millions of dollars. And this responsibility will exist, whether there be a stipulation in the treaty or not expressly assuming the payment of the debt of Texas. For I suppose it to be undeniable that, if one nation becomes incorporated in another, all the debts, and obligations, and incumbrances, and wars of the incorporated nation, become the debts, and obligations, and incumbrances, and wars of the common nation created by the incorporation.

If any European nation entertains any ambitious designs upon Texas, such as that of colonizing her, or in any way subjugating her, I should regard it as the imperative duty of the government of the United States to oppose such designs the most firm and determined resistance, to the extent, if necessary, of appealing to arms to prevent the accomplishment of any such designs. The executive of the United States ought to be informed as to the aims and views of foreign powers with regard to Texas, and I presume that, if there be any of the exceptionable character which I have indicated, the executive will disclose to the co-ordinate departments of the government, if not to the public, the evidence of them. From what I have seen and heard, I believe that Great Britain has recently formally and solemnly disavowed any such aims or purposes—has declared that she is desirous only of the independence of Texas, and that she has no intention to interfere in her domestic institutions. If she has made such disavowal and declaration, I presume they are in the possession of the executive.

In the future progress of events, it is probable that there will be a voluntary or forcible separation of the British North American possessions from the parent country. I am strongly inclined to think that it will be best for the happiness of all parties that, in that event, they should be erected into a separate and independent republic. With the Canadian republic on one side, that of Texas on the other, and the United States, the friend of both, between them, each could advance its own happiness by such constitutions, laws, and measures, as were best adapted to its peculiar condition. They would be natural allies, ready, by co-operation, to repel any European or foreign attack upon either. Each would afford a secure refuge to the persecuted and oppressed driven into exile by either of the others. They would emulate each other in improvements, in free institutions, and in the science of self-government. Whilst Texas has adopted our constitution as the model of hers, she has, in several important particulars, greatly improved upon it.

Although I have felt compelled, from the nature of the inquiries addressed to me, to extend this communication to a much greater length than I could have wished, I could not do justice to the subject, and fairly and fully expose my own opinions in a shorter space. In conclusion, they may be stated in a few words to be, that I consider the annexation of Texas, at this time, without the assent of Mexico, as a measure compromising the national character, involving us certainly in war with Mexico, probably with other foreign powers, dangerous to the integrity of the Union, inexpedient in the present financial condition of the country, and not called for by any general expression of public opinion.

        I am, respectfully, your obedient
           servant,

                         Henry Clay

Martin Van Buren
Letter to W. H. Hammet
April 20, 1844

Niles Register, May 4, 1844, 153-57.

My Dear Sir: Your letter of the 28th of March last, was duly received.

Acting as an unpledged delegate to the Baltimore convention you ask my opinion in regard to the constitutionality and expediency of an immediate annexation of Texas to the United States, or as soon as the assent of Texas may be had to such annexation.—Upon the receipt of your letter, I caused you to be forthwith informed that your request should be complied with in full season for the convention. This promise I shall now perform. But, lest my motives in making a public avowal of my opinions, whilst a negotiation is supposed to be pending, should be misconstrued, I shall send this to a friend who will delay its delivery as long as that can be done consistently with a faithful compliance with the requirements of your letter, and the general objects for which it was written.

You by no means overrate the importance of the subject upon which you have been pleased to address me. It is not only a question of intense interest to every part of the country, but is unhappily also one in regard to which we may not promise ourselves that unanimity in opinions which is so important when great national questions like this are to be decided. That those which I am about to express will, in at least one important particular, differ from that of many friends, political and personal, whose judgments and purity of views I hold in high and habitual respect, I can well imagine; and it is quite evident, from the tenor of your letter, that they will not in all respects correspond with your own. If, however, such of my fellow citizens as are neither influenced by prejudices, nor warped by self-interest, concede to my opinions the merit of having been formed under views directed to the preservation and advancement of the honor and best interests of our common country, as a whole, and expressed with a sincerity which has overlooked, as far as our feeble natures will permit us to do, all personal considerations, my most favorable anticipations will be realized.

It has already been made my duty to act officially on at least two several occasions, but in different forms, upon the subject matter to which your questions have reference.

Having charge of the department of state in 1829, I prepared, by direction of the president, instructions to our minister at Mexico, by which he was directed to open without delay, a negotiation with the Mexican government for the purchase of a greater part of the then province of Texas, and by which he was likewise authorized to insert in the treaty a provision similar to that in the Louisiana and Florida treaties, for the incorporation of the inhabitants of Texas into the Union as soon as it could be done consistently with the principles of the federal constitution. The reasons in favor of this measure I stated at large in that document.

In taking this step, the administration of president Jackson renewed (but, as was supposed, under more favorable circumstances) an attempt to accomplish the same object which had been made by its immediate predecessor. Instructions, similar in their general object, had, in the second year of the latter administration, been sent from the department of state to the same American minister at Mexico. I am not aware that there were any material differences between them, other than those of 1827 proposed an acquisition of territory as far west as the Rio del Norte—being, I believe, the extreme western boundary of Texas—whilst the cession asked for by president Jackson extended only as far west as the centre of the Desert or Grand Prairie, which lies east of the river Nueces; and that for the frontier the payment of one million of dollars was authorized whilst, by the administration of president Jackson, the American minister was permitted to go as high as four, and, if indispensable, five millions. Both authorized agreements for smaller portions of territory, and the payments were modified accordingly. In respect for the proposed stipulations for the ultimate incorporation of the inhabitants into the Union, both instructions were identical.

In August, 1837, a proposition was received at the department of state, from the Texian minister at Washington, proposing a negotiation for the annexation of Texas to the United States. This was the first time the question of a foreign independent state has ever been presented to this government. In deciding upon the disposition that ought to be made of it, I did not find it necessary to consider the question of constitutional power, nor the manner in which the object should be accomplished, if deemed expedient and proper. Both these points were therefore, in terms, passed over in the reply of the secretary of state to the Texan minister, as subjects the consideration of which had not been entered upon by the executive.

The first of these, viz: constitutional power—is now presented by your inquiries, not, however, in precisely the same form. Then the application was for the immediate admission of Texas into the Union as an independent state; your question looks only to its annexation as part of the territory of the United States. There is no express power giving to any department of the government to purchase territory except for the objects specified in the constitution, viz: for arsenals, etc ; but the power has, on several very important occasions, been regarded as embraced in the treaty-making power; and territories have been so annexed with a view and under engagements for their ultimate admission into the Union as states.

If there be nothing in the situation or condition of the territory of Texas, which would render its admission hereafter into the Union as a new state improper, I cannot perceive any objection, on constitutional grounds, to its annexation as a territory. In speaking of the right to admit new states, I must, of course, be understood as referring to the power of congress. The executive and senate may, as I have already observed, by the exercise of the treaty-making power, acquire territory; but new states can only be admitted by congress; and the sole authority over the subject, which is given to it by the constitution, is contained in the following provision, viz: "new states may be admitted by the congress into this Union." The only restrictions imposed upon this general power are, 1st, That no new states shall be formed or erected within the jurisdiction of any other state; nor 2dly, "Any state formed by the junction of two or more states, or parts of states, without the consent of the legislatures concerned, as well as of congress"—restrictions which have no bearing upon the present question. The matter, therefore, stands as it would do if the constitution said "new states may be admitted by the congress into this Union," without addition or restriction. That these words, taken by themselves, are broad enough to authorize the admission of the territory of Texas, cannot, I think, be well doubted; nor do I perceive upon what principle we can set up limitations to a power so unqualifiedly recognized by the constitution in the plain simple words I have quoted, and with which no other provision of that instrument conflicts in the slightest degree. But if, with no other guides than our own discretion, we assume limitations upon a power so general, we are at least bound to give to them some intelligible and definite character. The most natural, and indeed the only one of that nature which has been suggested, and which was presented by Mr. Jefferson whilst he entertained doubts in respect to the constitutional power to admit Louisiana, is, that the new states to be admitted must be formed out of territory, not foreign, but which constituted a part of the United States, at the declaration of independence, or the adoption of the constitution. So far from there being any thing in the language of the constitution, or to be found in the extraneous and cotemporaneous circumstances which preceded and attended its adoption, to show that such was the intentions of its framers, they are, in my judgment, all strongly the other way. In the first place, the articles of confederation, under which the Union was originally formed, and which gave place to the present constitution, looked directly to a broader extension of the confederacy. It contained a provision that "Canada, acceding to the constitution, and joining in the measures of the United States, shall be admitted into, and entitled to all the advantages of this Union; but no other colony shall be admitted into the same, *unless* such admission be agreed to by nine states." The practicability, as well as expediency, of making Canada a member of the Union, did certainly, to some extent at least, occupy the minds of our public men, as well before the close of the revolution, as between that event and the formation of the new constitution. This is, however, only a link in the chain of evidence, to make probable what subsequent events make certain, that the framers of the constitution had their eyes upon this very question, when this section was finally settled. That part of the constitution, as appears by the journal of the proceedings of the convention, was presented in a variety of forms before it assumed the shape in which it was finally adopted.

In the resolutions offered by Mr. Edward Randolph, as a basis for the new constitution, and which contained the first propositions of that character which were submitted to it, the power in question was described as follows, viz: "that provisions ought to be made for the admission of states *lawfully arising within the limits of the United States,* whether arising from a voluntary junction of government or otherwise, with the consent of a number of voices in the legislature, less than the whole." In Mr. Charles Pinckney's draft, it was proposed that "the legislature shall have power to admit new states into the Union, on the same terms with the original states, provided two-thirds of the members present in both houses agree—leaving out the clause in respect to the character of the territory. Mr. Randolph's proposition, containing the restriction confining the power to states lawfully arising within the limits of the United States, was at one time adopted in committee of the whole; and, in that state, referred with others to the committee of detail. In a draft of a constitution, reported by that committee, the article upon this subject contained the following propositions: 1st. That new states, lawfully constituted or established within the limits of the United States might be admitted by the legislature in this government. 2d. That to such admission, the consent of two-thirds of the members present in each house should be necessary. 3d. That if a new state should arise within the limits of any of the present states, the consent of the legislature of such states should also be necessary to its admission. 4th. That if the admission was consented to, the new states should be admitted on the same terms with the original states; and 5th. That the legislature might make conditions with new states concerning the public debt then subsisting. The 2d, 4th, and 5th clauses were stricken out by the votes of the convention; and after that had been done, the following was adopted as a substitute for the whole, viz: "New states may be admitted by the legislature into the union; but no new state shall be erected within the limits of any of the present states, without the consent of the legislature of such state, as well as of the general legislature"—leaving out that part of the first clause which related to the domestic character of the territory; and this substitute was consequently revised and amended, so as to make it conform in its phraseology to the section as it now stands in the constitution. These proceedings show that the proposition to restrict the power to admit new states to the territory without the original limits of the United States, was distinctly before the convention, once adopted by it, and finally rejected in favor of a clause making the power in this respect general. Whatever differences of opinion may exist as to the propriety of referring to extraneous matter to influence the construction of the constitution where its language is explicit, there can certainly be no objections to a resort to such aids to test the correctness of interferences, having no other basis than supposed improbabilities. I have not, therefore, been able to bring my mind to any other satisfactory conclusion than that it was the intention of the convention to give the power of admitting new states to congress, with no other limitation than those which are specified in that instrument. The language employed, the specifications of certain restrictions, the adoption and subsequent exclusion of that which is now referred to, together with the subsequent and continued action of the new government, all seem to combine to render this interpretation of the constitution the true one. Propositions for annexation can certainly be imagined, of a character so unwise and improvident as to strike the minds of all with repugnance. But if we look over the conceded powers of congress, we shall also find many others, the abuse of which might involve, to an equally great extent, the well being of the republic, and against which abuse the constitution has provided no other safeguards than the responsibilities to their constituents and to the laws of the land, of those whose sanction is necessary to the validity of an act of congress. Nor is it very unreasonable to suppose that those who based their government upon the great principle that it is the right of the people to alter or abolish it, and to institute new ones, in such form as they may think most likely to effect their safety and happiness, should feel themselves secure in trusting to their representatives in the house, in the senate, and in the executive chair, the right to admit new members into the confederacy, with no other restrictions than those which they have thought proper to specify.

It was under this view of the constitution that the purchase of Louisiana in 1803, only fifteen years after the adoption of the constitution, promising the incorporation of the ceded territory into the Union, and the admission, as soon as possible, of the inhabitants to the enjoyment of all the rights, advantages, and immunities of citizens of the United States, was ratified, confirmed, and finally executed by every branch of the federal government whose co-operation is required by the constitution. It is true that Mr. Jefferson, in the interval between the negotiation and submission of the treaty to the senate, thought that the opinion that the constitution had made no provision for our holding foreign territory, nor for incorporating foreign states into the Union. The fact of his approving the treaty, and the laws necessary to its execution, must, however, be regarded as conclusive proof that, upon looking further into the matter, his opinion was changed. The attempt to convince him of his error was made by his friend, governor Nicholas, as appears by Mr. Jefferson's letter to him; and I have little doubt that, if his letters to Breckenridge and Nicholas had been published in his life-time, or his attention been in any other way directed to their contents, he would, from his habitual care in such matters, have avowed the change, and explained the grounds on which it was based. It is equally true that the acceptance of the cession, as well as the admission of the state, became party questions, and were contested with partisan warmth. Of the vital importance of that great acquisition to the safety, prosperity, and honor of the whole Union, there can however, now be no diversity of opinion. But the councils of the nation, in the course of time, cease to be at all divided upon the question of constitutional power to accept a cession of foreign territory, with the view of its ultimate admission into the Union. In 1819 the Spanish treaty for the cession of east and west Florida containing the usual stipulation for ultimate incorporation into the Union was ratified and upon the call of the names of the senators present, it appeared that every one voted for the ratification. Upon the question of constitutional power, so far that case went, the senate of the Unites States has therefore, become unanimous.

Certainly no remarks are necessary to show that there can be no possible difference produced in the constitutional question by the relative positions of the territory comprising Louisiana, the Floridas, and Texas, in respect to the old United States.

I have gone thus fully and minutely into this matter, as well from a deep sense of the vast importance of the question, as from a sincere desire to satisfy those of my friends who may differ from me on this point, and whose opinions I hold in the highest respect, that I have not yielded my assent hastily or unadvisedly to the views I have here taken of the subject.

Having thus given you my views upon the constitutional question, I will, with the same frankness answer the remaining portion of your inquiries, viz. the expediency of immediately annexing Texas to the United States, or so soon as her consent to such annexation may be obtained.

I have already referred to an application for the accomplishment of the same object that was made to this government by Texas, whilst I was president.

The history of the Texan revolution, and the condition of that republic, as well as the probable advantages to result to both from the proposed annexation, were placed before us in an elaborate communication. It can scarcely be necessary to say that the application was considered with that attention and care which were due to so grave a proposition, and under the full influence of feeling of sincere solicitude for the prosperity and permanent welfare of a young and neighboring state, whose dependence we had been the first to acknowledge feelings which constitute, and I sincerely hope, will constitute, the prevailing sentiment of the people of the United States. In coming to the decision which it became my duty to make, I was aided in addition to the other members of my cabinet, by the counsel and constitutional advice of two distinguished citizens of your own section of the Union, of the first order of intellect, great experience in public affairs, and whose devotion to their own, as well as every other section of the Union, was above all question.—The result of our united opinions was announced to the Texian minister, (Gen. Hunt,) in a communication from the late Mr. Forsyth, the substance of which I cannot better express than by incorporating one or two brief extracts from it in this letter. Upon the general subjects, my own views, as well as those of the cabinet, were thus stated:

So long as Texas shall remain at war, while the United States are at peace with her adversary, the proposition of the Texan minister plenipotentiary necessarily involves the question of war with that adversary. The United States are bound to Mexico by a treaty of amity and commerce, which will be scrupulously observed on their part so long as it can be reasonably hoped that Mexico will perform her duties, and respect our rights under it. The United States might justly be suspected of a disregard of the friendly purposes of the compact, if the overture of General Hunt were to be even reserved for future consideration, as this would imply a disposition on our part to espouse the quarrel of Texas with Mexico—a disposition wholly at variance with the spirit of the treaty with the uniform policy and all the obvious welfare of the United States.

The inducements mentioned, by general Hunt for the United States to annex Texas to their territory, are duly appreciated; but, powerful and weighty as certainly they are, they are light when opposed in the scale of reason to treaty obligations, and respect for that integrity of character by which the United States have sought to distinguish themselves since the establishment of their right to claim a place in the great family of nations.

The intimation in general Hunt's letter that Texas might be induced to extend commercial advantages to other nations to the prejudice of the United States, was thus noticed:

"It is presumed, however, that the motives by which Texas has been governed in making this overture, have equal force in impelling her to preserve, as an independent power, the most liberal commercial relations with the United States. Such a disposition will be cheerfully met, in a corresponding spirit, by this government. If the answer which the undersigned has been directed to give to the proposition of general Hunt should unfortunately work such a change in the sentiments of that government as to induce an attempt to extend commercial relations elsewhere, upon terms prejudicial to the United States, this government will be consoled by the rectitude of its intentions, and a certainty that, although the hazard of transient losses may be incurred by a rigid adherence to just principles, no lasting prosperity can be secured when they are disregarded." That these views were not altogether satisfactory to General Hunt, nor probably to his government, has been seen. But I think I may safely say that seldom, if ever, has the decision, by this government, of a question of equal magnitude, been more decidedly or more unanimously approved by the people of the U. States. The correspondence was, very soon after it took place, communicated to congress, and although the public mind was at the time in a state of the highest excitement, and the administration daily assailed through every avenue by which it was deemed approachable, I am yet to see the first sentence of complaint upon that point, in any quarter of the Union. Even a resolution offered in the senate, declaring annexation, "whenever it could be effected *consistently with the public faith and treaty stipulations of the United States*, desirable," was ordered to be laid upon the table; and a similar disposition was made in the house of the papers upon the subject, which had been referred to the committee on foreign relations, and that committee discharged from the further consideration of the matter, upon its own application:—Nor were the friendly relations then existing between that republic and the United States—to its honor be it said—in any perceptible degree impaired by this decision.

Standing in this position before the country, it becomes my duty to consider whether either the nature of the question, or the circumstances of the case, have so far changed as to justify me in now advising a policy from which I then, in the most solemn form, dissented.

In giving to you, and, through you to the public, the result of a very careful and dispassionate examination of this grave question, I should neither do justice to yourself, to the patriotic state which you, in conjunction with others, are to represent in the convention, to the people of the United States, nor to my own position, if I failed to accompany it with a brief exposition of the grounds upon which I have proceeded. It is in that way only that justice can be done to my intentions; and that is all I desire. The annexation of the territory, and the consequent assumption by us of a responsibility to protect and defend its inhabitants, would, in respect to the consideration to which I am about to refer, stand upon the same footing with that of its admission as a state. The recognition of Texas as an independent state, was a measure which received, in various and appropriate forms, the sanction of every department of the government, whose co-operation was necessary to its validity, and had my hearty concurrence. From this act of our government just and proper in all respects as it was; an inference has, however, been drawn and brought to bear upon the present question, not only very far beyond its real bearing, but by which its true character is entirely reversed. Many persons who enter upon the consideration of the subject with the purest intention and are incapable of knowingly giving a false interpretation to anything connected with it, take it for granted that the United States, in recognising the independence of Texas, declared to the world, not only that she was independent *in fact*, but also that she was such *of right*. Acting upon this erroneous construction, they very naturally conclude, that having gone thus far, having examined into and passed not only upon the existence of her independence, but also upon her right to its enjoyment, it is now (and more especially after the lapse of several years) too late to hesitate upon the question of annexation on the ground of any existing controversy upon those points. The fallacy of this reasoning will be apparent when it is considered that the usage of nations to acknowledge the government, *de facto*, of every country, was established for the express purpose of avoiding all inquiry into, or the expression of any opinion upon, the question of *right* between the contending parties. They acknowledge no other power in any country than that which is in fact supreme. They cannot inquire beyond that point without interfering with the internal concerns of other nations—a practice which all disclaim, and a disclaimer which it has been our invariable usage not only to make, but to enforce with scrupulous fidelity. To recognise the independence of the government *de facto*, is also a matter of state necessity; for without it, neither commercial nor diplomatic intercourse between any such power and the nations of the world could be carried on with success, and the social interests of mankind require that these should not be arrested by quarrels between contesting parties, in regard to their respective right to the supreme power. In respect to all beyond this, the laws and usages of nations require the observance of a strict neutrality between the contending parties, as long as the war lasts. It is due, also, from every government to its own citizens, to declare when a revolted colony shall be regarded as an independent nation. Because "it belongs to the government alone to make the declaration," and because "until it is made, or the parent state relinquishes her claims, courts of justice must consider the ancient state of things as remaining unaltered, and the sovereign power of the parent state over that colony as still subsisting." But nothing can be farther from giving to the act of recognition its true character, than to suppose that it has the slightest bearing upon the rights of the parties; it being, as I have already said resorted to for the express purpose of avoiding any such construction. Such is not only the law and usage of nations, but such also have been the reiterated avowals of our own government. I do not remember that the recognition of Texan independence gave rise to any correspondence between Mexico and our government; and if it did, I have not the means of stating its character. But the principles upon which all such acts are based, were fully set forth by this government upon the occasion of the recognition of the independence of the Spanish American States.—In the message of president Monroe, to the house of representatives, suggesting the propriety of that recognition, it was expressly declared that, in proposing this measure, it was "not contemplated to change thereby, in the slightest manner, our friendly relations with either of the parties; but to observe in all respects, as heretofore, should the war be continued, the most perfect neutrality between them." The committee on foreign affairs in their elaborate report upon the subject says: "our recognition must necessarily be co-existent only with the fact on which it is founded, and cannot survive it. While the nations of South America are actually independent, it is simply to speak the truth to acknowledge them to be so. *Should Spain, contrary to her avowed principle and acknowledged interest, renew the war for the conquest of South America, we shall, indeed, regret it; but we shall observe, as we have done between the independent parties an honest and impartial neutrality.*" The secretary of state, in defence of the act of recognition said to the Spanish minister: "This recognition is neither intended to invalidate any right of Spain, *nor to affect the employment of any means which she may yet be disposed or enabled to use, with the view of re-uniting those provinces to the rest of her dominions.*" That these avowals were in strict conformity to the true principles of the law of nations, there can be no doubt.—They were, at all events, those which this government has solemnly announced as its rule of action in regard to contests between rival parties for the supreme power in foreign states. That the admission of Texas as a member of this confederacy, whilst the contest for the maintenance of the independence she has acquired was still pending, and a consequent assumption of the responsibility of protecting her against invasion, would have been a plain departure from the laws and usages of nations, and a violation of the principles to which we had avowed our adherence in the face of the world, was too clear to be doubted. Thus believing, I had on the occasion to which I have referred, in the faithful discharge of the trust which the people had reposed in me, but one course to pursue; and that was promptly, but respectfully adopted.

I return now to the question. Has the condition of the contest between Texas and Mexico, for the sovereignty of the former, so far changed as to render these principles now inapplicable? What is the attitude which these two states at this moment occupy towards each other? Are they at war, or are they not? We cannot evade this question if we would.—To enumerate all the circumstances bearing upon it, in a communication like this, would be impracticable, nor is it necessary. In respect to the parties themselves, there would seem to be no misunderstanding upon the subject. Mexico has been incessant in her avowal, as well to our government as to others, of the continuance of the war, and of her determination to prosecute it. How does Texas regard her position in respect to the war with Mexico? Three years subsequent to our recognition of her independence, we find her entering into a stipulation with a foreign power to accept of her mediation to bring about a cession of hostilities between her and Mexico, engaging to assume a million sterling of the debt due from Mexico to the subjects of that power, if she, through her influence, obtained from Mexico an unlimited truce in respect to the war then raging between her and Texas within one month and a treaty of peace in six. As late as last June, we see a proclamation of the president of Texas, declaring a suspension of hostilities between the two powers during the pendency of negotiations to be entered upon between them, issued on the supposition that a similar proclamation would be issued by Mexico; and actual hostilities are now only suspended by an armistice to be continued for a specified and short period, for the sake of negotiation. Nor are our own views upon the point less explicit. In the published letter of the late secretary of state, to the Mexican minister at Washington, written in December last, he says: "Nearly eight years have elapsed since Texas declared her independence. During *all that time* Mexico has asserted her right of jurisdiction and dominion over that country, and has endeavored to enforce it by arms." In the president's message to congress, it is stated "that the war which has existed for so long a time between Mexico and Texas, has, since the battle of San Jacinto, consisted for the most part of predatory incursions, which, while they have been attended with much of suffering to individuals, and kept the borders of the two countries in a state of constant alarm *have failed to approach to any definite result.*" And after commenting with much truth upon the insufficiency of the armaments which Mexico has fitted out for the subjection of Texas—on the length of time which has elapsed since the latter declared her independence—on the perseverance, notwithstanding, in plans of reconquest by Mexico—on her refusal to acknowledge the independence of Texas, and on the evils of border warfare, the message adds: "The United States have an immediate interest in seeing an end put to the state of hostilities between Mexico and Texas;" following up the remark with a forcible remonstrance against the continuance of the war, and a very just and impressive statement of the reasons why it should cease. This remonstrance is, in my opinion, entirely just and perfectly proper. The government of the United States should be at all times ready to interpose its good offices to bring about a speedy, and, as far as practicable a satisfactory adjustment of this long pending controversy. Its whole influence should be exerted constantly zealously and in good faith, to advance so desirable an object, and in the process of time it can, without doubt, be accomplished. But what, my dear sir, is the true and undisguised character of the remedy for those evils, which would be applied by the "immediate annexation of Texas to the United States?" Is it more or less than saying to Mexico, We feel ourselves aggrieved by the continuance of this war between you and Texas; we have an interest in seeing it terminated; we will accomplish that object by taking the disputed territory to ourselves, we will make Texas a part of the United States, so that those plans of reconquest which we know you are maturing, to be successful, must be made so against the power that we can bring into the contest; if the war is to be continued as we understand to be your design, the United States are henceforth to be regarded as one of the belligerents?

We must look at this matter as it really stands —We shall act under the eye of an intelligent, observing world; and the affair cannot be made to wear a different aspect from what it deserves if even we had the disposition (which we have not) to throw over it disguises of any kind. We should consider whether there is any way in which the peace of the country can be preserved, should an immediate annexation take place, save one—and that is, according to present appearances, the improbible event that Mexico will be deterred from the farther prosecution of the war by the apprehension of our power. How does that matter stand? She has caused us to be informed, both at Mexico and here, in a manner the most formal and solemn, that she will feel herself constrained, by every consideration that can influence the conduct of a nation, to regard the fact of annexation as an act of war on the part of the United States and that she will, notwithstanding, prosecute her attempts to regain Texas, regardless of consequences. Exceptions are, however, taken by the president, and I think very justly taken, to the manner in which this determination has been announced. The Mexican government should certainly have applied in a becoming spirit to ours for explanation of its intention. If it found this government under the impression that Mexico, although it might not be willing to acknowledge its independence, had abandoned all serious hope of re-conquering Texas, Mexico should have assured us of our error, and remonstrated against any action on our part based on that erroneous assumption and declared firmly, if it pleased, but in that courteous and respectful manner which is alone suited to the intercourse between nations who profess to be friends, its determination to oppose us. Instead of taking a course, the propriety of which was so obvious, she first assumes, upon grounds which were neither proper nor safe for her to act upon, that this government had designs upon Texas; then denounces the annexation as a great national crime, and forthwith proclaims instant war as the penalty of our persisting in such an attempt; and all this in language bearing certainly (although subsequently disavowed) every appearance of menace.

But this is a besetting and very ancient foible of the mother country, as well as of her descendants, in their diplomatic intercourse. Every one conversant with the subject of Spanish relations, knows that, at least from the time of Don Louis d'Onis to the present day, this government has been frequently—not to say continually—subjected to this species of diplomatic dogmatism. Partly in consequence of the genius of their language; partly from their peculiar temperament; much from habit, but more from a radical defect of judgment,—they continue the use of language in their state papers, which better tempered, if not wiser diplomatists have almost every where laid aside as worse than useless. But at no time has our government suffered its actions upon great national questions to be influenced by such petulance. From the time of the modest, yet firm Madison, to the late Mr. Upshur, (whose melancholy fate is so justly and generally lamented,) has every secretary of state, acting under the direction of the executive, deemed it sufficient to place the government and minister employing it in the wrong, by showing its injustice as well as its futility. We have then heretofore, as I hope we shall now, decided to act in the matter under consideration in a manner which was deemed due to justice and to our own character, without being in any degree influenced by such unavailing menaces. It is foreign to my habit, and repugnant to my feelings, to say any thing that should offend the pride of any nation, if the declarations of individuals could possibly have that effect, being sincerely desirous that the United States should cultivate friendly relations with all. But with a population not equal to half that of the United States, and laboring under many and serious disadvantages, from which we are comparatively free, Mexico could not with propriety, be offended by the assumption that this government may act as it would have done had no such menaces been made, without the slightest danger of being regarded by the rest of the world—as having been intimidated by threats of war from that republic. So at least I should act, if the direction of public affairs were in my hands. The question then recurs, if, as sensible men, we cannot avoid the conclusion that the immediate annexation of Texas would, in all human probability, draw after it a war with Mexico, can it be expedient to attempt it? Of the consequences of such a war, the character it might be made to assume, the entanglements with other nations which the position of a belligerent almost unavoidably draws after it, and the undoubted injuries which might be inflicted upon each,—notwithstanding the great desparity of their respective forces, I will not say a word. God forbid that an American citizen should ever count the cost of any appeal to what is appropriately denominated the last resort of nations, whenever that resort becomes necessary either for the safety or to vindicate the honor of his country. There is, I trust, not one so base as not to regard himself and all he has to be forever and at all times subject to such a requisition. But would a war with Mexico, brought on under such circumstances, be a contest of that character? Could we hope to stand justified in the eyes of mankind for entering into it; more especially if its commencement is to be preceded by the appropriation to our own uses of the territory, the sovereignty of which is in dispute between two nations one of which we are to join in the struggle? This sir, is a matter of the very gravest import, one in respect to which no American statesman or citizen can possibly be indifferent. We have a character among the nations of the earth to maintain.—All our public functionaries, as well those who advocate this measure as those who oppose it, however much they may differ as to its effects, will I am sure, be equally solicitous for the performance of this first of duties. It has hitherto been our pride and our boast, that whilst the lust of power, with fraud and violence in its train, has led other and differently constituted governments to aggression and conquest, our movements in these respects have always been regulated by reason and justice. A disposition to detract from our pretensions in this respect, will in the nature of things be always prevalent elsewhere; and has, at this very moment,—and from special causes assumed, in some quarters, the most rabid character. Should not every one, then who sincerely loves his country—who venerates its time-honored and glorious institutions—who dwells with pride and delight on associations connected with our rise, progress and present condition—on the steady step with which we have advanced to our present eminence, in despite of the hostility, and in contempt of the bitter revilings of the enemies of freedom in all parts of the globe,—consider and think deeply whether we would not by the immediate annexation of Texas, place a weapon in the hands of those who now look upon us and our institutions with distrustful and envious eyes, that would do us more real, lasting injury as a nation, than the acquisition of such a territory, valuable as it undoubtedly is, could possibly repair? It is said, and truly said, that this war between Texas and Mexico has already been of too long duration. We are and must continue to be more or less annoyed by its prosecution, and have undoubtedly, as has been remarked, an interest in seeing it terminated. But can we appeal to any principle in the law of nations, to which we practise a scrupulous adherence, that would, under present circumstances, justify us in interfering for its suppression in a manner that would unavoidably make us a party to its prosecution? Can this position be made sufficiently clear to justify us in committing the peace and honor of the country to its support.

In regard to the performance by us of that duty, so difficult for any government to perform,—the observance of an honest neutrality between nations at war—we can now look through our whole career, since our first admission into the family of nations, not only without a blush, but with feelings of honest pride and satisfaction. The way was opened by President Washington himself, under circumstances of the most difficult character, and at no less a hazard than that of exposing ourselves to plausible, yet unjust, imputations of infidelity to treaty stipulations. The path he trod with such unfaltering steps—and which led to such beneficial results, has hitherto been pursued with unvarying fidelity by every one of his successors of whom it becomes me to speak.

If our sympathies could induce a departure from a policy which has so much in its commencement to consecrate it, and such advantages to recommend its continuance, they would doubtless draw us to the side of Texas. That the happiness of her people would be promoted by the maintenance of her independence, I have no doubt. Few, if any, efforts for the extension of the blessings of free government in any part of the world have been made since the establishment of our own independence, that have failed to excite our earnest and sincere wishes for their success. But they have never been permitted to withdraw us from the faithful performance of our duty as a neutral nation. They were excited, and deeply too, at the commencement of the French revolution; they were revived in the struggle of the South American states for the establishment of their independence; they have been put to their severest trial in this very contest between Texas and Mexico. Yet, in that whole period of time, amidst the convulsions of empires and the lawlessness of power by which many of its possessors have been distinguished, it has been a cardinal point in the administration of the affairs of this republic to adhere with the strictest fidelity to the rule which was laid down by Washington, enforced by Jefferson and respected with unabated sincerity by his successors.

There is another circumstance which is well calculated to mislead us upon this subject. Many, if not most, of the persons to be affected by the decision of this question, were once citizens of the U. States, and have still their relatives and friends amongst us. I am not unaware of the hazard to which I expose my standing with the latter, in speaking thus unreservedly upon a point so well calculated to excite deep feelings. This is perhaps more particularly applicable to the portion of my fellow citizens, of whom it was aptly and appropriately said by one of their own number, that "they are the children of the sun, and partake of its warm fire."—Yet, whether we stand or fall in the estimation of our countrymen, it is always true wisdom, as well as true morality, to hold fast to the truth. It is, moreover, a consolation to know, that if to nourish enthusiasm is one of the effects of a genial climate, it at the same time seldom fails to give birth to a chivalrous spirit, which will not permit itself to be outdone in the extent or sincerity of its sacrifices at the shrine of patriotism. To preserve our national escutcheon untarnished, has, consequently, if reliance can be placed upon our public archives, been an object of unceasing solicitude with southern statesmen.

Nothing is either more true or more extensively known than that Texas was wrested from Mexico, and her independence established through the instrumentality of citizens of the United States. Equally true is it that this was done not only against the wishes, but in direct contravention of the best efforts of our government to prevent our citizens from engaging in the enterprise. Efforts have nevertheless, not been wanting on the part of those who are not over-anxious for the credit of republican governments, to misrepresent our views in this respect—to cause it to be believed that our efforts to prevent unlawful participation by our citizens in that struggle were insincere; that we coveted this portion of the territory of Mexico; and having failed to obtain it by fair purchase, or by negotiation, we saw in this movement a preliminary step, which would, in the end, be equally subservient to our views upon Texas. No one can have had better opportunities of knowing how unfounded these injurious imputations were than myself. As early as when president Houston first went to Texas, I believe in 1829, I was consulted by general Jackson upon the subject of a private letter addressed by him to the honorable Mr. Fulton, now senator of the United States, then secretary of the territory of Arkansas, requesting him to cause the movements of general Houston to be watched, and to apprize the president of the first indication on his part of any intention to violate the laws of the United States by an armed incursion into Mexico. From that period to the end of general Jackson's term of office, I am as well satisfied as I can be of any fact, that he was sincerely desirous to perform his whole duty as chief magistrate of the country, and to prevent in this respect, the slightest violation of the laws, with the execution of which he was charged. He no doubt sincerely believed that the incorporation of Texas into the Federal Union would be alike advantageous to her, to Mexico, and to the United States and was ever ready to adopt all proper measures for the accomplishment of that object. But they know very little of general Jackson's true character, who can for a moment permit themselves to believe him capable of doing, countenancing, or advising, a single act which he believed, or had even reason to apprehend, would violate the plighted faith of his country, or infringe upon the duty which it owes to the great family of nations. To prevent our people from going to Texas, and embarking in the war, was an impossibility which neither he nor any other chief magistrate could have accomplished. If they went there without military organization, or armaments, and chose to place themselves beyond the protection of this government, we had no right to control their action; nor do other governments exercise any such right in similar cases. For the suppression of military enterprises, organized and armed here against a nation with which we are at peace, the provisions of our laws are ample. But of the difficulties of enforcing them with a frontier and seaboard like those which open our communication with Texas, no sensible and well informed mind can be ignorant.

For the voluntary action of our government in regard to the subject of annexation, we can have no such explanation to give. The acquisition of so valuable a territory by means which are of questionable propriety, would be a departure from those just principles upon which this government has ever added and which have excited the admiration and secured the respect of the dispassionate and enlightened friends of freedom throughout the world. But I am very sure that we shall all, in the end, so act upon this subject as to put it out of the power of the national enemies of republican institutions to make a plausible charge of infidelity to our avowed principles in respect to it. No one was more deeply sensible of the necessity of the greatest prudence in this particular, or more anxious to secure its observance, than general Jackson. As late as December, 1836—only a few months before the recognition—he thus expresses himself, in a special message to the senate: "But there are circumstances in the relations of the two countries which require us to act, on this occasion, with ever more than our wonted caution. Texas was once claimed as a part of our property; and there are those among our citizens who, always reluctant to abandon that claim, cannot but regard with solicitude the prospect of the union of the territory to this country; a large proportion of its civilived inhabitants are emigrants from the United States, speak the same language with ourselves, cherish the same principles, political and religious, and are bound to many of our citizens by ties of friendship and kindred blood; and, more than all, it is known that the people of that country have instituted the same form of government with our own, and have, since the close of your session, openly resolved on the acknowledgment of their independence, to seek admission into the Union as one of the federal States. This last circumstance is a matter of peculiar delicacy, and forces upon us considerations of the gravest character. The title of Texas to the territory she claims, is identified with her independence. She asks us to acknowledge that title to the territory, with an avowed design to treat immediately of its transfer to the United States. It becomes us to beware of a early movement, as it might subject us, however unjustly to the imputation of seeking to establish the claims of our neighbors to a territory, with a view to its subsequent acquisition by ourselves."

It has been urged, from a quarter entitled to great respect, and reasoned, too, with no inconsiderable degree of cogency, that the acquisition of Texas now, in the mode proposed, would be liable to no greater objection than the accomplishment of the same object would have been either in 1827 or 1829, when it was attempted by two successive administrations to purchase it from Mexico. If I were to go into a discussion of this question, and the facts necessarily connected with it, I should be writing a book instead of a letter; nor is it necessary that I should. I will therefore content myself with saying, that with every disposition to look at the subject in all its bearings with an impartial eye, I have not been able to see the analogy which is claimed to exist between the two cases. But if it were even admitted that the able men who were, at those respective periods, at the end of the government, under strong convictions of the importance of the acquisition of Texas to the U. States, so far precipitated their measures for the accomplishment of that object, as to have endangered the good faith and pacific relations of the United States (which I do not admit), we could still only convince ourselves on their failure, but could not thereby justify the present movement, if it is not right in itself, and capable of justification on other grounds. I by no means contend that a formal recognition of the independence of Texas by Mexico is necessary to justify us in assenting to her annexation to the United States. Time and circumstances may work such a change in the relations between those two countries, as to render an act of that character, on the part of Mexico, unnecessary and unimportant. What I mean to say, is, that from all the information I have been able to acquire upon the subject, no change has yet taken place in those regions that would make the objections, which I have here detailed, inapplicable.

It is said, also, that if Texas is not acquired now, the opportunity will be forever lost—that some other power will acquire it; and, indeed, some of the rumors of the day have gone so far as to say that the Texan minister is already instructed, in case of failure here, to proceed forthwith to Europe, with all authority for the accomplishment of that object. We must not forget, that besides great public considerations, there are extensive private interests involved in this matter; and we may therefore well be distrustful of the thousand rumors which are from day to day put afloat upon this subject. What a comparatively few individuals, acting under the influence of personal interest, may not desire to have done, I will not undertake to say, or to conjecture. But that the people of Texas—so many of whom carry in their veins the blood of our revolutionary ancestors—thousands of whom are thoroughly imbued with democratic principles—who achieved by their own gallantry that independence which we were the first to acknowledge—who have established and subsequently maintain institutions similar to our own; that such a people and such a government will ever be found capable of sending a minister to the crowned heads of Europe, to barter away their young and enterprising republic, and all that they have purchased with their blood, to the highest bidder, is what I cannot believe; in the possibility of "so apostate and unnatural a connexion?" I can have no faith.

It is also apprehended by many, that the British authorities, will attempt to make Texas a British colony or dependency. I find it difficult to credit the existence of such infatuation on the part of any European power. I cannot bring myself to believe that any European government which has not already made up its mind to provoke a war with this country, will ever attempt to colonize Texas, either in form or in substance. If there be any such power, the considerations to which I have adverted, would soon lose most of their importance; for opportunities would not then be slow in presenting themselves for the conquest of whatever territory might, in that event, be deemed necessary to our security, in legitimate self defence. Commercial favors Texas has, to the same extent as other independent powers, the right to dispose of as she thinks proper; subject only to the penalties which are certain, sooner or later, to follow in the wake of national injustice. But European colonization of Texas is another and a very different matter—a matter in respect to the ultimate consequence of which no European nation can possibly deceive either herself or us. I have no access to the sources of true information in respect to the degree of credit which may be due to these rumors; but our government ought, without doubt, to exercise a most jealous vigilance against the extension of British influence, and indeed foreign influence, or dominion of any kind, or from any quarter, either in Texas, or in any portions of the continent bordering on the Gulf of Mexico. If the time ever comes when the question resolves itself into whether Texas shall become a British dependency or colony, or a constitutional portion of this union, the great principle of self-defence, applicable as well to nations as to individuals, would, without doubt, produce as great a unanimity amongst us in favor of the latter alternative, as can ever be expected on any great question of foreign or domestic policy.

Having now replied, in the fullest and frankest manner, to both the questions which you have propounded to me, I might here close this letter; but being sincerely anxious to put you, and others occupying the same position, in possession of my views and opinions upon the whole subject, as far as they can with propriety be now formed and expressed, I will go a few steps farther.

Occasions do sometimes present themselves, in the administration of public affairs, when the decisions of great questions can be safely anticipated by those whose subsequent duty it may become to pass upon them; but to justify such a course, those questions must be such as are unavoidably dependent upon circumstances and considerations of a fixed and settled character. I have not been able to regard this as being, in all its respects, a case of that description. It is a matter affecting our foreign relations, in respect to which every enlightened nation makes it a rule to avoid, as far as practicable, public annunciation of its proceedings and intentions beyond what is deemed necessary either to justify its past course, or to make others sensible of its determination to resist aggression, whether present or prospective. As the action of the executive upon all questions that affect our relations with other countries, must be more or less influenced by their conduct towards us, it is, in general, desirable that his future course should not be embarrassed by assurances given at a period when no safe opinion could be formed of what that conduct would be. In respect even to motives of a domestic character, it could scarcely be deemed consistent with that prudence and calm discretion which, in public as well as private affairs, is of such inestimable value, to bind ourselves in advance in respect to the particular line of conduct we will hereafter adopt in a case of such magnitude as the present. When the period for definitive action shall have arrived, the considerations now taken into view may have lost its weight they at present possess in the estimation of the public; and others, not now regarded as of any value, may, in the mean time, arise to affect materially, if not to change, the whole aspect of the subject. The present condition of the relations between Mexico and Texas may soon be so far changed as to weaken, and perhaps to obviate entirely, the objections against the immediate annexation of the latter to the United States, which I have here set forth, and to place the question on different grounds. Should such a state of things arise, and I be found in charge of the responsible duties of president, you may be assured that I would meet the question, if then presented to me, with a sincere desire to promote the result which I believed best calculated to advance the permanent welfare of the whole country. In the discharge of this, the common duty of all our public functionaries, I would not allow myself to be influenced by local or sectional feelings. I am not, I need hardly say to you, an untried man in respect to my disposition or ability to disregard any feelings of that character in the discharge of official duties. You, as well as all others, have therefore at least some grounds on which to form an opinion as to the probable fidelity with which these assurances would be observed.

I shall add a few words on another aspect of the question, and then dismiss the subject. Mexico may carry her persistance in refusing to acknowledge the independence of Texas, and in destructive but fruitless efforts to reconquer that state, so far as to produce, in connexion with other circumstances, a decided conviction on the part of a majority of the people of the United States, that the permanent welfare, if not absolute safety to all, make it necessary that the proposed annexation should be effected, be the consequences what they may. The question may be asked, what, under such circumstances, would be the use you would make of the executive power, if intrusted to your hands? Would it be wielded to defeat, or to carry into effect the ascertained wishes of our people? My reply to such a supposition is, that I can conceive of no public questions, in respect to which it is more eminently proper that the opinions and wishes of the people of the different states, should be consulted, and being ascertained, treated with greater respect than those which relate either to the admission of a new member into the confederacy, or the acquisition of additional territory, with a view to such a result; and that, if any application for annexation, under such circumstances, were made to me, I would feel it to be my duty to submit the same to congress for a public expression of their opinion, as well upon the propriety of annexation, as to regard to the terms upon which it should take place. If, after the whole subject had been brought before the country, and fully discussed, as it now will be, the senate and house of representatives, a large portion of the former, and the whole of the latter having been chosen by the people, after the question of annexation had been brought before the country for its mature consideration, should express an opinion in favor of annexation, I would hold it to be my farther duty to employ the executive power to carry into full and fair effect the wishes of a majority of the people of the existing states, thus constitutionally and solemnly expressed.

There may, notwithstanding, be those, on both sides of this great question, who are unwilling to confer their suffrages on one who is not prepared to give them specific pledges in regard to the course he would, if elected, pursue in respect to the various aspects in which this matter may hereafter be presented. To all such I have only to say—and I do so with the greatest sincerity—that I have not the slightest disposition to question their right so to regulate their conduct, and will be the last to complain of its exercise. If there be any one who they believe can be more safely intrusted with their interest in this or any other of the great questions of public policy which are likely to arise in the administration of the government, or whose assurances as to his future course are more satisfactory to them, they will, without doubt, be well warranted in giving him the preference, and they may be assured that no one will more cheerfully acquiesce in a decision made from such motives, than myself. I have expressed a willingness to discharge, to the best of my abilities, the responsible duties of the highest office in question, should the democracy of the U. States be able and willing to re-elect me to the same. But I can take no steps to obtain it by which my ability to discharge its duties impartially and usefully to every portion of our common country would be impaired; nor can I in any extremity, be induced to cast a shade over the motives of my past life, by changes or concealments of opinions maturely formed upon a great national question, for the unworthy purpose of increasing my chances for political promotion.

    I am, sir, very respectfully, your
    friend and obedient servant,

                                        M. Van Buren

    Van Buren's statement on the annexation of Texas, as in Clay's case based primarily upon principle and not political expediency, unquestionably cost him the Democratic nomination in 1844, and might well have led to the Mexican War. If Van Buren had not spoken out so unequivocally, he would have received the Democratic nomination, and neither he nor Clay, when elected President, would have continued Tyler's policy of immediate annexation, thus provoking Mexico into war. Both men were statesmen as well as politicians; however, in Clay's case, he gambled on the speculation that his statement would win more votes in the North than it would lose in the South, a calculation he further undermined by his continued vacillation on this issue and on the slavery issue throughout the campaign. If either Clay or Van Buren had gone to the White House, the chances are that they would have negotiated a settlement with Mexico in time to avert war.[45] What the Mexicans wanted above all else was some sign of humility on the part of the United States, in the face of their great loss of land and prestige—some recognition of their dignity and rights. They received precious little of either from the Tyler or the Polk administrations.
    But both Clay and Van Buren did speak out on this issue, and it cost Van Buren the nomination and Clay the election. It also provided the rationale for Polk's last-minute "dark horse" candidacy. Van Buren had the nomination all but sewn up at the time he released his annexation letter, but the concern and growing opposition which his views produced within his party stimulated forces which were later able to

block his nomination. They would include members of his party in Congress who were horrified by his position—Calhounites, Texans, southerners of all types and descriptions, and from all states, and Democrats throughout the country who had been bitten by the "manifest destiny" bug. Washington was in an uproar as Democratic congressmen caucused to hear anti-Van Buren speeches. Clay, who was in Washington at the time, observed that he had never seen the Democratic party in "such a state of utter disorder, confusion and decomposition" as developed in the wake of the Van Buren letter.[46] Even once loyal Virginia "abandoned ship," and the New York-Virginia axis flew apart as the Virginia leaders realized they could not continue to hold their supporters in line in the face of Van Buren's statement.

Polk was the principal beneficiary of this uproar and dissension. He had been maneuvering slowly and very quietly to capture the vice presidential nomination, having failed in his effort to obtain that nomination in 1840. His first and most formidable obstacle was the dissension within his own state party. The two statewide defeats the Democrats suffered in Tennessee shattered their confidence, and encouraged opposition to the established leadership. The state party was divided over their preference in the presidential sweepstakes, and although Polk favored Van Buren over Cass, he succeeded in sending a noncommitted delegation to the national convention, but they were firmly committed to supporting his candidacy for the vice presidency.

The scene abruptly changed with Van Buren's letter. Jackson was furious and urged that it disqualified Van Buren from seeking the presidency in 1844. The aging warrior was emotionally distraught over the episode and physically wracked with pain and sickness; he was hardly in any position to rally his faculties to intervene. But he did, nevertheless, in one of his last acts of supreme will. Jackson was at first torn between his affection for Van Buren and his strong convictions on annexation, but he soon made up his mind to write to his old Kitchen Cabinet advisor, Francis Preston Blair, that he was "for the annexation regardless of all consequences."[47] For a time he considered the possibility that a strong convention resolution on annexation might swing Van Buren into line, but his sense of political reality convinced him that this would not work and that Van Buren would have to withdraw so the Democratic party could go before the country as the party of annexation; this they could never do with Martin Van Buren as their candidate for President. Jackson was also convinced that if this advice was not heeded, the party would lose the election. Without question, he was right.

Meanwhile Polk had been out of political circulation, visiting his plantation in Mississippi. When he returned to Tennessee in mid-April, he was interrogated from several sources with regard to his opinion on immediate annexation. His response was prompt; he answered that he favored "immediate re-annexation," arguing as Jackson did that Texas had originally been part of the United States until it was unwisely ceded to Spain in the Florida Treaty of 1819.[48] He argued that United States authority should replace British influence in Texas and in the Oregon Territory and

> let the fixed policy of our government be, not to permit Great Britain or any other foreign power to plant a colony or hold dominion over any portion of the people or territory of either.[49]

Tennessee Democrats flocked around Polk after he published this statement. A rally was held in Nashville to exploit the great advantage they had over the Whigs on the issue of Texas. By then they were familiar with Clay's position on annexation and they compared Polk's statement favorably with it, but they were still unaware that the Democratic standard-bearer was in agreement with the Whig candidate on this question. When Tennessee Democrats learned of Van Buren's letter they were demoralized. There was no longer any chance of holding the support of the state delegation for him. Many talked openly of a "southern Ticket for President & V. Prest.," and Polk's name was mentioned by more than one of his supporters as a possibility, not simply for Vice President but for President.[50] But it was Andrew Jackson who put the real force behind this proposal. Two weeks after receiving word of Van Buren's letter, Jackson summoned his friend Polk to the Hermitage for an historic interview. The former President had written a detailed refutation of Van Buren's arguments and he was determined to make the document public. It contained an affectionate expression of regard for his former Vice President who had succeeded him in the White House, for "Old Hickory" wrote, "No difference on this subject can change my opinion of his character"; but this did not interfere with his criticisms which were based primarily on the argument that Van Buren failed to consider seriously enough "the probability of a dangerous interference with the affairs of Texas by a foreign power."[51]

Other visitors to the Hermitage indicated that the General's "dander is up," and that he felt Van Buren had cut his own throat politically by publishing his letter. Jackson wanted the New Yorker to remove himself and make way for "an annexation man" from the southwest who could redeem Tennessee and some of its neighboring states from the recent ascendancy of the Whigs. He concluded his analysis of the situation, according to Polk's account to Cave Johnson, by suggesting that Polk was "the most available man," and should choose his Vice President from the North.[52]

This was heady wine for the man who would later be referred to as "Young Hickory." As a veteran and successful politician, Polk certainly was not without personal ambition. However, it is somewhat doubtful whether before this the presidency ever seemed to be remotely within his grasp.[53] And yet Silas Wright, esteemed senator from New York and Van Buren's closest confidant, indicated to a close associate of Polk's that in the event that Van Buren did step aside, Polk would be "the only man he thought the Northern democrats would support . . . because [the Tennessean] was known to be firm and true to the cause."[54]

In reply to Jackson's proposal, Polk answered modestly that he had "never aspired so high, and that in all probability the attempt to place me in the first position would be utterly abortive."[55] But he went on, "In the confusion which will prevail and I fear distract your counsels at Baltimore—there is no telling what may occur."[56] He pointed out that the current sentiment in favor of the annexation of Texas was overwhelming and any man who opposed it "will be crushed by it."[57]

I have stood by *Mr. V. B.* and will stand by him as long as there is hope, but I now dispair of his election—even if he is nominated.[58]

Tongue in cheek, Polk insisted that he was interested in the vice presidential nomination, but that his friends "can use my name in any way that they may think proper."[59] He meant them to be cautious, but not to miss any opportunities.

Van Buren entered the Democratic Convention of 1844 in a condition very similar to that of Clay at Harrisburg in 1839. He possessed a majority of the delegates' votes, but his opposition was well organized, very shrewd and the momentum was all in their direction. The delegates were not seriously supporting any single candidate, but were determined to prevent Van Buren from capturing the nomination. There were three procedural measures essential for the convention to adopt in order for the opposition to achieve their goal. The first was to capture the position of presiding officer of the gathering, and this they proceeded to do by simply bullying their way to the front of the auditorium, taking over the platform and then proceeding to nominate and elect a permanent president to the convention, who was favorable to their interests. This was all accomplished before most of the delegates were properly seated.

The anti-Van Buren forces were also intent upon readopting the two-thirds majority rule for the presidential nomination. Van Buren had a majority but it was extremely doubtful if he could increase it to two-thirds under any circumstances. When the Van Buren forces finally woke up, they discovered that the convention was being stolen from them. Their only chance to defeat the adoption of the two-thirds majority rule was to force the convention to record its votes on a unit basis; that is each state would vote its full weighted delegation in favor of the candidate who commanded the most votes among the delegates, thus neutralizing the opposition strength in some of the major Van Buren delegations. But Van Buren lost this opportunity when the opposition's presiding officer ruled against this procedure. The real reason for this series of early defeats was not only that the Van Buren forces were caught asleep at the starting gate, but also that there was substantial anti-Van Buren opposition lurking behind the facades of many of the well-instructed Van Buren delegates, and when an issue of procedure was forced to a vote, they voted their sentiments rather than their mandates.

After the adoption of the two-thirds majority rule, it was all but hopeless for Van Buren. Although Cass continued to gain strength, it was clear that he was not an overwhelming convention favorite either. The underlying sentiment for a strong annexation candidate was substantial, but no candidate could hope to amass a two-thirds majority without adding the Van Buren supporters to his camp. Polk, who had surmised this would be the case weeks before the convention, had bent over backwards to convince Van Buren of his personal integrity and his full support as long as he had a chance to win. He could not swing the Tennessee delegation behind his candidacy because of the Texas issue, but he did his best to neutralize their outright opposition to the New Yorker.

After the fifth ballot when Van Buren lost even his numerical majority over Cass, his supporters realized it was hopeless and that their only chance of maintaining some semblance of influence was to help determine the alternate candidate. At this point the first American presidential "dark horse" emerged, smelling sweet and innocent as a rose. It took several ballots for the convention to realize that he was the only candidate it could really agree upon, but once the steam roller began moving with the Van Buren supporters leading the way, the result was inevitable. A miracle had taken place in Baltimore, and the Democratic party selected a candidate for President on the ninth ballot who had not had a single pledged delegate before the convention began.

Many factors entered into this unexpected victory, but the most essential were Van Buren's letter on immediate annexation, the reaction of the regular Democratic leadership in Congress to his arguments, and the strong, perhaps overwhelming, sentiment in the country (or at least within the Democratic party) not only for annexation, but manifest destiny, as applied to Oregon and California and all of the territory east of these areas and north of the Rio Grande (del Norte). Polk stated his position on these questions early and unequivocally. This was the principal reason why the Democrats turned to him to lead their campaign to capture the national government.

It is also probably the reason why he won the presidency in his close battle against Henry Clay. Clay was far better known throughout the country than Polk, and over the years had built up a legion of followers in most states. He was the acknowledged intellectual and political leader of the Whig party and a man well-liked, even by some of his strongest opponents. He was clearly in command of his party, and unlike Polk, he was a consistent winning candidate in his own state. But like Van Buren, the public understood him to be on the wrong side of the annexation question, and for that reason, he lost many of the critical votes which would have put him over the top.

The Whigs clearly wanted Clay as their candidate. They had previously been betrayed by pseudo-Whig John Tyler, and too late they realized their mistake in not having nominated their real leader in 1839. In 1844 he captured the party nomination by unanimous acclamation, and the party was united behind him. Clay expected to face Van Buren, and correctly guessed that they were in agreement on the annexation issue and could neutralize it in the campaign. Under these circumstances their fight would be over traditional issues—a well-regulated currency, a tariff for revenue, with discriminating protection for "the domestic labor of the country," distribution of land sale proceeds and, of course, reform of "executive unsurpation." But the mood of the country had changed in four years, and these issues no longer triggered the enthusiastic response they had in 1840. Furthermore Van Buren was not nominated by the Democrats and Clay was forced to contend with James Polk, a fervent annexationist and a typical American expansionist.

Clay would not have been so vulnerable if he had not written so many letters on the subject of Texas. He had opposed the original treaty with Spain when Texas was traded away for the Floridas, and his record on Texas was clear of any recorded votes or statements that revealed any opposition to eventual statehood for the territory. But he had been appalled by Tyler's secret diplomacy, and outraged by his provoking insults to Mexico, and he sensed very surely that the President's policy would lead to war. Furthermore, the leaders of his party agreed with him on this issue, and their conservative bias favored diplomacy and negotiations with Mexico as well as with Texas. In addition to all this, he probably reasoned that there were more votes to be gained in the North by opposing immediate annexation, than to be salvaged in the South by joining Tyler and Calhoun in supporting it.

This was a costly error in judgment, however. It lost critical votes in the South and did not gain that many in the North. Clay (and Van Buren too) had the only reasonable and honorable position on the annexation of Texas. They certainly were not opposed to annexation per se, but they would not consider it apart from and until the question of borders was resolved with the heretofore friendly neighbor to the South. This position was weak politically, for although it was supported by many thoughtful Americans, it gained no new adherents for the candidate who needed enthusiasm and new supporters to win. If the Whigs had consolidated their victory in 1840 with a brilliantly successful administration, they probably would have held the support they had attracted and perhaps have added substantially to them in 1844. But they won the election and lost the victory. The White House was in hostile hands, their policies defeated or untried, the patronage distributed elsewhere to would-be Tyler supporters, most of whom were Democrats and the rest turncoat Whigs. In short they had lost the initiative, the historical momentum they had going for them in 1840, and what momentum there was left in the American environment was generated by the expansionist dream. Polk's unequivocal statement on Texas and Oregon attracted these forces, helped regroup and consolidate a badly divided Democratic party, and won the election.

Once it was clear that a Democratic candidate who was an unequivocal champion of annexation had been nominated, there was absolutely no chance for the third party candidacy of John Tyler, who was nominated by a convention of essentially patronage serving officeholders. Tyler refused to withdraw from the presidential race, however, until he had the assurance of Polk's representatives that members of his administration would be favorably considered for reappointment by Polk. The Tennessean was shrewd enough not to handle these negotiations himself, nor to commit himself to anything in writing, but very skilfully maneuvered Jackson into the picture and used future Secretary of the Treasury Robert J. Walker and others to handle this sensitive problem.

Much has been made of the marginal gains Polk achieved by his carefully wrought statement on the protective tariff, which was aimed at the iron moulders and allied industries in Pennsylvania and the abolitionist Liberty party voters, most of whom were former Whigs who Clay alienated by what they considered his equivocations on slavery. Clay, himself, attributed the loss primarily to the strong immigrant vote against him. All of this was true and has been carefully documented, along with the fact that with 5,000 more votes Clay would not have had to carry votes from marginal groups, had he led a still dynamic and successful party in the election of 1844. Despite the fact that they returned to power in 1848 (again for very special reasons), the Whigs lost their golden opportunity to govern the nation in 1841 by reason of their own internal conflicts and ideological contradictions. As a result, in 1844 they were just another political party struggling to maintain power but with no clear sense of national destiny, nor the sureness or the confidence that such an historical mission provides.

Polk on the other hand acted like a man who had that sense of destiny in his bones. His nomination, of course, came to him as an unexpected accident of fortune, but once in the White House, he seemed to know what he was about and precisely where he was going. He revealed none of the misgivings and hesitations that a man might usually exhibit, particularly if he questions the rightness or the morality of his actions and objectives. Polk was not only determined, he was convinced that his determination was right, and he never wavered or hesitated for long in pursuing his objectives. This is a good part of what constitutes greatness. If he had been right, he would have possessed the other part of the formula. But right or wrong, he unquestionably advanced the war powers of the President beyond anything yet imagined by his predecessors, and established the foundations of the modern presidency and its agonizing problems in the middle of the nineteenth century.

Tyler's outrageous unconstitutional behavior led Polk to the brink of this experience. He brought the annexation question to the boiling point, only to be frustrated by Thomas Hart Benton and the Senate's overwhelming defeat of his treaty. But he certainly did not give up. He went on to suggest to the House of Representatives that he would look favorably upon annexation through another means (a joint resolution possibly?) if the treaty method had been excluded. Here Polk's successful Democratic campaign aided Tyler in his ambition to crown his four years in the White House by achieving the annexation of Texas. Polk unified the badly divided Democratic party in the course of this campaign and succeeded in neutralizing the strong opposition to annexation within its ranks. Some of his methods smacked of deception, but Polk was no moralist, and the successful achievement of a desired end, justified for him the employment of methods which might have seemed questionable under other circumstances.

Deceit in High Office

Tyler's hairshirt in his effort to achieve ratification of the annexation treaty had been Benton and his followers who joined with the Whigs in defeating the measure. But even without Benton, the treaty would probably not have had the necessary two-thirds vote. Only a majority vote was necessary to carry a joint resolution, however, and in this instance Benton and company were critically important, yet the winds were shifting. Senator Benton had run into substantial criticism on the home front for his stand against the treaty, and was instructed by the Missouri legislature to drop his condition for Mexican consent and to work in favor of annexation. In addition, the question had become a source of dispute between the senator and some of his former allies, including Jackson and Polk, and he was ready to modify his stand somewhat. Tyler and Calhoun, however, were trying to cram the defeated treaty down the throats of Congress in the form of a joint resolution embodying all of the provisions of the original treaty. The stage was set for another impasse.

Benton's original position was that a treaty of annexation could be approved only after agreement between Mexico and the United States on the question of the Texas border. This was the principal argument of those like Clay and Van Buren who had opposed the treaty. Under pressure Benton waived this critical condition, and in the post-election session of Congress he submitted a second resolution calling for the President to negotiate the terms of a new treaty of annexation with the Texas authorities. Agreement crystallized around this proposal, but again Calhoun intervened and used his influence to convince southern Democrats to oppose the Benton proposal and favor a resolution which embodied the defeated treaty provisions. The compromise resolution which finally passed the House called for Texas being admitted to the Union as a state without having to undergo again the treaty-making procedure in the Senate; four additional states were to be formed out of her territory, and slavery would be barred from any such state north of the Missouri Compromise line. Another impasse developed when it became clear that the Benton and the Van Buren forces would not support this proposal. Among their more serious objections was the fact that the proposal clearly incorporated provisions which were in the nature of a treaty, while obviously circumventing the treaty-making procedures of the Constitution.

Another serious objection to the resolution by the northern Whigs and some Democrats was the proliferation of additional slave states, embodying the two-thirds representation but "no vote" principle, which had been adopted as a compromise at the Constitutional Convention. Subject to considerable re-examination and protest, the principle caused much irritation as the northern states realized how it continued to diminish their electoral power. This particular development will be discussed in greater detail further on.

President-elect Polk arrived in Washington just about that time and used his influence to bring about a compromise. On several occasions he had expressed his strong desire to achieve annexation before his inauguration, which was also the day that Congress adjourned. He felt that the question had been settled in the presidential election of 1844 and he did not want it to erupt all over again at the beginning of his administration. The President-elect was already showing something of his grasp of the nature of his office, and also of his ability to cope with its problems. Although Polk was adamant in declining to pass judgment on the steps being taken by the outgoing administration, he was not adverse to using his potential power with the Congress to bring about actions consistent with his objectives.

Polk worked closely with two members of his future cabinet who were in the Senate, Robert J. Walker, senator from Mississippi, who was to become secretary of the treasury, and James Buchanan from Pennsylvania, who would be the next secretary of state. They attempted to press the House resolution on the Benton and Van Buren forces, but to no avail. Finally Polk intervened personally and proposed that both the Benton proposal and the House resolution be incorporated into a resolution which would give the President the option of selecting either one. Both groups eventually were persuaded to accept this compromise, but not until Polk had secretly assured the Benton and Van Buren representatives that he would choose the Benton proposal when it came before him in the White House.

This was assurance enough and they went along with the combined resolution, incorporating both alternatives. Calhoun was outraged by all of this, and although not entirely satisfied himself with the House plan, he persuaded Tyler rather than Polk to make the choice between the alternative methods and put his decision immediately into effect. Tyler followed this advice and two days before the new President was to be inaugurated, he dispatched a special courier to Texas, with instructions to present the House proposal to the Texas authorities. He had first informed Polk that he intended to do this and requested his opinion, but the President-elect refused to pass judgment on the outgoing President's actions. Later it may become evident why this was not simply a silence motivated by principle, but rather a conscious and devious method of avoiding his previous agreement with Benton's supporters.

Polk could have easily indicated his disapproval of Tyler's action at their pre-inaugural interview, and even if the outgoing President had acted in defiance of his opinion, Polk could have countermanded Tyler's decision and selected the Benton alternative, as he had promised to do. He could even have done so had he refrained from commenting on Tyler's decision on the basis of principle, as he claimed. The truth is that he was in favor of ramming through the annexation of Texas as quickly as possible, and he too favored the House proposal. He simply used Tyler and Calhoun's outraged action as a means of justifying a decision of which he had already approved. In fact, after he was inaugurated, President Polk did send another courier off to Texas who overtook the Tyler messenger before he arrived, but his instructions were to reinforce immediate annexation rather than to employ the procedure laid down in the Benton proposal.

Polk quickly revealed in this incident and in subsequent actions that there would be no retreat from the expanded use of presidential power, nor would he allow an overly strict interpretation of the Constitution to hamstring his decisions when he considered the national interest to be at stake. He wanted Texas and this was the safest way to acquire it. The treaty-making procedure might forestall annexation for many more months, or defeat it once again, and he was not willing to run that risk. The reasoning was no doubt correct, but the implications of it were unwise and unconstitutional. In the long reach of history, the precedent established in this situation by both Tyler and Polk was harmful to the best interests of the country and to the future of a responsible theory and practice of presidential power.

Polk Prepares for War

As early as 1843 Mexico warned the United States that annexation of Texas would lead to war between the two countries. When annexation was finally accomplished, the Mexican ambassador to the United States, General Juan Almonte, demanded his passport, and this country was confronted with a diplomatic crisis tottering on the brink of war. The serious problem of the sovereignty of huge areas of land, which was triggered by the annexation crisis, had never really been discussed by the two countries. Clearly some extraordinary diplomacy would have to be used.

The annexation procedure dragged through the first nine months of the Polk administration, and the President was not at all hasty in approaching the Mexican government. On the other hand, right from the beginning of his tenure in Washington, Polk alerted the military commander most directly involved, General Zachary Taylor, and informed him that hostilities might develop over annexation. As early as June 15, 1845, General Taylor was informed that Texas would probably ratify the annexation proposal by July 4, 1845; realizing this, he was instructed to move his troops into Texas, with the banks of the Rio Grande[61] as his eventual line of defense. Up to that time no diplomatic overtures by this country to Mexico had been initiated. On July 11, 1845, similar orders relevant to patrolling the coastal waters of Mexico were issued to Commander David Conner of the United States Navy.

On July 30, 1845, General Taylor was given a direct order to cross the Nueces River and to deploy his troops on the disputed Mexican territory:

> While avoiding, as you have been instructed to do, all aggressive measures towards Mexico, as long as the relations of peace exist between that republic and the United States, you are expected to occupy, protect and defend, the territory of Texas. The Rio Grande is claimed to be the boundary between the two countries, and up to this boundary you are to extend your protection, only excepting any posts on the eastern side thereof, which are in the actual occupancy of Mexican forces, or Mexican settlements over which the republic of Texas did not exercise jurisdiction at the period of annexation, or shortly before that event. It is expected that, in selecting the establishment for your troops, you will approach as near the boundary line, the Rio Grande, as prudence will dictate. With this view, the President desires that your position, for part of your forces at least, should be West of the river Nueces.[62]

Polk's later argument was that war had come about as a defensive action in repelling an attack, and in effect an invasion by the Mexican army. It is interesting to note in the order of July 30 that the defensive action that the secretary of war and the President were preparing, on territory claimed by Mexico to be under her sovereign jurisdiction, was against a threatened attack, about which the War Department had almost no information, as the following instructions from the secretary of war to General Taylor indicate:

> You are directed to ascertain and communicate to this department, the number of Mexican troops now at Matamoras, and the other Mexican posts along the border, their position, the condition of them, and particularly the measures taken or contemplated to increase or strengthen them. If you should have any reason to believe that the government of Mexico is concentrating forces on the boundaries of the two countries, you will not only act with reference to such a state of things, but give the earliest information to this department.[63]

James Polk was one of the few Presidents of the United States to keep a regular and quite accurate diary of the day-to-day affairs of his office.[64] He started it several months after he was in office, reflecting one day that it would be useful to have an accurate record of a long discussion he had the previous day with his secretary of state, James Buchanan. That first day he recorded his recollections on several sheets of paper, but the next day he procured a blank book, and everyday thereafter (except when he was preoccupied, could find no time, or if he had nothing of importance to record) he kept a condensed record of the day's developments. On the third day of his diarykeeping, the President summarized an important cabinet meeting on the Mexican situation.

President James K. Polk
Diary Entry on Relations with Mexico
August 29, 1845

Milo Milton Quaife, ed., *The Diary of James K. Polk, During His Presidency, 1845-1849* (Chicago, 1910) I, 8-10.

The President called a special meeting of the Cabinet at 12 O'Clock, all the members present except Mr. Mason. The President brought up for consideration our relations with Mexico, and the threatened invasion of Texas with [by] that power. He submitting the following propositions which were unanimously agreed to as follows, *viz.*, If Mexico should declare War or actual hostilities should be commenced by that power, orders to be issued to Gen'l Taylor to attack and drive her back across the Del Norte. Gen'l Taylor shall be instructed that the crossing the Del Norte by a Mexican army in force shall be regarded as an act of War on her part, and in that event Gen'l Taylor to be ordered, if he shall deem it advisable, not to wait to be attacked but to attack her army first. Gen'l Taylor in case of invasion by Mexico to be ordered not only to drive the invading army back to the West of the Del Norte, but to dislodge and drive back in like manner the Mexican post now stationed at Santiago. Gen'l Taylor to be vested with discretionary authority to pursue the Mexican army to the West of the Del Norte, and take Matamoras or any other Spanish Post West of that River, but not to penetrate any great distance into the interior of the Mexican Territory.

Commodore Conner commanding the Home Squadron in the Gulf to be ordered, on hearing that war existed as above described, to Blockade all Mexican ports on the Gulf, to attack and take them if deemed practicable; except of Yucatan and Tobasco, which Departments it is reported refuse to take part in the threatened war against Texas or the U. States. These he is to visit at Campeache and Tobasco, communicate with the inhabitants and inform them that they should not be molested, provided they would agree to take no part in the war.

These orders it was agreed should be prepared by the Secretaries of War and the Navy to be submitted to the Cabinet on to-morrow.

These decisions were translated into official orders to General Taylor the next day by the War Department. By this time Taylor was well encamped on St. James Island, off Aransas Bay in Corpus Christi, Texas, and was preparing for a movement further south and west along the banks of the Rio Grande. He had at his disposal approximately 1,500 regular United States Army troops, and this body was soon increased by auxiliary aid from Texas and the surrounding states of Louisiana, Alabama and Mississippi. The secretary of war, William M. Marcy, called upon the governors of these three states, along with Texas officials, to cooperate with General Taylor in providing military assistance. All of these preparations were very much in progress before any formal diplomatic approach to Mexico was initiated.

By October Taylor had approximately 3,900 officers and men under his command.[65]

These efforts clearly indicated Polk was preparing for war. Was it Polk's opinion that war with Mexico was inevitable and that it was only a question of weeks or months before the shooting began or was there any attempt on the part of his administration to introduce diplomatic initiatives? Certainly the President was not necessarily a warlike person, and if there was a chance that he could obtain peacefully what the country might otherwise acquire through the agony of war, he would certainly have chosen the former. Apart from anything else, however, James Knox Polk was purposeful and determined. Once he set his mind upon an objective, he was not easily discouraged. As James Schouler put it: "What he [Polk] went for he fetched."[66] At the outset of his administration, he told historian George Bancroft, his secretary of the navy:

> There are four great measures which are to be the measures of my administration: one, a reduction of the tariff; another, the independent treasury; a third, the settlement of the Oregon boundary question; and, lastly, the acquisition of California.[67]

It is important to note that Polk was not simply interested in settling the Texas boundary dispute with Mexico. He wanted more land than even the Texans claimed, and he was determined to use the present dispute to achieve this goal. Thus when one raises the question of whether or not Polk wanted peace or war, the answer would be that of course he preferred peace to war, if he could have achieved his goals by means of peace. But that would have been a large order. It was not simply a matter of negotiating a satisfactory settlement of the Texas-Mexican border, but of acquiring all of the land west of the Rio Grande to the shores of the Pacific. Of course the President was willing to pay Mexico for the land (perhaps as much as 40 million dollars), but he was determined he would get it.[68]

Under these circumstances he never entertained the notion of negotiating from a position of weakness, and this explains his ruthless military seizure of land to which Mexico had every legal and historical claim. This also explains why he waited six months before initiating formal diplomatic negotiations with Mexico. He wanted his army and navy in a position to strike, and all of the logistical problems well in hand before he opened negotiations. But he did not initiate informal, even "secret" diplomacy prior to this date. Following his inauguration he recalled the United States minister in Mexico, Wilson Shannon, who had become a source of embarrassment (even to the previous administration), as a result of his heated disputes with the Mexican foreign office. He was not immediately replaced, but the President soon dispatched a "secret agent," a dentist named William S. Parrott, to advance American interests in Mexico. Before undertaking his mission, Parrott had been in Washington, presumably to lobby for his personal claim upon Mexico, which was part of the collective sum the international arbitration commission had awarded to United States citizens who had filed claims against the Mexican government. Polk's biographer, Charles Sellers, points out that the Parrott claims were probably wildly inflated, and that he was particularly hated by the Mexicans.

However, he spoke Spanish well, and moreover was available, so Polk sent him back to Mexico to attempt to exact an agreement from the Mexican government that she sit down and negotiate her complaints with the United States.

Sellers called this Polk's "peace offensive," certainly with tongue in cheek, because he quickly demonstrated why it was just the opposite. It was an inept effort, bound to fail. Every aspect of it was colored with the arrogant and patronizing sense of a superior attempting to "buy off " an inferior. It was conducted against a background of the illegal seizure of sovereign Mexican territory, under the threat of the advancing rifles, muskets and cannons of the United States Army, and by a "secret agent" who was a hated foreigner and was in the process of attempting to extort widely expanded debts from a bankrupt government. The next American representative Polk sent to Mexico was a haughty Louisiana white supremacist who looked down on all non-white races, which of course predominated in Mexico.

This is not to say that Polk wanted the effort to fail. If peace could have been preserved under these circumstances, and his ends still accomplished, so much the better. But one did not go about pacifying an outraged nation in this fashion. Mexico had been defeated in combat by an upstart and disorganized group of American settlers in Texas; she had been deprived of recently won sovereign territory without even as much as a diplomatic apology; finally she was expected to place her seal of legality upon these assaults on her pride and sovereignty for a relatively small sum of money. On top of all this, the United States was to offer to "relieve" Mexico, for further financial considerations, of hundreds of thousands of additional acres of some of the best land on the continent. This was Polk's planned "peace offensive."

Parrott was first dispatched to Mexico to attempt to determine whether or not the Mexican government would receive an American representative authorized to negotiate all differences between the two countries. The annexation of Texas was, of course, not subject to further negotiation. It was to be considered an accomplished fact, although the procedure would not be completed until the following fall. The Polk administration's newly acquired official mouthpiece, the Washington *Union*, however, gave voice to the real expansionist objectives of the mission. "Let the great measure of annexation be accomplished, and with it the questions of boundary and claims," stated Polk's personally selected editor.[69]

The immediate emphasis was placed upon the boundary and claims questions, but once they had been removed, manifest destiny took over. "For who can arrest the torrent that will pour onward to the West? The road to California will be open to us. Who will stay the march of our Western people?" he asked.[70] Would the Mexicans dare resist, this official administration spokesman inquired. Indeed if they did, he left no doubts as to what lay in store for them:

> A corps of properly organized volunteers (and they might be obtained from all quarters of the Union) would invade, overrun, and occupy Mexico. They would enable us not only to take California, but to keep it.[71]

Secretary of State Buchanan's instructions to Parrott indicated that the Polk administration was quite anxious to resolve its misunderstanding with the Mexican government, but certainly not on the basis of yielding any of its claims to the territory which would be incorporated into the Union upon the final resolution of the annexation process.

Secretary of State James Buchanan
Instructions to William S. Parrott,
Confidential Agent of the United States to Mexico
March 28, 1845

William R. Manning, ed., *Diplomatic Correspondence of the United States, Inter-American Affairs: 1831-1860* (Washington, D. C., 1937) VIII, 164-66.

Sir: All diplomatic intercourse having been suspended between the governments of the United States and Mexico, it is the desire of the President to restore such an intercourse if this can be effected consistently with the national honor. To accomplish this purpose he has deemed it expedient to send a confidential agent to Mexico, and reposing confidence in your abilities and patriotism, has selected you as a proper person to execute this important trust. Your success may mainly depend upon your perfect command of temper in all situations and under all circumstances, and upon your prudence in refraining from the least intimation that you are a Government agent, unless this should become indispensable to the success of your mission. The trust confided to you is one of a delicate and important character and may involve the public peace. Should you execute it with skill, ability and success, you will deserve and receive the thanks of the President and of the country. From your long residence in Mexico and your thorough acquaintance with the Mexican people and their language, the President considers you peculiarly qualified for the trust and indulges in favorable anticipations of your success.

You will proceed without delay by the most expeditious route to the City of Mexico, and will there ascertain the temper and tone of the present Mexican Government towards the United States. Such previous knowlege is necessary to enable you to decide upon the manner of approaching the chief officers of that government. From the nature of the case, it is impossible to give you specific instructions as to your mode of proceeding. Nearly all must depend upon your own prudence and discretion. The great object of your mission and that which you will constantly keep in view in all your proceedings, is to reach the President and other high officers of the Mexican government and especially the Minister of Foreign Affairs; and by every honorable effort to convince them that it is the true interest of their country, as it certainly is, to restore friendly relations between the two Republics. Should you clearly ascertain that they are willing to renew our diplomatic intercourse, then and not till then you are at liberty to communicate to them your official character and to state that the United States will send a Minister to Mexico as soon as they receive authentic information that he will be kindly received.

The policy which The President will pursue towards Mexico is best illustrated by the following extract from my note to General Almonte under date of the 10th instant, in answer to his note to Mr. Calhoun of the 6th, protesting against the

Resolution of the late Congress for annexing Texas to the United States, and demanding his passports.

In answer, the Undersigned is instructed to say that the admission of Texas as one of the States of this Union, having received the sanction both of the Legislative and Executive Departments of the Government, is now irrevocably decided, so far as the United States are concerned. Nothing but the refusal of Texas to ratify the terms and conditions on which her admission depends, can defeat this object. It is, therefore, too late at present to reopen a discussion which has already been exhausted and again to prove that Texas has long since achieved her independence of Mexico and now stands before the world, both *de jure* and *de facto*, as a sovereign and independent State amid the family of nations. Sustaining this character and having manifested a strong desire to become one of the members of our Confederacy, neither Mexico nor any other nation will have just cause of complaint against the United States for admitting her into this Union.

The President nevertheless sincerely regrets that the Government of Mexico should have taken offence at these proceedings, and he earnestly trusts that it may hereafter be disposed to view them in a more favorable and friendly light. Whilst entering upon the duties of the Presidential office, he cheerfully declares in advance that his most strenuous efforts shall be devoted to the amicable adjustment of every cause of complaint between the two governments and to the cultivation of the kindest and most friendly relations between the sister Republics.

Whilst, therefore, you ought not to conceal that the reunion of Texas with the United States is already decreed and can never under any circumstances be abandoned, you are at liberty to state your confident belief that in regard to all unsettled questions, we are prepared to meet Mexico in a most liberal and friendly spirit.

You will ascertain the nature and causes of the late revolution in Mexico, and whether the new Government will most probably be permanent, the character of the chiefs of that revolution and what are their dispositions towards the United States and other foreign nations. This and all other information in relation to your mission you will communicate to the Department of State as often as you can obtain safe and secret opportunities.

If upon your arrival at Vera Cruz you should find that the government of Mexico have commenced open hostilities against the United States, you will return immediately. In that unfortunate event we shall be prepared to act promptly and vigorously in maintaining the rights and honor of the country.

Your compensation will be at the rate of eight dollars per day from the time of your departure on the business of your mission, until your return; and you will be allowed your travelling and other expenses during your absence, for which you will take vouchers when they may be obtainable. The sum of one thousand dollars is advanced to you on account.

I am [etc.].

The "Peace Offensive"

Almost six months after the War Department set in motion its plans for quartering a relatively large army on the Mexican border, the Polk administration prepared to launch its formal diplomatic "peace offensive." It was agreed upon at a cabinet meeting in mid-September 1845 to communicate with John Black, the United States consul in Mexico, to confirm reports that had come to the President from Parrott that the Mexican government "is desirous to re-establish Diplomatic relations with the U. States, and that a minister from the U. S. would be received."[72] The cabinet reacted favorably and agreed that Congressman John Slidell from Louisiana should undertake the mission. The following day the cabinet had second thoughts and decided to write to Black to confirm Parrott's information, and to obtain a formal confirmation from the Mexican government as to whether "a Minister would be received."[73] A positive reply was received from Black in about six weeks, and a few weeks later the mission to Mexico was dispatched.

It is instructive to review the correspondence between the major parties involved in this diplomatic prelude to the Mexican war, since it clearly reveals the clumsiness of the much vaunted American "peace offensive." War between Mexico and the United States may have been inevitable under any circumstances, but the diplomatic record indicates the fundamental insensitivity of this nation's diplomats to the interests and aspirations of a different sovereign people. It is clear that Polk and Buchanan would have preferred to avoid war with Mexico if peace could have been obtained on their terms. But they gave no real indication of appreciating how costly and politically dangerous such a "bargain" could be to any Mexican regime which desired to retain power. It involved after all the *de jure* as well as the *de facto* recognition of the Texas-American seizure of huge areas of land, which even the United States had previously acknowledged by treaty to be sovereign Mexican territory. Moreover, it is clear from Secretary Buchanan's instructions to Slidell, that this country's real objectives in these negotiations went considerably beyond the immediate matters at hand, namely the private American indemnity claims against the Mexican government and the settlement of the border dispute. Polk was intent upon asserting American control over all of the territory west of the Rio Grande to the Pacific Ocean, including the port of San Francisco. He was of course willing to pay what he considered to be a fair price for this land, but he intended to obtain it, and if peaceful negotiations did not succeed, military efforts would have to.

Buchanan's instructions to Slidell established the guidelines and also the parameters of the events which followed. They represented a distillation of previous cabinet decisions, and were reflective of the clear objectives and strong determination of the President. There is no question that in his capacity as the directing force of the nation's foreign relations, the President did not exceed his authority in initiating any diplomatic approach to Mexico, but there is considerable question as to whether his support of these diplomatic overtures by utilizing his other role as Commander in Chief of the Armed Forces to issue orders to General Taylor, which were in fact violations of sovereign Mexican territory recognized by this country in previous treaties with Mexico, and never terminated with congressional approval, did not constitute a serious abuse of presidential power, and an expansion of the President's power as Commander in Chief considerably beyond any precedent set in the earlier history of the office.

The secretary's instructions began with his strong emphasis upon the importance of the negotiations to the interests of this country, and his insistence upon excluding from the dispute the countries of Europe, which had previously expressed colonial interest in the affairs of this continent and particularly in matters concerning Mexico. He went on to discuss at length the question of American private party claims against the Mexican government, referring to them in the strongest terms, and asserting:

> The history of no civilized nation presents, in so short a period of time, so many wanton attacks upon the rights of persons and property as have been endured by citizens of the United States from the Mexican authorities.[74]

Buchanan argued that there could be no "serious doubt" with "regard to the right of Texas to the boundary of the Del Norte (Rio Grande) from its mouth to the Paso," but of greater significance to this study were the references to the justifications for the Texas-American claim to this Mexican territory west of the Rio Grande River and south of the Nueces River. Other instructions related to the greatly expanded territorial goals of obtaining additional Mexican territory in the southwest, running from the western border of Texas (whatever that was) to the Pacific Ocean. The American secretary of state admitted that although the United States claimed such territory at the time of the Louisiana Purchase and during the Jefferson and Madison administrations, these claims were negated by the Florida treaty with Spain in 1819, when the United States ceded this area to Spain in return for territory stretching from the mouth of the Mississippi River at New Orleans east to the tip of Florida (including the adjacent islands). The sole basis, then, for claiming this territory in 1845 was the assertion by the Republic of Texas prior to annexation that the Rio Grande was her border. Buchanan made this clear in his instructions to Slidell:

> You have been perfectly familiar with the subject from the beginning, and know that the jurisdiction of Texas has been extended beyond that river [the Nueces] and that the representatives from that country between it and the Del Norte have participated in the deliberations both of her Congress and her Convention. Besides, this portion of the territory was embraced within the limits of ancient Louisiana.[75]

Certainly this must be one of the weakest territorial claims ever made upon a sovereign country by an aggressive and land-hungry neighbor. The claim was based upon assertions advanced by equally greedy Texans. The reference to the claim made prior to the Treaty of Florida when the land was ceded to Spanish Mexico is absurd, and yet it is quite revealing of the lack of substance to the American case in this dispute. One could place the problem in a contemporary context by recalling Adolf Hitler's campaign prior to World War II in which he argued for *lebensraum* for Germany, and her right to annex all territory like the Sudetenland on Germany's border, where a sizeable number of Germans were living. Texas could, of course, advance its claims to this territory as justifiable spoils of its war of independence, but the United States did not even recognize this border (which had been established by Texas fiat) in its annexation resolution, where it referred to "the territory properly included within and rightfully belonging to the Republic of Texas. . . ."[76] Furthermore, Polk ignored his agreement with the Bentonites to carry out their proposal for prior negotiations with Mexico before the annexation process began; he did just the opposite. He also agreed to the most extreme interpretation of the "rights" of Texas, and there is considerable evidence available that his agents (with or without his approval) attempted to further stir up Texas discontent and apprehension about a Mexican military invasion and the need for Texas volunteers to attack the enemy first.[77] In addition to all of this, he marched General Taylor at the head of an army of 3,500 men into the disputed area and ordered them deployed at a critical point along the Rio Grande River, which happened to form the extreme limits of the territory in question. This was hardly the background to the "peace offensive."

In completing his instructions, Buchanan explained to Slidell that his mission was "the most delicate and important which has ever been confided to a citizen of the United States."[78] He warned him that the Mexicans

> are proverbially jealous, and they have been irritated against the United States by recent events and by the intrigues of foreign Powers. To conciliate their good will is indispensable to your success. I need not warn you against wounding their national vanity. You may probably have to endure their unjust reproaches with equanimity. It would be difficult to raise a point of honor between the United States and so feeble and degraded a power as Mexico. This reflection will teach you to bear and forbear much for the sake of accomplishing the great objects of your mission.[79]

A closer look at the negotiations between Slidell and the Mexican foreign minister, Manuel de la Peña y Peña, will indicate how well Slidell responded to this Polonian advice.

Secretary of State James Buchanan
Letter to John Slidell,
United States Minister to Mexico
November 10, 1845

Manning, VIII, 172-82.

Sir: I transmit herewith copies of a despatch, addressed by me under date the 17th September, 1845, to John Black, Esqr., Consul of the United States at the City of

Mexico; of a note written by the Consul to the Mexican Minister for Foreign Affairs, dated 13th October, 1845; and of the answer of that Minister, under date October 15th, 1845.

From these papers you will perceive that the Mexican Government have accepted the overture of the President for settling all the questions in dispute between the two Republics by negotiation; and that consequently the contingency has occurred, in which your acceptance of the trust tendered to you by the President is to take effect. You will, therefore, repair without delay to your post and present yourself to the Mexican Government, as the Envoy Extraordinary and Minister Plenipotentiary of the United States.

In the present crisis of the relations between the two countries, the office for which you have been selected is one of vast importance. To counteract the influence of foreign Powers, exerted against the United States in Mexico, & to restore those ancient relations of peace and good will which formerly existed between the Governments and the citizens of the sister Republics, will be principal objects of your mission. The wretched condition of the internal affairs of Mexico, and the misunderstanding which exists between her Government and the Ministers of France and England, seem to render the present a propitious moment for the accomplishment of these objects. From your perfect knowledge of the language of the country, your well known firmness and ability, and your taste and talent for society, the President hopes that you will accomplish much in your intercourse with the Mexican authorities and people. The early and decided stand which the people of the United States and their Government took and maintained in favor of the independence of the Spanish American Republics on this Continent, secured their gratitude and good will. Unfortunate events have since estranged from us the sympathies of the Mexican people. They ought to feel assured that their prosperity is our prosperity and that we cannot but have the strongest desire to see them elevated, under a free, stable and Republican Government, to a high rank among the nations of the earth.

The nations on the continent of America have interests peculiar to themselves. Their free forms of Government are altogether different from the monarchical institutions of Europe. The interests and the independence of these sister nations require that they should establish and maintain an American system of policy for their own protection and security, entirely distinct from that which has so long prevailed in Europe. To tolerate any interference on the part of European sovereigns with controversies in America; to permit them to apply the worn out dogma of the balance of power to the free States of this continent; and above all, to suffer them to establish new Colonies of their own, intermingled with our free Republics, would be to make, to the same extent, a voluntary sacrifice of our independence. These truths ought everywhere, throughout the continent of America, to be impressed on the public mind. If therefore in the course of your negotiations with Mexico, that Government should propose the mediation or guarantee of any European Power, you are to reject the proposition without hesitation. The United States will never afford, by their conduct, the slightest pretext for any interference from that quarter in American concerns. Separated as we are from the old world, and still further removed from it by the nature of our political institutions, the march of free Government on this continent must not be trammeled by the intrigues and selfish interests of European powers. Liberty here must be allowed to work out its natural results; and these will, ere long, astonish the world.

Neither is it for the interest of those powers to plant colonies on this continent. No settlement of the kind can exist long. The expansive energy of free institutions must soon spread over them. The colonists themselves will break from the mother country, to become free and independent States. Any European nation which should plant a new colony on this continent would thereby sow the seeds of troubles and wars, the injury from which, even to her own interests, would far outweigh all the advantages which she could possibly promise herself from any such establishment.

The first subject which will demand your attention is, the claims of our citizens on Mexico. It would be useless here to trace the history of these claims and the outrages from which they spring. The archives of your Legation will furnish all the necessary information on this subject. The history of no civilized nation presents, in so short a period of time, so many wanton attacks upon the rights of persons and property as have been endured by citizens of the United States from the Mexican authorities. These never would have been tolerated by the United States from any nation on the face of the earth, except a neighbouring and sister Republic.

President Jackson, in his message to the Senate, of the 7th February, 1837, uses the following language with great justice and truth: "The length of time since some of these injuries have been committed, the repeated and unavailing applications for redress, the wanton character of some of the outrages upon the property and persons of our citizens, upon the officers and flag of the United States, independent of recent insults to this Government and people by the late Extraordinary Mexican Minister, would justify, in the eyes of all nations, immediate war."

Still, he was unwilling to resort to this last extremity, without "giving to Mexico one more opportunity to atone for the past, before we take redress into our own hands." Accordingly, he recommended, "that an Act be passed, authorizing reprisals, and the use of the naval force of the United States by the Executive against Mexico, to enforce them, in the event of a refusal by the Mexican Government to come to an amicable adjustment of the matters in controversy between us, upon another demand thereof, made from on board one of our vessels of war on the coast of Mexico."

This message was referred to the Committee on Foreign Relations, which, on the 19th of February, 1837, made a report to the Senate, entirely in accordance with the message of the President in regard to the outrages and wrongs committed by Mexico on citizens of the United States. They recommended, however, that another demand should be made for redress upon the Mexican Government, in pursuance of the form required by the 34th Article of our Treaty with Mexico, and the result submitted to Congress for their decision, before actual hostilities should be authorized. The Committee say, "After such a demand, should prompt justice be refused by the Mexican Government, we may appeal to all nations, not only for the equity and moderation with which we have acted towards a sister republic, but for the necessity which will then compel us to seek redress for our wrongs by actual war or by reprisals. The subject will then be presented before Congress at the commencement of the next session, in a clear and distinct form; and the committee cannot doubt but that such measures will be immediately adopted as may be necessary to vindicate the honor of the country and ensure ample reparation to our injured fellow citizens."

The Resolution with which this report concluded, was, on the 27th February, adopted by the unanimous vote of the Senate.

The report of the Committee on Foreign Affairs, made to the House of Representatives on the 24th February, 1837, breathes the same spirit with that of the Senate.

In pursuance of the suggestion of the Committee on Foreign Relations of the Senate, a special messenger was sent to Mexico, to make a final demand for redress, with the documents required by the 34th Article of the Treaty. This demand was made on the 20th July, 1838. The answer to it contained fair promises. How these were evaded from time to time, you will learn by an examination of the archives of your Legation.

Finally, on the 11th April, 1839, a convention was concluded, "for the adjustment of claims of citizens of the United States of America upon the Government of the Mexican Republic."

The Board of Commissioners was not organized under this Convention, until the 25th August, 1840; and, under its terms, they were obliged to terminate their duties within eighteen months from that date. Four of these eighteen months were spent in preliminary discussions, which had arisen on objections raised by the Mexican Commissioners; and at one time there was great danger that the Board would separate without hearing or deciding a single case. It was not until the 24th December, 1840, that they commenced the examination of the claims of our citizens. Fourteen months only were left, to examine and decide upon these numerous and complicated cases.

The claims allowed by the Commissioners, without reference to the umpire, amounted, principal and interest, to $439,393.82

The amount, principal and interest, subsequently awarded by the umpire, was   1,586,745.86

$2,026,139.68

The Mexican Government finding it inconvenient to pay the amount awarded, either in money or in an issue of Treasury notes, according to the terms of the Convention, a new Convention was concluded between the two Governments on the 30th January, 1843, to relieve that of Mexico from this embarrassment. Under its terms, the interest due on the whole amount awarded was to be paid on the 30th April, 1843; and the principal, with the accruing interest, was made payable in five years, in equal instalments every three months.

Under this new agreement, made to favor Mexico, the claimants have yet received only the interest up to the 30th April, 1843, and three of the twenty instalments.

But this is not all. There were pending before the umpire, when the Commission expired, claims which had been examined and awarded by the

American Commissioners, amounting to $928,627.88. Upon these he refused to decide, alleging that his authority had expired. This was a strange construction of the Treaty. Had he decided that his duties did not commence until those of the Commissioners had ended, this would have been a more natural interpretation.

To obviate this injustice and to provide for the decision of other claims of American citizens, amounting to $3,336,837.05, which had been submitted too late to be considered by the Board, a third Convention was signed at Mexico on the 20th November, 1843, by Mr. Waddy Thompson on the part of the United States, and Messrs. Bocanegra and Trigueros on the part of Mexico. On the 30th January, 1844, this Convention was ratified by the Senate of the United States, with two amendments. The one changed the place of meeting of the Commissioners from Mexico to Washington; and the other struck out the 16th article, which referred the claims of a pecuniary nature that the two Governments might have against each other, to the Commissioners, with an appeal to the umpire, in case a majority of them could not agree.

These amendments were manifestly reasonable and necessary. To have compelled the claimants, all of whom are citizens of the United States, to go to Mexico with their documents and testimony, would, in a great degree, have frustrated the object of the Commission. Besides, the new Commission was, in fact, but a continuance of the old one; and its duties simply were, to complete the business which had been left unfinished in the City of Washington.

It was something new in the history of sovereign nations, to refer their mutual claims to the arbitrament of a Board composed of their own citizens, with an appeal to a subject appointed by a foreign sovereign. The dignity of sovereign States forbade such a proceeding. Besides, it never had been suggested that either of the two Governments had claims upon the other, or that there were any claims in existence except those of American citizens on Mexico.

It is difficult to conceive why this Convention, departing from that of the 11th April, 1839, should have embraced any such provision; or why it should have stipulated for claims of citizens of Mexico against the United States, when no such claims had ever been alleged to exist.

Upon a reference of these amendments to the Government of Mexico, it interposed the same evasions, difficulties and delays which have always characterized its policy towards the United States. It has never yet decided whether it would or would not accede to them, although the subject has repeatedly been pressed upon its consideration by our Ministers.

The result of the whole is, that the injuries and outrages committed by the authorities of Mexico on American citizens, which, in the opinion of President Jackson, would, so long ago as February, 1837, have justified a resort to war or reprisals for redress, yet remain wholly unredressed, excepting only the comparatively small amount received under the Convention of April, 1839.

It will be your duty in a prudent and friendly spirit, to impress the Mexican Government with a sense of their great injustice towards the United States, as well as of the patient forbearance which has been exercised by us. This cannot be expected to endure much longer, and these claims must now speedily be adjusted in a satisfactory manner. Already have the Government of the United States too long omitted to obtain redress for their injured citizens.

But in what manner can this duty be performed consistently with the amicable spirit of your mission? The fact is but too well known to the world, that the Mexican Government are not now in a condition to satisfy these claims by the payment of money. Unless the debt should be assumed by the Government of the United States, the claimants cannot receive what is justly their due. Fortunately, the Joint Resolution of Congress, approved 1st March, 1845, "For annexing Texas to the United States," presents the means of satisfying these claims in perfect consistency with the interest as well as the honor of both Republics. It has reserved to this Government the adjustment "of all questions of boundary that may arise with other Governments." This question of boundary may, therefore, be adjusted in such a manner between the two Republics, as to cast the burden of the debt due to American claimants upon their own Government, whilst it will do no injury to Mexico.

In order to arrive at a just conclusion upon this subject, it is necessary briefly to state what at present are the territorial rights of the parties. The Congress of Texas, by the Act of December 19th, 1836, have declared the Rio del Norte, from its mouth to its source, to be a boundary of that Republic.

In regard to the right of Texas to the boundary of the Del Norte, from its mouth to the Paso, there cannot, it is apprehended, be any very serious doubt. It would be easy to establish by the authority of our most eminent statesmen—at a time, too, when the question of the boundary of the Province of Louisiana was better understood that it is at present,—that, to this extent at least, the Del Norte was its western limit. Messrs. Monroe and Pinckney, in their communication of January 28th 1805, to Don Pedro Cevallos, then the Spanish Minister of Foreign Relations, assert, in the strongest terms, that ["] the boundaries of that Province are the River Perdido, to the East; and the Rio Bravo to the West." They say, "the facts and principles which justify this conclusion are so satisfactory to our Government, as to convince it that the United States have not a better right to the Island of New Orleans, under the cession referred to, (that of Louisiana) than they have to the whole District of territory which is above described." Mr. Jefferson was at that time President, and Mr. Madison Secretary of State; and you well know how to appreciate their authority. In the subsequent negotiation with Mr. Cevallos, Messrs. Monroe and Pinckney conclusively vindicated the right of the United States as far west as the Del Norte. Down to the very conclusion of the Florida Treaty, the United States asserted their right to this extent, not by words only, but by deeds. In 1818, this Government, having learned that a number of adventurers, chiefly Frenchmen, had landed at Galveston, with the avowed purpose of forming a settlement in that vicinity, despatched George Graham, Esquire, with instructions to warn them to desist. The following is an extract from these instructions, dated 2nd June, 1818:

> The President wishes you to proceed with all convenient speed, to that place (Galveston) unless, as is not improbable, you should, in the progress of the journey, learn that they have abandoned or been driven from it. Should they have removed to Matagorda, or any other place North of the Rio Bravo, and within the territory claimed by the United States, you will repair thither, without however exposing yourself to be captured by any

Spanish military force. When arrived, you will, in a suitable manner, make known to the chief or leader of the expedition your authority from the Government of the United States, and express the surprise with which the President has seen possession thus taken, without authority from the United States, of a place within their territorial limits, and upon which no lawful settlement can be made without their sanction. You will call upon him explicitly to avow under what national authority they profess to act, and take care that due warning be given to the whole body, that the place is within the United States, who will suffer no permanent settlement to be made there, under any authority other than their own.

It cannot be denied, however, that the Florida Treaty of 22nd February, 1819, ceded to Spain all that part of ancient Louisiana within the present limits of Texas; and the more important enquiry now is, what is the extent of the territorial rights which Texas has acquired by the sword, in a righteous resistance to Mexico?

In your negotiations with Mexico, the independence of Texas must be considered a settled fact, and is not to be called in question.

Texas achieved her independence on the plain of San Jacinto, in April, 1836, by one of the most decisive and memorable victories recorded in history. She then convinced the world by her courage and her conduct, that she deserved to rank as an independent nation. To use the language of Mr. Webster, Secretary of State, in a despatch to our Minister at Mexico, dated 8th July, 1842,

> From the time of the battle of St. Jacinto, in April, 1836, to the present moment, Texas has exhibited the same external signs of national independence as Mexico herself, and with quite as much stability of Government. Practically free and independent, acknowledged as a political sovereignty by the principal powers of the world; no hostile foot finding rest within her territory, for six or seven years; and Mexico herself refraining, for all that period, from any further attempt to reestablish her own authority over the territory.

Finally, on the 29th March, 1845, Mexico consented, in the most solemn form, through the intervention of the British and French Governments, to acknowledge the independence of Texas, provided she would stipulate not to annex herself or become subject to any country whatever.

It may, however, be contended on the part of Mexico, that the Nueces and not the Rio del Norte, is the true western boundary of Texas. I need not furnish you arguments to controvert this position. You have been perfectly familiar with the subject from the beginning, and know that the jurisdiction of Texas has been extended beyond that river and that representatives from the country between it and the Del Norte have participated in the deliberations both of her Congress and her Convention. Besides, this portion of the territory was embraced within the limits of ancient Louisiana.

The case is different in regard to New Mexico. Santa Fe, its capital, was settled by the Spaniards more than two centuries ago; and that province has been ever since in their possession and that of the Republic of Mexico. The Texans never have conquered or taken possession of it, nor have its people ever been represented in any of their Legislative Assemblies or Conventions.

The long and narrow valley of New Mexico or Santa Fe is situated on both banks of the upper Del Norte, and is bounded on both sides by mountains. It is many hundred miles remote from other settled portions of Mexico, and from its distance, it is both difficult and expensive to defend the inhabitants against the tribes of fierce and warlike savages that roam over the surrounding country. For this cause it has suffered severely from their incursions. Mexico must expend far more in defending so distant a possession than she can possibly derive benefit from continuing to hold it.

Besides, it is greatly to be desired that our boundary with Mexico should now be established in such a manner as to preclude all future difficulties and disputes between the two Republics. A great portion of New Mexico being on this side of the Rio Grande and included within the limits already claimed by Texas, it may hereafter, should it remain a Mexican province, become a subject of dispute and a source of bad feeling between those who, I trust, are destined in future to be always friends.

On the other hand, if in adjusting the boundary, the province of New Mexico should be included within the limits of the United States, this would obviate the danger of future collisions. Mexico would part with a remote and disturbed province, the possession of which can never be advantageous to her; and she would be relieved from the trouble and expense of defending its inhabitants against the Indians. Besides, she would thus purchase security against their attacks for her other provinces West of the Del Norte, as it would at once become the duty of the United States to restrain the savage tribes within their limits and prevent them from making hostile incursions into Mexico. From these considerations and others which will readily suggest themselves to your mind, it would seem to be equally the interest of both Powers, that New Mexico should belong to the United States.

But the President desires to deal liberally by Mexico. You are therefore authorized to offer to assume the payment of all the just claims of our citizens against Mexico, and, in addition, to pay five millions of dollars, in case the Mexican Government shall agree to establish the boundary between the two countries from the mouth of the Rio Grande, up the principal stream to the point where it touches the line of New Mexico, thence west of the river, along the exterior line of that province and so as to include the whole within the United States until it again intersects the river, thence up the principal stream of the same to its source and thence due north until it intersects the forty second degree of north latitude.

A boundary still preferable to this, would be an extension of the line from the north west corner of New Mexico, along the range of mountains, until it would intersect the forty second parallel.

Should the Mexican authorities prove unwilling to extend our boundary beyond the Del Norte, you are, in that event, instructed to offer to assume the payment of all the just claims of citizens of the United States against Mexico, should she agree that the line shall be established along the boundary defined by the Act of Congress of Texas, approved December 19th, 1836, to wit; beginning at "the mouth of the Rio Grande, thence up the principal stream of said river to its source, thence due north to the forty second degree of north latitude.["] It is scarcely to be supposed, however, that Mexico would relinquish five millions of dollars for the sake of retaining the narrow strip of territory in the valley of New Mexico, west of the Rio Grande, and thus place under two distinct Governments the small settlements closely identified with each other, on the opposite banks of the river. Besides, all the inconveniences to her from holding New Mexico, which I have pointed out, would be seriously aggravated by her continuing to hold that small portion of it which lies west of the river.

There is another subject of vast importance to the United States, which will demand your particular attention. From information possessed by this Department, it is to be seriously apprehended that both Great Britain and France have designs upon California. The views of the Government of the United States on this subject you will find presented in my despatch to Thomas O. Larkin, Esqr. our Consul at Monterey, dated October 17, 1845, a copy of which is herewith transmitted. From it you will perceive that, whilst this Government does not intend to interfere between Mexico and California, it would vigorously interpose to prevent the latter from becoming either a British or a French colony. You will endeavor to ascertain whether Mexico has any intention of ceding it to the one or the other power; and if any such design exists, you will exert all your energies to prevent an act which, if consummated, would be so fraught with danger to the best interests of the United States. On this subject, you may freely correspond with Mr. Larkin, taking care that your letters shall not fall into improper hands.

The possession of the Bay and harbour of San Francisco, is all important to the United States. The advantages to us of its acquisition are so striking, that it would be a waste of time to enumerate them here. If all these should be turned against our country, by the cession of California to Great Britain, our principal commercial rival, the consequences would be most disastrous.

The Government of California is now but nominally dependent on Mexico; and it is more than doubtful whether her authority will ever be re-instated. Under these circumstances, it is the desire of the President that you shall use your best efforts to obtain a cession of that Province from Mexico to the United States. Could you accomplish this object, you would render immense service to your country and establish an enviable reputation for yourself. Money would be no object when compared with the value of the acquisition. Still the attempt must be made with great prudence and caution, and in such a manner as not to alarm the jealousy of the Mexican Government. Should you, after sounding the Mexican authorities on the subject, discover a prospect of success, the President would not hesitate to give, in addition to the assumption of the just claims of our citizens on Mexico, twenty five millions of dollars for the cession. Should you deem it expedient, you are authorized to offer this sum for a boundary, running due West from the southern extremity of New Mexico to the Pacific ocean, or from any other point on its western boundary, which would embrace Monterey within our limits. If Monterey cannot be obtained, you may, if necessary, in addition to the assumption of those claims, offer twenty millions of dollars for any boundary, commencing at any point on the western line of New Mexico, and running due West to the Pacific, so as to include the bay and harbour of San Francisco. The larger the territory South of this Bay, the better. Of course, when I speak of any point on the Western boundary of New Mexico, it is understood, that, from the Del Norte to that point, our boundary shall run according to the first offer which you have been authorized to make. I need scarcely add, that, in authorizing the offer of five millions or twenty five millions or twenty millions of dollars, these are to be considered as maximum sums. If you can accomplish either of the objects contemplated for a less amount, so much more satisfactory will it prove to the President.

The views and wishes of the President are now before you, and much at last must be left to your own discretion. If you can accomplish any one of the specific objects which have been presented in these instructions, you are authorized to conclude a Treaty to that effect. If you cannot, after you have ascertained what is practicable, you will ask for further instructions, and they shall be immediately communicated.

Your mission is one of the most delicate and important which has ever been confided to a citizen of the United States. The people to whom you will be sent are proverbially jealous, and they have been irritated against the United States by recent events and by the intrigues of foreign Powers. To conciliate their good will is indispensable to your success. I need not warn you against wounding their national vanity. You may probably have to endure their unjust reproaches with equanimity. It would be difficult to raise a point of honor between the United States and so feeble and degraded a Power as Mexico. This reflection will teach you to bear and forbear much for the sake of accomplishing the great objects of your mission. We are sincerely desirous to be on good terms with Mexico, and the President reposes implicit confidence in your patriotism, sagacity and ability to restore the ancient relations of friendship between the two Republics.

Herewith you will also receive your full powers to conclude a Treaty, together with two maps, the one Arrowsmiths and the other Emory's, on which are designated the limits of New Mexico.

You will keep the Department advised of your progress as often as safe opportunities may offer.

You are aware that Congress, at their last session, made the following appropriation:

"For paying the April and July instalments of the Mexican indemnities due in eighteen hundred and forty four, the sum of two hundred and seventy five thousand dollars: Provided it shall be ascertained to the satisfaction of the American Government, that said instalments have been paid by the Mexican Government to the agent appointed by the United States to receive the same in such manner as to discharge all claim on the Mexican Government, and said agent to be delinquent in remitting the money to the United States."

The whole transaction between Emilio Voss, Esquire, the agent of the United States and the Mexican authorities is yet involved in mystery which this Government has not been able to unravel. You will endeavor, with as little delay as possible, to ascertain the true state of the case in relation to the alleged payment of these instalments by the Mexican Government to our agent, and give the

Department the earliest information on the subject. A copy of his receipt ought to be obtained if possible.

I am [etc.].

In all probability two developments set these diplomatic negotiations in motion. The first was President Polk's feeling of confidence after General Taylor and his forces were encamped on the Gulf of Mexico at Corpus Christi; the second was that word had come to the President from his secret agent in Mexico, William Parrott, that the officials of Mexican government would probably be receptive to American overtures regarding a settlement of the border dispute. Before acting precipitously however, Polk, on Buchanan's advice, instructed John Black, the American consul in the capital, to obtain from the government written assurances that a representative would be welcome. Acting on these instructions, Black met with the Mexican foreign minister, Manuel de la Peña y Peña, to receive from him written confirmation of earlier discussions they had held. It is important to note that this meeting was secret and was conducted in the foreign minister's own home. Black's report to the secretary of state explained why such precautions were necessary and also revealed the almost paranoid fear on the part of the Mexican officials that information regarding this matter could be used against the current government in order to trigger another revolution.

John Black, American Consul in Mexico
Letter (Extract) to Secretary of State James Buchanan
October 17, 1845

House Executive Document No. 60, 30th Cong., 1st sess., 13-14.

I had the honor, on the 10th instant, of receiving your communication of the 17th ultimo. . . . On Saturday evening, the 11th instant, I obtained a confidential interview with the minister of foreign relations of the Mexican republic, in relation to the important charge which his excellency the President of the United States was pleased to confide to me, and am happy now to have it in my power to advise my government of a favorable result; the proceedings had with the Mexican government in this affair will be seen by reference to the enclosed documents, Nos. 1 and 2.

No. 1 is a copy of a confidential communication addressed by this consulate to his excellency the minister of foreign relations of the Mexican government; and No. 2 is a copy of the said minister's answer to said communication.

When I handed the aforesaid communications to his excellency on Monday, the 13th instant, I requested that an answer might be given as early as possible, and desired to be informed at what time it would likely be given. He promised that on Wednesday evening, the 15th, and requested at that time a private interview with me, to be at eight o'clock in the evening, (not at the department, he said, but at his private dwelling,) in order, as he said, that the affair might be kept as close and as little exposed to public view as possible, to avoid suspicion. At the time appointed, I went to his house; he (being alone in his study) received me cordially and politely, and told me the answer was ready, and only wanted his signature, which he placed to it in my presence, stating, at the same time, that he would accompany the answer with some verbal, frank, and confidential explanations; which, after reading to me the answer, he did, in the following manner:

He said that the Mexican government, notwithstanding it felt itself very much aggrieved and offended by the acts of that of the United States, in relation to the affairs of Texas, yet it would appear to be out of place to express these feelings in a communication of this nature; and that, if the government had but itself to consult, the expression of these feelings would have been left out of the communication, as they only tend to irritate; but that I knew, as well as he did, that governments like ours must endeavor to reconcile the feelings and opinions of the people to their public acts; and that I also knew very well that a strong opposition were daily calling the attention of the public to, and scrutinizing and condemning every act of the government, and that the government endeavored to give them as little pretext as possible; and, therefore, wished me to make this explanation to my government.

And that, in relation to the qualities he had recommended to be possessed by the person to be sent out by the government of the United States for the settlement of existing differences, it was the wish of the Mexican government, and would be for the good of both countries, that a person suitable in every respect should be sent, endued with the necessary qualities, and not one against whom the government or people of Mexico should unfortunately entertain a fixed prejudice, which would be a great obstacle in the way to an amicable adjustment of the differences. . . .

And that, in order that the coming of the commissioner might not have the appearance of being forced on them by threat, his government wished the naval force of the United States, now in sight of Vera Cruz, should retire from that place before his arrival; and requested that I should inform his government, by a communication, as soon as I should know the fact, of their having left. These things he repeated more than once, and with the appearance of a great deal of earnestness, and enjoined it upon me not to fail to advise my government; and that he communicated these things to me not as a minister, but as an individual and friend, who wished for the good exit of the contemplated mission.

Notwithstanding my communication to the Mexican government of the 13th instant was of the most confidential character, as well as all the proceedings in relation to the affair, and this at the request of the Mexican minister, who himself enjoined secrecy upon me, and promised the strictest adherence to it on his part. . . . So you will be able to see what reliance can be placed on the most solemn injunctions of secrecy, as far as this government is concerned.

John Black, American Consul in Mexico
Letter to Manuel de la Peña y Peña,
Foreign Minister of Mexico
October 13, 1845

House Executive Document No. 60, 30th Cong., 1st sess., 14-16.

The undersigned, consul of the United States of America, in a confidential interview with his excellency Manuel de la Peña y Peña, minister of foreign relations and government of the Mexican republic, which took place on the evening of the 11th instant, had the honor to advise his excellency that he, the undersigned, had received a communication from the Secretary of State of the United States; and having, in that interview, made known to his excellency the substance of said communication, which contained a reiteration of the sentiments which, at the time of the suspension of the diplomatic relations between the two countries, had been expressed to General Almonte, and which were now renewed, and offered to the consideration of the Mexican government.

His excellency having heard, and considered with due attention, the statement read from the communication aforesaid, and having stated that, as the diplomatic relations between the two governments had been and were still suspended, the present interview could and should have no other character than that of a confidential meeting, which was assented to, and only considered in that light by the undersigned.

His excellency was then pleased to request that the undersigned might, in the same confidential manner, communicate in writing what had thus been made known verbally. In conformity to that request, the undersigned has now the honor to transcribe, herewith, that part of the communication of the Secretary of State of the United States referred to, and is in the following words, viz:

At the time of the suspension of the diplomatic relations between the two countries, General Almonte was assured of the desire felt by the President to adjust amicably every cause of complaint between the governments, and to cultivate the kindest and most friendly relations between the sister republics. He still continues to be animated by the same sentiments. He desires that all existing differences should be terminated amicably by negotiation, and not by the sword.

Actuated by these sentiments, the President has directed me to instruct you, in the absence of any diplomatic agent in Mexico, to ascertain from the Mexican government whether they would receive an envoy from the United States, entrusted with full power to adjust all the questions in dispute between the two governments. Should the answer be in the affirmative, such an envoy will be immediately despatched to Mexico.

The undersigned can assure his excellency that it is with the most heartfelt satisfaction he sees, in the preceding proposition on the part of the President of the United States, (notwithstanding the preparations for war on both sides,) that a door is still left open for conciliation, whereby all existing differences may be amicably and equitably adjusted, and the honor of both nations preserved inviolate, and their friendly relations restored and fixed upon a firmer foundation than they unfortunately have hitherto been; and the undersigned has reason to believe that they will not be blinded to their mutual interest, nor suffer themselves to become the victims of the mechinations of their mutual enemies.

If the President of the United States has been disposed to stand upon a mere question of etiquette, he would have waited until the Mexican government, which had suspended the diplomatic relations between the two countries, should have asked that they might be restored; but his desire is so strong to terminate the present unfortunate state of our relations with this republic, that he has even consented to waive all ceremony, and take the initiative.

In view of what is hereinbefore set forth, the undersigned is fully persuaded that the Mexican government will not misconstrue the benevolent sentiments of the President of the United States, nor mistake his motives.

His excellency will be pleased to return an answer with as little delay as possible, and in the meantime, the undersigned avails himself of the occasion to renew to his excellency Manuel de la Peña y Peña, minister of foreign relations and government of the Mexican republic, the assurances of his distinguished consideration and personal regard.

John Black

Manuel de la Peña y Peña, Foreign Minister of Mexico Letter to John Black, American Consul in Mexico
October 15, 1845

House Executive Document No. 60, 30th Cong., 1st sess., 16-17.

Sir: I have informed my government of the private conference which took place between you and myself on the 11th instant, and have submitted it to the confidential letter which you, in consequence of, and agreeably to what was then said, addressed to me yesterday. In answer, I have to say to you, that, although the Mexican nation is deeply injured by the United States, through the acts committed by them in the department of Texas, which belongs to this nation, my government is disposed to receive the commissioner of the United States, who may come to this capital with full powers from his government to settle the present dispute in a peaceable, reasonable, and honorable manner; thus giving a new proof that, even in the midst of its injuries, and of its firm decision to exact adequate reparation for them, it does not repel with contumely the measure of reason and peace to which it is invited by its adversary.

As my government believes this invitation to be made in good faith, and with the real desire that it may lead to a favorable conclusion, it also hopes that the commissioner will be a person endowed with the qualities proper for the attainment of this end; that his dignity, prudence, and moderation, and the discreetness and reasonableness of his proposals will contribute to calm as much as possible the just irritation of the Mexicans; and, in fine, that the conduct of the commissioner on all points may be such as to persuade them that they may obtain satisfaction for their injuries, through the means of reason and peace, and without being obliged to resort to those of arms and force.

What my government requires above all things, is, that the mission of the commissioner of the United States, and his reception by us, should appear to be always absolutely frank, and free from every sign of menace or coercion. And thus, Mr.•Consul, while making known to your government the disposition on the part of that of Mexico to receive the commissioner, you should impress upon it, as indispensable, the previous recall of the whole naval force now lying in sight of our port of Vera Cruz. Its presence would degrade Mexico, while she is receiving the commissioner, and would justly subject the United States to the imputation of contradicting by acts the vehement desire of conciliation, peace, and friendship, which is professed and asserted by words.

I have made known to you, Mr. Consul, with the brevity which you desired, the disposition of my government; and in so doing, I have the satisfaction to assure you of my consideration and esteem for you personally.

The correspondence between Black, Buchanan and Peña y Peña very clearly revealed the sensitive nature of the problem. The situation of the Herrera government was extremely tenuous; it might have been toppled at any time through a misstep in negotiations. The Mexican foreign minister appeared to be acting in good faith; he seemed to want to move ahead in the negotiations, but he was extremely wary of the possibility that American blunders and/or bad faith might undercut his government. He sought to prevent such an occurrence by attempting to convince the American consul of the critical nature of the situation—proposing explicitly and implicitly how the Americans could cooperate with Mexico.

The conditions set out by the Mexican foreign minister are quickly summarized. He wanted the menacing American fleet to be withdrawn from the Mexican coast. The representative from the United States was to be a commissioner (commissionado) "who may come to this capital with full powers from his government to settle the present dispute in a peaceable, reasonable, and honorable manner. . . ."[80] It is clear from this description that the Mexican government was not suggesting a restoration of normal relations between the two powers nor the re-establishment of mutual representatives of ministerial rank, but instead, the very tentative exploration of existing problems by special representatives named for that explicit purpose. The Mexican foreign minister also stressed the point that such a representative be a person "with the qualities proper for the attainment of this end."[81] Those qualities, he said, should be "dignity, prudence, and moderation," along with discretion and reason. The original letter in which Black described his meeting with Peña contained a reference to a former minister to the republic of Mexico, Joel R. Poinsett, who the Mexican foreign minister described as not meeting these qualifications. This was deleted from the State Department documents submitted to the House of Representatives.

Difficulties set in immediately after Slidell's arrival in Mexico. The Mexican government had not been informed of his presence before their agents discovered him lying off Vera Cruz in an American ship which had arrived during the last few days of November. The Mexican foreign minister appeared to be totally unprepared for this turn of events and was quite flustered by it. There is no indication that even the American consul was prepared for his appearance. Given the very sensitive circumstances which prevailed, this signaled an ominous beginning for the negotiations. Peña quickly explained to Black that the Mexican government was not prepared to receive Slidell at that time and that his very appearance in the capital "might prove destructive to the government."[82] He had not been expected for another month, the Mexican government assuming that his appointment would have to await Senate approval. Slidell's presence in Mexico before adequate preparations for the negotiations could be undertaken was considered a source of embarrassment for the government, and from that point on, everything was done to delay the meetings.

John Black, American Consul in Mexico
Letter to Secretary of State James Buchanan
December 18, 1845

House Executive Document No. 60, 30th Cong., 1st sess., 22-23.

On Wednesday, the 3d instant, I received a letter from our consul at Vera Cruz, dated the 29th of November, informing me that a vessel had just arrived at Sacrificios, on board of which was the Hon. John Slidell, who had sent for him, the said consul, to come down to that place, as he wished to leave Vera Cruz for this capital by that night's diligence, but he, the consul, was of opinion he would not be able to leave until the next stage.

On the receipt of this letter I called at the foreign department of this government, to see the minister of foreign affairs, and was informed by Mr. Monasterio, the chief clerk, that the minister was up stairs with the President, and that he was going up to see him, and would advise him of my wish. He soon returned, and requested me to go up, as the minister wished to see me. I went up to the President's quarters, when the minister came out into the ante-chamber and met me, and accosted me, saying that the government was informed that there was an arrival at Vera Cruz from the United States, bringing out a commissioner, by which the government was taken by surprise, and asked me who could this commissioner be, and what had he come for? I told him I did not know, but I presumed it was the envoy which the Mexican government had agreed to receive from the government of the United States; all the information which I had upon the subject was, that the consul of the United States at Vera Cruz had advised me in a letter under date of the 29th of November, that the Hon. John Slidell had just arrived at Sacrificios, and wished to leave Vera Cruz for this capital by the first diligence, and that I was under the impression that this person was an envoy from the government of the United States to that of Mexico, as we had good reason to expect one about this time. He said that ought not to be; the government did not expect an envoy from the United States until January, as they were not prepared to receive him; and he desired, if possible, that he would not come to the capital, nor even disembark at this time, and that I should endeavor to prevent his doing so, as his appearance in the capital at this time might prove destructive to the government, and thus defeat the whole affair. You know the opposition are calling us traitors, for entering into this arrangement with you. I told him I regretted this had not been known in time, as the envoy would be now on his way to this capital, and that the Mexican government had set no time for his arrival, and it was to be presumed that they would be ready to receive him whenever he arrived. I know, he said, there was no time set; but from the conversations which I have had with yourself, and what I have heard from others, I had good reason to believe the envoy would not have been appointed by your government, or, at least, not have started on his mission, until after the meeting of Congress; which, he said, he understood would not meet until the first of this month.

He said that the government itself was well disposed, and ready to proceed in the negotiation, but that if the affair was commenced now, it would endanger its existence; that the government were preparing the thing, collecting the opinion and consent of the departments, which they expected to have finished by January, and then they would be able to proceed in the affair with more security; that the government were afraid that the appearance of the envoy at this time would produce a revolution against it, which might terminate in its destruction.

It was impossible to prevent Slidell from travelling from Vera Cruz to Mexico City, although Black intercepted him at Puebla and attempted to brief him on the complexities of the problem. His presence in the capital city occasioned new attacks upon the government for treasonous activity, and it soon appeared that the days of the government might be numbered. The Mexican foreign minister informed the American consul and Slidell that the American envoy's papers had been submitted to the very prestigious Council of State for its consideration and approval. This body was independent of the Executive and contained some of the most extreme opponents, some of whom advocated his overthrow. It hardly appeared likely that this council would approve the negotiations or that the government was in any position to defy the council.

Slidell relayed the decision of the council to Buchanan in a report to the secretary of state, dated December 17, 1845 and written from Mexico City. After reviewing Slidell's papers the council had decided to recommend against recognizing the American envoy. The reasons advanced for this breach of diplomatic etiquette were the following. First, the representative of the United States' appointment and mission had not been approved by the Senate of the United States. Second, the credentials carried by the envoy were identical to those submitted by the previous minister to Mexico, Wilson Shannon. The understanding of the Mexican government was that the envoy from the United States was to be an ad hoc commissioner, specially authorized to deal with outstanding disputes between the two countries. Congressman Slidell's papers indicated that he was sent to replace Shannon as a regular minister representing the United States in Mexico. Finally, further confirming the above argument was the title Mr. Slidell bore— Envoy Extraordinary and Minister Plenipotentiary to Mexico. This was the title reserved by Mexico and other countries for the regular ministerial representative, and in accepting his credentials as such, Mexico would be reversing its previous action taken in protest against the annexation of Texas, by withdrawing their diplomatic representative from Washington. In short, the acceptance of Slidell's credentials would amount to a *de facto* withdrawal of Mexico's serious complaints against the United States.

John Slidell, United States Minister to Mexico
Letter (Extract) to Secretary of State James Buchanan
December 17, 1845

House Executive Document No. 60, 30th Cong., 1st sess., 23-27.

By my letter of 30th ultimo, I had the honor to inform you of my safe arrival at Vera Cruz. I reached this city on Saturday, the 6th instant, having been detained two days by the stoppage of the mail coach at Jalapa. At Puebla, I was met by our consul, Mr. Black, who in some measure prepared me for the delays and difficulties which I should have to contend with, in placing myself in relation with this government, by informing me that in a private interview which he had had with the minister of foreign affairs, Mr. Manuel de la Peña y Peña, for the purpose of announcing to him my arrival at Vera Cruz, that functionary had manifested great surprise that a minister should have presented himself so soon, and intimated that the state of things was such that he should have preferred less promptness on the part of our government. On Monday, the 8th instant, I addressed to the minister of foreign affairs a note, in the usual form, announcing my arrival in the capital, accompanying it with a copy of my letter of credence, and your official communication to the minister of foreign affairs, and asking to be informed when and where I should be admitted to present my credentials to the President. Of this note I annex a copy. It was handed by Mr. Black to the minister, who assured him that I should have an answer on the following Wednesday, and requested him to call and receive it. On that day, however, Mr. Black received a note from the secretary of the minister, stating that it was necessary to submit the matter to the council of government, and that he would be advised when the answer would be given. Mr.

Black has since had another interview with Mr. Peña, and has prepared, at my request, a statement of what passed between them, which I send you.

This council of government is a permanent body of a very anomalous character, composed of persons not removable by the executive; its functions, so far as I can understand them, are, with a few exceptions, and these not applying to foreign relations, merely advisory; and no obligation exists on the part of the executive, but in the exceptionable cases, to consult the council. The council was not consulted when the executive determined to renew diplomatic relations with the United States, and a recourse to it at this moment was altogether gratuitous. It is a notorious fact, that several of the members of this council are not only in open and violent opposition to the present administration, but are endeavoring to get up a revolutionary movement to overthrow it; and it is generally understood that a majority of them are unfavorably disposed towards it.

The impression here, among the best informed persons, is, that while the president and his cabinet are really desirous to enter frankly upon a negotiation which would terminate all their difficulties with the United States. . . .

This, at least, is certain; the administration, in referring a matter entirely within their own competence to a body whose decision they cannot control, and upon whose sympathies they cannot rely, manifest either a weakness or a bad faith, which renders the prospect of any favorable issue to negotiations with them, at best, very problematical.

The deliberations of the council, although ostensibly confidential, soon became known out of doors. It has been twice or thrice convoked for the purpose of deliberating upon my reception, and it is perfectly well known that it has advised against it. The most absurd reasons have there been advanced against my recognition; so absurd, indeed, that they would appear scarcely credible to anyone not upon the spot. . . .

The objections started were, that my credentials did not appear to have been given with the sanction of Congress; that my appointment had not been confirmed by the Senate; that this government had agreed only to receive a commissioner, and that, consequently, the appointment of an envoy extraordinary and minister plenipotentiary was not in accordance with the letter of the 15th October from the minister of foreign affairs to Mr. Black; that this letter only contemplated negotiations upon the subject of Texas; and finally, to cap the climax of absurdity, that my powers were not sufficient. I hope, before the closing of this despatch, to obtain information of the precise grounds upon which the council finally decided to recommend that I should not be received.

Having received no reply to my note of the 8th instant, and no assurance of the time when I might expect one, I addressed another on the 15th instant, (a copy of which you will find herewith,) stating my desire to communicate speedily with my government, and requesting to know when I might expect an answer.

I have, while writing this, received a communication from the minister of foreign relations, of which I shall furnish you a copy. You will observe that it is dated yesterday, although I have no doubt that it was written after the final negative decision of the council, which was rendered on that day. You will find it evasive and unsatisfactory, intimating difficulties respecting my credentials, and that negotiations were, by the terms of his letter to our consul, to be confined to the subject of Texas. It concludes with an assurance that I shall be informed, at the earliest moment, of the decision of the council, to whom the matter had been submitted.

You will observe that this note is not addressed to me in my official capacity; the omission to do so is certainly not an accidental one. I feel considerably embarrassed as to the proper course to pursue in relation to this circumstance, unimportant in itself, but not without significancy when taken in connexion with other circumstances. Your instructions direct me bear and forbear much, for the purpose of promoting the great objects of my mission. . . .

As for myself, personally, I should feel very indifferent to any questions of mere etiquette; but in my representative capacity, I ought not silently to suffer any mark of disrespect. Although not yet recognized by this government as the person with whom it is willing to enter upon official relations, so far as my own is concerned, I am its representative here, and all other considerations apart, the interests of my mission with a people attaching peculiar importance to forms, require that I should not allow any violation of accustomed courtesies to pass unnoticed. My present intention is, to address a note to the minister of foreign relations, couched in the most respectful terms, attributing the omission to address me by my proper title, to inadvertence, and suggesting the expectation that it will not be repeated. This, however, I shall not do without proper reflection and consultation of precedents, if any such can be found. There is less reason for immediate reply, as I am satisfied that nothing is to be gained by pressing upon the government at this moment; their existence hangs by a thread, and they retain power, not by their own force, but solely by the inability of their opponents to agree among themselves. The greatest object of the administration, in all matters, is to gain time; to do nothing to compromit themselves in the hope that if they can hold over until the meeting of the new congress, which will take place on the 1st of January, they will then be enabled to maintain their position. It would seem presumptuous in me, having so recently arrived, and with my necessarily very limited acquaintance and means of information, to express any opinion on this subject, but I give it to you for what it may be worth. A revolution, and that before the meeting of congress, is a probable event; a change of ministers almost a certain one. Notwithstanding the desire, which I believe the present administration really entertains, to adjust all their difficulties with us, so feeble and inert is it, that I am rather inclined to the opinion that the chances of a successful negotiation would be better with one more hostile, but possessing greater energy. The country, torn by conflicting factions, is in a state of perfect anarchy; its finances in a condition utterly desperate. . . .

A refusal to treat with, or even receive me at all, in the only capacity in which I am authorised to act, under pretexts more or less plausible, is a possible (I aught, perhaps, to say a probable) event. This is a contingency which could not have been anticipated, and for which your instructions have, consequently, not provided. It will place me in a novel, awkward, and most embarrassing position, and impose upon me a grave responsibility. Should it occur, I shall endeavor so to conduct myself as to throw the whole odium of the failure of the negotiation upon this government; point out, in the most temperate manner, the inevitable consequences of so unheard of a violation of all the usages which govern the intercourse between civilized nations; and declare my intention to remain here until I can receive instructions adapted to the exigencies of the case. I trust that no time will be lost in furnishing me with instructions that will enable me to act promptly and decisively; and, to assure the requisite despatch, I would recommend that they be sent by a steamer from Pensacola. Sailing vessels are frequently from fifteen to twenty days making the passage from Havana, or the Balize, to Vera Cruz.

I send you files of the three principal papers published here, viz: the Diario, Siglo, and Amigo del Pueblo, which will enable you to form some idea of the state of public opinion as indicated by the press. The first is the official government paper; it has not made the slightest allusion to my arrival, and preserves upon all other debatable subjects a silence equally oracular. The second, although it has had a sort of semi-official character, and had heretofore supported the administration, has recently commented very freely upon its feebleness and inefficiency. The third is the leading opposition journal; it breathes the fiercest hostility against the United States, denounces the proposed negotiation as treason; and, in the last number, openly calls upon the troops and the people to put down the government by force. . . .

The rest of the story can be told briefly. Slidell demonstrated no sensitivity to the situation in which the Herrera government found itself and continued to ignore the legitimate questions the Mexicans raised regarding his credentials. He even arrogantly objected to Peña's failure to address him by his full title, again not acknowledging the fact that such an address would have constituted a recognition of precisely the point which the Mexican government was challenging. A diplomat who wanted to cut through the formalities and seek out what faint possibilities still existed for peace, would have scrapped the titles, kept out of Mexico City and met clandestinely with the Mexican leaders to explore the conditions upon which the two countries might have worked out a satisfactory settlement. No Mexican government which publicly recognized a formal minister from the United States or hinted at waiving claims to the land west of the Rio Grande could have hoped to stay in power for even a few days, let alone weeks. Under the constant pressure of rival warlords seeking power, no real rapprochement was possible. But it was worth trying, worth any effort to forestall a costly and bloody struggle. The American envoy was above or beyond making such an effort. He was acting out a charade to justify the later bloodletting; true statesmanship would have tried to avoid such a disaster.

The communications between John Slidell and Manuel de la Peña y Peña continued for the next few weeks as Herrera precariously clung to power. Slidell, with what he correctly assessed as solid support back in Washington, did not yield an inch; Herrera, with the hot breath of several dissident generals breathing down his neck, could not afford to appear to grant the Americans anything. So the magic moment escaped, and soon men would again begin killing one another.

By the end of December the Herrera government was overthrown, but Slidell was instructed to linger on in Mexico for several more weeks to ascertain whether or not the new Mexican President, General Parades, would reverse his predecessor's position. When he did not, Slidell demanded his passport and returned to the United States. The final exchange of notes between Slidell and Foreign Minister J. M. de Castillo y Lanzas indicated how far both sides had travelled since the American envoy's arrival.

John Slidell, United States Minister to Mexico
Letter to Joaquın M. de Castillo y Lanzas,
Minister of Foreign Affairs of Mexico
March 1, 1846

Manning, VIII, 814-15.

The undersigned Envoy Extraordinary and Minister Plenipotentiary of the United States of America, to the Mexican Republic, had the honor on the eighth day of December last, to address to His Excellency Manuel de la Peña y Peña, then Minister of Foreign Relations, a copy of his credentials, with a request that he might be informed, when he would be admitted to present the original to the President of the Mexican Republic.

On the 16th December, the undersigned was informed by Mr. Peña y Peña, that difficulties existed in relation to the tenor of his credentials, which made it necessary to consult the Council of Government thereon, and on the twentieth of the same month, he was advised by Mr. Peña y Peña, that the Mexican Government had decided not to recognize him in his capacity of Envoy Extraordinary and Minister Plenipotentiary.

To these communications of the Minister of Foreign Relations, the undersigned replied under dates of 20th & 24th December, refuting the reasoning by which the refusal to recognize him, was attempted to be sustained, vindicating the course pursued by his Government, and declaring his intention to proceed to Jalapa, there to await instructions adapted to an emergency so entirely unlooked for. He has now received these instructions.

The President of the United States entirely approves the course pursued by the undersigned, and the Communications by him addressed to the Mexican Government—Had the then existing Government continued in power, as no alternative would have remained, the undersigned would have been directed to demand his passports, the President of the United States would have submitted the whole case to Congress and called upon the nation to assert its just rights and avenge its injured honor. The destinies of the Mexican Republic, however, having since been committed to other hands, the President is unwilling to take a course which would inevitably result in war, without making another effort to avert so great a calamity. He wishes by exhausting every honorable means of conciliation, to demonstrate to the civilized world, that if its peace shall be disturbed, the responsibility must fall upon Mexico alone. He is sincerely desirous to preserve that peace; but the state of quasi hostility which now exists on the part of Mexico, is one which is incompatible with the dignity and interests of the United States, and it is for the Mexican Government to decide whether it shall give place to friendly negotiations, or lead to an open rupture.

It would be idle to repeat the arguments which the undersigned had the honor to present in his notes of 20th and 24th December above referred to; he has nothing to add to them, but is instructed again to present them to the consideration of the President ad-interim of the Mexican Republic, General Mariano Paredes y Arrillaga—

The undersigned begs leave to suggest most respectfully to Your Excellency, that inasmuch as ample time has been afforded for the most mature reflection upon the momentous interests involved in the question of his recognition, as little delay as possible may occur in notifying him of the final decision of His Excellency the President ad-interim—He cannot but indulge the hope that it will be such as to result in the establishment of cordial and lasting amity between the two Republics.

The undersigned avails himself of this opportunity of presenting to his excellency Don Joaquın Castillo y Lanzas the assurances of his distinguished consideration.

Joaquın M. de Castillo y Lanzas,
Minister of Foreign Affairs of Mexico
Letter to John Slidell,
United States Minister to Mexico
March 12, 1846

Manning, VIII, 818-23.

The Undersigned, Minister of Foreign Relations and Government of the Republic, has the honor to acknowledge receipt of the note, addressed to him from Jalapa, under date the 1st instant, by His Excellency John Slidell, appointed Minister Plenipotentiary and Envoy Extraordinary of the United States of America.

So soon as the said communication was received by the undersigned, he proceeded to communicate it to His Excellency the President ad interim; and he, after deliberately considering its contents, and maturely meditating upon the business, has seen fit to order the undersigned to make known to Mr. Slidell, in reply, as he now has the honour of doing, that the Mexican Government cannot receive him as Envoy Extraordinary & Minister Plenipotentiary to reside near it.

And here might the undersigned terminate his note, if reasons of great weight did not convince him of the necessity of making some reflections in this place; not through fear of the consequences which may result from this decisive resolve, but through the respect which he owes to reason and to justice.

It is true that this warlike display, with which the American Union presents herself,—by sea, with her squadrons on both coasts; by land, with her invading forces advancing by the northern frontiers—at the same time, that by her Minister Plenipotentiary propositions are made for conciliation, and accommodation, would be a sufficiently powerful reason for not listening to them, so long as all threatening should not be withdrawn, even to the slightest appearance of hostility. But even this is waived by the Government of the Republic, in order that it may in all frankness & loyalty enter into the discussion, relying solely upon reason and facts. A simple reference to the truth, plainly stated, suffices to show the justice by which Mexico is upheld in the question now under discussion.

The vehement desire of the Government of the United States, to extend its already immense territory at the expense of that of Mexico, has been manifest for many years; and it is beyond all doubt, that in regard to Texas at least, this has been their firm and constant determination: for it has been so declared categorically & officially by an authorized representative of the Union, whose assertion, strange & injurious as was its frankness, has nevertheless not been belied by the United States.

Putting out of view, now, all the events to which this marked intent has given rise through a long series of years, events which have served not only to prove it more & more strongly, but also to show, that no means, of whatever kind they might be, were to be spared for its accomplishment; it is sufficient to attend to what occurred last year: this is the important part to the present case.

Considering the time as having come for carrying into effect the annexation of Texas, the United States, in union & by agreement with their natural allies & adherents in that territory, concerted the means for the purpose. The project was introduced into the American Congress. It was at first frustrated, thanks to the prudential considerations, the circumspection and the wisdom, with which the Senate of the Union then proceeded.

Nevertheless, the project was reproduced in the following sessions, and was then approved and sanctioned in the form & terms known to the whole world.

A fact such as this, or to speak with greater exactness, so notable an act of usurpation created an imperious necessity that Mexico, for her own honour, should repell it with proper firmness & dignity. The Supreme Government had before hand declared that it would look upon such an act as a *casus belli*; and as a consequence of this declaration, negotiation was by its very nature at an end, and war was the only recourse of the Mexican Government.

But before it proceeded to recover its outraged rights, propositions were addressed to it from the so called President of the Republic of Texas, which had for object to enter into an amicable accommodation upon the basis of her independence, and the Government agreed to hear them and consented to receive the Commissioners who with this view were sent to it from Texas.

Moments so precious were not thrown away by the agents of the United States in Texas. Availing themselves of the *statu quo* of Mexico, they so prepared matters and directed affairs, that the already concerted annexation to the American Union should follow almost immediately.

Thus, this incorporation of a territory which had constituted an integral part of that of Mexico during the long period of the Spanish dominion, and after her emancipation for so long a term without any interruption whatever, and which moreover had been recognized & sanctioned by the Treaty of limits between the Mexican Republic and the United States of America; this annexation was affected by the reprobated means of violence and fraud.

Civilized nations have beheld with amazement, at this enlightened and refined epoch, a powerful & well consolidated State, availing itself of the internal dissensions of a neighbouring nation, putting its vigilance to sleep by protestations of friendship, setting in action all manner of springs and artifices, alternately plying intrigue & violence, and seizing a moment to despoil her of a precious part of her territory, regardless of the incontrovertible rights of the most unquestionable ownership and the most uninterrupted possession.

Here, then, is the true position of the Mexican Republic: despoiled, outraged, contemned, it is now attempted to subject her to a humiliating degradation. The sentiment of her own dignity will not allow her to consent to such ignominy.

After the definite & clear explanations rendered to His Excellency Mr. Slidell, in the note of the 20th December last, referred to by him, it is not easy to comprehend how the Executive of the United States should still think it can find reasons for insisting upon that which was then refuted upon grounds the most conclusive.

The Consul of the United States in this capital addressed, on the 13th of October, to the then Minister of Foreign Relations a confidential note, wherein, referring to what he had previously stated to the Minister in an interview of the same character, he says: "that in suspending diplomatic relations between the two countries, the assurance was given to General Almonte that the President desired that all reasons for complaint between the two governments be settled in a friendly manner and that the most amicable and kindly relations with the sister republics be cultivated. He is still animated by the same sentiments. He desires that all the existing differences be terminated in a *friendly manner* and not by means of arms. The President, moved by these sentiments, has directed me to notify you, on account of there being no diplomatic agent in Mexico to ascertain from the Mexican Government whether it will receive an envoy of the United States vested with full powers to adjust all the questions which are in dispute between the two governments. If the reply should be in the affirmative the said envoy will be despatched to Mexico immediately."

To this the Ministry now in charge of the undersigned replied, on the 15th of the same month, "that although the Nation is gravely offended by that of the United States by reason of the acts committed by the latter towards the Department of Texas, the property of the former, my Government is disposed to receive the Commissioner who may come from the United States to this capital, with full powers from his Government to arrange, in a pacific, reasonable & decorous manner, the present controversy; thereby giving a new proof that, even in the midst of injuries and of its firm determination to exact the adequate reparation, it does not repell nor despise the pact of reason & of peace to which it is invited by its adversary."

From these extracts it is manifest that it was the firm intention of the Mexican Government to admit only a Plenipotentiary from the United States clothed with powers *ad hoc*; that is to say, special powers to treat upon the question of Texas, and upon this alone, as preliminary to the renewal of friendly relations between the two countries, if the result should be such as to admit of their restoration, and then, but not before, of the reception of an Envoy Extraordinary & Minister Plenipotentiary near the same government.

Nor could the Government of the Republic, on that occasion extend its engagement beyond this: for to admit any person sent by the United States in character simply of the ordinary agents between friendly nations, whilst the grave question of Texas was still pending, directly & immediately affecting as it does the integrity of the Mexican territory and the very nationality itself, would be equivalent to an acknowledgment that this question was at an end, thus prejudging it without even touching it, and to a recognition that the relations of friendship & harmony between the two nations were, from that moment, in fact reestablished.

So very simple a truth is this, that the appointment of an Envoy Extraordinary & Minister Plenipotentiary by the Executive of the United States, and the subsequent ratification of this appointment, notwithstanding all that was set forth on the subject by the Government of Mexico, causes this act to appear as an attempt which the undersigned does not permit himself to qualify.

If good faith presides, as is to be supposed, over the dispositions of the Government of the United States: what motive could exist for repelling the indispensable restriction with which Mexico has acceded to the proposal spontaneously made by the former? If it was really & positively desired to tie up again the bonds of good understanding & friendship between the two nations, the way was very easy: the Mexican Government offered to admit the Plenipotentiary or Commissioner who should come clothed with special powers to treat upon the question of Texas.

Upon this point the resolve of the Mexican Government is immutable. And since, in the extreme case, it is the rights of the Mexican Nation which will have to be affirmed, for it is her honor which has been outraged & which will have to be avenged, her Government will, if this necessity arise, call upon all her citizens to fulfil the sacred duty of defending their country.

A lover of peace, she would wish to ward off this sad contigency; and without fearing war, she would desire to avoid so great a calamity for both countries. For this she has offered herself, and will continue to offer herself, open to all honorable means of conciliation, and she anxiously desires that the present controversy may terminate in a reasonable and decorous manner.

In the actual state of things, to say that Mexico maintains a position of quasi hostility with respect to the United States, is to add a new offence to her previous injuries. Her attitude is one of defence, because she sees herself unjustly attacked; because a portion of her territory is occupied by the forces of a nation, intent, without any right whatever, to possess itself of it; because her ports are threatened by the squadrons of the same power. Under such circumstances, is she to remain inactive, without taking measures suited to so rigorous an emergency?

It is then, not upon Mexico, seeing her present state, that it devolves to decide if the issue shall be a friendly negotiation or an open rupture. It is long since her interests have made this necessary, and her dignity has demanded it; but in the hope of an accommodation, at once honourable & pacific, she has silenced the clamour of these imperious exigencies.

It follows, that if war should finally become inevitable, and if in consequence of this war the peace of the civilized world should be disturbed, the responsibility will not fall upon Mexico. It will all rest upon the United States, to them will the whole of it belong. Not upon Mexico, who, with a generosity unequalled, admitted the American citizens who wished to colonize in Texas; but upon the United States, who, bent upon possessing themselves, early or late, of that territory, encouraged emigration thither, with that view; in order that, in due time, its inhabitants, converting themselves from colonists into its masters, should claim the country as their own, for the purpose of transferring it to the United States. Not upon Mexico, who having in due season protested against so enormous a transgression, wished to remove all cause for controversy & hostility; but upon the United States, who, to the scandal of the world, and in manifest violation of treaties, gave protection and aid to those guilty of a rebellion so iniquitous. Not upon Mexico, who, in the midst even of injuries so great & so repeated, has shewn herself disposed to admit propositions for conciliation; but upon the United States, who pretending sincerely to desire a friendly and honourable accommodation, has belied by their acts the sincerity of their words. Finally, not upon Mexico, who, putting out of view her own dearest interests, through her deference for peace, has entertained as long as was wished the propositions which with this view might be made to her: but upon the United States, who, by frivolous pretexts, evade the conclusion of such an arrangement; proposing peace, at the very moment when they are causing their squadrons & their troops to advance upon the ports & the frontiers of Mexico; exacting an humiliation, impossible to be submitted to, in order to find a pretext, if no reason can be found, which may occasion the breaking out of hostilities.

It is therefore upon the United States, and not upon Mexico that it devolves to determine in the alternative presented by Mr. Slidell: that is, between a friendly negotiation and an open rupture.

The undersigned doubts not that he makes His Excellency Mr. Slidell sensible, that, in view of what is set forth in the present note, the Mexican Government trusts that the Executive of the United States, in coming to the determination which it shall deem proper, will act with the deliberation and mature consideration demanded by the exceedingly grave interests involved in this very thorny question.

The Mexican Government, preparing for war, should circumstances require it, will keep alive its flattering hope that peace will not be disturbed on the new continent; and in making this declaration in the face of the world, it emphatically disclaims all responsibility for the evils which may attend a struggle which it has not provoked, and which it has made every effort to avoid.

In communicating all this, by order of his Government, to His Excellency John Slidell, the undersigned avails himself of the opportunity to offer him the assurance of his very distinguished consideration.

John Slidell, United States Minister to Mexico
Letter to Joaquın M. de Castillo y Lanzas,
Minister of Foreign Affairs of Mexico
March 17, 1846

Manning, VIII, 824-28.

The undersigned Envoy Extraordinary and Minister Plenipotentiary of the United States of America, has the honor to acknowledge the receipt of the note of Y. E. of the 12th instant, by which he is informed that the Mexican Government cannot receive him in his capacity of Envoy Extraordinary and Minister Plenipotentiary to reside near that Government.

As it is the intention of the Undersigned, in conformity with his instructions, to return to the United States, with the least possible delay, embarking at Vera Cruz, he has now to request that he may be furnished with the necessary passports, which he will await at this place.

As Y. E. has advanced no new arguments in support of the refusal to receive the undersigned as Envoy Extraordinary and Minister Plenipotentiary, he will abstain from commenting upon that portion of the note of Y. E. which with a mere difference of phraseology presents, substantially the same reasoning as that urged by Mr. Peña y Peña in his note of 20th December last, but he cannot permit, by his silence, the inference which would naturally be implied of his assent to the correctness of the statements made by Y. E. in relation to the question of Texas, and to the general course of policy which is so gratuitously ascribed to the Government of the United States. In the review of these statements, which it becomes his duty to make, he will strive to preserve that calmness of tone and reserve of language, which is most consistent with the consciousness of right and the power to vindicate it if necessary, and of which he regrets to find that Y. E. has not given him the example. The United States can confidently appeal to the history of the events of the last twenty years, as affording the most conclusive refutation of the charges of usurpation, violence, fraud, artifice, intrigue and bad faith so lavishly scattered through the note of Y. E.

It has never been pretended that the scheme of colonization of the territory of Texas by citizens of the United States was suggested by their Government, it was in conformity with a policy deliberately adopted by that of Mexico, and she must accuse herself alone, for results which the slightest foresight must have anticipated from the introduction of a population whose character, habits, and opinions were so widely divergent from those of the people, with whom it was attempted to amalgamate them. There is no ground for the assertion that "the United States, profiting by the generosity with which their citizens had been invited to Texas, and resolved sooner or later to take possession of that territory, encouraged emigration thither with the view that its inhabitants, changing the character of colonists for that of masters, should seize upon the territory for the purpose of transferring it to the United States." It is true that no obstacles to this emigration were interposed by them, for it has ever been one of the most cherished articles of the political creed of the American people, that every citizen has the absolute and uncontrollable right to divest himself of his allegiance, and to seek, if he think proper, the advancement of his fortunes, in foreign lands. Stimulated by the gratuitous allotment of lands to emigrants and by the similarity, approaching, with the exception of religious toleration, almost to identity, of the political institutions of the Mexican Republic to those under which they had been reared, the population of Texas soon attained a development that authorised the demand of a privilege which had been solemnly guarantied to them by the Constitution of 1824—admission into the Mexican Union as a separate State. A convention was held and a State Constitution formed in conformity with the provisions of the fundamental compact of 1824. It was presented to the General Congress with a petition to be admitted into the Union: the application was rejected and the delegate imprisoned. Soon after the Constitutional Congress of Mexico was dissolved by military force, the same arbitrary power convened a new Congress, by which the Federal Constitution was abrogated, and a consolidated or central Government established in its stead. Texas, as she had an unquestionable right to do, refused to acknowledge the authority of a Government which had been imposed upon the other States, by a successful military usurpation. The compact which had bound her to the Mexican Republic was dissolved, and an abortive effort having been made to reduce her to subjection, she, on the 3rd March 1836, declared herself an independent Republic, and nobly sustained that declaration on the battle field of San Jacinto, by the complete defeat and destruction of a numerous, and well appointed army, commanded by the President of the Mexican Republic in person. She then demanded the recognition of her independence, and asked to be annexed to the United States. The language of President Jackson in a communication by him addressed to Congress on the subject, affords a striking illustration of the good faith and forbearance towards Mexico which has ever characterised the conduct of the United States. He advised that no Change should be made in the attitude of the United States, "if not until Mexico herself or one of the great foreign powers should recognise the independence of the new Government, at least, until the lapse of time or course of events should have proved beyond cavil or dispute the ability of the people of Texas to maintain their sovereignty or to uphold the Government constituted by them." These overtures on the part of Texas were pending for several years, but were not entertained by the Government of the United States, until the period had arrived, when, in the language of President Jackson above quoted, the lapse of time and course of events, had proved beyond cavil or dispute, the ability of her people, to maintain her separate sovereignty. Her independence must be considered as a settled fact, which cannot be called in question. Nearly four years since, Mr. Webster, then Secretary of State, in a despatch to the Minister of the United States at Mexico, said; "From the time of the battle of San Jacinto, in April 1836, to the present moment, Texas has exhibited the same external signs of national independence as Mexico herself, and with quite as much stability of Government. Practically free and independent, acknowledged as a political sovereignty by the principal powers of the world; no hostile foot finding rest within her territory, for six or seven years; and Mexico herself refraining, for all that period, from any further attempt to reestablish her own authority over the territory." Three additional years of inaction on the part of Mexico, elapsed, before the final action of the United States upon the question of annexation, with the assent to the same Senate, whose prudence, circumspection and wisdom, Y. E. so justly eulogises; And if any additional sanction could have been required to a measure so evidently just and proper, it has been afforded by Mexico herself, who through her Minister of Foreign Affairs, Mr. Cuevas, authorised by the National Congress, on the 19th May last, declared. "The supreme Government receives the four articles above mentioned as the preliminaries of a formal and definitive treaty, and further, that it is disposed to commence the negotiation as Texas may desire and to receive the Commissioners which she may name for this purpose." The first condition was, "Mexico consents to acknowledge the independence of Texas": true it is that, by the second condition, Texas engaged that she would stipulate in the treaty, not to annex herself or become subject to any country whatever. When it is recollected that this preliminary arrangement was made through the intervention of the Ministers of Great Britain and France, consequent upon the passage of the act of annexation, it cannot be denied that it was intended to apply solely to the United States, and that while Mexico acknowledged her inability to contest the independence of Texas, and was prepared to abandon all her pretentions to that territory, she was induced to make this tardy and reluctant recognition, not by any abatement of her hostile sentiments towards her, so called, rebellious subjects, but in the hope of gratifying her unfriendly feelings against the United States.

The undersigned cannot but express his unfeigned surprise, that in the face of this incontrovertible evidence that Mexico had abandoned all intention or even hope of ever reestablishing her authority over any portion of Texas. Y. E. should have asserted that, "Texas had been an integral part of Mexico, not only during the long period of the Spanish dominion, but since its emancipation, *without any interruption whatever*, during so long a space of time," and again that, "the United States had despoiled Mexico of a valuable portion of her territory, regardless of the incontrovertible rights of the most unquestionable property and of the *most constant possession*." How weak must be the cause which can only be sustained by assertions so inconsistent with facts that are notorious to all the world, and how unfounded are all these vehement declamations against the usurpations, and thirst for territorial aggrandisement of the United States. The independence of Texas then, being a fact conceded by Mexico herself, she had no right to prescribe restrictions as to the form of Government Texas might choose to assume, nor can she justly complain that Texas, with a wise appreciation of her true interests, has thought proper to merge her sovereignty in that of the United States.

The Mexican Government cannot shift the responsibility of war upon the United States, by assuming that they are the aggressors. A plain unanswerable fact responds to all the subtleties and sophistries by which it is attempted to obscure the real question. That fact is, the presence in Mexico, of a Minister of the United States, clothed with full power to settle all the questions in dispute, between the two nations, and among them that of Texas. Their complaints are mutual, the consideration of them cannot be separated, and they must be settled by the same negotiation, or by the arbitrament which Mexico herself has elected. With what reason does Mexico attribute to the United States the desire of finding a pretext to commence hostilities? The appearance of a few ships of war on the Mexican coasts, and the advance of a small military force to the frontier of Texas, are cited as evidence, that the declarations of a desire to preserve peace are insincere. Surely, it cannot be necessary to remind Your Excellency, that the menaces of war have all proceeded from Mexico, and it would seem that the elevation to power of its actual Government, was too recent to have afforded Y. E.. time to forget the ostensible reasons for which that, which preceeded it, was overthrown. The crime imputed to the then President, a crime so odious as to justify his forcible expulsion from the Presidency to which he had been, but a few months previous, elected with unparrallelled unanimity, and in accordance with all the forms of the Constitution, was that of not having prosecuted the war against Texas, or in other words, against the United States; a crime, of which the enormity was aggravated in a tenfold degree, by his having accepted the proposal of the United States to negotiate. To suppose that the present Government has not always, intended, and does not still intend, vigorously, to prosecute an offensive war, would be to insinuate the degrading charge of making declarations which it did not design to fulfil, with the unworthy motive of supplanting a rival.

With these avowed intentions on the part of Mexico and, so far as words can constitute war, that state actually existing; with what fairness can she complain of precautions having been taken by the United States, to guard against the attacks with which they have been menaced; so far at least, as their very moderate peace establishment, would permit them to do so. Are they patiently and meekly to abide the time when Mexico shall be prepared to strike with due effect the threatened blow?

Y. E. has alluded to the internal dissentions of Mexico and accused the United States "of taking advantage of them, beguiling its vigilance by protestations of friendship, bringing into play every kind of device and artifice and appealing alternately to intrigue and violence." Were the disposition of the United States such as Y. E. is pleased to attribute to them, they would have eagerly availed themselves of the opportunity afforded by the first refusal to receive the undersigned, and certainly no moment more propitious than the present, to carry their ambitious schemes, into effect, could have been selected. Instead of availing themselves of it, they have, with a degree of forbearance, that by many, perhaps by most impartial observers, will be considered humiliating: repeated the overtures for negotiation which had been rejected under circumstances the best calculated to offend national pride: and this most conciliatory advance, made by the aggrieved party, is said by Y. E. to be an attempt, which he cannot permit himself, to call by its proper name. *(Una tentativa que el infrascrito no se permite calificar.)* This reserve is remarkable when contrasted with the terms of vituperation so freely employed in other parts of the note: or, is it, that Y. E. could discover no epithet sufficiently energetic to stigmatize an offence so enormous as, a renewed proposition to enter upon negotiations?

The undersigned has already exceeded the limits which he had prescribed to himself for reply: the question has now reached a point where words must give place to acts. While he deeply regrets a result so little contemplated when he commenced the duties of his mission of peace, he is consoled by the reflection that no honorable efforts, to avert the calamities of war, have been spared by his Government, and that, these efforts cannot fail to be properly appreciated, not only by the people of the United States, but by the world.

The undersigned begs leave [etc.].

Polk and Tyler's War Begins

Back in Washington, all was in readiness for Polk's war in defense of American honor. Slidell had thrown down the gauntlet when he bid farewell to that country with a ringing challenge: "the question has now reached a point where words must give place to acts."[83] Polk and Buchanan instructed Slidell to act out this last scene of the charade before returning home. They were maneuvering to place the responsibility for the war, which they knew would follow, on the Mexicans and they insisted that the American envoy to Mexico establish a clear record of having offered to negotiate with the new government and of waiting to be formally rejected before returning to the states. "It will then become the duty of the President to submit the whole case to Congress and call upon the nation to assert its just rights and avenge its injured honor."[84]

Two months earlier General Taylor was ordered by the secretary of war to break camp at Corpus Christi and to "advance and occupy, with troops under your command, positions on or near the east bank of the Rio del Norte [Rio Grande]...."[85] But it had taken Taylor until March 8, 1846 to leave Corpus Christi and another 12 days before he reached the Rio Grande and established fortifications near the Mexican town of Matamoras on the opposite bank of the river. Taylor's guns were trained on the town square. With the players poised on the stage, the curtain was almost ready to go up on the Mexican War.

Secretary of War William L. Marcy
Orders to Brigadier General Zachary Taylor
January 13, 1846

House Executive Document No. 60, 30th Cong., 1st sess., 90-91.

Sir: I am directed by the President to instruct you to advance and occupy, with the troops under your command, positions on or near the east bank of the Rio del Norte, as soon as it can be conveniently done with reference to the season and the routes by which your movements must be made. From the views heretofore presented to this department, it is presumed Point Isabel will be considered by you an eligible position. This point, or some one near it, and points opposite Matamoras and Mier, and in the vicinity of Laredo, are suggested for your consideration; but you are left to your better knowledge to determine the post or posts which you are to occupy, as well as the question of dividing your forces with a view to occupying two or more positions.

In the positions you may take in carrying out these instructions and other movements that may be made, the use of the Rio del Norte may be very convenient, if not necessary. Should you attempt to exercise the right which the United States have in common with Mexico to the free navigation of this river, it is probable that Mexico would interpose resistance. You will not attempt to enforce this right without further instructions.

You are requested to report to this department, without delay, what means you may require, if any, beyond those you now possess, to enforce and maintain our common right to navigate this river, as well as your views of the importance of this right in the defence and protection of the State of Texas.

It is not designed, in our present relations with Mexico, that you should treat her as an enemy; but, should she assume that character by a declaration of war, or any open act of hostility towards us, you will not act merely on the defensive, if your relative means enable you to do otherwise.

Since instructions were given you to draw aid from Texas, in case you should deem it necessary, the relations between that State and the United States have undergone some modification. Texas is now fully incorporated into our union of States, and you are hereby authorized by the President to make a requisition upon the executive of that State for such of its militia force as may be needed to repel invasion or to secure the country against apprehended invasion.

> I have the honor to be, with great
> respect, your obedient servant,
>
> *Wm. L. Marcy*
> Secretary of War

Slidell returned from Mexico and met with the President on May 8, 1846. Polk recorded their meeting in his diary and indicated that he hoped to act on the Mexican question "very soon." The next day the President met with his cabinet and they discussed the matter.

President James K. Polk
Diary Entry Contemplating the
Declaration of War on Mexico
May 8, 1846

Quaife, I, 382.

Friday—Saw company until 12 o'clock to-day. Among others the Hon. John Slidell, late U. S. Minister to Mexico, called in company with the Secretary of State. Mr. Buchanan retired after a few minutes, and Mr. Slidell remained about an hour in conversation concerning his mission and the state of our relations with Mexico. Mr. Slidell's opinion was that but one course towards Mexico was left to the U.S. and that was to take the redress of the wrongs and injuries which we had so long borne from Mexico into our own hands, and to act with promptness and energy. In this I agreed with him, and told him it was only a matter of time when I would make a communication to Congress on the subject, and that I had made up my mind to do so very soon.

Once Taylor's army was in position, the President was prepared to begin his "defensive" war against Mexico. He met with his cabinet on Saturday, May 9, 1846, and after extended discussion he decided to draft a message to Congress recommending an immediate declaration of war. This decision was not based upon any information of a Mexican attack on General Taylor's troops, but rather on considerations of what the President and his cabinet interpreted as indignities suffered by this country at the hands of Mexico. These same indignities had been carefully outlined in the President's State of the Union Message the previous December and were to be reiterated again in his special message, delivered to the Congress 48 hours later. There was nothing new in these charges. They referred once again to the outrageous actions of the Mexican government in defaulting on its scheduled payments of arbitration awards to private American citizens, and to the recent breakdown of the negotiations in Mexico.

President James K. Polk
Diary Entry Concerning his Discussions of
The Mexican Situation with his Cabinet
May 9, 1846

Quaife, I, 384-85.

Saturday—The Cabinet held a regular meeting to-day; all the members present. I brought up the Mexican question, and the question of what was the duty of the administration in the present state of our relations with that country. The subject was very fully discussed. All agreed that if the Mexican forces at Matamoras committed any act of hostility on Gen'l Taylor's forces I should immediately send a message to Congress recommending an immediate declaration of War. I stated to the Cabinet that up to this time, as they knew, we had heard of no open act of aggression by the Mexican army, but that the danger was imminent that such acts would be committed. I said that in my opinion we had ample cause of war, and that it was impossible that we could stand in *statu quo*, or that I could remain silent much longer; that I thought it was my duty to send a message to Congress very soon & recommend definitive measures. I told them that I thought I ought to make such a message by tuesday next, that the country was excited and impatient on the subject, and if I failed to do so I would not be doing my duty. I then propounded the distinct question to the Cabinet and took their opinions individually, whether I should make a message to Congress on tuesday, and whether in that message I should recommend a declaration of War against Mexico. All except the Secretary of the Navy gave their advice in the affirmitive. Mr. Bancroft dissented but said if any act of hostility should be committed by the Mexican forces he was then in favour of immediate war. Mr. Buchanan said he would feel better satisifed in his course if the Mexican forces had or should commit any act of hostility, but that as matters stood we had ample cause of war against Mexico, & he gave his assent to the measure. It was agreed that the message should be prepared and submitted to the Cabinet in their meeting on tuesday. A history of our causes of complaint against Mexico had been at my request previously drawn up by Mr. Buchanan. I stated that what was said in my annual message in December gave that history as succinctly and satisfactorily as Mr. Buchanan's statement, that in truth it was the same history in both, expressed in different language, and that if I repeated that history in [a] message to Congress now I had better employ the precise language used in my message of December last. Without deciding this point the Cabinet passed to the consideration of some other subjects of minor importance. The Cabinet adjourned about 2 O'Clock P.M. Before they separated I directed the Secretary of State to have all the correspondence of Mr. Slidell with the Mexican Government, & such portions of his correspondence with the Department of State as it was proper to communicate copied; and in like manner I directed the Secretary of War to have all his orders to Gen'l Taylor commanding the army in Texas copied, so as to have these documents ready to be communicated to Congress with my message. . . .

The cabinet adjourned at about two o'clock on the afternoon of May 9: at about six that evening Adjutant General R. Jones came to the White House and informed the President that elements of the Mexican army had crossed the Rio Grande and attacked two dragoons of General Taylor's army, killing or capturing 63 officers and men. The cabinet was recalled at 7:30 p.m. and Polk set about putting the war machinery into motion. It was decided that an even stronger war message would be sent to the Congress on Monday morning. Not a great deal of redrafting of the original message was necessary, but this time there was no need to plead for a declaration of war. It stated simply that "In further vindication of our rights and defense of our territory, I invoke the prompt action of Congress to recognize the existence of the war, and to place at the disposition of the Executive the means of prosecuting the war with vigor, and thus hastening the restoration of peace."[86] The President also submitted a preamble to an appropriations measure which would authorize the expenditure of $10,000.000 and permit the President to call out 50,000 troops. In the preamble, the President inserted a phrase recognizing that "by the act of the Republic of Mexico, a state of war exists between that government and the United States."

The diary entries for the rest of Saturday, after the news of the Mexican attack had been received, and of the following two days provide a fascinating record of the President's efforts to organize political support to sustain his war effort. They reveal the calm assurance he possessed as he saw the goal he had pursued coming to fruition; they embroider the tremendous energy he put into this effort. He accepted all the developments with no apparent alarm and with a firm conviction of the righteousness of his actions and the soundness of his decisions. As a constitutional leader he moved quickly to consolidate the support of Congress in favor of increasing the territorial dominion of the United States, having no serious reservations about the justice or the integrity of these aims.

President James K. Polk
Diary Entry (Extract) Explaining his Efforts
To Put War Machinery into Action
May 9, 1846

Quaife, I, 386-87.

. . . About 6 o'clock P.M. Gen'l R. Jones, the Adjutant General of the army, called and handed to me despatches received from Gen's Taylor by the Southern mail which had just arrived, giving information that a part of [the] Mexican army had crossed to the Del Norte, [crossed the Del Norte] and attacked and killed and captured two companies of dragoons of Gen'l Taylor's army consisting of 63 officers & men. The despatch also stated that he had on that day (26th April) made a requisition on the Governors of Texas & Louisiana for four Regiments each, to be sent to his relief at the earliest practicable period. Before I had finished reading the despatch, the Secretary of War called. I immediately summoned the Cabinet to meet at 7½ O'Clock this evening. The Cabinet accordingly assembled at that hour; all the members present. The subject of the despatch received this evening from Gen'l Taylor, as well as the state of our relations with Mexico, were fully considered. The Cabinet were unanimously of opinion, and it was so agreed, that a message should be sent to Congress on Monday laying all the information in my possession before them and recommending vigorous & prompt measure[s] to enable the Executive to prosecute the War. The Secretary of War & Secretary of State agreed to put their clerks to work to copy the correspondence between Mr. Slidell & the Mexican Government & Secretary of State and the correspondence between the War Department & Gen'l Taylor, to the end that these documents should be transmitted to Congress with my message on Monday. The other members of the Cabinet tendered the services of their clerks to aid in preparing these copies.

Mr. Senator Houston, Hon. Barkley Martin, & several other members of Congress called in the course of the evening, & were greatly excited at the news brought by the Southern mail from the army. They all approved the steps which had been taken by the administration, and were all of opinion that war with Mexico should now be prosecuted with vigor.

The Cabinet adjourned about 10 O'Clock, & I commenced my message; Mr. Bancroft and Mr. Buchanan, the latter of whom had prepared a history of our causes of complaint against Mexico, agreed to assist me in preparing the message.

President James K. Polk
Diary Entry Describing the Preparation
Of his War Message to Congress
May 10, 1846

Quaife, 1, 387-90.

Sunday—As the public excitement in and out of Congress was very naturally very great, and as there was a great public necessity to have the prompt action of Congress on the Mexican question, and therefore an absolute necessity for sending my message to Congress on tomorrow, I resumed this morning the preparation of my message. About 9½ O'Clock Mr. Bancroft called, and with his assistance I was engaged in preparing it until 11 O'Clock, at which time I suspended my labours in order to attend church. I left the part of the message which had been written to be copied by my Private Secretary, and accompanied Mrs. Polk, my niece, Miss Rucker, & my nephew, Marshall T. Polk, to church. As we were leaving for church the Hon. Mr. Haralson & the Hon. Mr. Baker, [Edward Dickinson Baker of Illinois, killed in the battle of Ball's Bluff, October 21, 1861. Footnote in Quaife.] members of the Committee of Military affairs, called to see me on the subject of the legislative action proper to be had to provide for the vigorous prosecution of the war with Mexico. I told them I would see them at 5 O'Clock this afternoon.

On my return from church about 1 O'Clock P.M. I resumed the preparation of my message. In the course of half an hour Mr. Bancroft & Mr. Buchanan called and the part of the message which had been written was examined & approved. At 2 O'Clock my family dinner was announced. I invited Mr. Buchanan and Mr. Bancroft to dine with me. Mr. Buchanan declined and Mr. Bancroft dined with me. After dinner Mr. Bancroft and myself returned to the prepartion of the message. Two confidential Clerks, *viz.*, H. C. Williams from the War Department an[d]——, from the Navy Department were engaged in assisting my Private Secretary in making two copies of my message, one for the Senate and one for the House.

At 5 O'Clock Mr. Haralson & Mr. Baker called according to the appointment made this morning. They informed me that deeming the present a great emergency they had called the Committee on Military affairs of the Ho. Repts. together this morning and that they had unanimously agreed to support a Bill appropriating ten millions of Dollars, and authorizing the President to raise fifty thousand dollars [men] to prosecute the war with Mexico. They showed to me a copy of the Bill which they proposed to pass. I pointed out some defects in it & advised them to consult with the Secretary and officers connected with the War Department, including Gen'l Scott and Adj't Gen'l Jones. They said they would do so. I discovered in the course of the conversation that both Mr. Haralson and Mr. Baker desired to be appointed to high commands in the army of Volunteers which their Bill proposed to raise. I talked civilly to them but made no promises.

After night and whilst the clerks were still copying my message in my Private Secretary's office, the Secretaries of State, of the Treasury, of the Navy, the P.M. Gen'l, and [the] Atto. Gen'l called, but were not all present at any one time. The Secretary of War was indisposed as I learned, and did not call during the day. Senator Houston & Bartley Martin & Ch. J. Ingersoll called to consult me on the Mexican question, and to learn what I intended to recommend in my message. The two former had retired before Mr. Ingersoll called. I addressed notes to Senator Allen, Ch. of the Comm. of Foreign Affairs of the Senate, & Mr. McKay of N. C., Ch. of the Com. of Ways and Means of the Ho. Repts. requesting them to call at my office to-night. In the course of half an hour they called, and the message being copied, I read it to them and Mr. Ingersoll in presence of some of the members of [the] Cabinet who had remained. They all approved it.

At 10½ O'Clock the company left and I retired to rest. It was a day of great anxiety to me, and I regretted the necessity which had existed to make it necessary for me to spend the Sabbath in the manner I have.

President James K. Polk
Diary Entry on the Delivery of
The War Message to Congress
May 11, 1846

Quaife, I, 390-93.

Monday—I refused to see company generally this morning. I carefully revised my message on the Mexican question, but had no time to read the copies of the correspondence furnished by the War & State Departments which was to accompany it. I had read the original correspondence and presume the copies are correct.

I addressed [notes] to Senators Cass and Benton this morning requesting them to call. Gen'l Cass called first. The message was read to him and he highly approved it. Col. Benton called before Gen'l Cass left, and I gave him the copy of the message and he retired to an adjoining room and read it. After he had read it I had a conversation with him alone. I found he did not approve it in all its parts. He was willing to vote men and money for defence of our territory, but was not prepared to make aggressive war on Mexico. He disapproved the marching of the army from Corpus Christi to the left Bank of the Del Norte, but said he had never said so to the public. I had a full conversation with him, and he left without satisfying me that I could rely upon his support of the measures recommended by the message, further than the mere defence of our territory. I inferred, too, from his conversation that he did not think the territory of the U.S. extended West of the Nueces River.

At 12 O'Clock I sent my message to Congress. It was a day of great anxiety with me. Between 5 and 6 O'Clock P.M. Mr. Slidell, U. S. Minister to Mexico, called and informed me that the Ho. Repts. had passed a Bill carrying out all the recommendations of the message by a vote of 173 ayes to 14 noes, and that the Senate had adjourned after a debate without coming to any decision.

My Private Secretary brought me a note from Col. Benton desiring information as to the number of men and amount of money required to defend the country. There was nothing in his note to commit him to any course of policy beyond what he had intimated in his conversation this morning. My Private Secretary informed me that Col. Benton would call for an answer at 8 O'Clock this evening. I immediately sent his note to the Secretary of War and requested him to call at that hour. The Secretaries of War and State called a few minutes before 8 O'Clock but before I had consulted him [the former] in relation to Col. Benton's note, Col. Benton came in. I told Col. B. that the Secretary of War had just come in & that I had no opportunity to consult him on the subject of his note. I told him that my own opinion was that it was at present impossible to say what number of troops would be wanted, and that until Congress acted I could not tell what authority would be given to the Executive; but that if the Bill which had passed the House to-day should also pass the Senate, no more men would be called out and no more money expended than would be absolutely necessary to bring the present state of hostilities to an end. I told him if the war [was] recognized by Congress, that with a large force on land and sea I thought it could be speedily terminated. Col. B. said that the Ho. Repts. had passed a Bill to-day declaring war in two hours, and that one and [a] half hours of that time had been occupied in reading the documents which accompanied my message, and that in his opinion in the 19th Century war should not be declared without full discussion and much more consideration than had been given to it in the Ho. Repts. Mr. Buchanan then remarked that War already existed by the act of Mexico herself & therefore it did not require much deliberation to satisfy all that we ought promptly and vigorously to meet [it]. Mr. Marcy and Mr. Buchanan discussed the subject for some time with Mr. Benton, but without any change of the opinions which he had expressed to me in conversation this morning. I saw it was useless to debate the subject further with him & therefore I abstained from engaging further in the conversation. After reminaing near an hour Col. Benton left. Mr. Buchanan, Mr. Marcy, and myself were perfectly satisfied that he would oppose the Bill which had passed the House to-day, and that if the Whigs on party grounds acted with him the Bill might be defeated.

Gov. Yell of Arkansas, Senator Houston, & other members of Congress called in in the course of the evening, and were highly gratified at the action of the House in passing the Bill by so overwhelming a majority. The part taken by Mr. Calhoun in the Senate to-day satisfies me that he too will oppose the Bill passed by the House to-day if he thinks he can do so safely in reference to public opinion. The Whigs in the Senate will oppose it on party grounds probably, if they can get Mr. Calhoun, Mr. Benton, and two or three other Senators professing to belong to the Democratic party to join them, so as to make a majority against the Bill. Should the Bill be defeated by such a combination, the professed Democratic members who by their votes aid in rejecting it will owe a heavy responsibility not only to their party but to the country. I am fully satisfied that all that can save the Bill in the Senate is the fear of the people by the few Democratic Senators who wish it defeated.

President James K. Polk
Special War Message to Congress
May 11, 1846

Richardson, V, 2287-93.

To the Senate and House of Representatives:
   The existing state of the relations between the United States and Mexico renders it proper that I should bring the subject to the consideration of Congress. In my message at the commencement of your present session the state of these relations, the causes which led to the suspension of diplomatic intercourse between the two countries in March, 1845, and the long-continued and unredressed wrongs and injuries committed by the Mexican Government on citizens of the United States in their persons and property were briefly set forth.
   As the facts and opinions which were then laid before you were carefully considered, I can not better express my present convictions of the condition of affairs up to that time than by referring you to that communication.
   The strong desire to establish peace with Mexico on liberal and honorable terms, and the readiness of this Government to regulate and adjust our boundary and other causes of difference with that power on such fair and equitable principles as would lead to permanent relations of the most friendly nature, induced me in September last to seek the reopening of diplomatic relations between the two countries. Every measure adopted on our part had for its object the furtherance of these desired results. In communicating to Congress a succinct statement of the injuries which we had suffered from Mexico, and which have been accumulating during a period of more than twenty years, every expression that could tend to inflame the people of Mexico or defeat or delay a pacific result was carefully avoided. An envoy of the United States repaired to Mexico with full powers to adjust every existing difference. But though present on the Mexican soil by agreement between the two Governments, invested with full powers, and bearing evidence of the most friendly dispositions, his mission has been unavailing. The Mexican Government not only refused to receive him or listen to his propositions, but after a long-continued series of menaces have at last invaded our territory and shed the blood of our fellow-citizens on our own soil.
   It now becomes my duty to state more in detail the origin, progress, and failure of that mission. In pursuance of the instructions given in September last, an inquiry was made on the 13th of October, 1845, in the most friendly terms, through our consul in Mexico, of the minister for foreign affairs, whether the Mexican Government "would receive an envoy from the United States intrusted with full powers to adjust all the questions in dispute between the two Governments," with the assurance that "should the answer be in the affirmative such an envoy would be immediately dispatched to Mexico." The Mexican minister on the 15th of October gave an affirmative answer to this inquiry, requesting at the same time that our

naval force at Vera Cruz might be withdrawn, lest its continued presence might assume the appearance of menace and coercion pending the negotiations. This force was immediately withdrawn. On the 10th of November, 1845, Mr. John Slidell, of Louisiana, was commissioned by me as envoy extraordinary and minister plenipotentiary of the United States to Mexico, and was intrusted with full powers to adjust both the questions of the Texas boundary and of indemnification to our citizens. The redress of the wrongs of our citizens naturally and inseparably blended itself with the question of boundary. The settlement of the one question in any correct view of the subject involves that of the other. I could not for a moment entertain the idea that the claims of our much-injured and long-suffering citizens, many of which had existed for more than twenty years, should be postponed or separated from the settlement of the boundary question.

Mr. Slidell arrived at Vera Cruz on the 30th of November, and was courteously received by the authorities of that city. But the Government of General Herrera was then tottering to its fall. The revolutionary party had seized upon the Texas question to effect or hasten its overthrow. Its determination to restore friendly relations with the United States, and to receive our minister to negotiate for the settlement of this question, was violently assailed, and was made the great theme of denunciation against it. The Government of General Herrera, there is good reason to believe, was sincerely desirous to receive our minister; but it yielded to the storm raised by its enemies, and on the 21st of December refused to accredit Mr. Slidell upon the most frivolous pretexts. These are so fully and ably exposed in the note of Mr. Slidell of the 24th of December last to the Mexican minister of foreign relations, herewith transmitted, that I deem it unnecessary to enter into further detail on this portion of the subject.

Five days after the date of Mr. Slidell's note General Herrera yielded the Government to General Paredes without a struggle, and on the 30th of December resigned the Presidency. This revolution was accomplished solely by the army, the people having taken little part in the contest; and thus the supreme power in Mexico passed into the hands of a military leader.

Determined to leave no effort untried to effect an amicable adjustment with Mexico, I directed Mr. Slidell to present his credentials to the Government of General Paredes and ask to be officially received by him. There would have been less ground for taking this step had General Paredes come into power by a regular constitutional succession. In that event his administration would have been considered but a mere constitutional continuance of the Government of General Herrera, and the refusal of the latter to receive our minister would have been deemed conclusive unless an intimation had been given by General Paredes of his desire to reverse the decision of his predecessor. But the Government of General Paredes owes its existence to a military revolution, by which the subsisting constituional authorities had been subverted. The form of government was entirely changed, as well as all the high functionaries by whom it was administered.

Under these circumstances, Mr. Slidell, in obedience to my direction, addressed a note to the Mexican minister of foreign relations, under date of the 1st of March last, asking to be received by that Government in the diplomatic character to which he had been appointed. This minister in his reply, under date of the 12 of

March, reiterated the arguments of his predecessor, and in terms that may be considered as giving just grounds of offense to the Government and people of the United States denied the application of Mr. Slidell. Nothing therefore remained for our envoy to demand his passports and return to his own country.

Thus the Government of Mexico, though solemnly pledged by official acts in October last to receive and accredit an American envoy, violated their plighted faith and refused the offer of a peaceful adjustment of our difficulties. Not only was the offer rejected, but the indignity of its rejection was enhanced by the manifest breach of faith in refusing to admit the envoy who came because they had bound themselves to receive him. Nor can it be said that the offer was fruitless from the want of opportunity of discussing it; our envoy was present on their own soil. Nor can it be ascribed to a want of sufficient powers; our envoy had full powers to adjust every question of difference. Nor was there room for complaint that our propositions for settlement were unreasonable; permission was not even given our envoy to make any proposition whatever. Nor can it be objected that we, on our part, would not listen to any reasonable terms of their suggestion; the Mexican Government refused all negotiation, and have made no proposition of any kind.

In my message at the commencement of the present session I informed you that upon the earnest appeal both of the Congress and convention of Texas I had ordered an efficient military force to take a position "between the Nueces and the Del Norte." This had become necessary to meet a threatened invasion of Texas by the Mexican forces, for which extensive military preparations had been made. The invasion was threatened solely because Texas had determined, in accordance with a solemn resolution of the Congress of the United States, to annex herself to our Union, and under these circumstances it was plainly our duty to extend our protection over her citizens and soil.

This force was concentrated at Corpus Christi, and remained there until after I had received such information from Mexico as rendered it probable, if not certain, that the Mexican Government would refuse to receive our envoy.

Meantime Texas, by the final action of our Congress, had become an integral part of our Union. The Congress of Texas, by its act of December 19, 1836, had declared the Rio del Norte to be the boundary of that Republic. Its jurisdiction had been extended and exercised beyond the Nueces. The country between that river and the Del Norte had been represented in the Congress and in the convention of Texas, had thus taken part in the act of annexation itself, and is now included within one of our Congressional districts. Our own Congress had, moreover, with great unanimity, by the act approved December 31, 1845, recognized the country beyond the Nueces as a part of our territory by including it within our own revenue system, and a revenue officer to reside within that district has been appointed by and with the advice and consent of the Senate. It became, therefore, of urgent necessity to provide for the defense of that portion of our country. Accordingly, on the 13th of January last instructions were issued to the general in command of these troops to occupy the left bank of the Del Norte. This river, which is the southwestern boundary of the State of Texas, is an exposed frontier. From this quarter invasion was threatened; upon it and in its immediate vicinity, in the judgment of high military experience, are the proper stations for the protecting forces of the

Government. In addition to this important consideration, several others occurred to induce this movement. Among these are the facilities afforded by the ports at Brazos Santiago and the mouth of the Del Norte for the reception of supplies by sea, the stronger and more healthful military positions, the convenience for obtaining a ready and a more abundant supply of provisions, water, fuel, and forage, and the advantages which are afforded by the Del Norte in forwarding supplies to such posts as may be established in the interior and upon the Indian frontier.

The movement of the troops to the Del Norte was made by the commanding general under positive instructions to abstain from all aggressive acts toward Mexico or Mexican citizens and to regard the relations between that Republic and the United States as peaceful unless she should declare war or commit acts of hostility indicative of a state of war. He was specially directed to protect private property and respect personal rights.

The Army moved from Corpus Christi on the 11th of March, and on the 28th of that month arrived on the left bank of the Del Norte opposite to Matamoras, where it encamped on a commanding position, which has since been strengthened by the erection of fieldworks. A depot has also been established at Point Isabel, near the Brazos Santiago, 30 miles in rear of the encampment. The selection of his position was necessarily confided to the judgment of the general in command.

The Mexican forces at Matamoras assumed a belligerent attitude, and on the 12th of April General Ampudia, then in command, notified General Taylor to break up his camp within twenty-four hours and to retire beyond the Nueces River, and in the event of his failure to comply with these demands announced that arms, and arms alone, must decide the question. But no open act of hostility was committed until the 24th of April. On that day General Arista, who had succeeded to the command of the Mexican forces, communicated to General Taylor that "he considered hostilities commenced and should prosecute them." A party of dragoons of 63 men and officers were on the same day dispatched from the American camp up the Rio del Norte, on its left bank, to ascertain whether the Mexican troops had crossed or were preparing to cross the river, "became engaged with a large body of these troops, and after a short affair, in which some 16 were killed and wounded, appear to have been surrounded and compelled to surrender."

The grievous wrongs perpetrated by Mexico upon our citizens throughout a long period of years remain unredressed, and solemn treaties pledging her public faith for this redress have been disregarded. A government either unable or unwilling to enforce the execution of such treaties fails to perform one of its plainest duties.

Our commerce with Mexico has been almost annihilated. It was formerly highly beneficial to both nations, but our merchants have been deterred from prosecuting it by the system of outrage and extortion which the Mexican authorities have pursued against them, whilst their appeals through their own Government for indemnity have been made in vain. Our forbearance has gone to such an extreme as to be mistaken in its character. Had we acted with vigor in repelling the insults and redressing the injuries inflicted by Mexico at the commencement, we should doubtless have escaped all the difficulties in which we are now involved.

Instead of this, however, we have been exerting our best efforts to propitiate her good will. Upon the pretext that Texas, a nation as independent as herself, thought proper to unite its destinies with our own she has affected to believe that we have severed her rightful territory, and in official proclamations and manifestoes has repeatedly threatened to make war upon us for the purpose of reconquering Texas. In the meantime we have tried every effort at reconciliation. The cup of forbearance had been exhausted even before the recent information from the frontier of the Del Norte. But now, after reiterated menaces, Mexico has passed the boundary of the United States, has invaded our territory and shed American blood upon the American soil. She has proclaimed that hostilities have commenced, and that the two nations are now at war.

As war exists, and, notwithstanding all our efforts to avoid it, exists by the act of Mexico herself, we are called upon by every consideration of duty and patriotism to vindicate with decision the honor, the rights, and the interests of our country.

Anticipating the possibility of a crisis like that which has arrived, instructions were given in August last, "as a precautionary measure" against invasion or threatened invasion, authorizing General Taylor, if the emergency required, to accept volunteers, not from Texas only, but from the States of Louisiana, Alabama, Mississippi, Tennessee, and Kentucky, and corresponding letters were addressed to the respective governors of those States. These instructions were repeated, and in January last, soon after the incorporation of "Texas into our Union of States," General Taylor was further "authorized by the President to make a requisition upon the executive of that State for such of its militia force as may be needed to repel invasion or to secure the country against apprehended invasion." On the 2d day of March he was again reminded, "in the event of the approach of any considerable Mexican force, promptly and efficiently to use the authority with which he was clothed to call to him such auxiliary force as he might need." War actually existing and our territory having been invaded, General Taylor, pursuant to authority vested in him by my direction, has called on the governor of Texas for four regiments of State troops, two to be mounted and two to serve on foot, and on the governor of Louisiana for four regiments of infantry to be sent to him as soon as practicable.

In further vindication of our rights and defense of our territory, I invoke the prompt action of Congress to recognize the existence of the war, and to place at the disposition of the Executive the means of prosecuting the war with vigor, and thus hastening the restoration of peace. To this end I recommend that authority should be given to call into the public service a large body of volunteers to serve for not less than six or twelve months unless sooner discharged. A volunteer force is beyond question more efficient than any other description of citizen soldiers, and it is not to be doubted that a number far beyond that required would readily rush to the field upon the call of their country. I further recommend that a liberal provision be made for sustaining our entire military force and furnishing it with supplies and munitions of war.

The most energetic and prompt measures and the immediate appearance in arms of a large and overpowering force are recommended to Congress as the most certain and efficient means of bringing the existing collision with Mexico to a speedy and successful termination.

In making these recommendations I deem it proper to declare that it is my anxious desire not only to terminate hostilities speedily, but to bring all matters in dispute between this Government and Mexico to an early and amicable adjustment; and in this view I shall be prepared to renew negotiations whenever Mexico shall be ready to receive propositions or to make propositions of her own.

I transmit herewith a copy of the correspondence between our envoy to Mexico and the Mexican minister for foreign affairs, and so much of the correspondence between that envoy and the Secretary of State and between the Secretary of War and the general in command on the Del Norte as is necessary to a full understanding of the subject.

James K. Polk

There was substantial opposition to "Polk's War," particularly in the Senate, where the combined forces of the Whig party, Calhoun and MacDuffie (both of whom had strongly advocated and in fact energetically pursued the annexation of Texas, but who were now in bitter opposition to Polk's war moves), and Senator Benton could have defeated the declaration of war in the Senate. Polk's diary reveals something of the pressure that was directed towards Colonel Benton, as Polk always referred to him, that he go along with the measure.[87] Benton's support of the President's position was particularly critical, not only because the votes were close and his was needed, but also because his motion on Monday succeeded in separating the war declaration from the appropriations measure, thus sending them to separate Senate committees, one of which (the Military Affairs Committee which received the appropriations section of the measure) was headed by Benton himself:

That night the administration threw all its energies into arousing Benton's "fear of the people." Polk, Buchanan, and Marcy remonstrated with him, and his friends of the Van Buren group were enlisted to warn him of the political consequences of siding with Calhoun, the Whigs, and Mexico. When these entreaties failed to move the stubborn Missourian, Senator Dix "in distress" summoned Frank Blair from his suburban home. Blair hastened to town early Tuesday morning, played adroitly on Benton's suspicions of Calhoun, and concluded by telling his old friend bluntly "that he was bound to stick to the War party or he was a ruined man." Finally Benton said, "I see *you are right.*" Hastily he assembled the Military Affairs Committee, while Allen was convening the Foreign Relations Committee [where the preamble had been directed by Benton's motion for consideration]; and at a Senate Democratic caucus later that morning Benton and Allen announced that their committees would support the House war bill [which had already triumphed overwhelmingly] and press it to a vote before adjournment that day.[88]

**President James K. Polk
Diary Entry as War Is
Declared against Mexico**
May 12, 1846

Quaife, I, 393-95.

Tuesday—The Cabinet held a regular meeting to-day; all members present except the P. M. Gen'l, who was understood to be engaged in his office in examining the bids for mail contracts at the late letting in the Western & S. Western States.

The Mexican question was the subject of conversation, and all had doubts whether the Bill which passed the House on yesterday would pass the Senate to-day. Should it pass, the course of operations was considered. Mr. Bancroft at my request brought from his office all the orders and letters of instruction to our squadrons in the Pacific & Gulf of Mexico, and they were read. This was done 1st, because I desired to refresh my memory of what they were, & 2nd, because they may be called for by Congress.

Some other business of minor importance was considered; & the Cabinet adjourned about 2 O'Clock P.M.

At 7 O'Clock P.M. my Private Secretary returned from the Capitol and announced to me that the Bill which passed the Ho. Repts. on yesterday, making a formal declaration of War against Mexico, had passed the Senate by a vote of 42 ayes to 2 noes, with some immaterial amendment in its details. He represented to me that the debate in the Senate to-day was most animating and thrilling, and that Mr. Calhoun, who spoke in opposition to the Bill, but finally did not vote, had suffered much in the discussion. Mr. Crittenden and other Whigs, he informed me, had made speeches against portions of the Bill & made indirect opposition to it, [but had] finally voted for it. He represented the whole debate as a great triumph for the administration. The Senate, he informed me, adjourned as soon as the Bill was passed. The Ho. of Repts., he informed me, had adjourned to meet this evening at 7½ O'Clock with a view to receive the Bill from the Senate, if that body should act upon it to-day. At 8½ o'clock P.M. I learned that the House had concurred in the amendments of the Senate to the Bill, so that when the Bill is signed by the President War will be declared against Mexico. . . .

Polk had succeeded; war was now a reality, and California and the New Mexico area lay ahead.

Polk's Critics

The Mexican War was never a very popular war and from the very beginning serious criticism was leveled against its origins and its conduct in the Congress and elsewhere. Calhoun and many of the Whigs launched severe attacks on the presidential policies that had led to war, and during the next few years Polk would face renewed attacks upon his conduct of the war. A jingoist mood overcame the American people for a short time, but they soon tired of the conflict when the casualty figures continued to increase and the appropriations skyrocketed. Calhoun had denounced Polk's message as "making war on the Constitution," and called the war "monstrous."[89] Congressman Giddings of Ohio, one of the strongest leaders in the Congress, denounced the war, calling it "illegal, unrighteous and damnable. . . . We had seen an American President, without provocation, and without right, planting the standard of the United States on foreign soil, and using the military forces of the United States to violate every principle of international law and of moral justice."[90] Another Whig congressman charged that the "war had been planned and declared" against Mexico because "we wanted to get her territory. . . .[91] Where was his right to enter into a country which did not belong to us, and point his cannon at a Mexican town to which we could have no pretensions."[92]

The voices of criticism, whose tenor rose quickly in all parts of the country during the course of the war, were more harsh than those that had been heard in Congress. The most knowledgeable and experienced statesman in the field of international relations in the country was Albert Gallatin, who had served exceptionally in both Jefferson and Madison's cabinets and who had represented the country abroad on a number of different missions. Gallatin presented a devastating analysis of Polk's policy vis à vis Mexico with such eloquent and forceful style that it appeared to be unanswerable. His pamphlet—"Peace with Mexico"—should be read in its entirety to capture the graceful and controlled manner in which he argued his cogent case against the Polk administration's handling of the Mexican question; and it is worth noting some of the highlights of that analysis for further study.

Gallatin wrote in 1847 from the vantage point of hindsight, but there is no doubt that he held these views throughout the crisis; furthermore, they are reflective of his own thinking and conduct during his long and brilliant career in public service. He began his analysis by recognizing the outstanding military feats of the American army in the field, the inevitability of its total victory over its enemy and its ability to impose its own terms upon the defeated. He did, however, raise the question as to whether or not the victory in the field, achieved at a price measured in lives lost, could ever be compensated for by any negotiated terms.

He next reviewed the question of Mexican indemnities to citizens of the United States, concluding that such citizens were fully entitled to just indemnity, but added that "before the annexation of Texas there was every prospect of securing such indemnity."[93] He also reminded his American readers that historically such claims by citizens of one nation against the government of another had a tendency to involve "long-protracted negotiations"; such had been the experience of the United States, both as claimant and debtor. He pointed out that some of the claims demanded by Great Britain against the United States and secured by the Treaty of

1783 were not settled until 1803; and American claims against France for depredations committed in the years 1806 to 1813 were not settled until late in the second Jackson administration. In both these cases, and in many others, Gallatin pointed out, "peace was preserved by patience and forebearance."[94]

In a third section the former secretary of the treasury stated that however justifiable from our own point of view and that of Texas, the annexation of that territory to the United States was, from the perspective of international law

> tantamount to a declaration of war against Mexico. Nothing can be more clear and undeniable than that, whenever two nations are at war, if a third power shall enter into a treaty of alliance, offensive and defensive, with either of the belligerents, and if such a treaty is not contingent, and is to take effect immediately and pending the war, such a treaty is a declaration of war against the other belligerent.
>
> ... Mexico, sensible of her weakness, declined war, and only resorted to a suspension of diplomatic intercourse; but a profound sense of the injury inflicted by the United States has ever rankled in their minds. It will be found through all their diplomatic correspondence, through all their manifestos, that the Mexicans, even to this day, perpetually recur to this never-forgotten offensive measure. *And on the other hand, the subsequent Administration of our government seems to have altogether forgotten this primary act of injustice, and in their negotiations to have acted as if this was only an accomplished fact and had been a matter of course.*[95]

Gallatin recognized the affinity of most of the citizens of Texas with those of the United States and accepted the arguments for such an affiliation, and yet he wanted to show to the self-righteous Americans who took annexation in stride, accepted it and justified it solely in terms of their own interests, that there were other interests involved in this dispute, namely the historical and legal claim to the territory held by the Mexicans. To ignore such claims or to put them on the same level as one would a handful of aggrieved citizens attempting to recover lost speculative interests, was to defy a decent sense of international morality.

He dealt systematically with other points in dispute. He carefully examined Texan and American claims to the land lying between the Nueces and del Norte (Rio Grande) Rivers, and "in vain sought for any document emanating from the republic or state of Texas . . . sustaining its claim either to New Mexico or to the country bordering on the lower portion of the del Norte."[96] All he could find was President Polk's statement laying claim to such territory, based entirely upon support for Texas' claim.

Referring to the disruption of negotiations which took place between the two countries after they were belatedly initiated, he deplored the attitude and manner in which this country approached the negotiations. He pointed out that President Herrera was well disposed to settling such disagreements, but that the instability of his government, and the constant watchful eye of the opposition, made such negotiations difficult if not impossible:

> The questions at issue might have been discussed and settled as easily, fully, and satisfactorily by commissioners appointed for that special

purpose as by residing ministers or envoys. It is well known that whenever diplomatic relations have been superceded by war, treaties of peace are always negotiated by commissioners appointed for that special purpose, who are personally amply protected by the law of nations, but who are never received as resident ministers till after peace has restored ordinary diplomatic intercourse. Thus, the treaty of peace of 1783, between France and England, was negotiated by and concluded at Paris by British commissioners, whom it would have been deemed absurd to admit as resident envoys or ministers before peace had been made.

The only distinction which can possibly be made between the two cases is that there was not yet actual war between Mexico and the United States. But the annexation of Texas was no ordinary occurrence. It was a most clear act of unprovoked aggression; a deep and most offensive injury; in fact, a declaration of war, if Mexico had accepted it as such. In lieu of this, that country had only resorted to a suspension of the ordinary diplomatic relations. It would seem as if our government had considered this an act of unparalleled audacity, which Mexico must be compelled to retract before any negotiations for the arrangement of existing difficulties could take place; as an insult to the government and to the nation, which must compel it to assert its just rights and *to avenge its injured honor*.

. . . Yet when Mexico refused to receive Mr. Slidell as an envoy extraordinary and minister plenipotentiary, the United States should have remembered that we had been the aggressors, that we had committed the an act acknowledged, as well by the practical law of nations as by common sense and common justice, to be tantamount to a declaration of war; and they should have waited with patience till the feelings excited by our own conduct had subsided.[97]

Gallatin's conclusions were disturbing for a nation intoxicated by a series of rousing military victories and consumed with an almost insatiable hunger for land and westward expansion into territory where Mexico held prior historical and legal claims. In a very real sense Gallatin was the last of the Founding Fathers. Although he was not present at the Constitutional Convention in Philadelphia, he had served at Madison's side in the early Congresses, had helped Jefferson and Madison forge the early Republican party, and had served with great distinction for more than a dozen years as the most successful secretary of the treasury in this country's history. It was Gallatin who initiated and administered the wise and frugal policies which transformed this country from a weak profligate debtor nation to a strong and solvent power with which to be reckoned.

At that critical juncture in American history, Gallatin's words should have been taken seriously, particularly since he sensed that the war policy was a significant deviation from the earlier direction and purposes of American society— the mission of the United States—as he termed it. His warning, although certainly not heeded by the government in power as it prepared to enjoy the spoils of conquest, may perhaps have even greater meaning for Americans of a later period. Beset by some of the same temptations and perhaps inclined to use, or better, misuse their tremendous power in a world setting where national expansion is no longer necessarily confined to geographical conquest, Americans may consider the warning when pondering the far more subtle question of the expansion of political and economic influence on a world-wide level.

Albert Gallatin
"The Mission of the United States"
1847

Albert Gallatin, "Peace With Mexico," in Henry Adams, ed., *The Writings of Albert Gallatin* (Philadelphia, Pennsylvania, 1879) III, 581-87.

The people of the United States have been placed by Providence in a position never before enjoyed by any other nation. They are possessed of a most extensive territory, with a very fertile soil, a variety of climates and productions, and a capacity of sustaining a population greater in proportion to its extent than any other territory of the same size on the face of the globe.

By a concourse of various circumstances, they found themselves, at the epoch of their independence, in the full enjoyment of religious, civil, and political liberty, entirely free from any hereditary monopoly of wealth or power. The people at large were in full and quiet possession of all those natural rights for which the people of other countries have for a long time contended and still do contend. They were, and you still are, the supreme sovereigns, acknowledged as such by all. For the proper exercise of these uncontrolled powers and privileges you are responsible to posterity, to the world at large, and to the Almighty Being who has poured on you such unparalleled blessings.

Your mission is to improve the state of the world, to be the "model republic," to show that men are capable of governing themselves, and that this simple and natural form of government is that also which confers most happiness on all, is productive of the greatest development of the intellectual faculties, above all, that which is attended with the highest standard of private and political virtue and morality.

Your forefathers, the founders of the republic, imbued with a deep feeling of their rights and duties, did not deviate from those principles. The sound sense, the wisdom, the probity, the respect for public faith, with which the internal concerns of the nation were managed made our institutions an object of general admiration. Here, for the first time, was the experiment attempted with any prospect of success, and on a large scale, of a representative democratic republic. If it failed, the last hope of the friends of mankind was lost or indefinitely postponed; and the eyes of the world were turned towards you. Whenever real or pretended apprehensions of the imminent danger of trusting the people at large with power were expressed, the answer ever was, "Look at America!"

In their external relations the United States, before this unfortunate war, had, whilst sustaining their just rights, ever acted in strict conformity with the dictates of justice, and displayed the utmost moderation. They never had voluntarily injured any other nation. Every acquisition of territory from foreign powers was honestly made, the result of treaties not imposed, but freely assented to by the other party.

The preservation of peace was ever a primary object. The recourse to arms was always in self-defence. On its expediency there may have been a difference of opinion; that in the only two instances of conflict with civilized nations which occurred during a period of sixty-three years (1783 to 1846) the just rights of the United States had been invaded by a long-continued series of aggressions is undeniable. In the first instance war was not declared, and there were only partial hostilities between France and England. The Congress of the United States, the only legitimate organ of the nation for that purpose, did, in 1812, declare war against Great Britain. Independent of depredations on our commerce, she had for twenty years carried on an actual war against the United States. I say actual war, since there is now but one opinion on that subject; a renewal of the impressment of men sailing under the protection of our flag would be tantamount to a declaration of war. The partial opposition to the war of 1812 did not rest on a denial of the aggressions of England and of the justice of our cause, but on the fact that, with the exception of impressments, similar infractions of our just rights had been committed by France, and on the most erroneous belief that the Administration was partial to that country and insincere in their apparent efforts to restore peace.

At present all these principles would seem to have been abandoned. The most just, a purely defensive war, and no other is justifiable, is necessarily attended with a train of great and unavoidable evils. What shall we say of one, iniquitous in its origin, and provoked by ourselves, of a war of aggression, which is now publicly avowed to be one of intended conquest?

If persisted in, its necessary consequences will be a permanent increase of our military establishment and of executive patronage; its general tendency to make man hate man, to awaken his worst passions, to accustom him to the taste of blood. It has already demoralized no inconsiderable portion of the nation.

The general peace which has been preserved between the great European powers during the last thirty years may not be ascribed to the purest motives. Be these what they may, this long and unusual repose has been most beneficial to the cause of humanity. Nothing can be more injurious to it, more lamentable, more scandalous, than the war between two adjacent republics of North America.

Your mission was to be a model for all other governments and for all other less-favored nations, to adhere to the most elevated principles of political morality, to apply all your faculties to the gradual improvement of your own institutions and social state, and by your example to exert a moral influence most beneficial to mankind at large. Instead of this, an appeal has been made to your worst passions; to cupidity; to the thirst of unjust aggrandizement by brutal force; to the love of military fame and of false glory; and it has even been tried to pervert the noblest feelings of your nature. The attempt is made to make you abandon the lofty position which your fathers occupied, to substitute for it the political morality and heathen patriotism of the heroes and statesmen of antiquity.

I have said that it was attempted to pervert even your virtues. Devotedness to country, or patriotism, is a most essential virtue, since the national existence of any society depends upon it. Unfortunately, our most virtuous dispositions are perverted not only by our vices and selfishness, but also by their own excess. Even the most holy of our attributes, the religious feeling, may be perverted from that cause, as was but too lamentably exhibited in the persecutions, even unto death, of those who were deemed heretics. It is not, therefore, astonishing that patriotism carried to excess should also be perverted. In the entire devotedness to their country, the people everywhere and at all times have been too apt to forget the duties imposed upon them by justice towards other nations. It is against this natural propensity that you should be specially on your guard. The blame does not attach to those who, led by their patriotic feelings, though erroneous, flock around the national standard. On the contrary, no men are more worthy of admiration, better entitled to the thanks of their country, than those who, after war has once taken place, actuated only by the purest motives, daily and with the utmost self-devotedness brave death and stake their own lives in the conflict against the actual enemy. I must confess that I do not extend the same charity to those civilians who coolly and deliberately plunge the country into any unjust or unnecessary war.

We should have but one conscience; and most happy would it be for mankind were statesmen and politicians only as honest in their management of the internal or external national concerns as they are in private life. The irreproachable private character of the President and of all the members of his Administration is known and respected. There is not one of them who would not spurn with indignation the most remote hint that, on similar pretences to those alleged for dismembering Mexico, he might be capable of an attempt to appropriate to himself his neighbor's farm.

In the total absence of any argument that can justify the war in which we are now involved, resort has been had to a most extraordinary assertion. It is said that the people of the United States have an hereditary superiority of race over the Mexicans, which gives them the right to subjugate and keep in bondage the inferior nation. This, it is also alleged, will be the means of enlightening the degraded Mexicans, of improving their social state, and of ultimately increasing the happiness of the masses.

Is it compatible with the principle of democracy, which rejects every hereditary claim of individuals, to admit an hereditary superiority of races? You very properly deny that the son can, independent of his own merit, derive any right or privilege whatever from the merit or any other social superiority of his father. Can you for a moment suppose that a very doubtful descent from men who lived one thousand years ago has transmitted to you a superiority over your fellow-men? But the Anglo-Saxons were inferior to the Goths, from whom the Spaniards claim to be descended; and they were in no respect superior to the Franks and to the Burgundians. It is not to their Anglo-Saxon descent, but to a variety of causes, among which the subsequent mixture of Frenchified Normans, Angevins, and Gascons must not be forgotten, that the English are indebted for their superior institutions. In the progressive improvement of mankind much more has been due to religious and political institutions than to races. Whenever the European nations which from their language are presumed to belong to the Latin or to the Sclavonian race shall have conquered institutions similar to those of England, there will be no trace left of the pretended superiority of one of those races above the other. At this time the claim is but a pretext for covering and justifying unjust usurpation and unbounded ambition.

But admitting, with respect to Mexico, the superiority of race, this confers no superiority of rights. Among ourselves the most ignorant, the most inferior, either in physical or mental faculties, is recognized as having equal rights, and he has an equal vote with any one, however superior to him in all those respects. This is founded on the immutable principle that no one man is born with the right of governing another man. He may, indeed, acquire a moral influence over others, and no other is legitimate. The same principle will apply to nations. However superior the Anglo-American race may be to that of Mexico, this gives the Americans no right to infringe upon the rights of the inferior race. The people of the United States may rightfully, and will, if they use the proper means, exercise a most beneficial moral influence over the Mexicans and other less enlightened nations of America. Beyond this they have no right to go.

The allegation that the subjugation of Mexico would be the means of enlightening the Mexicans, of improving their social state, and of increasing their happiness, is but the shallow attempt to disguise unbounded cupidity and ambition. Truth never was or can be propagated by fire and sword, or by any other than purely moral means. By these, and by these alone, the Christian religion was propagated, and enabled, in less than three hundred years, to conquer idolatry. During the whole of that period Christianity was tainted by no other blood than that of its martyrs.

The duties of the people of the United States towards other nations are obvious. Never losing sight of the divine precept, "Do to others as you would be done by," they have only to consult their own conscience. For our benevolent Creator has implanted in the hearts of men the moral sense of right and wrong, and that sympathy for other men the evidences of which are of daily occurrence.

It seems unnecessary to add anything respecting that false glory which, from habit and the general tenor of our early education, we are taught to admire. The task has already been repeatedly performed, in a far more able and impressive manner than anything I could say on the subject. It is sufficient to say that at this time neither the dignity or honor of the nation demand a further sacrifice of invaluable lives, or even of money. The very reverse is the case. The true honor and dignity of the nation are inseparable from justice. Pride and vanity alone demand the sacrifice. Though so dearly purchased, the astonishing successes of the American arms have at least put it in the power of the United States to grant any terms of peace without incurring the imputation of being actuated by any but the most elevated motives. It would seem that the most proud and vain must be satiated with glory, and that the most reckless and bellicose should be sufficiently glutted with human gore.

A more truly glorious termination of the war, a more splendid spectacle, an example more highly useful to mankind at large, cannot well be conceived than that of the victorious forces of the United States voluntarily abandoning all their conquests, without requiring anything else than that which was strictly due to our citizens.

Disregarded as it was, Gallatin's appeal counselled his country to reject territorial conquest and return to the prewar boundaries before entering into mutually satisfactory negotiations with Mexico. The national leadership which had led the country into the war had done so in order to obtain an excuse for taking whatever territory they desired. Although such objectives were not made explicit in President Polk's war message, they were communicated to members of his official family on more than one occasion. Reference has already been made to his post-inaugural assertion to Secretary of the Navy George Bancroft that the acquisition of California was one of his administration's primary objectives. At a cabinet meeting where Buchanan proposed telling the heads of all foreign states that the United States had no explicit designs on California or New Mexico and had gone to war simply to defend the Texas border on the Del Norte River, he was cut short by the President.

President James K. Polk
Diary Entry (Extract) Explaining his
Actions and Intentions in Mexico
May 13, 1846

Quaife, I, 396-97.

Mr. Buchanan read the draft of a despatch which he had prepared to our Ministers at London, Paris, & other Foreign Courts, announcing the declaration of War against Mexico, with a statement of the causes and objects of the War, with a view that they should communicate its substance to the respective Governments to which they are accredited. Among other things Mr. Buchanan had stated that our object was not to dismember Mexico or to make conquests, and that the Del Norte was the boundary to which we claimed; or rather that in going to war we did not do so with a view to acquire either California or New Mexico or any other portion of the Mexican territory. I told Mr. Buchanan that I thought such a declaration to Foreign Governments unnecessary and improper; that the causes of the war as set forth in my message to Congress and the accompanying documents were altogether satisfactory. I told him that though we had not gone to war for conquest, yet it was clear that in making peace we would if practicable obtain California and such other portion of the Mexican territory as would be sufficient to indemnify our claimants on Mexico, and to defray the expenses of the war which that power by her long continued wrongs and injuries had forced us to wage. I told him it was well known that the Mexican Government had no other means of indemnifying us. . . .

Polk had his eye on California from the very beginning of his administration. Later, alarmed by reports of possible British and French interest in acquiring this valuable area covering the greater part of the long Pacific coastline, with its warm valleys and snow-capped mountains, he instructed (through his secretary of state) the American consul in Monterey, who was also made a confidential State

248

Department agent, to assess the possibility of a settlers' revolt in those parts. Polk probably had in mind a set of developments similar to those of the Texas revolt, but this time the country would be prepared to support such an action.

Secretary of State James Buchanan
Letter to Thomas O. Larkin,
United States Consul and Confidential Agent
October 17, 1845

Manning, VIII, 169-71.

Sir: I feel much indebted to you for the information which you have communicated to the Department from time to time in relation to California. The future destiny of that country is a subject of anxious solicitude for the Government and people of the United States. The interests of our commerce and our whale fisheries on the Pacific ocean demand that you should exert the greatest vigilance in discovering and defeating any attempt, which may be made by foreign governments to acquire a control over that country. In the contest between Mexico and California we can take no part, unless the former should commence hostilities against the United States; but should California assert and maintain her independence, we shall render her all the kind offices in our power, as a sister Republic. This Government has no ambitious aspirations to gratify and no desire to extend our federal system over more territory than we already possess, unless by the free and spontaneous wish of the independent people of adjoining territories. The exercise of compulsion or improper influence to accomplish such a result, would be repugnant both to the policy and principles of this Government. But whilst these are the sentiments of the President, he could not view with indifference the transfer of California to Great Britain or any other European Power. The system of colonization by foreign monarchies on the North American continent must and will be resisted by the United States. It could result in nothing but evil to the colonists under their dominion who would naturally desire to secure for themselves the blessings of liberty by means of republican institutions; whilst it must prove highly prejudicial to the best interests of the United States. Nor would it in the end benefit such foreign monarchies. On the contrary, even Great Britain, by the acquisition of California, would sow the seeds of future war and disaster for herself; because there is no political truth more certain than that this fine Province could not long be held in vassalage by any European Power. The emigration to it of people from the United States would soon render this impossible.

I am induced to make these remarks in consequence of the information communicated to this Department in your despatch of the 10th July, last. From this it appears that Mr Rea, the Agent of the British Hudson Bay Company, furnished the Californians with arms and money in October and November, last, to enable them to expel the Mexicans from the country; and you state that this policy has been reversed and now no doubt exists there, but that the Mexican troops about to invade the province have been sent for this purpose at the instigation of the British

Government; and that "it is rumored that two English houses in Mexico have become bound to the new General to accept his drafts for funds to pay his troops for eighteen months." Connected with these circumstances, the appearance of a British Vice Consul and a French Consul in California at the present crisis, without any apparent commercial business, is well calculated to produce the impression, that their respective governments entertain designs on that country which must necessarily be hostile to its interests. On all proper occasions, you should not fail prudently to warn the Government and people of California of the danger of such an interference to their peace and prosperity; to inspire them with a jealousy of European dominion, and to arouse in their bosoms that love of liberty and independence so natural to the American Continent. Whilst I repeat that this Government does not, under existing circumstances, intend to interfere between Mexico and California, it would vigorously interpose to prevent the latter from becoming a British or French Colony. In this they might surely expect the aid of the Californians themselves.

Whilst the President will make no effort and use no influence to induce California to become one of the free and independent States of this Union, yet if the people should desire to unite their destiny with ours, they would be received as brethren, whenever this can be done without affording Mexico just cause of complaint. Their true policy for the present in regard to this question, is to let events take their course, unless an attempt should be made to transfer them without their consent either to Great Britain or France. This they ought to resist by all the means in their power, as ruinous to their best interests and destructive of their freedom and independence.

I am rejoiced to learn that "our countrymen continue to receive every assurance of safety and protection from the present Government" of California and that they manifest so much confidence in you as Consul of the United States. You may assure them of the cordial sympathy and friendship of the President and that their conduct is appreciated by him as it deserves.

In addition to your Consular functions, the President has thought proper to appoint you a confidential agent in California; and you may consider the present despatch as your authority for acting in this character. The confidence which he reposes in your patriotism and discretion is evinced by conferring upon you this delicate and important trust. You will take care not to awaken the jealousy of the French and English agents there by assuming any other than your Consular character. Lieutenant Archibald H. Gillespie of the Marine Corps will immediately proceed to Monterey, and will probably reach you before this despatch. He is a gentleman in whom the President reposes entire confidence. He has seen these instructions and will cooperate as a confidential agent with you, in carrying them into execution.

You will not fail by every safe opportunity to keep this Department advised of the progress of events in California and the disposition of the authorities and people towards the United States and other Governments. We should, also, be pleased to learn what is the aggregate population of that province and the force it can bring into the field.

What is the proportion of Mexican, American, British and French citizens and the feelings of each class towards the United States; the names and character of the principal persons in the Executive, Legislative and Judicial Departments of the Government and of other distinguished and influential citizens. Its financial system and resources; the amount and nature of its commerce with foreign nations, its productions which might with advantage be imported into the United States and the productions of the United States which might with advantage be received in exchange.

It would also be interesting to the Department to learn in what part of California the principal American settlements exist, the rate at which the settlers have been and still are increasing in number;—from what portions of the Union they come and by what routes they arrive in the country.

These specifications are not intended to limit your inquiries. On the contrary, it is expected that you will collect and communicate to the Department all the information respecting California which may be useful or important to the United States.

Your compensation will be at the rate of six dollars per day from the time of the arrival of this Despatch or of Lieutenant Gillespie at Monterey. You will also be allowed your necessary travelling and other expenses incurred in accomplishing the objects of your appointment; but you will be careful to keep an accurate account of the expenditures and procure vouchers for them in all cases where this is practicable without interfering with the successful performance of your duties. For these expenses and your per diem allowance, you are authorized to draw from time to time on the Department.

I am [etc.].

Perhaps nothing revealed President Polk's desire to obtain California more than his curious dealings with a certain Colonel Atocha, a representative of the exiled Mexican leader, General Santa Anna, who was brooding in Havana, plotting a return to power in his country. Atocha conveyed the message to Polk that Santa Anna, if and when he returned to power in Mexico, would agree to cede New Mexico and upper California to the United States for the sum of $30,000,000, as well as giving recognition to the American claim for the extended Texas border along the Rio Grande. But he warned the President that no Mexican government could hope to remain in power after agreeing to such terms, unless it was clear to the Mexican people that the superior naval and military forces of the United States were poised to attack the country if agreement was not reached upon these terms. The President described in detail conversations with Colonel Atocha and also subsequent discussions with his cabinet concerning these proposals in his diary. The colonel sought the immediate payment to Santa Anna of $500,000 to expedite his return to Mexico and also to repay a debt of the government's to the archbishop, who would be reassured by this action of the value of such a settlement. Polk was intrigued by the specific advice from Santa Anna that the United States should mobilize a very large fleet off the coast of Vera Cruz and send a strong army along the Rio Grande to support the enforcement of this policy. He attempted to implement this arrangement by assisting Santa Anna's return through orders to the fleet commander to pass the Mexican general through any blockade, but he was finally frustrated by Congress which refused to appropriate funds designed for this activity. Santa Anna's subsequent behavior, however, casts some doubt as to whether he was serious or merely trying to hoodwink the President into assisting him to get through the American naval blockade and back into office in Mexico City.

Stung by the continuing criticism of the Whigs, in and out of Congress, President Polk, through the remaining years of his single term in office, continued to justify the war with Mexico on the grounds of the Mexican army's initial attack upon Taylor's forces on the banks of the Rio Grande in the spring of 1846. He coupled that argument with a review of what he termed "years of endurance of aggravated and unredressed wrongs" committed by that country, which had compromised the honor and integrity of the United States. In his Second Annual Message he devoted many pages to this defense. His rationalizations so aggravated a freshman congressman from Illinois, a man named Abraham Lincoln, that he took upon himself a quite unprecedented series of interrogatories directed to the President and delivered a speech in the House, which locked horns squarely with the Chief Executive on the critical question of the responsibility for the war with Mexico. Below are the relevant sections of President Polk's message and Lincoln's interrogatories, or "Spot Resolutions," as they were referred to. These are followed by Lincoln's maiden speech before the House of Representatives.

President James K. Polk
Second Annual Message
Sections on the War with Mexico
December 8, 1847

Richardson, V, 2322-42.

. . .The existing war with Mexico was neither desired nor provoked by the United States. On the contrary, all honorable means were resorted to to avert it. After years of endurance of aggravated and unredressed wrongs on our part, Mexico, in violation of solemn treaty stipulations and of every principle of justice recognized by civilized nations, commenced hostilities, and thus by her own act forced the war upon us. Long before the advance of our Army to the left bank of the Rio Grande we had ample cause of war against Mexico, and had the United States resorted to this extremity we might have appealed to the whole civilized world for the justice of our cause. I deem it to be my duty to present to you on the present occasion a condensed review of the injuries we had sustained, of the causes which led to the war, and of its progress since its commencement. This is rendered the more necessary because of the misapprehensions which have to some extent prevailed as to its origin and true character. The war had been represented as unjust and unnecessary and as one of aggression on our part upon a weak and injured enemy. Such erroneous views, though entertained by but few, have been widely and extensively circulated, not only at home, but have been spread throughout Mexico and the whole world. A more effectual means could not have been devised to encourage the enemy and protract the war than to advocate and adhere to their cause, and thus give them "aid and comfort." It is a source of national pride and exultation that the great body of our people have thrown no such obstacles in the way of the Government in prosecuting the war successfully, but have shown themselves to be eminently patriotic and ready to vindicate their country's honor and interests at any sacrifice. The alacrity and promptness with which our volunteer forces rushed to the field on their country's call prove not only their patriotism, but their deep conviction that our cause is just.

The wrongs which we have suffered from Mexico almost ever since she became an independent power and the patient endurance with which we have borne them are without a parallel in the history of modern civilized nations. There is reason to believe that if these wrongs had been resented and resisted in the first instance the present war might have been avoided. One outrage, however, permitted to pass with impunity almost necessarily encouraged the perpetration of another, until at last Mexico seemed to attribute to weakness and indecision on our part a forbearance which was the offspring of magnanimity and of a sincere desire to preserve friendly relations with a sister republic.

Scarcely had Mexico achieved her independence, which the United States were the first among the nations to acknowledge, when she commenced the system of insult and spoliation which she has ever since pursued. Our citizens engaged in lawful commerce were imprisoned, their vessels seized, and our flag insulted in her ports. If money was wanted, the lawless seizure and confiscation of our merchant vessels and their cargoes was a ready resource, and if to accomplish their purposes it became necessary to imprison the owners, captains, and crews, it was done. Rulers superseded rulers in Mexico in rapid succession, but still there was no change in this system of depredation. The Government of the United States made repeated reclamations on behalf of its citizens, but these were answered by the perpetration of new outrages. Promises of redress made by Mexico in the most solemn forms were postponed or evaded. The files and records of the Department of State contain conclusive proofs of numerous lawless acts perpetrated upon the property and persons of our citizens by Mexico, and of wanton insults to our national flag. The interposition of our Government to obtain redress was again and again invoked under circumstances which no nation ought to disregard. It was hoped that these outrages would cease and that Mexico would be restrained by the laws which regulate the conduct of civilized nations in their intercourse with each other after the treaty of amity, commerce, and navigation of the 5th of April, 1831, was concluded between the two Republics; but this hope soon proved to be vain. The course of seizure and confiscation of the property of our citizens, the violation of their persons, and the insults to our flag pursued by Mexico previous to that time were scarcely suspended for even a brief period, although the treaty so clearly defines the rights and duties of the respective parties that it is impossible to misunderstand or mistake them. In less than seven years after the conclusion of that treaty our grievances had become so intolerable that in the opinion of President Jackson they should no longer be endured. In his message to Congress in February, 1837, he presented them to the consideration of that body, and declared that—

> The length of time since some of the injuries have been committed, the repeated and unavailing applications for redress, the wanton character of some of the outrages upon the property and persons of our citizens, upon the officers and flag of the United States, independent of recent insults to this Government and people by the late extraordinary Mexican minister, would justify in the eyes of all nations immediate war.

In a spirit of kindness and forbearance, however, he recommended reprisals as a milder mode of redress. He declared that war should not be used as a remedy "by just and generous nations, confiding in their strength for injuries committed, if it can be honorably avoided," and added:

> It has occurred to me that, considering the present embarrassed condition of that country, we should act with both wisdom and moderation by giving to Mexico one more opportunity to atone for the past before we take redress into our own hands. To avoid all misconception on the part of Mexico, as well as to protect our own national character from reproach, this opportunity should be given with the avowed design and full preparation to take immediate satisfaction if it should not be obtained on a repetition of the demand for it. To this end I recommend that an act be passed authorizing reprisals, and the use of the naval force of the United States by the Executive against Mexico to enforce them, in the event of a refusal by the Mexican Government to come to an amicable adjustment of the matters in controversy between us upon another demand thereof made from on board one of our vessels of war on the coast of Mexico.

Committees of both Houses of Congress, to which this message of the President was referred, fully sustained his views of the character of the wrongs which we had suffered from Mexico, and recommended that another demand for redress should be made before authorizing war or reprisals. The Committee on Foreign Relations of the Senate, in their report, say:

> After such a demand, should prompt justice be refused by the Mexican Government, we may appeal to all nations, not only for the equity and moderation with which we shall have acted toward a sister republic, but for the necessity which will then compel us to seek redress for our wrongs, either by actual war or by reprisals. The subject will then be presented before Congress, at the commencement of the next session, in a clear and distinct form, and the committee can not doubt but that such measures will be immediately adopted as may be necessary to vindicate the honor of the country and insure ample reparation to our injured fellow-citizens.

The Committee on Foreign Affairs of the House of Representatives made a similar recommendation. In their report they say that—

They fully concur with the President that ample cause exists for taking redress into our own hands, and believe that we should be justified in the opinion of other nations for taking such a step. But they are willing to try the experiment of another demand, made in the most solemn form, upon the justice of the Mexican Government before any further proceedings are adopted.

No difference of opinion upon the subject is believed to have existed in Congress at that time; the executive and legislative departments concurred; and yet such has been our forbearance and desire to preserve peace with Mexico that the wrongs of which we then complained, and which gave rise to these solemn proceedings, not only remain unredressed to this day, but additional causes of complaint of an aggravated character have ever since been accumulating. Shortly after these proceedings a special messenger was dispatched to Mexico to make a final demand for redress, and on the 20th of July, 1837, the demand was made. The reply of the Mexican Government bears date on the 29th of the same month, and contains assurances of the "anxious wish" of the Mexican Government "not to delay the moment of that final and equitable adjustment which is to terminate the existing difficulties between the two Governments;" that "nothing should be left undone which may contribute to the most speedy and equitable determination of the subjects which have so seriously engaged the attention of the American Government;" that the "Mexican Government would adopt as the only guides for its conduct the plainest principles of public right, the sacred obligations imposed by international law, and the religious faith of treaties," and that "whatever reason and justice may dictate respecting each case will be done." The assurance was further given that the decision of the Mexican Government upon each cause of complaint for which redress had been demanded should be communicated to the Government of the United States by the Mexican minister at Washington.

These solemn assurances in answer to our demand for redress were disregarded. By making them, however, Mexico obtained further delay. President Van Buren, in his annual message to Congress of the 5th of December, 1837, states that "although the larger number" of our demands for redress, "and many of them aggravated cases of personal wrongs, have been now for years before the Mexican Government, and some of the causes of national complaint, and those of the most offensive character, admitted of immediate, simple, and satisfactory replies, it is only within a few days past that any specific communication in answer to our last demand, made five months ago, has been received from the Mexican minister;" and that "for not one of our public complaints has satisfaction been given or offered, that but one of the cases of personal wrong has been favorably considered, and that but four cases of both descriptions out of all those formally presented and earnestly pressed have as yet been decided upon by the Mexican Government." President Van Buren, believing that it would be vain to make any further attempt to obtain redress by the ordinary means within the power of the Executive, communicated this opinion to Congress in the message referred to, in which he said:

On a careful and deliberate examination of their contents [of the correspondence with the Mexican Government], and considering the spirit manifested by the Mexican Government, it has become my painful duty to return the subject as it now stands to Congress, to whom it belongs to decide upon the time, the mode, and the measure of redress.

Had the United States at that time adopted compulsory measures and taken redress into their own hands, all our difficulties with Mexico would probably have been long since adjusted and the existing war have been averted. Magnanimity and moderation on our part only had the effect to complicate these difficulties and render an amicable settlement of them the more embarrassing. That such measures of redress under similar provocations committed by any of the powerful nations of Europe would have been promptly resorted to by the United States can not be doubted. The national honor and the preservation of the national character throughout the world, as well as our own self-respect and the protection due to our own citizens, would have rendered such a resort indispensable. The history of no civilized nation in modern times has presented within so brief a period so many wanton attacks upon the honor of its flag and upon the property and persons of its citizens as had at that time been borne by the United States from the Mexican authorities and people. But Mexico was a sister republic on the North American continent, occupying a territory contiguous to our own, and was in a feeble and distracted condition, and these considerations, it is presumed, induced Congress to forbear still longer.

Instead of taking redress into our own hands, a new negotiation was entered upon with fair promises on the part of Mexico, but with the real purpose, as the event has proved, of indefinitely postponing the reparation which we demanded, and which was so justly due. This negotiation, after more than a year's delay, resulted in the convention of the 11th of April, 1839, "for the adjustment of claims of citizens of the United States of America upon the Government of the Mexican Republic." The joint board of commissioners created by this convention to examine and decide upon these claims was not organized until the month of August, 1840, and under the terms of the convention they were to terminate their duties within eighteen months from that time. Four of the eighteen months were consumed in preliminary discussions on frivolous and dilatory points raised by the Mexican commissioners, and it was not until the month of December, 1840, that they commenced the examination of the claims of our citizens upon Mexico. Fourteen months only remained to examine and decide upon these numerous and complicated cases. In the month of February, 1842, the term of the commission expired, leaving many claims undisposed of for want of time. The claims which were allowed by the board and by the umpire authorized by the convention to decide in case of disagreement between the Mexican and American commissioners amounted to $2,026,139.68. There were pending before the umpire when the commission expired additional claims, which had been examined and awarded by the American commissioners and had not been allowed by the Mexican commissioners, amounted to $928,627.88, upon which he did not decide, alleging that his authority had ceased with the termination of the joint commission. Besides these claims, there were others of American citizens amounting to $3,336,837.05, which had been submitted to the board, and upon which they had not time to decide before their final adjournment.

The sum of $2,026,139.68, which had been awarded to the claimants, was a liquidated and ascertained debt due by Mexico, about which there could be no dispute, and which she was bound to pay according to the terms of the convention. Soon after the final awards for this amount had been made the Mexican Government asked for a postponement of the time of making payment, alleging that it would be inconvenient to make payment at the time stipulated. In the spirit of forbearing kindness toward a sister republic, which Mexico has so long abused, the United States promptly complied with her request. A second convention was accordingly concluded between the two Governments on the 30th of January, 1843, which upon its face declares that "this new arrangement is entered into for the accommodation of Mexico." By the terms of this convention all the interest due on the awards which had been made in favor of the claimants under the convention of the 11th of April, 1839, was to be paid to them on the 30th of April, 1843, and "the principal of the said awards and the interest accruing thereon" was stiupulated to "be paid in five years, in equal installments every three months." Notwithstanding this new convention was entered into at the request of Mexico and for the purpose of relieving her from embarrassment, the claimants have only received the interest due on the 30th of April, 1843, and three of the twenty installments. Although the payment of the sum thus liquidated and confessedly due by Mexico to our citizens as indemnity for acknowledged acts of outrage and wrong was secured by treaty, the obligations of which are ever held sacred by all just nations, yet Mexico has violated this solemn engagement by failing and refusing to make the payment. The two installments due in April and July, 1844, under the peculiar circumstances connected with them, have been assumed by the United States and discharged to the claimants, but they are still due by Mexico. But this is not all of which we have just cause of complaint. To provide a remedy for the claimants whose cases were not decided by the joint commission under the convention of April 11, 1839, it was expressly stipulated by the sixth article of the convention of the 30th of January, 1843, that—

A new convention shall be entered into for the settlement of all claims of the Government and citizens of the United States against the Republic of Mexico which were not finally decided by the late commission which met in the city of Washington, and of all claims of the Government and citizens of Mexico against the United States.

In conformity with this stipulation, a third convention was concluded and signed at the city of Mexico on the 20th of November, 1843, by the plenipotentiaries of the two Governments, by which provision was made for ascertaining and paying these claims. In January, 1844, this convention was ratified by the Senate of the United States with two amendments, which were manifestly reasonable in their character. Upon a reference of the amendments proposed to the Government of Mexico, the same evasions, difficulties, and delays were interposed which have so long marked the policy of that Government toward the United States. It has not even yet decided whether it would or would not accede to them, although the subject has been repeatedly pressed upon its consideration. Mexico has thus violated a second time the faith of treaties by failing or refusing to carry into effect the sixth article of the convention of January, 1843.

Such is the history of the wrongs which we have suffered and patiently endured from Mexico through a long series of years. So far from affording reasonable satisfaction for the injuries and insults we had borne, a great aggravation of them consists in the fact that while the United States, anxious to preserve a good understanding with Mexico, have been constantly but vainly employed in seeking redress for past wrongs, new outrages were constantly occurring, which have continued to increase our causes of complaint and to swell the amount of our demands. While the citizens of the United States were conducting a lawful commerce with Mexico under the guaranty of a treaty of "amity, commerce, and navigation," many of them have suffered all the injuries which would have resulted from open war. This treaty, instead of affording protection to our citizens, has been the means of inviting them into the ports of Mexico that they might be, as they have been in numerous instances, plundered of their property and deprived of their personal liberty if they dared insist on their rights. Had the unlawful seizures of American property and the violation of the personal liberty of our citizens, to say nothing of the insults to our flag, which have occurred in the ports of Mexico taken place on the high seas, they would themselves long since have constituted a state of actual war between the two countries. In so long suffering Mexico to violate her most solemn treaty obligations, plunder our citizens of their property, and imprison their persons without affording them any redress we have failed to perform one of the first and highest duties which every government owes to its citizens, and the consequence has been that many of them have been reduced from a state of affluence to bankruptcy. The proud name of American citizen, which ought to protect all who bear it from insult and injury throughout the world, has afforded no such protection to our citizens in Mexico. We had ample cause of war against Mexico long before the breaking out of hostilities; but even then we forbore to take redress into our own hands until Mexico herself became the aggressor by invading our soil in hostile array and shedding the blood of our citizens.

Such are the grave causes of complaint on the part of the United States against Mexico—causes which existed long before the annexation of Texas to the American Union; and yet, animated by the love of peace and a magnanimous moderation, we did not adopt those measures of redress which under such circumstances are the justified resort of injured nations.

The annexation of Texas to the United States constituted no just cause of offense to Mexico. The pretext that it did so is wholly inconsistent and irreconcilable with well-authenticated facts connected with the revolution by which Texas became independent of Mexico. That this may be the more manifest, it may be proper to advert to the causes and to the history of the principal events of that revolution.

Texas constituted a portion of the ancient Province of Louisiana, ceded to the United States by France in the year 1803. In the year 1819 the United States, by the Florida treaty, ceded to Spain all that part of Louisiana within the present limits of Texas, and Mexico, by the revolution which separated her from Spain and rendered her an independent nation, succeeded to the rights of the mother country over this territory. In the year 1824 Mexico established a federal constitution, under which the Mexican Republic was composed of a number of sovereign States confederated together in a federal union similar to our own. Each of these States had its own executive, legislature, and judiciary, and for all except federal purposes was as independent of the General Government and that of the other States as is Pennsylvania or Virginia under our Constitution. Texas and Coahuila united and formed one of these Mexican States. The State constitution which they adopted, and which was approved by the Mexican Confederacy, asserted that they were "free and independent of the other Mexican United States and of every other power and dominion whatsoever," and proclaimed the great principle of human liberty that "the sovereignty of the state resides originally and essentially in the general mass of the individuals who compose it." To the Government under this constitution, as well as to that under the federal constitution, the people of Texas owed allegiance.

Emigrants from foreign countries, including the United States, were invited by the colonization laws of the State and of the Federal Government to settle in Texas. Advantageous terms were offered to induce them to leave their own country and become Mexican citizens. This invitation was accepted by many of our citizens in the full faith that in their new home they would be governed by laws enacted by representatives elected by themselves, and that their lives, liberty, and property would be protected by constitutional guaranties similar to those which existed in the Republic they had left. Under a Government thus organized they continued until the year 1835, when a military revolution broke out in the City of Mexico which entirely subverted the federal and State constitutions and placed a military dictator at the head of the Government. By a sweeping decree of a Congress subservient to the will of the Dictator the several State constitutions were abolished and the States themselves converted into mere departments of the central Government. The people of Texas were unwilling to submit to this usurpation. Resistance to such tyranny became a high duty. Texas was fully absolved from all allegiance to the central Government of Mexico from the moment that Government had abolished her State constitution and in its place substituted an arbitrary and despotic central government. Such were the principal causes of the Texan revolution. The people of Texas at once determined upon resistance and flew to arms. In the midst of these important and exciting events, however, they did not omit to place their liberties upon a secure and permanent foundation. They elected members to a convention, who in the month of March, 1836, issued a formal declaration that their "political connection with the Mexican nation has forever ended, and that the people of Texas do now constitute a *free, sovereign, and independent Republic*, and are fully invested with all the rights and attributes which properly belong to independent nations." They also adopted for their government a liberal republican constitution. About the same time Santa Anna, then the Dictator of Mexico, invaded Texas with a numerous army for the purpose of subduing her people and enforcing obedience to his arbitrary and despotic Government. On the 21st of April, 1836, he was met by the Texan citizen soldiers, and on that day was achieved by them the memorable victory of San Jacinto, by which they conquered their independence. Considering the numbers engaged on the respective sides, history does not record a more brilliant achievement. Santa Anna himself was among the captives.

In the month of May, 1836, Santa Anna acknowledged by a treaty with the Texan authorities in the most solemn form "the full, entire, and perfect independence of the Republic of Texas." It is true he was then a prisoner of war, but it is equally true that he had failed to reconquer Texas, and had met with signal defeat; that his authority had not been revoked, and that by virtue of this treaty he obtained his personal release. By it hostilities were suspended, and the army which had invaded Texas under his command returned in pursuance of this arrangement unmolested to Mexico.

From the day that the battle of San Jacinto was fought until the present hour Mexico has never possessed the power to reconquer Texas. In the language of the Secretary of State of the United States in a dispatch to our minister in Mexico under date of the 8th of July, 1842—

> Mexico may have chosen to consider, and may still choose to consider, Texas as having been at all times since 1835, and as still continuing, a rebellious province; but the world has been obliged to take a very different view of the matter. From the time of the battle of San Jacinto, in April, 1836, to the present moment, Texas has exhibited the same external signs of national independence as Mexico herself, and with quite as much stability of government. Practically free and independent, acknowledged as a political sovereignty by the principal powers of the world, no hostile foot finding rest within her territory for six or seven years, and Mexico herself refraining for all that period from any further attempt to reestablish her own authority over that territory, it can not but be surprising to find Mr. De Bocanegra [the secretary of foreign affairs of Mexico] complaining that for that whole period citizens of the United States or its Government have been favoring the rebels of Texas and supplying them with vessels, ammunition, and money, as if the war for the reduction of the Province of Texas had been constantly prosecuted by Mexico, and her success prevented by these influences from abroad.

In the same dispatch the Secretary of State affirms that—

> Since 1837 the United States have regarded Texas as an independent sovereignty as much as Mexico, and that trade and commerce with citizens of a government at war with Mexico can not on that account be regarded as an intercourse by which assistance and succor are given to Mexican rebels. The whole current of Mr. De Bocanegra's remarks runs in the same direction, as if the independence of Texas had not been acknowledged. It has been acknowledged; it was acknowledged in 1837 against the remonstrance and protest of Mexico, and most of the acts of any importance of which Mr. De Bocanegra complains flow necessarily from that recognition. He speaks of Texas as still being "an integral part of the territory of the Mexican Republic," but he can not but understand that the United States do not so regard it. The real complaint of Mexico, therefore, is in substance neither more nor less than a complaint against the recognition of Texan independence. It may be thought rather late to repeat that complaint, and not quite just to confine it to the United States to the exemption of England, France, and Belgium, unless the United States, having been the first to acknowledge the independence of Mexico

herself, are to be blamed for setting an example for the recognition of that of Texas.

And he added that—

The Constitution, public treaties, and the laws oblige the President to regard Texas as an independent state, and its territory as no part of the territory of Mexico.

Texas had been an independent state, with an organized government, defying the power of Mexico to overthrow or reconquer her, for more than ten years before Mexico commenced the present war against the United States. Texas had given such evidence to the world of her ability to maintain her separate existence as an independent nation that she had been formally recognized as such not only by the United States, but by several of the principal powers of Europe. These powers had entered into treaties of amity, commerce, and navigation with her. They had received and accredited her ministers and other diplomatic agents at their respective courts, and they had commissioned ministers and diplomatic agents on their part to the Government of Texas. If Mexico, notwithstanding all this and her utter inability to subdue or reconquer Texas, still stubbornly refused to recognize her as an independent nation, she was none the less so on that account. Mexico herself had been recognized as an independent nation by the United States and by other powers many years before Spain, of which before her revolution she had been a colony, would agree to recognize her as such; and yet Mexico was at that time in the estimation of the civilized world, and in fact, none the less an independent power because Spain still claimed her as a colony. If Spain had continued until the present period to assert that Mexico was one of her colonies in rebellion against her, this would not have made her so or changed the fact of her independent existence. Texas at the period of her annexation to the United States bore the same relation to Mexico that Mexico had borne to Spain for many years before Spain acknowledged her independence, with this important difference, that before the annexation of Texas to the United States was consummated Mexico herself, by a formal act of her Government, had acknowledged the independence of Texas as a nation. It is true that in the act of recognition she prescribed a condition which she had no power or authority to impose—that Texas should not annex herself to any other power—but this could not detract in any degree from the recognition which Mexico then made of her actual independence. Upon this plain statement of facts, it is absurd for Mexico to allege as a pretext for commencing hostilities against the United States that Texas is still a part of her territory.

But there are those who, conceding all this to be true, assume the ground that the true western boundary of Texas is the Nueces instead of the Rio Grande, and that therefore in marching our Army to the east bank of the latter river we passed the Texas line and invaded the territory of Mexico. A simple statement of facts known to exist will conclusively refute such an assumption. Texas, as ceded to the United States by France in 1803, has been always claimed as extending west to the Rio Grande or Rio Bravo. This fact is established by the authority of our most eminent statesmen at a period when the question was as well, if not better, understood than it is at present. During Mr. Jefferson's Administration Messrs.

Monroe and Pinckney, who had been sent on a special mission to Madrid, charged among other things with the adjustment of boundary between the two countries, in a note addressed to the Spanish minister of foreign affairs under date of the 28th of January, 1805, assert that the boundaries of Louisiana, as ceded to the United States by France, "are the river Perdido on the east and the river Bravo on the west," and they add that "the facts and principles which justify this conclusion are so satisfactory to our Government as to convince it that the United States have not a better right to the island of New Orleans under the cession referred to than they have to the whole district of territory which is above described." Down to the conclusion of the Florida treaty, in February, 1819, by which this territory was ceded to Spain, the United States asserted and maintained their territorial rights to this extent. In the month of June, 1818, during Mr. Monroe's Administration, information having been received that a number of foreign adventurers had landed at Galveston with the avowed purpose of forming a settlement in that vicinity, a special messenger was dispatched by the Government of the United States with instructions from the Secretary of State to warn them to desist, should they be found there, "or any other place north of the Rio Bravo, and within the territory claimed by the United States." He was instructed, should they be found in the country north of that river, to make known to them "the surprise with which the President has seen possession thus taken, without authority from the United States, of a place within their territorial limits, and upon which no lawful settlement can be made without their sanction." He was instructed to call upon them to "avow under what national authority they profess to act," and to give them due warning "that the place is within the United States, who will suffer no permanent settlement to be made there under any authority other than their own." As late as the 8th of July, 1842, the Secretary of State of the United States, in a note addressed to our minister in Mexico, maintains that by the Florida treaty of 1819 the territory as far west as the Rio Grande was confirmed to Spain. In that note he states that—

> By the treaty of the 22nd of February, 1819, between the United States and Spain, the Sabine was adopted as the line of boundary between the two powers. Up to that period no considerable colonization had been effected in Texas; but the territory between the Sabine and the Rio Grande being confirmed to Spain by the treaty, applications were made to that power for grants of land, and such grants or permissions of settlement were in fact made by the Spanish authorities in favor of citizens of the United States proposing to emigrate to *Texas* in numerous families before the declaration of independence by Mexico.

The Texas which was ceded to Spain by the Florida treaty of 1819 embraced all the country now claimed by the State of Texas between the Nueces and the Rio Grande. The Republic of Texas always claimed this river as her western boundary, and in her treaty made with Santa Anna in May, 1836, he recognized it as such. By the constitution which Texas adopted in March, 1836, senatorial and representative districts were organized extending west of the Nueces. The Congress of Texas on the 19th of December, 1836, passed "An act to define the boundaries of the Republic of Texas," in which they declared the Rio Grande from its mouth to its source to be their boundary, and by the said act they extended their "civil and political jurisdiction" over the country up to that boundary. During a period of more than nine years which intervened between the adoption of her constitution and her annexation as one of the States of our Union Texas asserted and exercised many acts of sovereignty and jurisdiction over the territory and inhabitants west of the Nueces. She organized and defined the limits of counties extending to the Rio Grande; she established courts of justice and extended her judicial system over the territory; she established a custom-house and collected duties, and also post-offices and post-roads, in it; she established a land office and issued numerous grants for land within its limits; a senator and a representative residing in it were elected to the Congress of the Republic and served as such before the act of annexation took place. In both the Congress and convention of Texas which gave their assent to the terms of annexation to the United States proposed by our Congress were representatives residing west of the Nueces, who took part in the act of annexation itself. This was the Texas which by the act of our Congress of the 29th of December, 1845, was admitted as one of the States of our Union. That the Congress of the United States understood the State of Texas which they admitted into the Union to extend beyond the Nueces is apparent from the fact that on the 31st of December, 1845, only two days after the act of admission, they passed a law "to establish a collection district in the State of Texas," by which they created a port of delivery at Corpus Christi, situated west of the Nueces, and being the same point at which the Texas custom-house under the laws of that Republic had been located, and directed that a surveyor to collect the revenue should be appointed for that port by the President, by and with the advice and consent of the Senate. A surveyor was accordingly nominated, and confirmed by the Senate, and has been ever since in the performance of his duties. All these acts of the Republic of Texas and of our Congress preceded the orders for the advance of our Army to the east bank of the Rio Grande. Subsequently Congress passed an act "establishing certain post routes" extending west of the Nueces. The country west of that river now constitutes a part of one of the Congressional districts of Texas and is represented in the House of Representatives. The Senators from that State were chosen by a legislature in which the country west of that river was represented. In view of all these facts it is difficult to conceive upon what ground it can be maintained that in occupying the country west of the Nueces with our Army, with a view solely to its security and defense, we invaded the territory of Mexico. But it would have been still more difficult to justify the Executive, whose duty it is to see that the laws be faithfully executed, if in the face of all these proceedings, both of the Congress of Texas and of the United States, he had assumed the responsibility of yielding up the territory west of the Nueces to Mexico or of refusing to protect and defend this territory and its inhabitants, including Corpus Christi as well as the remainder of Texas, against the threatened Mexican invasion.

But Mexico herself has never placed the war which she has waged upon the ground that our Army occupied the intermediate territory between the Nueces and the Rio Grande. Her refuted pretension that Texas was not in fact an independent state, but a rebellious province, was obstinately persevered in, and her avowed purpose in commencing a war with the United States was to reconquer Texas and to restore Mexican authority over the whole territory—not to the Nueces only, but to the Sabine. In view of the proclaimed menaces of Mexico to this effect, I deemed it my duty, as a measure of precaution and defense, to order our Army to occupy a position on our frontier as a military post, from which our troops could best resist and repel any attempted invasion which Mexico might make. Our Army had occupied a position at Corpus Christi, west of the Nueces, as early as August, 1845, without complaint from any quarter. Had the Nueces been regarded as the true western boundary of Texas, that boundary had been passed by our Army many months before it advanced to the eastern bank of the Rio Grande. In my annual message of December last I informed Congress that upon the invitation of both the Congress and convention of Texas I had deemed it proper to order a strong squadron to the coasts of Mexico and to concentrate an efficient military force on the western frontier of Texas to protect and defend the inhabitants against the menaced invasion of Mexico. In that message I informed Congress that the moment the terms of annexation offered by the United States were accepted by Texas the latter became so far a part of our own country as to make it our duty to afford such protection and defense, and that for that purpose our squadron had been ordered to the Gulf and our Army to take a "position between the Nueces and the Del Norte" or Rio Grande and to "repel any invasion of the Texan territory which might be attempted by the Mexican forces."

It was deemed proper to issue this order, because soon after the President of Texas, in April, 1845, had issued his proclamation convening the Congress of that Republic for the purpose of submitting to that body the terms of annexation proposed by the United States the Government of Mexico made serious threats of invading the Texas territory. These threats became more imposing as it became more apparent in the progress of the question that the people of Texas would decide in favor of accepting the terms of annexation, and finally they had assumed such a formidable character as induced both the Congress and convention of Texas to request that a military force should be sent by the United States into her territory for the purpose of protecting and defending her against the threatened invasion. It would have been a violation of good faith toward the people of Texas to have refused to afford the aid which they desired against a threatened invasion to which they had been exposed by their free determination to annex themselves to our Union in compliance with the overture made to them by the joint resolution of our Congress. Accordingly, a portion of the Army was ordered to advance into Texas. Corpus Christi was the position selected by General Taylor. He encamped at that place in August, 1845, and the Army remained in that position until the 11th of March, 1846, when it moved westward, and on the 28th of that month reached the east bank of the Rio Grande opposite to Matamoras. This movement was made in pursuance of orders from the War Department, issued on the 13th of January, 1846. Before these orders were issued the dispatch of our minister in Mexico transmitting the decision of the council of government of Mexico advising that he should not be received, and also the dispatch of our consul residing in the City of Mexico, the former bearing date on the 17th and the latter on the 18th of December, 1845, copies of both of which accompanied my message to Congress of the 11th of May last, were received at the Department of State. These communications rendered it highly probable, if not absolutely certain, that our minister would not be received by the Government of General Herrera. It was also well known that but little hope could be entertained of a different result from General Paredes in case the revolutionary movement which he was prosecuting should prove successful, as was highly probable. The partisans of Paredes, as our minister in the dispatch referred to states, breathed the fiercest hostility against the United States, denounced the proposed negotiation as treason, and openly called upon the troops and the people to put down the Government of Herrera by force. The reconquest of Texas and war with the United States were openly threatened. These were the circumstances existing when it was deemed proper to order the Army under the command of General Taylor to advance to the western frontier of Texas and occupy a position on or near the Rio Grande.

The apprehensions of a contemplated Mexican invasion have been since fully justified by the event. The determination of Mexico to rush into hostilities with the United States was afterwards manifested from the whole tenor of the note of the Mexican minister of foreign affairs to our minister bearing date on the 12th of March, 1846. Paredes had then revolutionized the Government, and his minister, after referring to the resolution for the annexation of Texas which had been adopted by our Congress in March, 1845, proceeds to declare that—

A fact such as this, or, to speak with greater exactness, so notable an act of usurpation, created an imperious necessity that Mexico, for her own honor, should repel it with proper firmness and dignity. The supreme Government had beforehand declared that it would look upon such an act as a *casus belli*, and as a consequence of this declaration negotiation was by its very nature at an end, and war was the only recourse of the Mexican Government.

It appears also that on the 4th of April following General Paredes, through his minister of war, issued orders to the Mexican general in command on the Texan frontier to "attack" our Army "by every means which war permits." To this General Paredes had been pledged to the army and people of Mexico during the military revolution which had brought him into power. On the 18th of April, 1846, General Paredes addressed a letter to the commander on that frontier in which he stated to him: "At the present date I suppose you, at the head of that valiant army, either fighting already or preparing for the operations of a campaign;" and, "Supposing you already on the theater of operations and with all the forces assembled, it is indispensable that hostilities be commenced, yourself taking the initiative against the enemy."

The movement of our Army to the Rio Grande was made by the commanding general under positive orders to abstain from all aggressive acts toward Mexico or Mexican citizens, and to regard the relations between the two countries as peaceful unless Mexico should declare war or commit acts of hostility indicative of a state of war, and these orders he faithfully executed. Whilst occupying his position on the east bank of the Rio Grande, within the limits of Texas, then recently admitted as one of the States of our Union, the commanding general of the Mexican forces, who, in pursuance of the orders of his Government, had collected a large army on the opposite shore of the Rio Grande, crossed the river, invaded our territory, and commenced hostilities by attacking our forces. Thus, after all the injuries which we had received and borne from Mexico, and after she had insultingly rejected a minister sent to her on a mission of peace, and whom she had solemnly agreed to receive, she consummated her long course of outrage against our country by commencing an offensive war and shedding the blood of our citizens on our own soil.

The United States never attempted to acquire Texas by conquest. On the contrary, at an early period after the people of Texas had achieved their independence they sought to be annexed to the United States. At a general election in September, 1836, they decided with great unanimity in favor of "annexation," and in November following the Congress of the Republic authorized the appointment of a minister to bear their request to this Government. This Government, however, having remained neutral between Texas and Mexico during the war between them, and considering it due to the honor of our country and our fair fame among the nations of the earth that we should not at this early period consent to annexation, nor until it should be manifest to the whole world that the reconquest of Texas by Mexico was impossible, refused to accede to the overtures made by Texas. On the 12th of April, 1844, after more than seven years had elapsed since Texas had established her independence, a treaty was concluded for the annexation of that Republic to the United States, which was rejected by the Senate. Finally, on the 1st of March, 1845, Congress passed a joint resolution for annexing her to the United States upon certain preliminary conditions to which her assent was required. The solemnities which characterized the deliberations and conduct of the Government and people of Texas on the deeply interesting questions presented by these resolutions are known to the world. The Congress, the Executive, and the people of Texas, in a convention elected for that purpose, accepted with great unanimity the proposed terms of annexation, and thus consummated on her part the great act of restoring to our Federal Union a vast territory which had been ceded to Spain by the Florida treaty more than a quarter of a century before.

After the joint resolution for the annexation of Texas to the United States had been passed by our Congress the Mexican minister at Washington addressed a note to the Secretary of State, bearing date on the 6th of March, 1845, protesting against it as "an act of aggression the most unjust which can be found recorded in the annals of modern history, namely, that of despoiling a friendly nation like Mexico of a considerable portion of her territory," and protesting against the resolution of annexation as being an act "whereby the Province of Texas, an integral portion of the Mexican territory, is agreed and admitted into the American Union;" and he announced that as a consequence his mission to the United States had terminated, and demanded his passports, which were granted. It was upon the absurd pretext, made by Mexico (herself indebted for her independence to a successful revolution), that the Republic of Texas still continued to be, notwithstanding all that had passed, a Province of Mexico that this step was taken by the Mexican minister.

Every honorable effort has been used by me to avoid the war which followed, but all have proved vain. All our attempts to preserve peace have been met by insult and resistance on the part of Mexico. My efforts to this end commenced in the note of the Secretary of State of the 10th of March, 1845, in answer to that of the Mexican minister. Whilst declining to reopen a discussion which had already been exhausted, and proving again what was known to the whole world, that Texas had long since achieved her independence, the Secretary of State expressed the regret of this Government that Mexico should have taken offense at the resolution of annexation passed by Congress, and gave assurance that our "most strenuous efforts shall be devoted to the amicable adjustment of every cause of complaint between the two Governments and to the cultivation of the kindest and most friendly relations between the sister Republics." That I have acted in the spirit of this assurance will appear from the events which have since occurred. Notwithstanding Mexico had abruptly terminated all diplomatic intercourse with the United States and ought, therefore, to have been the first to ask for its resumption, yet, waiving all ceremony, I embraced the earliest favorable opportunity "to ascertain from the Mexican Government whether they would receive an envoy from the United States intrusted with full power to adjust all the questions in dispute between the two Governments." In September, 1845, I believed the propitious moment for such an overture had arrived. Texas, by the enthusiastic and almost unanimous will of her people, had pronounced in favor of annexation. Mexico herself had agreed to acknowledge the independence of Texas, subject to a condition, it is true, which she had no right to impose and no power to enforce. The last lingering hope of Mexico, if she still could have retained any, that Texas would ever again become one of her Provinces, must have been abandoned.

The consul of the United States at the City of Mexico was therefore instructed by the Secretary of State on the 15th of September, 1845, to make the inquiry of the Mexican Government. The inquiry was made, and on the 15th of October, 1845, the minister of foreign affairs of the Mexican Government, in a note addressed to our consul, gave a favorable response, requesting at the same time that our naval force might be withdrawn from Vera Cruz while negotiations should be pending. Upon the receipt of this note our naval force was promptly withdrawn from Vera Cruz. A minister was immediately appointed, and departed to Mexico. Everything bore a promising aspect for a speedy and peaceful adjustment of all our difficulties. At the date of my annual message to Congress in December last no doubt was entertained but that he would be received by the Mexican Government, and the hope was cherished that all cause of misunderstanding between the two countries would be speedily removed. In the confident hope that such would be the result of his mission, I informed Congress that I forbore at that time to "recommend such ulterior measures of redress for the wrongs and injuries we had so long borne as it would have been proper to make had no such negotiation been instituted." To my surprise and regret the Mexican Government, though solemnly pledged to do so, upon the arrival of our minister in Mexico refused to receive and accredit him. When he reached Vera Cruz, on the 30th of November, 1845, he found that the aspect of affairs had undergone an unhappy change. The Government of General Herrera, who was at that time President of the Republic, was tottering to its fall. General Paredes, a military leader, had manifested his determination to overthrow the Government of Herrera by a military revolution, and one of the principal means which he employed to effect his purpose and render the Government of Herrera odious to the army and people of Mexico was by loudly condemning its determination to receive a minister of peace from the United States, alleging that it was the intention of Herrera, by a treaty with the United Staes, to dismember the territory of Mexico by ceding away the department of Texas. The Government of Herrera is believed to have been well disposed to a pacific adjustment of existing difficulties, but probably alarmed for its own security, and in order to ward off the danger of the revolution led by Paredes, violated its solemn agreement and refused to receive or accredit our minister; and this although informed that he had been invested with full power to adjust all questions in dispute between the two Governments. Among the frivolous pretexts for this refusal, the principal one was that our minister had not gone upon a special mission confined to the question of Texas alone, leaving all the outrages upon our flag and our citizens unredressed. The Mexican Government well knew that both our national honor and the protection due to our citizens imperatively required that the two questions of boundary and indemnity should be treated of together, as naturally and inseparably blended, and they ought to have seen that this course was best calculated to enable the United States to extend to them the most liberal justice. On the 30th of December, 1845, General Herrera resigned the Presidency and yielded up the Government to General Paredes without a struggle. Thus a revolution was accomplished solely by the army commanded by Paredes, and the supreme power in Mexico passed into the hands of a military usurper who was known to be bitterly hostile to the United States.

Although the prospect of a pacific adjustment with the new Government was unpromising from the known hostility of its head to the United States, yet, determined that nothing should be left undone on our part to restore friendly relations between the two countries, our minister was instructed to present his credentials to the new Government and to ask to be accredited by it in the diplomatic character in which he had been commissioned. These instructions he executed by his note of the 1st of March, 1846, addressed to the Mexican minister of foreign affairs, but his request was insultingly refused by that minister in his answer of the 12th of the same month. No alternative remained for our minister but to demand his passports and return to the United States.

Thus was the extraordinary spectacle presented to the civilized world of a Government, in violation of its own express agreement, having twice rejected a minister of peace invested with full powers to adjust all the existing differences between the two countries in a manner just and honorable to both. I am not aware that modern history presents a parallel case in which in time of peace one nation has refused even to hear propositions from another for terminating existing difficulties between them. Scarcely a hope of adjusting our difficulties, even at a remote day, or of preserving peace with Mexico, could be cherished while Paredes remained at the head of the Government. He had acquired the supreme power by a military revolution and upon the most solemn pledges to wage war against the United States and to reconquer Texas, which he claimed as a revolted province of Mexico. He had denounced as guilty of treason all those Mexicans who considered Texas as no longer constituting a part of the territory of Mexico and who were friendly to the cause of peace. The duration of the war which he waged against the United States was indefinite, because the end which he proposed of the reconquest of Texas was hopeless. Besides, there was good reason to believe from all his conduct that it was his intention to convert the Republic of Mexico into a monarchy and to call a foreign European prince to the throne. Preparatory to this end, he had during his short rule destroyed the liberty of the press, tolerating that portion of it only which openly advocated the establishment of a monarchy. The better to secure the success of his ultimate designs, he had by an arbitrary decree convoked a Congress, not to be elected by the free voice of the people, but to be chosen in a manner to make them subservient to his will and to give him absolute control over their deliberations.

Under all these circumstances it was believed that any revolution in Mexico founded upon opposition to the ambitious projects of Paredes would tend to promote the cause of peace as well as prevent any attempted European interference in the affairs of the North American continent, both objects of deep interest to the United States. Any such foreign interference, if attempted, must have been resisted by the United States. My views upon that subject were fully communicated to Congress in my last annual message. In any event, it was certain that no change whatever in the Government of Mexico which would deprive Paredes of power could be for the worse so far as the United States were concerned, while it was highly probable that any change must be for the better. This was the state of affairs existing when Congress, on the 13th of May last, recognized the existence of the war which had been commenced by the Government of Paredes; and it became an object of much importance, with a view to a speedy settlement of our difficulties and the restoration of an honorable peace, that Paredes should not retain power in Mexico.

Before that time there were symptoms of a revolution in Mexico, favored, as it was understood to be, by the more liberal party, and especially by those who were opposed to foreign interference and to the monarchical form of government. Santa Anna was then in exile in Havana, having been expelled from power and banished from his country by a revolution which occurred in December, 1844; but it was known that he had still a considerable party in his favor in Mexico. It was also equally well known that no vigilance which could be exerted by our squadron would in all probability have prevented him from effecting a landing somewhere on the extensive Gulf coast of Mexico if he desired to return to his country. He had openly professed an entire change of policy, had expressed his regret that he had subverted the federal constitution of 1824, and avowed that he was now in favor of its restoration. He had publicly declared his hostility, in strongest terms, to the establishment of a monarchy and to European interference in the affairs of his country. Information to this effect had been received, from sources believed to be reliable, at the date of the recognition of the existence of the war by Congress, and was afterwards fully confirmed by the receipt of the dispatch of our consul in the City of Mexico, with the accompanying documents, which are herewith transmitted. Besides, it was reasonable to suppose that he must see the ruinous consequences to Mexico of a war with the United States, and that it would be his interest to favor peace.

It was under these circumstances and upon these considerations that it was deemed expedient not to obstruct his return to Mexico should he attempt to do so. Our object was the restoration of peace, and, with that view, no reason was perceived why we should take part with Paredes and aid him by means of our blockade in preventing the return of his rival to Mexico. On the contrary, it was believed that the intestine divisions which ordinary sagacity could not but anticipate as the fruit of Santa Anna's return to Mexico, and his contest with Paredes, might strongly tend to produce a disposition with both parties to restore and preserve peace with the United States. Paredes was a soldier by profession and a monarchist in principle. He had but recently before been successful in a military revolution, by which he had obtained power. He was the sworn enemy of the United States, with which he had involved his country in the existing war. Santa Anna had been expelled from power by the army, was known to be in open hostility to Paredes, and publicly pledged against foreign intervention and the restoration of monarchy in Mexico. In view of these facts and circumstances it was that when orders were issued to the commander of our naval forces in the Gulf, on the 13th day of May last, the same day on which the existence of the war was recognized by Congress, to place the coasts of Mexico under blockade, he was directed not to obstruct the passage of Santa Anna to Mexico should he attempt to return.

A revolution took place in Mexico in the early part of August following, by which the power of Paredes was overthrown, and he has since been banished from the country, and is now in exile. Shortly afterwards Santa Anna returned. It remains to be seen whether his return may not yet prove to be favorable to a pacific adjustment of the existing difficulties, it being manifestly his interest not to persevere in the prosecution of a war commenced by Paredes to accomplish a purpose so absurd as the reconquest of Texas to the Sabine. Had Paredes remained in power, it is morally certain that any pacific adjustment would have been hopeless.

Upon the commencement of hostilities by Mexico against the United States the indignant spirit of the nation was at once aroused. Congress promptly responded to the expectations of the country, and by the act of the 13th of May last recognized the fact that war existed, by the act of Mexico, between the United States and that Republic, and granted the means necessary for its vigorous prosecution. Being involved in a war thus commenced by Mexico, and for the justice of which on our part we may confidently appeal to the whole world, I resolved to prosecute it with the utmost vigor. Accordingly the ports of Mexico on the Gulf and on the Pacific have been placed under blockade and her territory invaded at several important points. The reports from the Departments of War and of the Navy will inform you more in detail of the measures adopted in the emergency in which our country was placed and of the gratifying results which have been accomplished. . . .

Representative Abraham Lincoln
"Spot Resolutions" Introduced
In the House of Representatives
December 22, 1847

Roy P. Basler, ed., *The Collected Works of Abraham Lincoln* (New Brunswick, New Jersey, 1953) I, 420-22.

Whereas the President of the United States, in his message of May 11th, 1846, has declared that "The Mexican Government not only refused to receive him" (the envoy of the U.S.) "or listen to his propositions, but, after a long continued series of menaces, have at last invaded *our teritory*, and shed the blood of our fellow *citizens* on *our own soil*"

And again, in his message of December 8, 1846 that "We had ample cause of war against Mexico, long before the breaking out of hostilities. But even then we forbore to take redress into our own hands, until Mexico herself became the aggressor by invading *our soil* in hostile array, and shedding the blood of our *citizens*"

And yet again, in his message of December 7—1847 that "The Mexican Government refused even to hear the terms of adjustment which he" (our minister of peace) "was authorized to propose; and finally, under wholly unjustifiable pretexts, involved the two countries in war, by invading the teritory of the State of Texas, striking the first blow, and shedding the blood of our *citizens* on *our own soil*"

And whereas this House desires to obtain a full knowledge of all the facts which go to establish whether the particular spot of soil on which the blood of our *citizens* was so shed, was, or was not, *our own soil*, at that time; therefore

Resolved by the House of Representatives, that the President of the United States be respectfully requested to inform this House—

First: Whether the spot of soil on which the blood of our *citizens* was shed, as in his messages declared, was, or was not, within the teritories of Spain, at least from the treaty of 1819 until the Mexican revolution

Second: Whether that spot is, or is not, within the teritory which was wrested from Spain, by the Mexican revolution.

Third: Whether that spot is, or is not, within a settlement of people, which settlement had existed ever since long before the Texas revolution, until it's inhabitants fled from the approach of the U.S. Army.

Fourth: Whether that settlement is, or is not, isolated from any and all other settlements, by the Gulf of Mexico, and the Rio Grande, on the South and West, and by wide uninhabited regions on the North and East.

Fifth: Whether the *People* of that settlement, or a *majority* of them, or *any* of them, had ever, previous to the bloodshed, mentioned in his messages, submitted themselves to the government or laws of Texas, or of the United States, by *consent*, or by *compulsion*, either by accepting office, or voting at elections, or paying taxes, or serving on juries, or having process served upon them, or in *any other way*.

Sixth: Whether the People of that settlement, did, or did not, flee from the approach of the United States Army, leaving unprotected their homes and their growing crops, *before* the blood was shed, as in his messages stated, and whether the first blood so shed, was, or was not shed, within the *inclosure* of the People, or some of them, who had thus fled from it.

Seventh: Whether our *citizens*, whose blood was shed, as in his messages declared, were, or were not, at that time, *armed* officers, and *soldiers*, sent into that settlement, by the military order of the President through the Secretary of War— and

Eighth: Whether the military force of the United States, including those *citizens*, was, or was not, so sent into that settlement, after Genl. Taylor had, more than once, intimated to the War Department that, in his opinion, no such movement was necessary to the defence or protection of Texas.

Representative Abraham Lincoln
"The War with Mexico"—His Maiden Speech
Before the House of Representatives
January 12, 1848

Basler, I, 431-42.

Mr. Chairman: Some, if not all the gentlemen on, the other side of the House, who have addressed the committee within the last two days, have spoken rather complainingly, if I have rightly understood them, of the vote given a week or ten days age, declaring that the war with Mexico was unnecessarily and unconstitutionally commenced by the President. I admit that such a vote should not be given, in mere party wantonness, and that the one given, is justly censurable, if it have no other, or better foundation. I am one of those who joined in that vote; and I did so under my best impression of the *truth* of the case. How I got this impression, and how it may possibly be removed, I will now try to show. When the war began, it was my opinion that all those who, because of knowing too *little*, or because of knowing too *much*, could not conscientiously approve the conduct of the President, in the beginning of it, should nevertheless, as good citizens and patriots, remain silent on that point, at least till the war should be ended. Some leading democrats, including Ex President Van Buren, have taken this same view, as I understand them; and I adhered to it, and acted upon it, until since I took my seat here; and I think I should still adhere to it, were it not that the President and his friends will not allow it to be so. Besides the continual effort of the President to argue every silent vote given for supplies, into an endorsement of the justice and widsom of his conduct—besides that singularly candid paragraph, in his late message in which he tells us that Congress, with great unanimity, only two in the Senate and fourteen in the House dissenting, had declared that, "by the act of the Republic of Mexico, a state of war exists between that Government and the United States," when the same journals that informed him of this, also informed him, that when that declaration stood disconnected from the question of supplies, sixtyseven in the House, and not fourteen merely, voted against it—besides this open attempt to prove, by telling the *truth*, what he could not prove by telling the *whole truth*—demanding of all who will not submit to be misrepresented, in justice to themselves, to speak out—besides all this, one of my colleagues (Mr. Richardson) [William A. Richardson, Democrat, from Rushville, Illinois, who had been elected to the House to fill the vacancy caused by the resignation of representative-elect Stephen A. Douglas. Footnote in Basler.] at a very early day in the session brought in a set of resolutions, expressly endorsing the original justice of the war on the part of the President. Upon these resolutions, when they shall be put on their passage I shall be *compelled* to vote; so that I can not be silent, if I would. Seeing this, I went about preparing myself to give the vote understandingly when it should come. I carefully examined the President's messages, to ascertain what he himself had said and proved upon the point. The result of this examination was to make the impression, that taking for true, all the

President states as facts, he falls far short of proving his justification; and that the President would have gone farther with his proof, if it had not been for the small matter, that the *truth* would not permit him. Under the impression thus made, I gave the vote before mentioned. I propose now to give, concisely, the process of the examination I made, and how I reached the conclusion I did. The President, in his first war message of May 1846, declares that the soil was *ours* on which hostilities were commenced by Mexico; and he repeats that declaration, almost in the same language, in each successive annual message, thus showing that he esteems that point, a highly essential one. In the importance of that point, I entirely agree with the President. To my judgment, it is the *very point*, upon which he should be justified, or condemned. In his message of Decr. 1846, It seems to have occurred to him, as is certainly true, that title—ownership—to soil, or any thing else, is not a simple fact; but is a conclusion following one or more simple facts; and that it was incumbent upon him, to present the facts, from which he concluded, the soil was ours, on which the first blood of the war was shed.

Accordingly a little below the middle of page twelve in the message last referred to, he enters upon that task; forming an issue, and introducing testimony, extending the whole, to a little below the middle of page fourteen. Now I propose to try to show, that the whole of this,—issue and evidence—is, from beginning to end, the sheerest deception. The issue, as he presents it, is in these words "But there are those who, conceding all this to be true, assume the ground that the true western boundary of Texas is the Nueces, instead of the Rio Grande; and that, therefore, in marching our army to the east bank of the latter river, we passed the Texan line, and invaded the teritory of Mexico." Now this issue, is made up of two affirmatives and no negative. The main deception of it is, that it assumes as true, that *one* river or the *other* is necessarily the boundary; and cheats the superficial thinker entirely out of the idea, that *possibly* the boundary is somewhere *between* the two, and not actually at either. A further deception is, that it will let in *evidence*, which a true issue would exclude. A true issue, made by the President, would be about as follows "I say, the soil *was ours*, on which the first blood was shed; there are those who say it was not."

I now proceed to examine the Presidents evidence, as applicable to such an issue. When that evidence is analized, it is all included in the following propositions:

1. That the Rio Grande was the Western boundary of Louisiana as we purchased it of France in 1803.

2. That the Republic of Texas always *claimed* the Rio Grande, as her Western boundary.

3. That by various acts, she had claimed it *on paper*.

4. That Santa Anna, in his treaty with Texas, recognised the Rio Grande, as her boundary.

5. That Texas *before*, and the U.S. *after*, annexation had *exercised* jurisdiction *beyond* the Nueces—*between* the two rivers.

6. That our Congress, *understood* the boundary of Texas to extend beyond the Nueces.

Now for each of these in its turn.

His first item is, that the Rio Grande was the Western boundary of Louisiana, as we purchased it of France in 1803; and seeming to expect this to be disputed, he argues over the amount of nearly a page, to prove it true; at the end of which he lets us know, that by the treaty of 1819, we sold to Spain the whole country from the Rio Grande eastward, to the Sabine. Now, admitting for the present, that the Rio Grande, was the boundary of Louisiana, what, under heaven, had that to do with the *present* boundary between us and Mexico? How, Mr. Chairman, the line, that once divided your land from mine, can *still* be the boundary between us, *after* I have sold my land to you, is, to me, beyond all comprehension. And how any man, with an honest purpose only, of proving the truth, could ever have *thought* of introducing such a fact to prove such an issue, is equally incomprehensible. [In the text of the *Congressional Globe Appendix*, Lincoln inserted at this point the following sentence: "The outrage upon common *right*, of seizing as our own what we have once sold, merely because it *was* ours *before* we sold it, is only equalled by the outrage on common *sense* of any attempt to justify it." Footnote in Basler.] His next piece of evidence is that "The Republic of Texas always *claimed* this river (Rio Grande) as her western boundary[.]" That is not true, in fact. Texas *has* claimed it, but she has not *always* claimed it. There is, at least, one distinguished exception. Her state constitution,—the republic's most solemn, and well considered act—that which may, without impropriety, be called her last will and testament revoking all others—makes no such claim. But suppose she had always claimed it. Has not Mexico always claimed the contrary? so that there is but *claim* against *claim*, leaving nothing proved, until we get back of the claims, and find which has the better *foundation*. Though not in the order in which the President presents his evidence, I now consider that class of his statements, which are, in substance, nothing more than that Texas has, by various acts of her convention and congress, claimed the Rio Grande, as her boundary, *on paper*. I mean here what he says about the fixing of the Rio Grande as her boundary in her old constitution (not her state constitution) about forming congressional districts, counties etc., etc. Now all of this is but naked *claim*; and what I have already said about claims is strictly applicable to this. If I should claim your land, by word of mouth, that certainly would not make it mine; and if I were to claim it by a deed which I had made myself, and with which, you had had nothing to do, the claim would be quite the same, in substance—or rather, in utter nothingness. I next consider the President's statement that Santa Anna in his *treaty* [the text of the so-called "treaty," printed following Lincoln's speech in the *Congressional Globe Appendix* is as follows:

> [*Articles of an agreement entered into between his Excellency David G. Burnet, President of the Republic of Texas, of the one part, and his Excellency General Santa Anna, President-General-in-Chief of the Mexican army, of the other part.*
>
> [Article 1. General Antonio Lopez de Santa Anna agrees that he will not take up arms, nor will he exercise his influence to cause them to be taken up, against the people of Texas, during the present war of independence.
>
> [Art. 2. All hostilities between the Mexican and Texan troops will cease immediately, both by land and water.
>
> [Art. 3. The Mexican troops will evacuate the territory of Texas, passing to the other side of the Rio Grande Del Norte.
>
> [Art. 4. The Mexican army, in its retreat, shall not take the property of

any person without his consent and just indemnification, using only such articles as may be necessary for its subsistence, in cases when the owner may not be present, and remitting to the commander of the army of Texas, or to the Commissioners to be appointed for the adjustment of such matters, on account of the value of the property consumed, the place where taken, and the name of the owner, if it can be ascertained.

[Art. 5. That all private property, including cattle, horses, negro slaves, or indentured persons, of whatever denomination, that may have been captured by any portion of the Mexican army, or may have taken refuge in the said army, since the commencement of the late invasion, shall be restored to the commander of the Texan army, or to such other persons as may be appointed by the Government of Texas to receive them.

[Art. 6. The troops of both armies will refrain from coming into contact with each other; and to this end, the commander of the army of Texas will be careful not to approach within a shorter distance than five leagues.

[Art. 7. The Mexican army shall not make any other delay, on its march, than that which is necessary to take up their hospitals, baggage, etc., and to cross the rivers, any delay not necessary to these purposes to be considered an infraction of this agreement.

[Art. 8. By an express to be immediately dispatched, this agreement shall be sent to General Vincente Filisola, and to General T. J. Rusk, commander of the Texan army, in order that they may be apprized of its stipulations; and to this end, they will exchange engagements to comply with the same.

[Art. 9. That all Texan prisoners now in the possession of the Mexican army, or its authorities, be forthwith released, and furnished with free passports to return to their homes; in consideration of which, a corresponding number of Mexican prisoners, rank and file, now in possession of the Government of Texas, shall be immediately released— the remainder of the Mexican prisoners that continue in the possession of the Government of Texas to be treated with due humanity; any extraordinary comforts that may be furnished them to be at the charge of the Government of Mexico.

[Art. 10. General Antonio Lopez de Santa Anna will be sent to Vera Cruz as soon as it shall be deemed proper.

[The contracting parties sign this instrument for the above mentioned purposes, in duplicate, at the port of Velasco, this 14th day of May, 1836.

> *David G. Burnet*
> *Jas. Collingsworth*
> *Antonio Lopez de Santa Anna*
> *B. Hardiman*
> *P. W. Grayson*

—Footnote in Basler.]

with Texas, recognised the Rio Grande, as the western boundary of Texas. Besides the position, so often taken that Santa Anna, while a prisoner of war—a captive— *could* not bind Mexico by a treaty, which I deem conclusive—besides this, I wish to say something in relation to this treaty, so called by the President, with Santa Anna. If any man would like to be amused by a sight of that *little* thing, which the President calls by that *big* name, he can have it, by turning to Niles' Register volume 50, page 336. And if any one should suppose that Niles' Register is a curious repository of so mighty a document, as a solemn treaty between nations, I can only say that I learned, to a tolerable degree [of] certainty, by enquiry at the State Department, that the President himself, never saw it any where else. By the way, I believe I should not err, if I were to declare, that during the first ten years of the existence of that document, it was never, by any body, *called* a treaty—that it was never so called, till the President, in his extremity, attempted, by so calling it, to wring something from it in justification of himself in connection with the Mexican war. It has none of the distinguishing features of a treaty. It does not call itself a treaty. Santa Anna does not therein, assume to bind Mexico; he assumes only to act as the President-Commander-in-chief of the Mexican Army and Navy; stipulates that the then present hostilities should cease, and that he would not *himself* take up arms, nor *influence* the Mexican people to take up arms, against Texas during the existence of the war of independence[.] He did not recognise the independence of Texas; he did not assume to put an end to the war; but clearly indicated his expectation of it's continuance; he did not say one word about boundary, and, most probably, never thought of it. It *is* stipulated therein that the Mexican forces should evacuate the teritory of Texas, *passing to the other side of the Rio Grande*; and in another article, it is stipulated that, to prevent collisions between the armies, the Texan army should not approach nearer than within five leagues—of *what* is not said—but clearly, from the object stated it is—of the Rio Grande. Now, if this is a treaty, recognising the Rio Grande, as the boundary of Texas, it contains the singular feature [*sic*], of stipulating, that Texas shall not go within five leagues of *her own* boundary.

Next comes the evidence of Texas before annexation, and the United States, afterwards, *exercising* jurisdiction *beyond* the Nueces, and *between* the two rivers. This actual *exercise* of jurisdiction, is the very class or quality of evidence we want. It is excellent so far as it goes; but does it go far enough? He tells us it went *beyond* the Nueces; but he does not tell us it went *to* the Rio Grande. He tells us, jurisdiction was exercised *between* the two rivers, but he does not tell us it was exercised over *all* the teritory between them. Some simple minded people, think it is *possible*, to cross one river and go *beyond* it without going *all the way* to the next—that jurisdiction may be exercised *between* two rivers without covering *all* the country between them. I know a man, not very unlike myself, who exercises jurisdiction over a piece of land between the Wabash and the Mississippi; and yet so far is this from being *all* there is between those rivers, that it is just one hundred and fiftytwo feet long by fifty wide, and no part of it much within a hundred miles of either. He has a neighbour between him and the Mississippi,—that is, just across the street, in that direction—whom, I am sure, he could neither *persuade* nor *force* to give up his habitation; but which nevertheless, he could certainly annex, if it were to be done, by merely standing on his own side of the street and *claiming* it, or even, sitting down, and writing a *deed* for it.

But next the President tells us, the Congress of the United States *understood* the state of Texas they admitted into the union, to extend *beyond* the Nueces. Well, I suppose they did. *I* certainly so understood it. But how *far* beyond? That Congress did *not* understand it to extend clear to the Rio Grande, is quite certain by the fact of their joint resolutions, for admission, expressly leaving all questions of boundary to future adjustment. And it may be added, that Texas herself, is proved to have had the same understanding of it, that our Congress had, by the fact of the exact conformity of her new constitution, to those resolutions.

I am now through the whole of the President's evidence; and it is a singular fact, that if any one should declare the President sent the army into the midst of a settlement of Mexican people, who had never submited, by consent or by force, to the authority of Texas or of the United States, and that *there*, and *thereby*, the first blood of the war was shed, there is not one word in all the President has said, which would either admit or deny the declaration. [At this point in the *Congressional Globe Appendix*, Lincoln emended the next sentence as follows: "In this strange omission chiefly consists the deception of the President's evidence—an omission which, it does seem to me, could scarcely have occurred but by design." Footnote in Basler.] This strange omission, it does seem to me, could not have occurred but by design. My way of living leads me to be about the courts of justice; and there, I have sometimes seen a good lawyer, struggling for his client's neck, in a desparate case, employing every artifice to work round, befog, and cover up, with many words, some [Lincoln emended "point arising in the case" to "position pressed upon him by the prosecution." Footnote in Basler.] point arising in the case, which he *dared* not admit, and yet *could* not deny. Party bias may help to make it appear so; but with all the allowance I can make for such bias, it still does appear to me, that just such, and from just such necessity, is the President's struggle in this case.

Some time after my colleague (Mr. Richardson) introduced the resolutions I have mentioned, I introduced a preamble, resolution, and interrogatories, intended to draw the President out, if possible, on this hitherto untrodden ground. To show their relevancy, I propose to state my understanding of the true rule for ascertaining the boundary between Texas and Mexico. It is, that *wherever* Texas was *exercising* jurisdiction, was hers; and *wherever Mexico* was exercising jurisdiction, was hers; and that *whatever* separated the actual exercise of jurisdiction of the one, from that of the other, was the true boundary between them. If, as is probably true, Texas was exercising jurisdiction along the western bank of the Nueces, and Mexico was exercising it along the eastern bank of the Rio Grande, then *neither* river was the boundary; but the uninhabited country between the two, was. The extent of our teritory in that region depended, not on any *treaty-fixed* boundary (for no treaty had attempted it) but on revolution. Any people anywhere, being inclined and having the power, have the *right* to rise up, and shake off the existing government, and form a new one that suits them better. This is a most valuable,—a most sacred right—a right, which we hope and believe, is to liberate the world. Nor is this right confined to cases in which the whole people of an existing government, may choose to exercise it. Any portion of such people that *can, may* revolutionize, and make their *own*, of so much of the teritory as they inhabit. More than this, a *majority* of any portion of such people may revolutionize, putting down a *minority*, intermingled with, or near about them, who may oppose their movement. Such minority, was precisely the case, of the tories of our own revolution. It is a quality of revolutions not to go by *old* lines, or *old* laws; but to break up both, and make new ones. As to the country now in question, we bought it of France in 1803, and sold it to Spain in 1819, according to the President's statements. After this, all Mexico, including Texas, revolutionized against Spain; and still later, Texas revolutionized against Mexico. In my view, just so far as she carried her revolution, by obtaining the *actual*, willing or unwilling, submission of the people, *so far*, the country was hers, and no farther. Now sir, for the purpose of obtaining the very best evidence, as to whether Texas had actually carried her revolution, to the place where the hostilities of the present war commenced, let the President answer the interrogatories, I proposed, as before mentioned, or some other similar ones. Let him answer, fully, fairly, and candidly. Let him answer with *facts*, and not with arguments. Let him remember he sits where Washington sat, and so remembering, let him answer, as Washington would answer. As a nation *should* not, and the Almighty *will* not, be evaded, so let him attempt no envasion—no equivocation. And if, so answering, he can show that the soil was ours, where the first blood of the war was shed—that it was not within an inhabited country, or, if within such, that the inhabitants had submitted themselves to the civil authority of Texas, or of the United States, and that the same is true of the site of Fort Brown, then I am with him for his justification. In that case I, shall be most happy to reverse the vote I gave the other day. I have a selfish motive for desiring that the President may do this. I expect to give some votes, in connection with the war, which, without his so doing, will be of doubtful propriety in my own judgment, but which will be free from the doubt if he does so. But if he *can* not, or *will* not do this—if on any pretence, or no pretence, he shall refuse or omit it, then I shall be fully convinced, of what I more than suspect already, that he is deeply conscious of being in the wrong—that he feels the blood of this war, like the blood of Abel, is crying to Heaven against him. [At this point Lincoln emended as follows: "; that he ordered General Taylor into the midst of a peaceful Mexican settlement, purposely to bring on a war; that originally . . ." etc. Footnote in Basler.] That originally having some strong motive—what, I will not stop now to give my opinion concerning—to involve the two countries in a war, and trusting to escape scrutiny, by fixing the public gaze upon the exceeding brightness of military glory—that attractive rainbow, that rises in showers of blood—that serpent's eye, that charms to destroy—he plunged into it, and has swept, *on* and *on*, till, disappointed in his calculation of the ease with which Mexico might be subdued, he now finds himself, he knows not where. How like the half insane mumbling of a fever-dream, is the whole war part of his late message! At one time telling us that Mexico has nothing whatever, that we can get, but teritory; at another, showing us how we can support the war, by levying contributions on Mexico. At one time, urging the national honor, the security of the future, the prevention of foreign interference, and even, the good of Mexico herself, as among the objects of the war; at another, telling us, that "to reject indemnity, by refusing to accept a cession of teritory, would be to abandon all our just demands, and to wage the war, bearing all it's expenses, *without a purpose or definite object*[.]" So then, the national honor, security of the future, and every thing but teritorial indemnity, may be considered the *no-purposes*, and *indefinite*, objects of the war! But, having it now settled that teritorial indemnity is the only object, we are urged to seize, by legislation here, all that he was content to take, a few months ago, and the whole province of lower California to boot, and to still carry on the war—to take *all* we are fighting for, and *still* fight on. Again, the President is resolved, under all circumstances, to have full teritorial indemnity for the expenses of the war; but he forgets to tell us how we are to get the *excess*, after those expenses shall have surpassed the value of the *whole* of the Mexican teritory. So again, he insists that the separate national existence of Mexico, shall be maintained; but he does not tell us *how* this can be done, after we shall have taken *all* her teritory. Lest the questions, I here suggest, be considered speculative merely, let me be indulged a moment in trying [to] show they are not. The war has gone on some twenty months; for the expenses of which, together with an inconsiderable old score, the President now claims about one half of the Mexican teritory; and that, by far the better half, so far as concerns our ability to make any thing out of it. *It* is comparatively uninhabited; so that we could establish land offices in it, and raise some money in that way. But the other half is already inhabited, as I understand it, tolerably densely for the nature of the country; and all it's lands, or all that are valuable, already appropriated as private property. How then are we to make any thing out of these lands with this incumbrance on them? or how, remove the incumbrance? I suppose no one will say we should kill the people, or drive them out, or make slaves of them, or even confiscate their property. How then can we make much out of this part of the teritory? If the prossecution of the war has, in expenses, already equalled the *better* half of the country, how long it's future prosecution, will be in equalling, the less valuable half, is not a *speculative*, but a *practical* question, pressing closely upon us. And yet it is a question which the President seems to never have thought of. As to the mode of terminating the war, and securing peace, the President is equally wandering and indefinite. First, it is to be done by a more vigorous prossecution of the war in the vital parts of the enemies country; and, after apparently, talking himself tired, on this point, the President drops down into a half despairing tone, and tells us that "with a people distracted and divided by contending factions, and a government subject to constant changes, by successive revolutions, *the continued success of our arms may fail to secure a satisfactory peace*[.]" Then he suggests the propriety of wheedling the Mexican people to desert the counsels of their own leaders, and trusting in our protection, to set up a government from which we can secure a satisfactory peace; telling us, that "*this may become the only mode of obtaining such a peace.*" But soon he falls into doubt of this too; and then drops back on to the already half abandoned ground of "more vigorous prossecution.["] All this shows that the President is, in no wise, satisfied with his own positions. First he takes up one, and in attempting to argue us *into* it, he argues himself *out* of it; then seizes another, and goes through the same process; and then, confused at being able to think of nothing new, he snatches up the old one again, which he has some time before cast off. His mind, tasked beyond it's power, is running hither and thither, like some tortured creature, on a burning surface, finding no position, on which it can settle down, and be at ease.

Again, it is a singular omission in this message, that it, no where intimates *when* the President expects the war to terminate. At it's beginning, Genl. Scott [Winfield

Scott. Both General Scott and General Taylor were Whigs, and administration leaders feared the increase of their popularity. Scott justifiably suspected the administration of withholding complete co-operation. On January 2, Scott was recalled; on January 31 and April 17, Lincoln voted in favor of resolutions requesting the President to explain the suspension. On April 22, Scott was superseded by General W. O. Butler. Footnote in Basler.] was, by this same President, driven into disfavor, if not disgrace, for intimating that peace could not be conquered in less than three or four months. But now, at the end of about twenty months, during which time our arms have given us the most splendid successes— every department, and every part, land and water, officers and privates, regulars and volunteers, doing all that men *could* do, and hundreds of things which it had ever before been thought men could *not* do,—after all this, this same President gives us a long message, without showing us, that, *as to the end*, he himself, has, ever an immaginary conception. As I have before said, he knows not where he is. He is a bewildered, confounded, and miserably perplexed man. God grant he may be able to show, there is not something about his conscience, more painful than all his mental perplexity!

Lincoln drew a barrage of criticism from some of his constituents, including his close friend and law partner, William H. Herndon, for these attacks upon the Commander in Chief. In his fascinating *Life of Lincoln*, Herndon relates some of the background of these events and describes his own reaction to Lincoln's position:

> He [Lincoln] doubtless felt he was taking rather advanced and perhaps questionable ground. And so he was, for very soon after, murmurs of dissatisfaction began to run through the Whig ranks. I did not, as some of Lincoln's biographers would have their readers believe, inaugurate this feeling of dissatisfaction. On the contrary, as the law partner of the Congressman, and as his ardent admirer, I discouraged the defection all I could. Still, when I listened to the comments of his friends everywhere after the delivery of his speech, I felt he had made a mistake. I therefore wrote him to that effect, at the same time giving him my own views, which I knew were in full accord with the views of his Whig constituents. My argument in substance was: That the President of the United States is Commander-in-Chief of the Army and Navy; that as such commander it was his duty, in the absence of Congress, if the country was about to be invaded and armies were organized in Mexico for that purpose, to go—if necessary—into the very heart of Mexico and prevent the invasion. I argued further that it would be a crime in the Executive to let the country be invaded in the least degree. The action of the President was a necessity. . . .[98]

The young congressman from Illinois was concerned but not distraught by the criticism, and soon turned his hand to convincing his friend, and hopefully his constituents, that he had been right in the stand that he took. He explained to Herndon that he had not opposed supplies to the American army in the field, but rather had voted and spoken to censure the President for his responsibility in initiating the war in the first place, because, as he put it, to do anything else would be to support what "you felt you knew to be a lie."[99] In a second letter Lincoln turned to the substance of their differences and in a masterful summation of the case against Polk, provides us with a fitting climax to this long chapter. It reveals not only the true greatness of this future President, but also defines as eloquently and explicitly as anyone has done before or since, the constitutional limits of presidential power.

Representative Abraham Lincoln
Letter to William H. Herndon
February 15, 1848

Basler, I, 451-52.

Dear William: Your letter of the 29th. Jany. was received last night. Being exclusively a constitutional argument, I wish to submit some reflections upon it in the same spirit of kindness that I know actuates you. Let me first state what I understand to be your position. It is, that if it shall become *necessary, to repel invasion*, the President may, without violation of the Constitution, cross the line, and *invade* the territory of another country, and that whether such *necessity* exists in any given case, the President is to be the *sole* judge.

Before going further, consider well whether this is, or is not your position. If it is, it is a position that neither the President himself, nor any friend of his, so far as I know, has ever taken. Their only positions are first, that the soil was *ours* where hostilities commenced, and second, that whether it was rightfully *ours* or not, *Congress had annexed it*, and the President, for that reason was bound to defend it, both of which are as clearly proved to be false in fact, as you can prove that your house is not mine. That soil was not ours; and Congress did not annex or attempt to annex it. But to return to your position: Allow the President to invade a neighboring nation, whenever *he* shall deem it necessary to repel an invasion, and you allow him to do so, *whenever he may choose to say* he deems it necessary for such purpose—and you allow him to make war at pleasure. Study to see if you can fix *any limit* to his power in this respect, after you have given him so much as you propose. If, to-day, he should choose to say he thinks it necessary to invade Canada, to prevent the British from invading us, how could you stop him? You may say to him, "I see no probability of the British invading us" but he will say to you "be silent; I see it, if you dont."

The provision of the Constitution giving the war-making power to Congress, was dictated, as I understand it, by the following reasons. Kings had always been involving and impoverishing their people in wars, pretending generally, if not always, that the good of the people was the object. This, our Convention understood to be the most oppressive of all Kingly oppressions; and they resolved to so frame the Constitution that *no one man* should hold the power of bringing this oppression upon us. But your view destroys the whole matter, and places our President where kings have always stood. Write soon again.

Yours truly,

A. Lincoln

The Retreat from Power

The 1850s and 1860s were the most tragic decades in American history. It was then that our original sin—slavery—emerged at the forefront of the American experience and imposed the wages of that sin upon society, first through aggravated national divisions already becoming apparent, and later by death and destruction of an unprecedented nature in the Civil War. It was also a period when the American presidency sank to its lowest ebb, producing its weakest and most unimpressive examples; it dangerously faltered for the first time in its more than half a century of creative experience. Yet tragedies often generate great moments of sublime understanding, of heroic grandeur and produce characters of a certain magnitude, tragic heroes, as Aristotle would define them, heroes who are able to raise their predicament to the highest level of human experience. That sad period also had its exalted moments, its deep understanding, its heroic figures. Perhaps they stood out in bolder relief because of the stark and forbidding background from which they emerged. The contrast was at times unbelievable. So it was with the greatest of these heroes—Abraham Lincoln—the sixteenth President of the United States.

Can there be serious doubt that Lincoln was the greatest American President? The years following his less than five years in the White House have been resonant with echoes of his mythical hold on the American conscience—an heroic figure who continues to inspire us and to wring both "pity and fear" from our sense of his overwhelming burden, the inevitability of his own personal tragic history, and the inspiration of his commanding presence, coupled with sadness at the recognition of its fatal consequences.

Lincoln filled a vacuum in national leadership which had existed since the administration of James Polk, who himself was a wartime exception to the drab set of predecessors who followed his political ally and fellow Tennessean, Andrew Jackson, into the White House. The reasons for this dearth of leadership are, of course, complex and go to the heart of the central problems of the period, but in a nutshell, the old parties faltered in the 1840s and broke down completely in the 1850s. The social and political system failed to respond effectively to the great problems of the society. And foremost among these, a stain upon the fabric of our body politic from the very beginning, was the permanent indentured servitude of the Black man in American civilization.

We have previously examined the breakdowns which resulted as the political leaders of "the Democracy"[100] and of "Whiggery" failed to resolve the critical economic problems of the period. The political institutions of the republic were weakened almost irreparably during the first Whig administration of John Tyler, and some of the frustration of that failure led to the inordinate and destructive drive for national expansion, the illegal and immoral exhortation to an aggressive war, and the breakdown and ultimate breakup of one of the major parties and the division and weakening of the other. That was the most recent legacy which the new Republican party inherited when it was founded in Jackson, Michigan in the summer of 1854. But before that significant event could take place, the realities of the severe social and political dislocation in society would have to come to the surface.

Slavery in this new society was present almost from the beginning, but its growth under the early struggling economy of the South was limited. The institution was condemned by the greatest of the early national leaders—Washington, Jefferson, Madison and Hamilton, all of whom advocated its gradual extinction—and it appeared before the turn of the century that that it would fade away in the free society of America. The Declaration of Independence declared that "all men are created equal," and Jefferson, its principal author, had wanted to go farther than that and denounce the slave trade in the document itself. The Northwest Ordinance of 1787 expressly outlawed slavery in the territories north of the Ohio River, and many Americans were confident that it would shortly "price itself out" of the competitive struggle for existence on this continent.

But the invention of the cotton gin changed all of that. It made slave labor relatively profitable in the agricultural economy of the South, with its fertile soil and mild climate. The slave trade bristled with activity, and the number of slaves multiplied many, many times beyond the highest numbers reached in the seventeenth and eighteenth centuries. In 1754 there were slightly over a quarter of a million slaves in this country, but 100 years later that number had increased to almost 4,000,000. Since cotton was the staple agricultural product throughout the South and slaves constituted the major source of agricultural labor, the institution of slavery became an integral part of the fabric of southern society. For a long while, Americans in other sections of the country were indifferent to slavery, and although it always had its moral opponents, it was not a major source of political disagreement in the early years of the republic. Neither the Federalists nor the Republicans had a position on slavery, and although there was a growing social distaste for it in the North, nothing much was done about it for the first 40-odd years in our history.[101]

The emergence of the anti-slavery abolitionist movement in the 1830s (the American Anti-Slavery Society—AASS) brought the issue to public attention. The objective of the AASS was to abolish slavery throughout the United States and to ameliorate the condition of the Black people "by encouraging their intellectual, moral and religious improvement, and by removing public prejudice that thus they may, according to their intellectual and moral worth, share an equality with the whites, of civil and religious privilege."[102] The movement was motivated by moral and spiritual rather than political zeal, and in the formative period of the society's growth, it gave very little time and consideration to political strategy. But as the movement gained adherents and its experience enlarged, political considerations prompted new developments.

The abolitionists soon discovered that aggressive social action led to political reprisal, and in order to protect themselves and advance their cause, they would have to exert political as well as "moral" influence. Post offices in the South refused to accept and distribute abolitionist newspapers and literature, and Congress even barred petitions of protest against slavery, particularly in the nation's capital, from being introduced on the floor of Congress (the so-called "gag rule"). By the end of the decade some abolitionists were convinced that political activity should become an integral part of their program, and their rapidly expanding numbers suggested that their influence might be of critical marginal political significance. Like the labor movement many decades later, they began by rewarding their friends and punishing their enemies. Although both the Jackson Democrats and the emerging anti-Jackson Whigs were national parties with supporters in every region, the Whigs claimed their greatest strength in the North, and they tended to be less hostile to the abolitionists than the Democratic party, which had its center of gravity and support in the South.

The movement of some of the radically oriented abolitionists into the political arena did not go unchallenged in the AASS. In fact the politicals represented the minority in most instances, and major leaders like William Lloyd Garrison remained at least formally nonpolitical and strongly criticized the defecting elements for weakening the unified moral force of the movement. But the political abolitionists had discovered what Aileen Kraditor has described as "a rationale for reversing the traditional attitude toward organized political action" based upon "the assumption that politics was sordid."[103] Instead, "some [abolitionist] leaders began to argue that politics was sordid because moral men left it to the politicians. Politics would not corrupt abolitionists, they discovered; abolitionists could regenerate politics.[104]

Most abolitionists did not quickly buy the new philosophy, and the political abolitionists had rough going of it. They were successful in helping to defeat several anti-abolitionist, pro-slavery government officials, including a United States congressman and the governor of a major state, but such negative campaigns were not very stimulating and failed to generate the enthusiasm and support that was needed to advance the cause. In 1839 in one county in Ohio, however, abolitionists found both candidates for the legislature unsatisfactory, and ran their own candidate who received 12 percent of the vote. In the presidential election year of 1840, radical abolitionists were convinced that this was the right direction in which to move and they met in a convention in Warsaw, New York, in 1839, to nominate one of their number, James G. Birney, a former slaveholder from Kentucky, as their candidate for President of the United States. They called themselves the Liberty party, but they did not succeed in getting their candidate on the ballot everywhere; they were pretty much lost in the hoopla and bluster of the 1840 campaign.[105]

But the Liberty party persisted and in the balloting of 1842 it elected five state legislators in Massachusetts and two in Maine. In the presidential race in 1844, the Liberty party made itself felt at the polls, not only increasing its dismal 1840 vote almost nine-fold, but Birney drew enough votes in New York State (15,812) to switch the margin between winner and loser. The result was a Democratic party victory, not only in the state, but also nationally, because the electoral votes in New York were decisive in the election of the President. There was little question that the presence of the Liberty party in the field cost Henry Clay the presidency.

The abolitionists were much closer to the Whigs than to the Democrats, and it was estimated that anywhere from 75 to 90 percent of the Birney vote would have otherwise gone to the Whig candidate. In what later came to be quite typical third party style, during the campaign Birney lambasted Clay more viciously than he did Polk, the real slave-state candidate. Clay's letters on annexation were mercilessly raked over by the Liberty party candidate and probably accounted for his strong showing in New York. The election demonstrated to the Whig party what a marginal defection could mean in terms of its national power, but ironically the cost of the lesson was electing a President who advocated a full pro-slavery position and moved ahead in the annexation of Texas as a slave state. Clay would not have gone that far to exacerbate the growing sectional divisions within the nation.

But the election also revealed the weakness of the Whigs and how vulnerable they were to their own dissident elements. During the next ten years the centrifugal pressures upon the unity of the party increased as the question of slavery, and more particularly, slavery in the territories, became the central political issue confronting both parties. The pressure bore down mainly upon centerists and moderates like Clay, who tried to hold the national coalition together against the polarity of the forces pulling in other directions. Both parties were subject to these centrifugal forces, but the Whigs were more vulnerable because anti-slavery thinking was strongest within their ranks and because the center of gravity of the Whig party was in the North, while the Democrats' strongest roots were in the South and in the northern cities which were unsympathetic to the anti-slavery movement.

The election defeat in 1844 was only the beginning of the agony for the Whigs. The annexation of Texas and the Mexican War had the effect of widening cleavages within the party, while the expansion of slavery became the pivotal issue in American politics. It generated increasing rancor and subsequent violence on both sides, as a moral issue was transformed into a political and economic struggle. At the eye of the storm were the abolitionists and the "conscience" Whigs who attacked the institution of slavery with all the fervor and outrage of religious zealots; but fanning out from this hard core at the center were increasing numbers of Americans who were apprehensive about the economic and political implications, not so much of the existing structure of a slave economy in the South, as of the expansion of slavery in the new states which were joining the Union.

Slavery represented a decided threat to free labor and to the small homesteader in these areas; there was also the possibility that additional slave states could rejuvenate the South's dwindling political power base. With the constitutional three-fifths vote advantage (according to the Constitution, three-fifths of the Negro population of each slave state was counted for purposes of political representation in congressional and ultimately presidential elections), the South had the opportunity of maintaining its present political strength, but also possibly recovering critical ground lost through far greater population increases in the North and in the West. The status of slavery in the territories and new states quickly became the most important and controversial issue that the country had ever faced. The mystery that it did so is only in the delay in the full development of the question, but having finally emerged in the 1840s, it exploded with a vengeance in the 1850s.

A strong indication of the increasing concern of larger and larger numbers of Americans was the number of petitions which began to pour into the Congress, protesting slavery, the slave trade in the District of Columbia and a number of others calling for the removal of the "three-fifths" clause in the Constitution by a constitutional amendment. The legislature of the state of Massachusetts voted such an amendment in 1843 and petitioned the House to consider it. Such a request could not be suppressed by the "gag rule" because it was a legislative request for a constitutional amendment; so after two days debate it was assigned to a special committee of nine for consideration.

The committee issued six different reports, reflecting a wide spectrum of opinions. President Tyler's close ally, Thomas Gilmer, wrote one report representing his views, as did another slave state representative on the committee. After reviewing the history of the constitutional compromise which enacted the three-fifths rule in the first place, Gilmer argued that it ought to be increased to five-fifths representation to compensate for the loss of slave state power brought about by the South's shrinking population base. Concerning Blacks, Gilmer indicated that "the livery of nature proclaims them, whether bond or free, the inferiors of the white man."[106] After such an introduction, he went on to express what he termed to be the outraged voice of the Negro, crying out against "the cruelty which would be perpetrated [by abolitionists] in the name of benevolence and equality":

> It pleads for protection against the hypocrisy or delusion of its friends and benefactors. It cites the happiness and comfort of the slave, in contrast with the misery and want [offered by] some of his pretended benefactors. It begs these philanthropists to remember the more cruel and hopeless bondage of Africa, from which the negro of American had escaped, and entreats them to forbear, from pity to the black, if they will not, from justice to the white man.[107]

John Quincy Adams was the chairman of that committee. Although surrounded by pro-slavery adherents, he filed his own report, a comprehensive analysis of and attack upon the three-fifths rule. His statement stands as a clarifying and piercing indictment of the powerful and fundamentally undemocratic nature of this aspect of the original constitutional system. It also suggested the potential power resources which were at stake in this developing struggle. Adams warned that the practical impact of that provision of the Constitution was as harmful as the theory it reflected:

> The first consequence has been a secret, imperceptible, combined and never-ceasing struggle, to engross all the offices and depositories of power to themselves. . . . At this day the President of the United States, the President of the Senate, the Speaker of the House of Representatives, and five, out of nine, of the Judges of the supreme judicial courts of the United States, are not only citizens of the slaveholding States, but individual

slaveholders themselves. So are, and constantly have been, with scarcely an exception, all the members of both Houses of Congress from the slaveholding States; and so are, in immensely disproportionate numbers, the commanding officers of the army and navy; the officers of the customs; the registers and receivers of the land offices, and the post-masters throughout the slaveholding States. The Biennial Register indicates the birthplace of all the officers employed in the government of the Union. If it were required to designate the owners of this species of property among them, it would be little more than a catalogue of slaveholders.

Among the offices thus monopolized by the silent but uniform operation of the slave representation, is that of Speaker of the House of Representatives. The members of the House from the free States, having no common centre of attraction to rally their forces upon any one of their own number, are reduced to the condition of mere auxiliaries to the rival candidates of the South; and though the choice is consummated by the votes of the Northern men with Southern principles, they are never admitted even to propose a candidate of their own, but are magnanimously permitted to choose between the slaveholders him whom they believe will prove to them the most complacent master.

The people of the free States have little conception of the power of influence exercised by the Speaker of the House of Representatives. First, by the appointment of all the committees, vested in him alone; and secondly, by the arbitrary power of deciding all questions of order. All the important business of the House is prepared or matured by the standing or select committees. By the recent practice of the House, the Speaker is always selected as a determined, uncompromising party-man. All the important committees are organized to fortify the ascendency of the slaveholding party. All questions of order are decided by the Speaker's arbitrary will; and, being decided on party grounds, are always sure of being sustained by a party majority in the House. A captious quibbling spirit of chicanery draws into the vortex of order, questions of vital interest to the whole Union. A single member of the ruling party can arrest and defeat any inquiry instituted, or any resolution offered by a member of the minority; while any leading member of the majority can carry any measure, if objected to, by the suspension of the rules.[108]

During the administration of President Zachary Taylor, what Allan Nevins[109] has described as the "gathering struggle" continued to escalate. Most Americans were not concerned with slavery *per se*, although there was significant opposition to it on moral grounds, but the real opposition was to the expansion of slavery into the territories and new states. Here the objections were primarily economic and political. Those in the North and the pioneers moving westward were well aware of the declining economy of the South in comparison with the dynamic growth in the North and West. They were not about to chain themselves to an institution which could only flourish under circumstances which could never be duplicated in the expanding areas of the country. Furthermore, slavery constituted a threat to free labor and to the small homesteader, for it could only be economically justified within the framework of the large plantation system. To allow slavery to gain a foothold in the new territories and states of the Union, would be to condemn them to an economy of stagnation, and to deprive them of the stabilizing force of middle-class homeowners who would dig their roots deep into the soil, and look hopefully to the future. This was the American dream, and the extension of slavery would annihilate it.

Presidential leadership and strong political party support was needed at that moment more than any other time in the history of the country, but many forces conspired to prevent it from emerging. The 1840s had demonstrated the validity of the principle that a loose and potentially divisive national coalition like the Whig party could survive only by moving as far to the center as possible and by suppressing as many controversial issues as allowable. The Whigs were able to recover from the defeat of 1844 by following that strategy. On the other hand, a longer historical perspective revealed a countervailing or dialectical principle also at work, indicating that if the political party moved so far towards the center that it was forced to suppress realistic policy responses to the major problems which confronted the country, the party would find itself obsolete or irrelevant, as was soon the experience of the Whigs. However, in 1848 the Whigs again applied the proven formula of running a military hero so removed from the problems at hand that his selection could not prove too offensive to any of the polarized groups in their ranks. This strategy resulted in a victory, but produced a President incapable of assuming national leadership during a critical period of developing crisis, lacking the understanding to grasp the full dimensions of the problem he confronted, and devoid of the skill to give direction to the engine of government, even if he did understand what needed to be done.[111] The old and partially discredited leaders, Clay and Webster, emerged at that moment to make their last attempt to contribute to the national interest to which both were devoted, but the compromise they negotiated brought neither satisfaction to the parties in dispute, nor solutions to the problems disputed, and the country plunged further into the morass of inflamed rhetoric and potential (and in some cases actual) violence, which were yet mild intimations of what was ahead.

One cannot do justice to this inept but fascinating period of American history without plunging into the detail which Professor Nevins has provided. Perhaps its appeal is because it possesses the sustained and mounting tension of an impending horror tale, the sense of an inevitable tragedy that grips one's attention. Americans are generally inclined to study success stories, but the truth is that one learns just as much, perhaps more, from the great failures of history. The inadequacies, the stupidities, the limitations of the species are frequently as significant occasions for learning as are the periods and characters of great strength and success. "Attention must be paid to these men" if only to perceive what they did not do and what they could not do in attempting to discover what they should have done. But that is an overwhelming assignment, and probably will never be done again for this period as well as Nevins' outstanding and comprehensive treatment.

As the skies darkened over the land during this tragic period, one can only note here some of the failures and the problems left unresolved, and lament the absence of the kind of leadership that might have identified those shortcomings and done something substantial about them. Zachary Taylor, to begin with, was just not adequate to the task. He was an excellent soldier, a man of integrity and courage, but totally unfamiliar with government and the problems eating away at the country. The story is told of Thurlow Weed meeting General Taylor's brother on a Hudson River steamboat shortly after "Ole Rough and Ready" routed the Mexican army under General Arista at Resaca de la Palma. Weed asked him about the general's political principles, and his brother replied that he had none, that he belonged to no party, had seldom voted and that the most he could say of his brother's outlook was that he held several strong prejudices: "he admired Clay, had disliked Jackson, and was so eager to protect American manufactures that he would not wear an imported garment."[111] Believing prejudice to be as important as principles, Weed responded, "Your brother is to be our next President."[112]

And so he was. Weed again maneuvered Clay out of the running at a bitter convention which drove many of the conscience Whigs to leave the convention hall and to walk out on the party. After several months of meetings, frantic negotiations, preconventions and the like, a great conglomeration of conscience Whigs, Liberty party members, dissident free soil Democrats, many who made up the "Barnburner" constituency of Martin Van Buren, gathered in Buffalo, New York, in August, founded the Free Soil party, and nominated Martin Van Buren and Charles Francis Adams, the son of John Quincy Adams, as their presidential ticket in 1848. The party attracted important figures from both major parties: William Cullen Bryant, Joshua Giddings, Salmon Chase, Samuel Tilden, John P. Hale, David Wilmot, Rockwood Hoar, Preston King and others. The fissures within the major party system were deepening, and it was not clear how long they could withstand the increasing level of centrifugal forces within their midst.

Again Weed manipulated correctly, if winning elections was the name of the game. His general won against the old Democratic campaigner, Lewis Cass, whose only military record was service in the War of 1812 many years earlier.[113] The Free Soilers did exceedingly well in the election, managing to corral over a quarter of a million votes. They obviously drew votes from both parties, but probably damaged the Democrats more severely in several states, particularly New York, where they polled almost half of their votes (120,510). In both New York and Massachusetts the combined Free Soil and Democratic ballots made up majorities, whereas Taylor took all the electoral votes in these states with a plurality. To claim all these votes for the Democracy would of course not be justified, because the Free Soil party was founded primarily by dissident conscience Whigs, but in New York State with its 36 electoral votes which were enough to change the outcome of the election, it is clear that a sufficient number to make the difference were so-called "Barnburner" followers of Martin Van Buren.

The election unity of the Whigs, however, was again short lived. Although General Taylor was a southerner and actually a slave owner, in office he became more of a nationalist with a western outlook. He appeared to most southerners to be under the influence of northern Whig advisors like William Seward. A new President who had appeared to many of them before the election as a fortunate replacement for the previously sympathetic southern, slave-holding inhabitant of the White House, now loomed as a threat to their precarious political position.

Taylor's highest policy priority was to establish stable government in the newly acquired territory. That was a reasonable objective, but it immediately opened up the most divisive of questions: would the new territories or states be free or slave? Taylor and his cabinet wanted them free and Whig, while Calhoun warned his southern colleagues against any unconditional arrangement of this nature. There was certainly no chance of slavery flourishing in California or of its operating profitably in New Mexico, but as the South saw its already eroding political strength suffering even greater losses by the addition of two (or even more) anti-slavery states, its paranoia increased and set the tone for the next decade. Of course this issue further polarized the Whig party, whose national bonds had been unravelling for some time, but it also produced some division within the ranks of the Democrats on a regional basis.

Under those conditions Henry Clay attempted his last experiment in statesmanship. He realized that the reasonable southerners understood that slavery would never take hold in the California-New Mexico areas, but they were concerned about granting the point without some substantial *quid pro quo*. The extremists from both sides would reject such a compromise, but Clay well understood that after they gave vent to their anguish and frustration, the realities of the circumstances would require such an arrangement. He also understood that the abolitionists and extreme Free Soil men of the North would not be happy with any compromise; but in a showdown, when the majority from both regions realized that strident advice and leadership from either end of the spectrum would lead nowhere, they would be ready to go along with and accept a compromise.

Clay proved right. He proposed a plan that encompassed eight different individual actions or resolutions of existing problems, all of which were directed towards preventing a constitutional crisis and establishing some solid basis for laying the escalating passions to rest. It was a plan which yielded some tangible satisfaction to each side of the struggle, and in the final agreement, something very close to Clay's proposal was accepted. Calhoun attacked it from the extreme southern position, and Seward from the point of view of an anti-slavery northern Whig, but Webster, in one of his most eloquent and prophetic speeches, supported the substance of the Clay proposals and threw his weight behind the compromise.

A long struggle ensued before the compromise was accepted and enacted into law. A protracted debate in Congress, which brought out a lot of sectional hostility, but produced little practical influence on the question, was the result. Clay, Calhoun and Webster all spoke in this their last important congressional encounter. Calhoun, who tried to enlist an emotional sentiment against the compromise, died during the debate, perhaps because he overtaxed himself in his vain attempt to stimulate strong opposition to it. Clay and Webster were successful, however, and the measure essentially embodying their recommendations finally passed both houses, but it was touch and go all the way. Without stipulating all of the provisions of the final compromise, it provided an immediate response to the most critical and pressing problems of the hour, but no lasting resolution to any of them.

First of all, California was to be admitted to the Union as a free state, having already written such a provision into her constitution; her present boundaries would remain unchanged. Texas presented more complex problems. She claimed territory which ran westward along the banks of the Rio Grande, with a panhandle running north as high as the 42nd parallel, but obviously all of that land went beyond the limits of any one state. Even when this area was greatly restricted, Texas was clearly the largest state in the Union. Perhaps more controversial than the extent of the territory, however, was the nature of the institutions which governed her people. Texas was the last slave state to enter the Union, and whether or not this new land area was under the jurisdiction of Texas or not would determine the fate of slavery within it. If incorporated under the existing Texas constitution it would unquestionably be slave territory, while if it came into the Union under its own charter, it would not.

The concept of barring slavery from such territory, as in the Wilmot Proviso, was rejected in the compromise, but boundary questions were settled by establishing the principle that all other states entering the Union carved out of or touching upon the area in question were to be free to determine their own laws governing the problem. It was also determined that Congress was "to redeem its compact with the Texan people" by granting admission of "any new State or States formed out of Texas."

— Territorial governments were to be established for New Mexico and Utah without any stipulation for or against slavery.
— Provisions respecting California, Utah and New Mexico, as constituting the territory obtained from Mexico, were to be bound up in the same bill.
— Texas was to be paid for surrendering her jurisdiction over the lands she claimed within the old boundaries of New Mexico, and her northern and western boundaries were to be fixed by the Rio Grande, "and up that river to the point commonly called El Paso, and running﹅ thence up that river twenty miles, measured thereon by a straight line, and then eastwardly to a point where the hundredth degree of west longitude crosses the Red River."
— A fugitive slave law was to be passed.
— The slave trade was to be abolished within the District of Columbia, though slavery was to continue therein.[114]

The moderates on both sides of the slavery question were satisfied with this settlement, for it did not violate the principle they were defending nor did it compromise any immediate interests they could possibly achieve. The South, or at least moderate southerners, realized slavery had little or no chance of thriving in the southwestern territories, and yet they were unwilling to accept the pejorative connotation of a statute barring it from those areas. Neither did they have an interest in defending the slave trade in the nation's capital, but they were unwilling to condemn and outlaw the institution of slavery in that community. In general, then, the terms imposed no hardships upon the South; they merely recognized without prejudice what in reality had to be accepted anyway.

On the other hand, the South did gain the acceptance of the principles of tightening up the Fugitive Slave Law and absolving the tremendous state debt with which Texas was burdened. The North and the West achieved their proximate ends in resolving their immediate territorial demands without having to accept the burden of slavery in any of these areas, or the principle that any additional land area be governed by "free soil" laws barring slavery. As a kind of dividend, the obnoxious slave market in Washington was also outlawed.

What aggravated the extremists on both sides of the question and drew their sharp opposition to the compromise was that it was equivocal on the central question of slavery. It postponed rather than settled this problem. The northern abolitionists and strong Free Soil men condemned the compromise as a whitewash of this intolerable condition. In fact, they interpreted it as official governmental approval of existing slave institutions. Some southerners saw in it a step backwards in the larger struggle, a default of their objective to extend the power and scope of the slave interests in the southwest and a general weakening of their political position. The real debate was not over the compromise itself, but over what it did not say and what it implied. It was an exceptionally pragmatic solution to a number of vexing and immediate problems, but it did not resolve the central issue which was tearing the nation apart. The moderates on both sides could live with it, however, and as they were in control for the time being, the compromise prevailed.

But the ugly undercurrent of opposition to any such settlement provided a warning of events to come. Extremists in the South talked of secession, and in the North, of war if necessary to defend the principles of freedom and justice. The compromise of 1850 was a gallant stroke of diplomacy on the part of statesmen like Clay and Webster who were making in this effort their last determined stand for the Union, but it succeeded only in delaying and not resolving the tragic conflict.

The most formidable obstacle towards the achievement of the compromise was not the extremists' opposition in the legislature, however, but rather the threat of a presidential veto. The President, who had pledged himself during the campaign never to veto any measure except for constitutional reasons, ironically a position developed in compliance with Clay and the Whigs' long struggle against "executive usurpation," had now forgotten that intention and was threatening a veto in order to kill the compromise. Taylor leaned heavily on the "free soil" Whig leader in the Senate, William Seward, who condemned both the compromise and Webster's attack upon the abolitionists, arguing that there was a "higher law than the Constitution" which condemned slavery and which should not be compromised by yielding a single foot of the land acquired from Mexico so that that institution could thrive.[115] Seward led the northern elements of his party in convincing the President to oppose the compromise and to insist upon the entry of California as a free state, with no conditions or concessions attached. Also opposed to the enactment of a new fugitive slave law, he was in favor of the abolition of slavery in the District of Columbia at the earliest possible moment.

The confrontation never came to a climax, however, for the rugged frontier fighter died in office before he completed a special message to Congress urging them to admit both California and New Mexico unconditionally, and asserting that he would never let Texas seize any land rightfully claimed by New Mexico. This had all the trappings of another nullification crisis, for Texas was not about to agree to such a settlement without some tangible *quid pro quo*, and the Texans would have found no difficulty in recruiting additional volunteers from other southern states. But death intervened before the struggle could take place.

President Taylor had been participating in a Fourth of July ceremony at the foot of the Washington monument when he first felt the symptoms of the typhoid fever from which he died. It was a hot day, and he was forced to remain standing in the sun for a protracted period of time. Returning to the White House, exhausted, he drank large quantities of ice water and cold milk, and ate some cherries. He was rapidly prostrated by cholera morbus. Old "Rough and Ready" had punished his stocky, bandy-legged frame for many years in the course of enduring army hardships on the frontier. Now his poor physical condition (he was over 65) was not strong enough to fight off the typhoid fever that developed rapidly; he died several days later. The message opposing the compromise and calling for singular action on California and New Mexico was never finished, and his successor, Millard Fillmore, signed the omnibus Clay compromise bills after they finally passed both houses of Congress.

Allan Nevins has described Fillmore as "a man of dignified bearing, suave manners, conciliatory temper and limited powers of mind."[116] His biography is another saga of the self-made American pulling himself up by his own bootstraps. The son of a poor upstate New York farmer, he recalled his early years as a friendless experience, when as an ill-clad, ill-fed young boy he was pressed into back-breaking toil in a textile mill without tasting most of the joys of a normal childhood and with little formal education. He was 17 before he was exposed to anything beyond a few elementary texts, but while he was laboring long shifts tending the carding machines in his mill, he doggedly consumed every piece of reading matter he could get his hands on. He memorized definitions of unknown words from a cheap dictionary he propped upon a desk and glanced at as he paced around his carding machines. With the assistance of a sympathetic Quaker judge, he received a legal education, practiced law in Buffalo and served three terms in the state legislature. Fillmore was one of the early founders of the Whig party, gained the respect and confidence of his upstate neighbors and was sent to Congress for eight years before he was elected to the vice presidency.

As contrasted with his fellow New Yorker, Senator Seward, who tended to be volatile and even erratic in his views and actions, Fillmore was very stable and conciliatory, but he really hated Seward and his extreme views and was very sympathetic towards states' rights and the southern position in general. In his inaugural he emphasized the fact the "United States is a limited government."[117]

> It is confined to the exercise of powers expressly granted, and such others
> as may be necessary for carrying those powers into effect; and it is at all
> times an especial duty to guard against any infringement on the just rights
> of the States.[118]

But where Fillmore was interested and effective in conciliating the two sections, he was not at all successful in bringing the warring factions of his own party together. He presided over the declining years of the Whigs in power. Never again would the grand old coalition of Henry Clay and Daniel Webster be a significant factor in national politics. The sectional cleavage became all but unbridgeable during the next few years and the Whig concept of a national party uniting the conservative and responsible interests of the North and South became a casualty of history.

The demise of the Whig party emphasized again the fatal ambivalence of American parties, which was discussed in section one. Throughout their short-lived existence as a powerful national party, the Whigs vacillated with respect to their definition of objectives as a party. In the beginning they concentrated upon an increasing attack, not only upon Jackson and Jacksonianism, but also upon the very concept of strong government and leadership. Much of the time they sounded very Madisonian as they emphasized the case against executive usurpation of power. But that was not their only thrust. Clay and his colleagues were truly ambivalent on the question of power once they actually achieved political office. Then they attempted to transform themselves into a responsible and creative political party, determining policy, unifying government and directing the force of party policy and power on the critical problems of the nation. Clay was very Burkean in this aspect of his ideas and actions. As the quintessential Whig he was the party leader, almost a prime minister in reality, drafting legislation, forcefully leading his party in the legislature, alternately inspiring, persuading and literally driving the Whigs on to support a constructive legislative program. He was defeated by Tyler's stubbornness and his conflicting ideology of the presidential office, but he pursued the positive and constructive party role, nevertheless, and brought the entire Whig party behind him in his effort.

The Whigs also reflected this basic ambivalance in the other decisive categories that were discussed in section one—responsibility and effectiveness. It was asserted that a successful political party should really incorporate both, but in the right proportions, for an overemphasis of either one tends to distort its role in the political process and damage the institutions of government as a consequence. In the first sense the Whigs certainly attempted to pursue a responsible party role. They conceived of themselves almost from the beginning as an alternative administration to the one in power; they mounted a serious critique of the opposition party, enumerated an alternative set of policies and presented an experienced and attractive slate of candidates who were capable of assuming the direction of the government and operating effectively within the system.

However they dissipated most of these advantages in their effort to transform the Whig party into an effective opposition in order to win the election. They took the public's pulse, decided what qualities appealed to it and came up with the extremely successful campaign of 1840, in which they swamped their opponents in one of the most colorful presidential elections in our history. Over 80 percent of the qualified electorate turned out to vote in that election, and the Whigs swept both houses of Congress, as well as the presidential office. The rub was that they thought they had to bypass their most recognized and effective leader in order to win, and replace him with a military hero, whose extremely modest military career was exaggerated out of all proportions, his humble origins fraudulently depicted, and who was totally inexperienced and untested as far as a responsible major office was concerned. The balance between responsibility and effectiveness was sacrificed and although the Whigs won, they suffered greatly for their extreme opportunism.

Once safely in office with a Whig President and a Whig majority in both houses of Congress, the Whigs soon discovered that there was a price attached to their "effective" campaign of 1840. Their war hero never got a chance to assume the presidency, for he died after a month in the White House, but the Vice President turned out to be an "effective" obstacle to the achievement of the Whig legislative program. He too had been an expedient choice, brought in to pacify some of the states' rights elements who were upset by Harrison's selection over Clay. In fact "when push came to shove," John Tyler turned out to be a states' rights man and not much of a Whig at all. He was rigid and fixed in his ideological principles, and he cared little if anything for the fate of the Whig party and the leadership he defied. Tyler vetoed the major Whig policies which emerged from the Whig majorities in Congress, and as a result the Whig experience in power was an utter failure; Clay resigned from the Senate in disappointment, the Whigs failed to consolidate their newly achieved national support and they were beaten in the next national election by the party they had defeated in 1840.

The Whigs were given a new lease on life by virtue of the serious divisions in the opposition party in the 1848 election; in that election they again ran an untested and inexperienced military hero for the presidency. But they were already beginning to unravel at the seams before Zachary Taylor was many months in office. The party had side-stepped the most serious problem facing the country for the past ten years, but now slavery rose to cast a shadow across the Whigs' continued life as a major political force. The issue of slavery, and more specifically, the expansion of slavery to the new territories, gripped the country in the 1850s but the Whigs were not prepared to deal with it. First, the slavery issue almost completely severed connections between southern and northern Whigs, who had earlier agreed upon questions of economics and material interests, but who now drew farther and farther apart. Even in the northern Whig party the divisions were severe and growing. While the moderate Whigs struggled to salvage the national party and unite the sections around the compromise of 1850, the conscience Whigs like Charles Francis Adams, Charles Sumner, Joshua Giddings, and others were finding it increasingly difficult to stay within the framework of the party. Their opposition to slavery was so important that it far overshadowed those other issues which they had in common with other members of their party.

In 1844 defectors from the Whig party in New York State, who joined the new abolitionist Liberty party, cost it the election. In 1848 defectors who followed Martin Van Buren into the Free Soil party lost both New York State and the presidential election for the Democrats. The Free Soilers were a mixed conglomeration of former Liberty party people, conscience Whigs and defecting Democratic Barnburners. They succeeded in weakening the existing parties but did not evidence any real possibility of replacing either one of the major parties in 1852. But the defections and the enlarging divisions in both parties were gradually undermining their ability to lead the nation and the people's confidence in their leadership. They selected compromise and usually weak candidates for the presidency who turned out to be even weaker when in office. The 1850s proved to be the moment of truth in American society, because it was no longer possible to paper over the internal conflicts within both major parties. Slavery and the question of the expansion of slavery were eating away at the foundations of the old political structure, and the performance of the leaders and the parties in power was increasingly unsatisfactory to all elements in American life. Minor parties appeared and disappeared with increasing frequency. They did not succeed at once in producing a new major party, but they whittled away at the power of the old parties, forced them into a defensive posture, and contributed to a long hiatus in which there was mounting confusion, violence, lack of leadership in the country, and increasing danger of permanent division and war. Herbert Croly, in *The Promise of American Life*, astutely assessed the situation:

> The two leading political parties deliberately and persistently sought to evade the issue [slavery]. The Western pioneers were so fascinated with the vision of millions of pale-faced democrats, leading free and prosperous lives as the reward for virtuously taking care of their own business, that the Constitutional existence of negro slavery did not in the least discommode them. Disunionism they detested and would fight to the end; but to waste valuable time in bothering about a perplexing and an apparently irremediable political problem was in their eyes the worst kind of economy. They were too optimistic and too superficial to anticipate any serious trouble in the Promised Land of America; and they were so habituated to inconsistent and irresponsible political thinking that they attached no importance to the moral and intellectual turpitude implied by the existence of slavery in a democratic nation. The responsibility of the Whigs for evading the issue is more serious than that of the Democrats. Their leaders were the trained political thinkers of their generation. They were committed by the logic of their party platform to protect the integrity of American national life and to consolidate its organization. But the Whigs, almost as much as the Democrats, refused to take seriously the legal existence of slavery. They shirked the problem whenever they could and for as long as they could; and they looked upon the men who persisted in raising it aloft as perverse fomenters of discord and trouble. The truth is, of course, that both of the dominant parties were merely representing the prevailing attitude towards slavery of American public opinion. That attitude was characterized chiefly by moral and intellectual cowardice. Throughout the whole of the Middle Period the increasing importance of negro servitude was the ghost in the house of the American democracy.[119]

The Democrats bounced back into power in the election of 1852. They picked up almost 400,000 additional votes, 39 percent of which came from New York, and represented, for the most part, the return of Van Buren and his Barnburners to the fold. Seward, Weed and the free soil Whigs controlled that party's convention, and turned aside Fillmore, who had essentially southern support. With it all their total national vote held up well, but this was to be the last national election in which it would. By the time the next presidential election rolled around, the Whig party was for all intents and purposes dead and so were its two great national leaders, Henry Clay and Daniel Webster. Southern Whigs, for the most part, passed over into the

Know Nothing (American National) party, while the free soil and conscience Whigs helped to found the Republican party, launching their first presidential candidate in 1856—John C. Frémont.

A word about the Know Nothings before turning to the emergence of the Republican party and Abraham Lincoln. In the 1840s the Whigs flirted with and encouraged blocs of anti-foreign, anti-Catholic voters in cities like New York and Boston, which had increasingly large foreign born populations. Most of these newcomers were different than the earlier flow of immigrants, almost all of whom had come from the Protestant areas of the British Isles. A large percentage of the recent arrivals were Irish, and some German Catholics, and it was essentially in opposition to their religion that the new American nativism arose. It started in New York City where a secret Order of the Star Spangled Banner, a super-patriotic fraternal order limited to native-born Protestants, was organized. Founded initially as a social organization, the order got the name of "Know Nothing" from the reply which members were instructed to give when interrogated about the nature of their secret order and rituals. The Know Nothings moved quickly into the political arena, attempting to pressure political parties to run no one but native Protestant Americans for public office; their support initially went to the Whigs, as the Democrats were the party traditionally hospitable to urban, working-class immigrants.

Under the normal circumstances of stable two party development, the Know Nothings would probably have gone no further than the ordinary ideological grouping that frequently emerges on the American political landscape and captures a few loyal supporters. Like the bee, it stings and sometimes infects, but kills itself in the process. But these were not normal times and the disintegrating state of the Whig party encouraged their unusually strong appeal during this critical period of American life. Furthermore, distrust and ignorance of the Catholic religion ran very deep in the consciousnesses of most native Americans, and in a divisive and disintegrating national political situation such a movement was more likely to attract attention and support than might be usual for that society.

The Whig party did not survive the Douglas initiated Kansas-Nebraska Act of 1854. Briefly, the senator from Illinois introduced his measure to pacify the southern alarm and discontent within his own party and perhaps also to promote the possibility of his own future presidential candidacy. The act nullified the free soil guarantees of the Missouri Compromise and so divided the Whig party that it never recovered, but disappeared entirely from the political landscape by the next presidential election, although some loyal and moderate Whigs supported the old Whig standard-bearer, Millard K. Fillmore, running on the Know Nothing ticket in that election. The Know Nothings were anxious and prepared to step into this political void, for the conscience and free soil Whigs had by that time despaired of the possibility of compromising their conflicts with their former southern allies and were in the process of organizing a new coalition of free soil dissenters from both the Whig and Democratic parties into the Republican party. But those ex-Whigs and others who were more alarmed by the threat of large masses of uneducated and essentially Catholic big city voters in the Democratic party than they were apprehensive of the sectional conflict and slavery, retreated to the Know Nothings as a political way-station in their longer pilgrimage to the northern-centered Republican party or the southern faction of the Democratic party. For a few short years this incredible party rose to hold substantial influence in the country, sweeping state legislatures in Massachusetts, New Hampshire, Rhode Island and Connecticut, and they made impressive showings in New York, Pennsylvania, and California. The party was also strong in many southern states. They had upwards of 70 members and sympathizers in the House of Representatives, and their influence was responsible for electing Nathaniel P. Banks, Speaker of the House in 1855.

The Know Nothings died out very quickly after the emergence of the Republican party and the exacerbation of the sectional struggle over slavery in the latter half of the decade. The party served briefly as an emotional release and a focus for pent-up hatreds and frustrations, but it was badly divided on the slavery issue and lacked the organizational strength and responsible character to develop into a major American political force. But the Republican party offered those potential strengths.

So much space in the study of the growth of presidential power has been devoted to analyzing the confusing disintegration of the Whig party, followed by the demise of the Democrats (who divided essentially over the same issue) during the next four years, because the sickness which plagued the major political parties manifested itself in a series of weak Presidents. The result was the total failure of leadership on the part of the American Chief Executive to cope with the dangerously mounting intensity of the sectional struggle. But any discussion of this sort demands some reference to this grim era, and certainly some recognition of the role Abraham Lincoln played in illuminating its tragic dilemma, clarifying its conflicting alternatives and finally establishing its historic mission.

Lincoln Draws the Line

The 1850s was a decade of impotence. There was continuing misunderstanding, increasing hatred and violence and agonizing powerlessness on the part of those in leadership positions, attempting to grapple with the problem. It was a period of drift, but the drift was in the direction of the great precipice—an armed conflict between the slave and the non-slave states of the Union. Historians since the war have been perplexed with the challenging problem of whether or not the Civil War could have been avoided. It is an impossible question to answer really, because it involves so many conditional themes and events that one is forced to totally reconstruct history in the process of attempting to explore a proper answer. If the existing political parties had been of a different character, if they had resolutely faced up to the problems of the period, if the country had elected Presidents who were willing to face the underlying issues and not try to hide from reality, to compromise the uncompromisable, to pacify and appease until there was almost no position of integrity left to defend—all of this involves too many "ifs," too much conjecture, too radical a reversal of men and events to be of any practical use.

What we do know, however, is that until the emergence of Abraham Lincoln and the Republican party there was no leader in this country who demonstrated the courage, the wisdom and the integrity to factor out the truth of the question, to appraise realistically the basic values held by most Americans during this period or to define the limits of their tolerance as well as the essence of their basic objectives, so that a realistic political position could be framed, around which imperfect but at least honest and non-self-destructive men could take a stand.

The emergence of Abraham Lincoln was not an overnight event. Lincoln, like a good barrel of whiskey, mellowed and aged in the American environment. He was the quintessential American, born on the frontier, nurtured in the rural towns and cities of the growing West, self-educated but rooted in the Bible, Blackstone, Euclid and Shakespeare. Lincoln chose the characteristically American profession of law as a livelihood, developing his understanding of the law as a foundation to his outlook on life. His great joy in the companionship of people, simple as well as profound, and yet his frequent desire to isolate himself from them in long periods of great, brooding silence, made him the most sensitive and appealing leader in our history.

Lincoln's career was not a rags to riches saga, a success story. It was a long and rugged struggle not simply for success, but for better understanding—of those around him, his neighbors, his colleagues, his family, and finally of his countrymen, North and South, and the reasons that divided them. Lincoln wandered through the turbulent, growing midwestern environment, not as a fellow booster and builder, but rather as a reflective friend and amiable critic, observing everything and sorting it out during the lonely train rides from one end of the state to the other and in the hours spent in cold waiting rooms as he followed the circuit, arguing cases before the courts, drinking deeply of the rich human drama that surrounded him wherever he went. I do not mean to imply that Lincoln was a sainted philosopher—far from it—nor that he lacked desire for personal success and accomplishment. His law partner, William Herndon, noted that "He was always calculating, and always planning ahead. His ambition was a little engine that knew no rest."[120] But for what purpose, towards what end, is an intriguing question. Ambition and success for Lincoln were not cast in a narrow or even a personal mold, but often went beyond the visions of those around him, touching the sensitive nerve of what we have come to refer to as "the public interest."

Yet there was always humor and a relaxed ability to laugh at himself in everything Lincoln did. Herndon relates that politicians always courted the press and that Lincoln was no exception to the rule:

> I remember a letter Lincoln once wrote to the editor of an obscure little country newspaper in southern Illinois in which he warms up to him in the following style. "Friend Harding: I have been reading your paper for three or four years and have paid you nothing for it." He then encloses ten dollars and admonishes the editor with innocent complacency: "Put it into your pocket and say nothing further about it." Very soon thereafter, he prepared an article on political matters and sent it to the rural journalist, requesting its publication in the editorial columns of his "valued paper," but the latter having followed Lincoln's directions and stowed the ten dollars away in his pocket, and alive to the importance of his journal's influence, declined, "because," he said, "I long ago made it a rule to

publish nothing as editorial matter not written by myself." Lincoln read the editor's answer to me. Although the laugh was on Lincoln he enjoyed the joke heartily. "That editor," he said, "has a rather lofty but proper conception of true journalism."[121]

It was fortunate for America that Abraham Lincoln did have "a little engine that knew no rest" purring inside of him. The country was infinitely better off for it, perhaps it was even salvaged from utter destruction. The 1850s were populated by hundreds of politicians who had little engines purring inside of them, but their thrust was directed towards personal power and aggrandizement, two objectives to which Lincoln gave relatively low priority. But as is frequently the case with leaders of extraordinary qualities of statesmanship, the crisis would have to ripen considerably before his neighbors and his countrymen would recognize him, heed his words and select him as their President.

At the same time the disintergration of parties, men and politics continued. Senator Stephen A. Douglas, attempting to unite the country behind his leadership of the Democratic party, introduced one of the most catastrophic pieces of legislation in all of American history—the Kansas-Nebraska Act. Its objective was to pacify the South by negating the Missouri Compromise, but it succeeded only in alienating what was left of the Whig party and many thousands of free soil Democrats, giving impetus to the founding of a new political coalition which united various groups and renegades into the Republican party. But the Kansas-Nebraska Act also created an unnecessary state of intermittent shooting warfare in the Kansas Territory. Missouri and other pro-slavery zealots crossed the border and attempted to frighten and intimidate the legitimate settlers into accepting a fraudulent slave-state constitution and government, saddling the inhabitants of the area with outside rulers and rules. Violence in Kansas erupted time and time again, John Brown's massacre at Osawatomie Creek set the cauldron boiling again, and the helpless President in Washington aggravated the chaos by his inept appointments and ruinous policies. When he finally stumbled upon an effective public servant like Governor John W. Geary, he failed to support him and allowed his administration to be cowed by the pro-slavery hoodlums.

Franklin Pierce ranks at the very bottom of any serious evaluation of American Presidents. His four years in office contributed nothing constructive towards the resolution of the major problems confronting the country; in fact his actions and his policies had a negative impact upon the situations affected. His clearly sympathetic attitude to the pro-slavery policies of the South made him an anathema to the free soil forces in the North and West, and drove Pierce to intervene on behalf of the corrupt and violent southern carpetbaggers who had invaded the Kansas Territory to claim it for the pro-slavery South. Rather than an even-handed policy which would sort out the fictitious claims of the rival governments in Kansas, Pierce supported every move and judgment favorable to the invading non-settler pro-slavery forces, literally keeping them in power. As the sectional conflict became more impelling, Pierce exacerbated its tempo by his failure to establish law and order and respect for the national government as a force capable of administering justice.

His successor, James Buchanan, not only betrayed a sympathy for the southern cause, but in office he became a captive of the very adept southern members of his cabinet, who manipulated him quite effectively in their own interests. These interests, however, could not be satisfied by constructive policies in the national interest, but could only be served by attempting to protect the regressive sectional claims of their dying social and political order, as they moved rapidly closer and closer to secession. The southern-dominated directory ruled the cabinet and the administration, yet there were no gains or tangible accomplishments for them to pursue save propping up causes at home (Kansas) and abroad (Cuba and the slave trade), which had no chance of success regardless of their support from the top. His one strong appointment, Robert Walker, as a successor to Geary in Kansas, was undermined by his straightforward efforts to bring law and order to that beseiged area. Buchanan betrayed his former good friend and failed to support his honest courageous efforts, even after persuading Walker to take the appointment "for the good of the country." The Pierce and Buchanan administrations reaped the sheer folly of the Kansas-Nebraska Act, aided and abetted by the infamous *Dred Scott* decision of the Taney Court. But the westward movement of the free soil forces and their ultimate triumph was inevitable; the lack of support and at times outright opposition and betrayal by two successive national administrations simply delayed rather than prevented that final victory.

The efforts of the Pierce and Buchanan administrations to support the invasion of Kansas by the pro-slavery forces and their fraudulent LeCompton constitution, finally drove Stephen Douglas into active opposition, and ultimately led to the break-up of the Democratic party. Douglas had staked his career on the principle of self determination, and when he became convinced that the pro-slavery forces in Kansas and their Democratic presidential and cabinet supporters in Washington intended to thwart that principle in order to establish a pro-slavery constitution and government in Kansas, the "little giant," as Douglas was sometimes referred to, did the honorable thing by opposing and defeating their cabal at the price of dividing his own party and sacrificing his chances of capturing the presidency.

With these dramatic actions the unravelling process of the formerly stable two-party system was complete and the way was cleared for the emergence and success of the new Republican party. Some very acute analysts of political parties have observed what was taking place at that point in American history, and have attempted to formulate some propositions derived from such developments.[122] The demise of what they refer to as the second party system is defined as a fundamental or organic party realignment. As James Sundquist writes:

> If a two-party system is visualized as an electorate divided by a line of party cleavage, an organic change in the system can be defined as a relocation of the line.[123]

The crises of the 1850s did bring about a realignment of political parties in this country, and Sundquist's linear model allows one to perceive it perhaps in its most simple and direct form. What was happening constituted what Walter Dean Burnham, building upon V.O. Key's earlier pioneering efforts, would call "a critical realignment." This critical realignment was one in which the line of party cleavage sliced through the electorate in a new direction, shifting the party structure on its axis. When things settled down, the changes had been so profound that in retrospect. . .a new party system can be seen to have replaced the old.[124]

However a critical realignment will not take place, Sundquist argues, if the "centrists are able to resolve the issue before the polar groups have achieved significant growth."[125] Then "both major parties will survive and the realignment will be minor.[126]

Clearly such was not the case in the 1850s. If Clay and Webster had been successful in holding the mainstream of the Whig party to their moderate-centrist position, realignment might have been minor, or at least prolonged the life of the second party system. But that did not happen. The gravity of the slavery issue was too forceful, and the Whig party could not stay together on the issue. "The center did not hold."[127] In hindsight it probably could not have held for long anyway. Burnham writes:

> The dramatic collapse of the second party system in the period from the mid 1850's to 1860 disclosed its essential fragility. Each party had been put together piecemeal from a bewildering variety of local cleavages and ethno-cultural hostilities. On the national level, each was an electoral machine which sought to make voting capital out of these local antagonisms and the national symbolic rhetoric of the democratic "revolution." But precisely because the two parties were both so nationwide in their coalitional base, they found it increasingly difficult to accommodate sectionally divergent interests among their elites and mass followings.[128]

In their attempts to achieve what Hofstadter called an "effective" role, both the Whigs and the Democrats extended their lines to a point where they simply broke in the middle. Richard P. McCormick argues that "If . . .each party is expected to mediate conflicting interests by aggregating the broad spectrum of those interests, the strain on the political system at the level of the parties may be disruptive."[129] If the parties had been less "effective" and more responsible to ideological principles, would they have been strong enough to respond to the slavery issue and still survive? McCormick suggests that the strains on such "responsible" parties may be equally disruptive:

> If in a democratic two-party system the parties became so aligned as to reflect crucial ideological, class, social, or sectional cleavages, and they therefore present the electorate with drastic alternatives, the strain on the political system as a whole, and particularly at the level of government, may be disruptive.[130]

What then is the answer to this dilemma? McCormick offers only a partially satisfactory answer:

> I have no solution to propose to this dilemma, other than to suggest that a party system that is *too* comprehensive—as was the second party system—

may be potentially as explosive as a party system that is polarized around drastic alternatives—as was the third party system in its formative years. Perhaps this is to say that threatening problems or the strains of crises must be shared between the party systems and the government.[131]

It appears that there is a close relationship between the character and development of the party and its ability to produce strong and competent leadership. The strong Presidents after Washington—Jefferson, Jackson and Lincoln—all emerged from relatively new and vigorous political parties which had a distinctly "responsible" character. Parties in a period of decline and fragmentation were able only to produce Presidents of the quality of Taylor, Pierce and Buchanan, men who succeeded to the office of Chief Executive because they were the products of desperate efforts to "cash in" on their wartime records, compromise candidates or partisans of factional interests attempting to capture the leadership of a national party. Abraham Lincoln could never squeeze his huge frame and high ideals into such confining circumstances.

The Republican party was born of frustration and hope from a relatively small group of men who were tired of being twisted and turned within the framework of both national parties. They wanted to clear the air, to establish a position they could reasonably adhere to and believe in, and resolve the national dilemma upon terms that were responsible and reflective of their commitment to the ideals of the American democratic tradition. Outraged by this last straw which broke the Whig party's back—the Kansas-Nebraska Act—a group of dissident Whigs joined together with Free Democrats to form a new party in 1854. Its predecessors had been the Liberty and Free Soil (now Free Democratic) parties, and although those political organizations had been able to draw a considerable number of dissidents from the major parties and to affect the outcome of numerous local and national elections, they had never attracted anywhere near the number of supporters required for major party status or influence.

But by 1854 the country was ready for a new major political party. Both of the existing national parties had failed to provide sustained leadership or direction throughout the crisis, and one of those parties was now in an almost complete state of decay. It was time for a new standard, new leadership, new policies. Perhaps such a party could have national appeal to voters in both sections, but it would have to be firmly rooted in the northern free soil environment and it could not equivocate on the issue of the expansion of slavery. On the other hand it dared not take on the character of an abolitionist movement, simply because that was not where the main stream of free soil thinking was. Although some like Lincoln had strong moral convictions in opposition to slavery, the center of gravity of the movement and the issue which bound it together was a firm opposition to the expansion of slavery in the new territories and states.

The day after the Kansas-Nebraska Act was reported to the Senate a small group of Free Democrats, including Salmon P. Chase, Charles Sumner, Joshua Giddings and Gerrit Smith, issued an appeal to the independent Democrats, characterizing Douglas' bill as "a gross violation of a sacred pledge; as a criminal betrayal of precious rights; as part and parcel of an atrocious plot to exclude from a vast unoccupied region immigrants from the Old World and free laborers from our own States, and convert it into a dreary region of despotism, inhabited by masters and slaves"[132] The outraged Free Democrats agreed to resist the measure "by speech and vote, and with all the abilities which God has given us."[133]

After the bill passed both houses with the extended efforts of Douglas and President Pierce, the Free Democrats realized that their only effective response would be to organize a political party capable of checking this "unholy alliance." The day after the final vote some 30 members of Congress met and agreed that a new party, preferably to be called Republican, should be formed. Earlier meetings in Detroit and Ripon, Wisconsin, recorded similar sentiments, and all these groups came together officially to found the Republican party at Jackson, Michigan on July 6, 1854. The gathering also adopted a platform opposing the extension of slavery and demanded the repeal of the Kansas-Nebraska Act and the Fugitive Slave Law.

The Republicans ran a candidate for the presidency in 1856, John C. Frémont, the California explorer and pioneer, and son-in-law of Thomas Hart Benton, but they were not yet well-enough organized to win a national election. Frémont, however, defeated Buchanan in the North and helped the Republicans to elect a large number of members to the House of Representatives. There were now 107 votes pledged to defeat the measure, although not all had been elected under the Republican party label. It was very close, but the Republicans still were not in control, and it took four more years before they were prepared to take over the reins of government.

Abraham Lincoln was something of a latecomer to the Republican party, having retired somewhat from active political life after his one term in the House of Representatives. But the passage of the Kansas-Nebraska Act and the outbreak of violence in Kansas brought him back into the center of public controversy, a position where he remained for the rest of his life. He did not rush to join the Republicans, and in this early period of the formation of the party, Lincoln retained his Whig identity and campaigned for candidates opposed to the Kansas-Nebraska Act on a fusion party basis. But in due time the Republican party emerged as the coalition with the greatest anti-slavery potential; and at the same time Lincoln began to attract attention for his carefully thought out arguments against Douglas and his "self determination" position.

Lincoln soon became better known and was considered a major force in his area on the free soil question. He was elected to the state legislature, resigned to seek election to the United States Senate, but was outmaneuvered by the Democrats and finally threw his support to Lyman Trumbull. In 1858, when Douglas himself came up for reelection, Lincoln was the obvious man to oppose him. He had already tackled Douglas on several occasions, and had bested him in several give-and-take exchanges. The Republicans in Illinois knew that if Douglas could be beaten, Lincoln was the only man who could do it. Before the party convention he was selected to run by 95 different county organizations.

Lincoln accepted the challenge; he opened the campaign with an acceptance speech at Springfield, material from which has since been quoted in every historical account of the period. Having an uncanny ability to go directly to the heart of the matter, and to express its essence in language that was both elegant and meaningful, people knew what Lincoln was talking about and they certainly knew where he stood. The opening sentences of his speech set the tone and direction for many events that developed during the next few years. They were simple and direct and went immediately to the issue troubling the nation. Lincoln did not retreat from this bold challenge. He explained, illuminated, and elaborated, for he was speaking for history, and he knew that the grain of that history flowed directly along with the spirit of his words:

> Mr. President and Gentlemen of the Convention: If we could first know where we are, and whither we are tending, we could better judge what to do and how to do it. We are now far into the fifth year since a policy was initiated with the avowed object and confident promise of putting an end to slavery agitation. Under the operation of that policy, that agitation has not only not ceased but has constantly augmented. In my opinion, it will not cease until a crisis shall have been reached and passed. "A house divided against itself cannot stand." I believe this government cannot endure permanently half slave and half free. I do not expect the Union to be disolved—I do not expect the house to fall—but I do expect it will cease to be divided. It will become all one thing, or all the other. Either the opponents of slavery will arrest the further spread of it, and place it where the public mind shall rest in the belief that it is in the course of ultimate extinction; or its advocates will push it forward till it shall become alike lawful in all the States, old as well as new, North as well as South. Have we no tendency to the latter condition?[134]

Lincoln debated with Douglas up and down the state of Illinois—in Ottawa, Freeport, Jonesboro, Charleson, Galesburg, Quincy, and Alton—during the course of the campaign. Thousands turned out to see the tall man with the high stove pipe hat do battle with the "little giant." They were stirring debates, if not great literary documents, but throughout Lincoln hewed the straight line, defined and re-defined his position taken at Springfield and held his ground. Slavery was wrong and it needed to be contained and prevented from any further growth, if the country was going to remain unified and free and to redeem its great promise. There was no talk of social equality of the races, no promise of citizenship, no commitment to an integrated society. In reading these debates many are disappointed when they find these worthy goals missing from Lincoln's speeches. In fact much that transpired in those debates, from both Douglas and Lincoln, would clearly be classified as racism today.

Lincoln was a product of his environment, and the American environment was racist in this sense from the very beginning. What Lincoln did was to stake out the highest political ground upon which decent men could take a stand. This position did not fulfill the democratic promise and it probably did not even fulfill Lincoln's true objectives. But it was the highest principle around which many men of that period could gather and hope to survive politically. It was the best expression of the general will and Lincoln realized it, saying it over and over again until its powerful message was irresistable among men of honor and feeling.

Looking back on these events many of us might want it to have been otherwise. Many of us would have had Lincoln struggle for the principle of full equality, not only before the law but in every other aspect affecting the humanity and integrity of the individual. I classify myself in that category. But it is a position made possible by earlier battles won, and lessons learned. Lincoln was not speaking from that vantage point, but he was seizing the opportunity to enunciate the clearest and most humane principles that could have been voiced in the America of his time. Lincoln understood this, and later he was able to overcome some of his limitations on this question. But politics is made of the reality of life, and Lincoln's words and actions spoke to the realities of mid-nineteenth century America. And he was the best there was. Only a great man could have hoped to rise to such an occasion, and only a great President could have implemented such goals. Lincoln was both.

In the Illinois state elections of 1858, Republican candidates for the state legislature who would support Lincoln received 4,000 more votes than his closest opponent, Stephen A. Douglas, but he was outmanuevered and outvoted in the legislature, where they actually elected the United States Senator. But the campaign was worthwhile in defeat. Abraham Lincoln had brought the anti-slavery message to the people more forcefully and effectively than had any other man of his period, and at some point he would not be denied.

To be right for the presidency is one thing, to be recognized as being right for the office by people in power who can act on such convictions is quite another thing. Some Presidents have been in line for the office by virtue of their positions in previous administrations, and others have had the advantage of battlefield notoriety or other prominent means of exposure to a nationwide audience. Lincoln was not that fortunate, but the Springfield speech and later the debates with Douglas gave him a national audience. Up to that time he had been well known only in his region. That can be a substantial handicap in the presidential sweepstakes, and any serious candidate for the presidency necessarily has to break out of his purely regional setting to convince opinion makers and others on the national scene that he has the presidential aura about him. The debates partially ameliorated Lincoln's national obscurity, but when he was invited to speak in New York City in the winter of 1859-60 at Henry Ward Beecher's prestigious Plymouth Church in Brooklyn, Lincoln readily accepted. The advantages of speaking before such an audience were obvious, but it was also dangerous, because a failure on such an occasion might kill his already improving chances of receiving the Republican nomination for the presidency later that year.

Lincoln arrived in New York after a tiring two-day journey from Chicago. He established himself at the Astor House and he was besieged by curious and interested powerful New York politicians. While some were already committed to native son William Seward, others, including the powerful editors, Horace Greeley and William Cullen Bryant, were open to new arguments, effectively advanced. In addition there was a certain coolness among New York conservatives with regard to Seward. His "higher law" speech had disturbed many and his somewhat erratic behavior and position statements did not always ring true. At any rate they wanted to hear what Lincoln had to say, and although it was a cold, snowy evening, 1500 people turned out to listen to the speech, among them a number of the most important political figures in the community. William Cullen Bryant presided, David Dudley Field escorted Lincoln to the platform, and Peter Cooper, G. P. Putnam, Abram S. Hewitt, Horace Greely, and ex-Governor John A. King were all

306

in the audience. (The meeting had been transferred to the new large hall at the Cooper Institute because of the indications of strong public interest in Lincoln's appearance.)

Both Lincoln's appearance and his speech were an extraordinary success. His tall, spare frame draped in a newly purchased homespun suit appeared impressive under the gaslight glow, and his speech electrified the audience. It was delivered in a slow and deliberate manner, but its careful and compelling logic cut through the maze of complex arguments, and rang with a sense of direct, simple but eloquent truth that his listeners had not heard before. The powerful *Tribune* reporter, Noah Brooks, was convinced that Lincoln was the greatest man since St. Paul; he rushed back to his office to write an article which asserted that "no man before made such an impression on his first appeal to a New York audience."[135] Lincoln had brought forth frequent cheers and shouting from his enthusiastic audience—the next day the newspapers and the city were full of enthusiastic reactions to his speech. The rail-splitter from Illinois scored with the New York "men of power," and from then on they took his candidacy for the presidency very seriously.

In an article discussing the speech, William Cullen Bryant mused, "it is wonderful how much a truth gains by a certain mastery of clear and impressive statement."[136] That was precisely the point. Lincoln was not saying anything new, anything radical, or even anything disturbing to the South or to the North. His Cooper Institute speech went well beyond the high flown phrases of the Springfield acceptance, for those phrases, as Randall has pointed out, offered themselves to various forms of misinterpretation, and in their substance, perhaps certain contradictions. Even the debates with Douglas had at times been long and tedious and were subject to certain distractions and circumlutions. But the Cooper Union speech was the most advanced, even the most conciliatory of Lincoln's preelection speeches. In it he clearly and with quite some scholarship established the historical continuities of the free soil position with the Declaration of Independence and the subsequent words and actions of the Founding Fathers. In substance, it is conciliatory to the South, cautious and sympathetic to their problems. But finally it is firm and resolute and marks out the irreducible principle from which the Republicans would not retreat. The speech established the position upon which Lincoln took his stand, and successfully convinced the party and later the American people that they too must take such a stand.

Abraham Lincoln
Cooper Institute Address
February 27, 1860

Basler, III, 522-50.

Mr. President and Fellow-Citizens of New-York:—The facts with which I shall deal this evening are mainly old and familiar; nor is there anything new in the general use I shall make of them. If there shall be any novelty, it will be in the mode of presenting the facts, and the inferences and observations following that presentation.

In his speech last autumn, at Columbus, Ohio, as reported in "The New-York Times," Senator Douglas said:

"Our fathers, when they framed the Government under which we live, understood this question just as well, and even better, than we do now."

I fully indorse this, and I adopt it as a text for this discourse. I so adopt it because it furnishes a precise and an agreed starting point for a discussion between Republicans and that wing of the Democracy headed by Senator Douglas. It simply leaves the inquiry: *"What was the understanding those fathers had of the question mentioned?"*

What is the frame of Government under which we live?

The answer must be: "The Constitution of the United States." That Constitution consists of the original, framed in 1787, (and under which the present government first went into operation,) and twelve subsequently framed amendments, the first ten of which were framed in 1789.

Who were our fathers that framed the Constitution? I suppose the "thirty-nine" who signed the original instrument may be fairly called our fathers who framed that part of the present Government. It is almost exactly true to say they framed it, and it is altogether true to say they fairly represented the opinion and sentiment of the whole nation at that time. Their names, being familiar to nearly all, and accessible to quite all, need not now be repeated.

I take these "thirty-nine" for the present, as being "our fathers who framed the Government under which we live."

What is the question which, according to the text, those fathers understood "just as well, and even better than we do now?"

It is this: Does the proper division of local from federal authority, or anything in the Constitution, forbid *our Federal Government* to control as to slavery in *our Federal Territories?*

Upon this, Senator Douglas holds the affirmative, and Republicans the negative. This affirmation and denial form an issue; and this issue—this question—is precisely what the text declares our fathers understood "better than we."

Let us now inquire whether the "thirty-nine," or any of them, ever acted upon this question; and if they did, how they acted upon it—how they expressed that better understanding?

In 1784, three years before the Constitution—the United States then owning the Northwestern Territory, and no other, the Congress of the Confederation had before them the question of prohibiting slavery in that Territory; and four of the "thirty-nine," who afterward framed the Constitution, were in that Congress, and voted on that question. Of these, Roger Sherman, Thomas Mifflin, and Hugh Williamson voted for the prohibition, thus showing that, in their understanding, no line dividing local from federal authority, nor anything else, properly forbade the Federal Government to control as to slavery in federal territory. The other of the four—James M'Henry—voted against the prohibition, showing that, for some cause, he thought it improper to vote for it.

In 1787, still before the Constitution, but while the Convention was in session framing it, and while the Northwestern Territory still was the only territory owned by the United States, the same question of prohibiting slavery in the territory again came before the Congress of the Confederation; and two more of the "thirty-nine" who afterward signed the Constitution, were in that Congress, and voted on the question. They were William Blount and William Few; and they both voted for the prohibition—thus showing that, in their understanding, no line dividing local from federal authority, nor anything else, properly forbade the Federal Government to control as to slavery in federal territory. This time the prohibition became a law, being part of what is now well known as the Ordinance of '87.

The question of federal control of slavery in the territories, seems not to have been directly before the Convention which framed the original Constitution; and hence it is not recorded that the "thirty-nine," or any of them, while engaged on that instrument, expressed any opinion of that precise question.

In 1789, by the first Congress which sat under the Constitution, an act was passed to enforce the Ordinance of '87, including the prohibition of slavery in the Northwestern Territory. The bill for this act was reported by one of the "thirty-nine," Thomas Fitzsimmons, then a member of the House of Representatives from Pennsylvania. It went through all its stages without a word of opposition, and finally passed both branches without yeas and nays, which is equivalent to an unanimous passage. In this Congress there were sixteen of the thirty-nine fathers who framed the original Constitution. They were John Langdon, Nicholas Gilman, Wm. S. Johnson, Roger Sherman, Robert Morris, Thos. Fitzsimmons, William Few, Abraham Baldwin, Rufus King, William Paterson, George Clymer, Richard Bassett, George Read, Pierce Butler, Daniel Carroll, James Madison.

This shows that, in their understanding, no line dividing local from federal authority, nor anything in the Constitution, properly forbade Congress to prohibit slavery in the federal territory; else both their fidelity to correct principle, and their oath to support the Constitution, would have constrained them to oppose the prohibition.

Again, George Washington, another of the "thirty-nine," was then President of the United States, and, as such, approved and signed the bill; thus completing its validity as a law, and thus showing that, in his understanding, no line dividing local from federal authority, nor anything in the Constitution, forbade the Federal Government, to control as to slavery in federal territory.

No great while after the adoption of the original Constitution, North Carolina ceded to the Federal Government the country now constituting the State of Tennessee; and a few years later Georgia ceded that which now constitutes the States of Mississippi and Alabama. In both deeds of cession it was made a condition by the ceding States that the Federal Government should not prohibit slavery in the ceded country. Besides this, slavery was then actually in the ceded country. Under these circumstances, Congress, on taking charge of these countries, did not absolutely prohibit slavery within them. But they did interfere with it—take control of it—even there, to a certain extent. In 1798, Congress organized the Territory of Mississippi. In the act of organization, they prohibited the bringing of slaves into the Territory, from any place without the United States, by fine, and giving freedom to slaves so brought. This act passed both branches of Congress without yeas and nays. In that Congress were three of the "thirty-nine" who framed the original

Constitution. They were John Langdon, George Read and Abraham Baldwin. They all, probably, voted for it. Certainly they would have placed their opposition to it upon record, if, in their understanding, any line dividing local from federal authority, or anything in the Constitution, properly forbade the Federal Government to control as to slavery in federal territory.

In 1803, the Federal Government purchased the Louisiana country. Our former territorial acquisitions came from certain of our own States; but this Louisiana country was acquired from a foreign nation. In 1804, Congress gave a territorial organization to that part of it which now constitutes the State of Louisiana. New Orleans, lying within that part, was an old and comparatively large city. There were other considerable towns and settlements, and slavery was extensively and thoroughly intermingled with the people. Congress did not, in the Territorial Act, prohibit slavery; but they did interfere with it—take control of it—in a more marked and extensive way than they did in the case of Mississippi. The substance of the provision therein made, in relation to slaves, was:

First. That no slave should be imported into the territory from foreign parts.

Second. That no slave should be carried into it who had been imported into the United States since the first day of May, 1798.

Third. That no slave should be carried into it, except by the owner, and for his own use as a settler; the penalty in all the cases being a fine upon the violator of the law, and freedom to the slave.

This act also was passed without yeas and nays. In the Congress which passed it, there were two of the "thirty-nine." They were Abraham Baldwin and Jonathan Dayton. As stated in the case of Mississippi, it is probable they both voted for it. They would not have allowed it to pass without recording their opposition to it, if, in their understanding, it violated either the line properly dividing local from federal authority, or any provision of the Constitution.

In 1819-20, came and passed the Missouri question. Many votes were taken, by yeas and nays, in both branches of Congress, upon the various phases of the general question. Two of the "thirty-nine"—Rufus King and Charles Pinckney—were members of that Congress. Mr. King steadily voted for slavery prohibition and against all compromises, while Mr. Pinckney as steadily voted against slavery prohibition and against all compromises. By this, Mr. King showed that, in his understanding, no line dividing local from federal authority, nor anything in the Constitution, was violated by Congress prohibiting slavery in federal territory; while Mr. Pinckney, by his votes, showed that, in his understanding, there was some sufficient reason for opposing such prohibition in that case.

The cases I have mentioned are the only acts of the "thirty-nine," or of any of them, upon the direct issue, which I have been able to discover.

To enumerate the persons who thus acted, as being four in 1784, two in 1787, seventeen in 1789, three in 1798, two in 1804, and two in 1819-20—there would be thirty of them. But this would be counting John Langdon, Roger Sherman, William Few, Rufus King, and George Read, each twice, and Abraham Baldwin, three times. The true number of those of the "thirty-nine" whom I have shown to have acted upon the question, which, by the text, they understood better than we, is twenty-three, leaving sixteen not shown to have acted upon it in any way.

Here, then, we have twenty-three out of our thirty-nine fathers "who framed the Government under which we live," who have, upon their official responsibility and their corporal oaths, acted upon the very question which the test affirms they "understood just as well, and even better than we do now;" and twenty-one of them—a clear majority of the whole "thirty-nine"—so acting upon it as to make them guilty of gross political impropriety and wilful perjury, if, in their understanding, any proper division between local and federal authority, or anything in the Constitution they had made themselves, and sworn to support, forbade the Federal Government to control as to slavery in the federal territories. Thus the twenty-one acted; and, as actions speak louder than words, so actions, under such responsibility, speak still louder.

Two of the twenty-three voted against Congressional prohibition of slavery in the federal territories, in the instances in which they acted upon the question. But for what reasons they so voted is not known. They may have done so because they thought a proper division of local from federal authority, or some provision or principle of the Constitution, stood in the way; or they may, without any such question, have voted against the prohibition, on what appeared to them to be sufficient grounds of expediency. No one who has sworn to support the Constitution, can conscientiously vote for what he understands to be an unconstitutional measure, however expedient he may think it; but one may and ought to vote against a measure which he deems constitutional, if, at the same time, he deems it inexpedient. It, therefore, would be unsafe to set down even the two who voted against the prohibition, as having done so because, in their understanding, any proper division of local from federal authority, or anything in the Constitution, forbade the Federal Government to control as to slavery in federal territory.

The remaining sixteen of the "thirty-nine," so far as I have discovered, have left no record of their understanding upon the direct question of federal control of slavery in the federal territories. But there is much reason to believe that their understanding upon that question would not have appeared different from that of their twenty-three compeers, had it been manifested at all.

For the purpose of adhering rigidly to the text, I have purposely omitted whatever understanding may have been manifested by any person, however distinguished, other than the thirty-nine fathers who framed the original Constitution; and, for the same reason, I have also omitted whatever understanding may have been manifested by any of the "thirty-nine" even, on any other phase of the general question of slavery. If we should look into their acts and declarations on those other phases, as the foreign slave trade, and the morality and policy of slavery generally, it would appear to us that on the direct question of federal control of slavery in federal territories, the sixteen, if they had acted at all, would probably have acted just as the twenty-three did. Among that sixteen were several of the most noted anti-slavery men of those times—as Dr. Franklin, Alexander Hamilton and Gouverneur Morris—while there was not one now known to have been otherwise, unless it may be John Rutledge, of South Carolina.

The sum of the whole is, that of our thirty-nine fathers who framed the original Constitution, twenty-one—a clear majority of the whole—certainly understood that no proper division of local from federal authority, nor any part of the

Constitution, forbade the Federal Government to control slavery in the federal territories; while all the rest probably had the same understanding. Such, unquestionably, was the understanding of our fathers who framed the original Constitution; and the text affirms that they understood the question "better than we."

But, so far, I have been considering the understanding of the question manifested by the framers of the original Constitution. In and by the original instrument, a mode was provided for amending it; and, as I have already stated, the present frame of "the Government under which we live" consists of that original, and twelve amendatory articles framed and adopted since. Those who now insist that federal control of slavery in federal territories violates the Constitution, point us to the provisions which they suppose it thus violates; and, as I understand, they all fix upon provisions in these amendatory articles, and not in the original instrument. The Supreme Court, in the Dred Scott case, plant themselves upon the fifth amendment, which provides that no person shall be deprived of "life, liberty or property without due process of law;" while Senator Douglas and his peculiar adherents plant themselves upon the tenth amendment, providing that "the powers not delegated to the United States by the Constitution," "are reserved to the States respectively, or to the people."

Now, it so happens that these amendments were framed by the first Congress which sat under the Constitution—the identical Congress which passed the act already mentioned, enforcing the prohibition of slavery in the Northwestern Territory. Not only was it the same Congress, but they were the identical, same individual men who, at the same session, and at the same time within the session, had under consideration, and in progress toward maturity, these Constitutional amendments, and this act prohibiting slavery in all the territory the nation then owned. The Constitutional amendments were introduced before, and passed after the act enforcing the Ordinance of '87; so that, during the whole pendency of the act to enforce the Ordinance, the Constitutional amendments were also pending.

The seventy-six members of that Congress, including sixteen of the framers of the original Constitution, as before stated, were pre eminently our fathers who framed that part of "the Government under which we live," which is now claimed as forbidding the Federal Government to control slavery in the federal territories.

Is it not a little presumptuous in any one at this day to affirm that the two things which that Congress deliberately framed, and carried to maturity at the same time, are absolutely inconsistent with each other? And does not such affirmation become impudently absurd when coupled with the other affirmation from the same mouth, that those who did the two things, alleged to be inconsistent, understood whether they really were inconsistent better than we—better than he who affirms that they are inconsistent?

It is surely safe to assume that the thirty-nine framers of the original Constitution, and the seventy-six members of the Congress which framed the amendments thereto, taken together, do certainly include those who may be fairly called "our fathers who framed the Government under which we live." And so assuming, I defy any man to show that any one of them ever, in his whole life, declared that, in his understanding, any proper division of local from federal authority, or any part of the Constitution, forbade the Federal Government to control as to slavery in the federal territories. I go a step further. I defy any one to show that any living man in the whole world ever did, prior to the beginning of the present century, (and I might almost say prior to the beginning of the last half of the present century,) declare that, in his understanding, any proper division of local from federal authority, or any part of the Constitution, forbade the Federal Government to control as to slavery in the federal territories. To those who now so declare, I give, not only "our fathers who framed the Government under which we live," but with them all other living men within the century in which it was framed, among whom to search, and they shall not be able to find the evidence of a single man agreeing with them.

Now, and here, let me guard a little against being misunderstood. I do not mean to say we are bound to follow implicitly in whatever our fathers did. To do so, would be to discard all the lights of current experience—to reject all progress—all improvement. What I do say is, that if we would supplant the opinions and policy of our fathers in any case, we should do so upon evidence so conclusive, and argument so clear, that even their great authority, fairly considered and weighed, cannot stand; and most surely not in a case whereof we ourselves declare they understood the question better than we.

If any man at this day sincerely believes that a proper division of local from federal authority, or any part of the Constitution, forbids the Federal Government to control as to slavery in the federal territories, he is right to say so, and to enforce his position by all truthful evidence and fair argument which he can. But he has no right to mislead others, who have less access to history, and less leisure to study it, into the false belief that "our fathers, who framed the Government under which we live," were of the same opinion—thus substituting falsehood and deception for truthful evidence and fair argument. If any man at this day sincerely believes "our fathers who framed the Government under which we live," used and applied principles, in other cases, which ought to have led them to understand that a proper division of local from federal authority or some part of the Constitution, forbids the Federal Government to control as to slavery in the federal territories, he is right to say so. But he should, at the same time, brave the responsibility of declaring that, in his opinion, he understands their principles better than they did themselves; and especially should he not shirk that responsibility by asserting that they "understood the question just as well, and even better, than we do now."

But enough! *Let all who believe that "our fathers, who framed the Government under which we live, understood this question just as well, and even better, than we do now," speak as they spoke, and act as they acted upon it. This is all Republicans ask—all Republicans desire—in relation to slavery. As those fathers marked it, so let it be again marked, as an evil not to be extended, but to be tolerated and protected only because of and so far as its actual presence among us makes that toleration and protection a necessity. Let all the guaranties those fathers gave it, be, not grudgingly, but fully and fairly maintained.* For this Republicans contend, and with this, so far as I know or believe, they will be content.

And now, if they would listen—as I suppose they will not—I would address a few words to the Southern people.

I would say to them:—You consider yourselves a reasonable and a just people; and I consider that in the general qualities of reason and justice you are not inferior to any other people. Still, when you speak of us Republicans, you do so only to denounce us as reptiles, or, at the best, as no better than outlaws. You will grant a hearing to pirates or murderers, but nothing like it to "Black Republicans." In all your contentions with one another, each of you deems an unconditional condemnation of "Black Republicanism" as the first thing to be attended to. Indeed, such condemnation of us seems to be an indispensable prerequisite—license, so to speak—among you to be admitted or permitted to speak at all. Now, can you, or not, be prevailed upon to pause and to consider whether this is quite just to us, or even to yourselves? Bring forward your charges and specifications, and then be patient long enough to hear us deny or justify.

You say we are sectional. We deny it. That makes an issue; and the burden of proof is upon you. You produce your proof; and what is it? Why, that our party has no existence in your section—gets no votes in your section. The fact is substantially true; but does it prove the issue? If it does, then in case we should, without change of principle, begin to get votes in your section, we should thereby cease to be sectional. You cannot escape this conclusion; and yet, are you willing to abide by it? If you are, you will probably soon find that we have ceased to be sectional, for we shall get votes in your section this very year. You will then begin to discover, as the truth plainly is, that your proof does not touch the issue. The fact that we get no votes in your section, is a fact of your making, and not of ours. And if there be fault in that fact, that fault is primarily yours, and remains so until you show that we repel you by some wrong principle or practice. If we do repel you by any wrong principle or practice, the fault is ours; but this brings you to where you ought to have started—to a discussion of the right or wrong of our principle. If our principle, put in practice, would wrong your section for the benefit of ours, or for any other object, then our principle, and we with it, are sectional, and are justly opposed and denounced as such. Meet us, then, on the question of whether our principle, put in practice, would wrong your section; and so meet us as if it were possible that something may be said on our side. Do you accept the challenge? No! Then you really believe that the principle which "our fathers who framed the Government under which we live" thought so clearly right as to adopt it, and indorse it again and again, upon their official oaths, is in fact so clearly wrong as to demand your condemnation without a moment's consideration.

Some of you delight to flaunt in our faces the warning against sectional parties given by Washington in his Farewell Address. Less than eight years before Washington gave that warning, he had, as President of the United States, approved and signed an act of Congress, enforcing the prohibition of slavery in the Northwestern Territory, which act embodied the policy of the Government upon that subject up to and at the very moment he penned that warning; and about one year after he penned it, he wrote La Fayette that he considered that prohibition a wise measure, expressing in the same connection his hope that we should at some time have a confederacy of free States.

Bearing this in mind, and seeing that sectionalism has since arisen upon this same subject, is that warning a weapon in your hands against us, or in our hands against you? Could Washington himself speak, would he cast the blame of that sectionalism upon us, who sustain his policy, or upon you who repudiate it? We respect that warning of Washington, and we commend it to you, together with his example pointing to the right application of it.

But you say you are conservative—eminently conservative—while we are revolutionary, destructive, or something of the sort. What is conservatism? Is it not adherence to the old and tried, against the new and untried? We stick to, contend for, the identical old policy on the point in controversy which was adopted by "our fathers who framed the Government under which we live;" while you with one accord reject, and scout, and spit upon that old policy, and insist upon substituting something new. True, you disagree among yourselves as to what that substitute shall be. You are divided on new propositions and plans, but you are unanimous in rejecting and denouncing the old policy of the fathers. Some of you are for reviving the foreign slave trade; some for a Congressional Slave-Code for the Territories; some for Congress forbidding the Territories to prohibit Slavery within their limits; some for maintaining Slavery in the Territories through the judiciary; some for the "gur-reat pur-rinciple" that "if one man would enslave another, no third man should object," fantastically called "Popular Sovereignty;" but never a man among you in favor of federal prohibition of slavery in federal territories, according to the practice of "our fathers who framed the Government under which we live." Not one of all your various plans can show a precedent or an advocate in the century within which our Government originated. Consider, then, whether your claim of conservatism for yourselves, and your charge of destructiveness against us, are based on the most clear and stable foundations.

Again, you say we have made the slavery question more prominent than it formerly was. We deny it. We admit that it is more prominent, but we deny that we made it so. It was not we, but you, who discarded the old policy of the fathers. We resisted, and still resist, your innovation; and thence comes the greater prominence of the question. Would you have that question reduced to its former proportions? Go back to that old policy. What has been will be again, under the same conditions. If you would have the peace of the old times, readopt the precepts and policy of the old times.

You charge that we stir up insurrections among your slaves. We deny it; and what is your proof? Harper's Ferry! John Brown!! John Brown was no Republican; and you have failed to implicate a single Republican in his Harper's Ferry enterprise. If any member of our party is guilty in that matter, you know it or you do not know it. If you do know it, you are inexcusable for not designating the man and proving the fact. If you do not know it, you are inexcusable for asserting it, and especially for persisting in the assertion after you have tried and failed to make the proof. You need not be told that persisting in a charge which one does not know to be true, is simply malicious slander.

Some of you admit that no Republican designedly aided or encouraged the Harper's Ferry affair; but still insist that our doctrines and declarations necessarily lead to such results. We do not believe it. We know we hold to no doctrine, and make no declaration, which were not held to and made by "our fathers who framed the Government under which we live." You never dealt fairly by us in relation to this affair. When it occurred, some important State elections were near at hand, and you were in evident glee with the belief that, by charging the blame upon us, you could get an advantage of us in those elections. The elections came, and your expectations were not quite fulfilled. Every Republican man knew that, as to himself at least, your charge was a slander, and he was not much inclined by it to cast his vote in your favor. Republican doctrines and declarations are accompanied with a continual protest against any interference whatever with your slaves, or with you about your slaves. Surely, this does not encourage them to revolt. True, we do, in common with "our fathers, who framed the Government under which we live," declare our belief that slavery is wrong; but the slaves do not hear us declare even this. For anything we say or do, the slaves would scarcely know there is a Republican party. I believe they would not, in fact, generally know it but for your misrepresentations of us, in their hearing. In your political contests among yourselves, each faction charges the other with sympathy with Black Republicanism; and then, to give point to the charge, defines Black Republicanism to simply be insurrection, blood and thunder among the slaves.

Slave insurrections are no more common now than they were before the Republican party was organized. What induced the Southampton insurrection, twenty-eight years ago, in which, at least, three times as many lives were lost as at Harper's Ferry? You can scarcely stretch your very elastic fancy to the conclusion that Southampton was "got up by Black Republicanism." In the present state of things in the United States, I do not think a general, or even a very extensive slave insurrection, is possible. The indispensable concert of action cannot be attained. The slaves have no means of rapid communication; nor can incendiary freemen, black or white, supply it. The explosive materials are everywhere in parcels; but there neither are, nor can be supplied, the indispensable connecting trains.

Much is said by Southern people about the affection of slaves for their masters and mistresses; and a part of it, at least, is true. A plot for an uprising could scarcely be devised and communicated to twenty individuals before some one of them, to save the life of a favorite master or mistress, would divulge it. This is the rule; and the slave revolution in Hayti was not an exception to it, but a case occurring under peculiar circumstances. The gunpowder plot of British history, though not connected with slaves, was more in point. In that case, only about twenty were admitted to the secret; and yet one of them, in his anxiety to save a friend, betrayed the plot to that friend, and, by consequence, averted the calamity. Occasional poisonings from the kitchen, and open or stealthy assassinations in the field, and local revolts extending to a score or so, will continue to occur as the natural results of slavery; but no general insurrection of slaves, as I think, can happen in this country for a long time. Whoever much fears, or much hopes for such an event, will be alike disappointed.

In the language of Mr. Jefferson, uttered many years ago, "It is still in our power to direct the process of emancipation, and deportation, peaceably, and in such slow degrees, as that the evil will wear off insensibly; and their places be, *pari passu*, filled up by free white laborers. If, on the contrary, it is left to force itself on, human nature must shudder at the prospect held up."

Mr. Jefferson did not mean to say, nor do I, that the power of emancipation is in the Federal Government. He spoke of Virginia; and, as to the power of emancipation, I speak of the slaveholding States only. The Federal Government, however, as we insist, has the power of restraining the extension of the institution—the power to insure that a slave insurrection shall never occur on any American soil which is now free from slavery.

John Brown's effort was peculiar. It was not a slave insurrection. It was an attempt by white men to get up a revolt among slaves, in which the slaves refused to participate. In fact, it was so absurd that the slaves, with all their ignorance, saw plainly enough it could not succeed. That affair, in its philosophy, corresponds with the many attempts, related in history, at the assassination of kings and emperors. An enthusiast broods over the oppression of a people till he fancies himself commissioned by Heaven to liberate them. He ventures the attempt, which ends in little else than his own execution. Orsini's attempt on Louis Napoleon, and John Brown's attempt at Harper's Ferry were, in their philosophy, precisely the same. The eagerness to cast blame on old England in the one case, and on New England in the other, does not disprove the sameness of the two things.

And how much would it avail you, if you could, by the use of John Brown, Helper's Book, and the like, break up the Republican organization? Human action can be modified to some extent, but human nature cannot be changed. There is a judgment and a feeling against slavery in this nation, which cast at least a million and a half of votes. You cannot destroy that judgment and feeling—that sentiment—by breaking up the political organization which rallies around it. You can scarcely scatter and disperse an army which has been formed into order in the face of your heaviest fire; but if you could, how much would you gain by forcing the sentiment which created it out of the peaceful channel of the ballot-box, into some other channel? What would that other channel probably be? Would the number of John Browns be lessened or enlarged by the operation?

But you will break up the Union rather than submit to a denial of your Constitutional rights.

That has a somewhat reckless sound, but it would be palliated, if not fully justified, were we proposing, by the mere force of numbers, to deprive you of some right, plainly written down in the Constitution. But we are proposing no such thing.

When you make these declarations, you have a specific and well-understood allusion to an assumed Constitutional right of yours, to take slaves into the federal territories, and to hold them there as property. But no such right is specifically written in the Constitution. That instrument is literally silent about any such right. We, on the contrary, deny that such a right has any existence in the Constitution, even by implication.

Your purpose, then, plainly stated, is, that you will destroy the Government, unless you be allowed to construe and enforce the Constitution as you please, on all points in dispute between you and us. You will rule or ruin in all events.

This, plainly stated, is your language. Perhaps you will say the Supreme Court has decided the disputed Constitutional question in your favor. Not quite so. But waiving the lawyer's distinction between dictum and decision, the Court have decided the question for you in a sort of way. The Court have substantially said, it is your Constitutional right to take slaves into the federal territories, and to hold them there as property. When I say the decision was made in a sort of way, I mean it was made in a divided Court, by a bare majority of the Judges, and they not quite agreeing with one another in the reasons for making it; that it is so made as that its avowed supporters disagree with one another about its meaning, and that it was mainly based upon a mistaken statement of fact—the statement in the opinion that "the right of property in a slave is distinctly and expressly affirmed in the Constitution."

An inspection of the Constitution will show that the right of property in a slave is not "*distinctly* and *expressly* affirmed" in it. Bear in mind, the Judges do not pledge their judicial opinion that such right is *impliedly* affirmed in the Constitution; but they pledge their veracity that it is "*distinctly* and *expressly*" affirmed there— "distinctly," that is, not mingled with anything else—"expressly," that is, in words meaning just that, without the aid of any inference, and susceptible of no other meaning.

If they had only pledged their judicial opinion that such right is affirmed in the instrument by implication, it would be open to others to show that neither the word "slave" nor "slavery" is to be found in the Constitution, nor the word "property" even, in any connection with language alluding to the things slave, or slavery, and that wherever in that instrument the slave is alluded to, he is called a "person;"—and wherever his master's legal right in relation to him is alluded to, it is spoken of as "service or labor which may be due,"—as a debt payable in service or labor. Also, it would be open to show, by contemporaneous history, that this mode of alluding to slaves and slavery, instead of speaking of them, was employed on purpose to exclude from the Constitution the idea that there could be property in man.

To show all this, is easy and certain.

When this obvious mistake of the Judges shall be brought to their notice, it is not reasonable to expect that they will withdraw the mistaken statement, and reconsider the conclusion based upon it?

And then it is to be remembered that "our fathers, who framed the Government under which we live"—the men who made the Constitution—decided this same Constitutional question in our favor, long ago—decided it without division among themselves, when making the decision; without division among themselves about the meaning of it after it was made, and, so far as any evidence is left, without basing it upon any mistaken statement of facts.

Under all these circumstances, do you really feel yourselves justified to break up this Government, unless such a court decision as yours is, shall be at once submitted to as a conclusive and final rule of political action? But you will not abide the election of a Republican President! In that supposed event, you say, you will destroy the Union; and then, you say, the great crime of having destroyed it will be upon us! That is cool. A highwayman holds a pistol to my ear, and mutters through his teeth, "Stand and deliver, or I shall kill you, and then you will be a murderer!"

To be sure, what the robber demanded of me—my money—was my own; and I had a clear right to keep it; but it was no more my own than my vote is my own; and the threat of death to me, to extort my money, and the threat of destruction to the Union, to extort my vote, can scarcely be distinguished in principle.

A few words now to Republicans. *It is exceedingly desirable that all parts of this great Confederacy shall be at peace, and in harmony, one with another. Let us Republicans do our part to have it so. Even though much provoked, let us do nothing through passion and ill temper. Even though the southern people will not so much as listen to us, let us calmly consider their demands, and yield to them if, in our deliberate view of our duty, we possibly can.* Judging by all they say and do, and by the subject and nature of their controversy with us, let us determine, if we can, what will satisfy them.

Will they be satisfied if the Territories be unconditionally surrendered to them? We know they will not. In all their present complaints against us, the Territories are scarcely mentioned. Invasions and insurrections are the rage now. Will it satisfy them, if, in the future, we have nothing to do with invasions and insurrections? We know it will not. We so know, because we know we never had anything to do with invasions and insurrections; and yet this total abstaining does not exempt us from the charge and the denunciation.

The question recurs, what will satisfy them? Simply this: We must not only let them alone, but we must, somehow, convince them that we do let them alone. This, we know by experience, is no easy task. We have been so trying to convince them from the very beginning of our organization, but with no success. In all our platforms and speeches we have constantly protested our purpose to let them alone; but this has had no tendency to convince them. Alike unavailing to convince them, is the fact that they have never detected a man of us in any attempt to disturb them.

These natural, and apparently adequate means all failing, what will convince them? This, and this only: cease to call slavery *wrong*, and join them in calling it *right*. And this must be done thoroughly—done in *acts* as well as in *words*. Silence will not be tolerated—we must place ourselves avowedly with them. Senator Douglas's new sedition law must be enacted and enforced, suppressing all declarations that slavery is wrong, whether made in politics, in presses, in pulpits, or in private. We must arrest and return their fugitive slaves with greedy pleasure. We must pull down our Free State constitutions. The whole atmosphere must be disinfected from all taint of opposition to slavery, before they will cease to believe that all their troubles proceed from us.

I am quite aware they do not state their case precisely in this way. Most of them would probably say to us, "Let us alone, *do* nothing to us, and *say* what you please about slavery." But we do let them alone—have never disturbed them—so that, after all, it is what we say, which dissatisfies them. They will continue to accuse us of doing, until we cease saying.

I am also aware they have not, as yet, in terms, demanded the overthrow of our Free-State Constitutions. Yet those Constitutions declare the wrong of slavery, with more solemn emphasis, than do all other sayings against it; and when all these other sayings shall have been silenced, the overthrow of these Constitutions will be demanded, and nothing be left to resist the demand. It is nothing to the contrary, that they do not demand the whole of this just now. Demanding what they do, and for the reason they do, they can voluntarily stop nowhere short of this consummation. Holding, as they do, that slavery is morally right, and socially elevating, they cannot cease to demand a full national recognition of it, as a legal right, and a social blessing.

Nor can we justifiably withhold this, on any ground save our conviction that slavery is wrong. If slavery is right, all words, acts, laws, and constitutions against it, are themselves wrong, and should be silenced, and swept away. If it is right, we cannot justly object to its nationality—its universality; if it is wrong, they cannot justly insist upon its extension—its enlargement. All they ask, we could readily grant, if we thought slavery right; all we ask, they could as readily grant, if they thought it wrong. Their thinking it right, and our thinking it wrong, is the precise fact upon which depends the whole controversy. Thinking it right, as they do, they are not to blame for desiring its full recognition, as being right; but, thinking it wrong, as we do, can we yield to them? Can we cast our votes with their view, and against our own? In view of our moral, social, and political responsibilities, can we do this?

Wrong as we think slavery is, we can yet afford to let it alone where it is, because that much is due to the necessity arising from its actual presence in the nation; but can we, while our votes will prevent it, allow it to spread into the National Territories, and to overrun us here in these Free States? If our sense of duty forbids this, then let us stand by our duty, fearless and effectively. Let us be diverted by none of those sophistical contrivances wherewith we are so industriously plied and belabored—contrivances such as groping for some middle ground between the right and the wrong, vain as the search for a man who should be neither a living man nor a dead man—such as a policy of "don't care" on a question about which all true men do care—such as Union appeals beseeching true Union men to yield to Disunionists, reversing the divine rule, and calling, not the sinners, but the righteous to repentence—such as invocations to Washington, imploring men to unsay what Washington said, and undo what Washington did.

Neither let us be slandered from our duty by false accusations against us, nor frightened from it by menaces of destruction to the Government nor of dungeons to ourselves. *Let us have faith that right makes might, and in that faith, let us, to the end, dare to do our duty as we understand it.*

Abraham Lincoln was a unique presidential candidate in many respects, but nothing was more unique and interesting than the fact that what he actually said had so much to do with his selection as a candidate and his later election to office. Some candidates have disparaged such speeches as mere "campaign oratory," but in Lincoln's case his preconvention and preelection words marked out the course upon which the serious people in the nation made the most important decision in its history. His words were carefully chosen and spoken with calm assurance. They succeeded in raising the issue above the din of confusing voices abroad in the land to present the alternatives in clear and unambiguous language. No one has described this contribution more accurately than Herbert Croly:

> Lincoln's peculiar service to his countrymen before the war was that of seeing straighter and thinking harder than did his contemporaries. No doubt he must needs have courage, also, for in the beginning he acted against the advice of his Republican associates. But in 1858 there were plenty of men who had the courage, whereas there were very few who had Lincoln's disciplined intelligence and his just and penetrating insight.

Lincoln's vision placed every aspect of the situation in its proper relations; and he was as fully competent to detect the logical weakness of his opponent's position as he was to explain his own lucidly, candidly, and persuasively. It so happened that the body of public opinion which he particularly addressed was that very part of the American democracy most likely to be deluded into allowing the Southern leaders to have their will, yet whose adhesion to the national cause was necessary to the preservation of the Union. It was into this mass of public opinion, after the announcement of his senatorial candidacy, that he hammered a new and a hard truth. He was the first responsible politician to draw the logical inference from the policy of the Republican party. The Constitution was inadequate to cure the ills it generated. By its authorization of slavery it established an institution whose legality did not prevent it from being anti-national. That institution must either be gradually reduced to insignificance, or else it must transform and take possession of the American national idea. The Union had become a house divided against itself; and this deep-lying division could not be bridged merely by loyal Constitutionalism or by an anti-national interpretation of democracy. The legal Union was being threatened precisely because American national integrity was being gutted by an undemocratic institution. The house must either fall or else cease to be divided. Thus for the first time it was clearly proclaimed by a responsible politician that American nationality was a living principle rather than a legal bond; and Lincoln's service to his country in making the Western Democracy understand that living Americans were responsible for their national integrity can scarcely be over-valued. The ground was cut from under the traditional point of view of the pioneer—which had been to feel patriotic and national, but to plan and to agitate only for the fulfillment of local and individual ends.

The virtue of Lincoln's attitude may seem to be as much a matter of character as of intelligence; and such, indeed, is undoubtedly the case. My point is, not that Lincoln's greatness was more a matter of intellect than of will, but that he rendered to his country a peculiar service, because his luminous and disciplined intelligence and his national outlook enabled him to give each aspect of a complicated and confused situation its proper relative emphasis.[137]

As early as his famous "House Divided" speech in Springfield, followed by his debates with Stephen Douglas and the Cooper Institute speech in New York, Abraham Lincoln clearly defined the issue between North and South upon which the presidential campaign of 1860 was to be fought and won. For all of his personal distaste of slavery, Lincoln maintained that the issue was not the existence of slavery in the southern states, but rather its extension into the new states and territories. The two major sections of the country took their stands on this question, and by 1860 the issue had evolved to center upon whether or not the South would remain a part of the Union if the North's position on the extension of slavery prevailed. At that point the question was largely one of principle because, realistically, the expansion of slavery into the free territories was not economically or politically feasible. The real issue was southern political power within the Union. If the South lost control of the presidency, its fate would be sealed, allowing for the inevitable transformation of territories into non-slave states, which would reduce its power in the Congress and ultimately render it subject to majority rule. Southerners believed that such an eventuality threatened the foundations of their society, and they were willing to fight to prevent it.

Between Lincoln's election and his inauguration six of the southern states withdrew from the Union. The slavery question took its place in the background, for the issue clearly became whether or not the Union was to survive. In his great inaugural address of 1861, Lincoln made this fact crystal clear, and although he inclined towards moderation and had an earnest desire to avoid bloodshed, he also insisted that he would carry out his duty to uphold the Constitution and the basic laws of the land. He sought to explain to the South that their basic rights were not in jeopardy, that even their ancient social institutions remained protected under law and they they had nothing to fear from the constitutional rule of the people. Yet he insisted that the Union would defend itself and maintain its laws under threat of violent attack. On the whole, it was an eloquent and a conciliatory address, firm in its principles, and yet magnanimous and even gentle in its bearing and style.

President Abraham Lincoln
First Inaugural Address
March 4, 1861

Basler, IV, 262-71.

Fellow citizens of the United States:
   In compliance with a custom as old as the government itself, I appear before you to address you briefly, and to take, in your presence, the oath prescribed by the Constitution of the United States, to be taken by the President "before he enters on the execution of his office."

   I do not consider it necessary, at present, for me to discuss those matters of administration about which there is no special anxiety, or excitement.

   Apprehension seems to exist among the people of the Southern States, that by the accession of a Republican Administration, their property, and their peace, and personal security, are to be endangered. There has never been any reasonable cause for such apprehension. Indeed, the most ample evidence to the contrary has all the while existed, and been open to their inspection. It is found in nearly all the published speeches of him who now addresses you. I do but quote from one of those speeches when I declare that "I have no purpose, directly or indirectly, to interfere with the institution of slavery in the States where it exists. I believe I have no lawful right to do so, and I have no inclination to do so." Those who nominated and elected me did so with full knowledge that I had made this, and many similar declarations, and had never recanted them. And more than this, they placed in the platform, for

322

my acceptance, and as a law to themselves, and to me, the clear and emphatic resolution which I now read:

"*Resolved,* That the maintenance inviolate of the rights of the States, and especially the right of each State to order and control its own domestic institutions according to its own judgment exclusively, is essential to that balance of power on which the perfection and endurance of our political fabric depend; and we denounce the lawless invasion by armed force of the soil of any State or Territory, no matter under what pretext, as among the gravest of crimes."

I now reiterate these sentiments: and in doing so, I only press upon the public attention the most conclusive evidence of which the case is susceptible, that the property, peace and security of no section are to be in anywise endangered by the now incoming Administration. I add too, that all the protection which, consistently with the Constitution and the laws, can be given, will be cheerfully given to all the States when lawfully demanded, for whatever cause—as cheerfully to one section, as to another.

There is much controversy about the delivering up of fugitives from service or labor. The clause I now read is as plainly written in the Constitution as any other of its provisions:

"No person held to service or labor in one State, under the laws thereof, escaping into another, shall, in consequence of any law or regulation therein, be discharged from such service or labor, but shall be delivered up on claim of the party to whom such service or labor may be due."

It is scarcely questioned that this provision was intended by those who made it, for the reclaiming of what we call fugitive slaves; and the intention of the law-giver is the law. All members of Congress swear their support to the whole Constitution—to this provision as much as to any other. To the proposition, then, that slaves whose cases come within the terms of this clause, "shall be delivered up," their oaths are unanimous. Now, if they would make the effort in good temper, could they not, with nearly equal unanimity, frame and pass a law, by means of which to keep good that unanimous oath?

There is some difference of opinion whether this clause should be enforced by national or by state authority; but surely that difference is not a very material one. If the slave is to be surrendered, it can be of but little consequence to him, or to others, by which authority it is done. And should any one, in any case, be content that his oath shall go unkept, on a merely unsubstantial controversy as to *how* it shall be kept?

Again, in any law upon this subject, ought not all the safeguards of liberty known in civilized and humane jurisprudence to be introduced, so that a free man be not, in any case, surrendered as a slave? And might it not be well, at the same time, to provide by law for the enforcement of that clause in the Constitution which guarranties that "The citizens of each State shall be entitled to all privileges and immunities of citizens in the several States?"

I take the official oath to-day, with no mental reservations, and with no purpose to construe the Constitution or laws, by any hypercritical rules. And while I do not choose now to specify particular acts of Congress as proper to be enforced, I do suggest, that it will be much safer for all, both in official and private stations, to conform to, and abide by, all those acts which stand unrepealed, than to violate any of them, trusting to find impunity in having them to be unconstitutional.

It is seventy-two years since the first inauguration of a President under our national Constitution. During that period fifteen different and greatly distinguished citizens, have, in succession, administered the executive branch of the government. They have conducted it through many perils; and, generally, with great success. Yet, with all this scope for precedent, I now enter upon the same task for the brief constitutional term of four years, under great and peculiar difficulty. A disruption of the Federal Union heretofore only menaced, is now formidably attempted.

I hold, that in contemplation of universal law, and of the Constitution, the Union of these States is perpetual. Perpetuity is implied, if not expressed, in the fundamental law of all national governments. It is safe to assert that no government proper, ever had a provision in its organic law for its own termination. Continue to execute all the express provisions of our national Constitution, and the Union will endure forever—it being impossible to destroy it, except by some action not provided for in the instrument itself.

Again, if the United States be not a government proper, but an association of States in the nature of contract merely, can it, as a contract, be peaceably unmade, by less than all the parties who made it? One party to a contract may violate it—break it, so to speak; but does it not require all to lawfully recind it?

Descending from these general principles, we find the proposition that, in legal contemplation, the Union is perpetual, confirmed by the history of the Union itself. The Union is much older than the Constitution. It was formed in fact, by the Articles of Association in 1774. It was matured and continued by the Declaration of Independence in 1776. It was further matured and the faith of all the then thirteen States expressly plighted and engaged that it should be perpetual, by the Articles of Confederation in 1778. And finally, in 1787, one of the declared objects for ordaining and establishing the Constitution, was "*to form a more perfect union.*"

But if destruction of the Union, by one, or by a part only, of the States, be lawfully possible, the Union is *less* perfect than before the Constitution, having lost the vital element of perpetuity.

It follows from these views that no State, upon its own mere motion, can lawfully get out of the Union,—that *resolves* and *ordinances* to that effect are legally void; and that acts of violence, within any State or States, against the authority of the United States, are insurrectionary or revolutionary, according to circumstances.

I therefore consider that, in view of the Constitution and the laws, the Union is unbroken; and, to the extent of my ability, I shall take care, as the Constitution itself expressly enjoins upon me, that the laws of the Union be faithfully executed in all the States. Doing this I deem to be only a simple duty on my part; and I shall perform it, so far as practicable, unless my rightful masters, the American people, shall withhold the requisite means, or, in some authoritative manner, direct the contrary. I trust this will not be regarded as a menace, but only as the declared purpose of the Union that it *will* constitutionally defend, and maintain itself.

In doing this there needs to be no bloodshed or violence; and there shall be none, unless it be forced upon the national authority. The power confided to me, will be used to hold, occupy, and possess the property, and places belonging to the government, and to collect the duties and imposts; but beyond what may be necessary for these objects, there will be no invasion—no using of force against, or among the people anywhere. Where hostility to the United States, in any interior locality, shall be so great and so universal, as to prevent competent resident citizens from holding the Federal offices, there will be no attempt to force obnoxious strangers among the people for that object. While the strict legal right may exist in the government to enforce the exercise of these offices, the attempt to do so would be so irritating, and so nearly impracticable with all, that I deem it better to forego, for the time, the uses of such offices.

The mails, unless repelled, will continue to be furnished in all parts of the Union. So far as possible, the people everywhere shall have that sense of perfect security which is most favorable to calm thought and reflection. The course here indicated will be followed, unless current events, and experience, shall show a modification, or change, to be proper; and in every case and exigency, my best discretion will be exercised, according to circumstances actually existing, and with a view and a hope of a peaceful solution of the national troubles, and the restoration of fraternal sympathies and affections.

That there are persons in one section, or another who seek to destroy the Union at all events, and are glad of any pretext to do it, I will neither affirm or deny; but if there be such, I need address no word to them. To those, however, who really love the Union, may I not speak?

Before entering upon so grave a matter as the destruction of our national fabric, with all its benefits, its memories, and its hopes, would it not be wise to ascertain precisely why we do it? Will you hazard so desperate a step, while there is any possibility that any portion of the ills you fly from, have no real existence? Will you, while the certain ills you fly to, are greater than all the real ones you fly from? You will risk the commission of so fearful a mistake?

All profess to be content in the Union, if all constitutional rights can be maintained. It is true, then, that any right, plainly written in the Constitution, has been denied? I think not. Happily the human mind is so constituted, that no party can reach to the audacity of doing this. Think, if you can, of a single instance in which a plainly written provision of the Constitution has ever been denied. If, by the mere force of numbers, a majority should deprive a minority of any clearly written constitutional right, it might, in a moral point of view, justify revolution—certainly would, if such right were a vital one. But such is not our case. All the vital rights of minorities, and of individuals, are so plainly assured to them, by affirmations and negations, guarranties and prohibitions, in the Constitution, that controversies never arise concerning them. But no organic law can ever be framed with a provision specifically applicable to every question which may occur in practical administration. No foresight can anticipate, nor any document of reasonable length contain express provisions for all possible questions. Shall fugitives from labor be surrendered by national or by State authority? The Constitution does not expressly say. *May* Congress prohibit slavery in the territories? The Constitution does not expressly say. *Must* Congress protect slavery in the territories? The Constitution does not expressly say.

From questions of this class spring all our constitutional controversies, and we divide upon them into majorities and minorities. If the minority will not acquiesce, the majority must, or the government must cease. There is no other alternative; for continuing the government, is acquiescence on one side or the other. If a minority, in such case, will secede rather than acquiesce, they make a precedent which, in turn, will divide and ruin them; for a minority of their own will secede from them, whenever a majority refuses to be controlled by such minority. For instance, why may not any portion of a new confederacy, a year or two hence, arbitrarily secede again, precisely as portions of the present Union now claim to secede from it. All who cherish disunion sentiments, are now being educated to the exact temper of doing this. Is there such perfect identity of interests among the States to compose a new Union, as to produce harmony only, and prevent renewed secession?

Plainly, the central idea of secession, is the essence of anarchy. A majority, held in restraint by constitutional checks, and limitations, and always changing easily, with deliberate changes of popular opinions and sentiments, is the only true sovereign of a free people. Whoever rejects it, does, of necessity, fly to anarchy or to despotism. Unanimity is impossible; the rule of a minority, as a permanent arrangement, is wholly inadmissable; so that, rejecting the majority principle, anarchy, or despotism in some form, is all that is left.

I do not forget the position assumed by some, that constitutional questions are to be decided by the Supreme Court; nor do I deny that such decisions must be binding in any case, upon the parties to a suit, as to the object of that suit, while they are also entitled to very high respect and consideration, in all paralel cases, by all other departments of the government. And while it is obviously possible that such decision may be erroneous in any given case, still the evil effect following it, being limited to that particular case, with the chance that it may be over-ruled, and never became a precedent for other cases, can better be borne than could the evils of a different practice. At the same time the candid citizen must confess that if the policy of the government, upon vital questions, affecting the whole people, is to be irrevocably fixed by decisions of the Supreme Court, the instant they are made, in ordinary litigation between parties, in personal actions, the people will have ceased, to be their own rulers, having, to that extent, practically resigned their government, into the hands of that eminent tribunal. Nor is there, in this view, any assault upon the court, or the judges. It is a duty, from which they may not shrink, to decide cases properly brought before them; and it is no fault of theirs, if others seek to turn their decisions to political purposes.

One section of our country believes slavery is *right*, and ought to be extended, while the other believes it is *wrong*, and ought not to be extended. This is the only substantial dispute. The fugitive slave clause of the Constitution, and the law for the suppression of the foreign slave trade, are each as well enforced, perhaps, as any law can ever be in a community where the moral sense of the people imperfectly supports the law itself. The great body of the people abide by the dry legal obligation in both cases, and a few break over in each. This, I think, cannot be perfectly cured; and it would be worse in both cases *after* the separation of the sections, than before. The foreign slave trade, now imperfectly suppressed, would be ultimately revived without restriction, in one section; while fugitive slaves, now only partially surrendered, would not be surrendered at all, by the other.

Physically speaking, we cannot separate. We cannot remove our respective sections from each other, nor build an impassable wall between them. A husband and wife may be divorced, and go out of the presence, and beyond the reach of each other; but the different parts of our country cannot do this. They cannot but remain face to face; and intercourse, either amicable or hostile, must continue between them. Is it possible then to make that intercourse more advantageous, or more satisfactory, *after* separation then *before*? Can aliens make treaties easier than friends can make laws? Can treaties be more faithfully enforced between aliens, than laws can among friends? Suppose you go to war, you cannot fight always; and when, after much loss on both sides, and no gain on either, you cease fighting, the identical old questions, as to terms of intercourse, are again upon you.

This country, with its institutions, belongs to the people who inhabit it. Whenever they shall grow weary of the existing government, they can exercise their *constitutional* right of amending it, or their *revolutionary* right to dismember, or overthrow it. I can not be ignorant of the fact that many worthy, and patriotic citizens are desirous of having the national constitution amended. While I make no recommendation of amendments, I fully recognize the rightful authority of the people over the whole subject, to be exercised in either of the modes prescribed in the instrument itself; and I should, under existing circumstances, favor, rather than oppose, a fair opportunity being afforded the people to act upon it.

I will venture to add that, to me, the convention mode seems preferable, in that it allows amendments to originate with the people themselves, instead of only permitting them to take, or reject, propositions, originated by others, not especially chosen for the purpose, and which might not be precisely such, as they would wish to either accept or refuse. I understand a proposed amendment to the Constitution—which amendment, however, I have not seen, has passed Congress, to the effect that the federal government, shall never interfere with the domestic institutions of the States, including that of persons held to service. To avoid misconstruction of what I have said, I depart from my purpose not to speak of particular amendments, so far as to say that, holding such a provision to now be implied constitutional law, I have no objection to its being made express, and irrevocable.

The Chief Magistrate derives all his authority from the people, and they have conferred none upon him to fix terms for the separation of the States. The people themselves can do this also if they choose; but the executive, as such, has nothing to do with it. His duty is to administer the present government, as it came to his hands, and to transmit it, unimpaired by him, to his successor.

Why should there not be a patient confidence in the ultimate justice of the people? Is there any better, or equal hope, in the world? In our present differences, is either party without faith of being in the right? If the Almighty Ruler of nations, with his eternal truth and justice, be on your side of the North, or on yours of the South, that truth, and that justice, will surely prevail, by the judgment of this great tribunal, the American people.

By the frame of the government under which we live, this same people have wisely given their public servants but little power for mischief; and have, with equal wisdom, provided for the return of that little to their own hands at very short intervals.

While the people retain their virtue, and vigilence, no administration, by any extreme of wickedness or folly, can very seriously injure the government, in the short space of four years.

My countrymen, one and all, think calmly and *well*, upon this whole subject. Nothing valuable can be lost by taking time. If there be an object to *hurry* any of you, in hot haste, to a step which you would never take *deliberately*, that object will be frustrated by taking time; but no good object can be frustrated by it. Such of you as are now dissatisfied, still have the old Constitution unimpaired, and, on the sensitive point, the laws of your own framing under it; while the new administration will have no immediate power, if it would, to change either. If it were admitted that you who are dissatisfied, hold the right side in the dispute, there still is no single good reason for precipitate action. Intelligence, patriotism, Christianity, and a firm reliance on Him, who has never yet forsaken this favored land, are still competent to adjust, in the best way, all our present difficulty.

In *your* hands, my dissatisfied fellow countrymen, and not in *mine*, is the momentous issue of civil war. The government will not assail *you*. You can have no conflict, without being yourselves the aggressors. *You* have no oath registered in Heaven to destroy the government, while *I* shall have the most solemn one to "preserve, protect and defend" it.

I am loth to close. We are not enemies, but friends, We must not be enemies. Though passion may have strained, it must not break our bonds of affection. The mystic chords of memory, streching from every battle-field, and patriot grave, to every living heart and hearthstone, all over this broad land, will yet swell the chorus of the Union, when again touched, as surely they will be, by the better angels of our nature.

The inaugural speech did not move or persuade those in power in the southern states. The national crisis escalated in the following weeks. Lincoln promised in his speech not to impose obnoxious federal officials from outside upon the recalcitrant states and communities where pressures prevented local citizens from maintaining federal offices. And yet the President insisted that the federal government would hold and occupy "the property, and places belonging to the government, and to collect the duties and imposts"[138] belonging to the government. What seemed to be a mild enough assertion by a supposedly powerful central government became the immediate cause of the war when the citizens of South Carolina forced Major Anderson at Fort Sumter to yield to superior forces. Civil war then became a reality with Lincoln's executive proclamations calling forth the militia to suppress the revolt and carry out the laws. Subsequent proclamations called for a blockade of southern ports, the conscription of thousands of volunteers and other emergency actions which seemed essential to the President as he acted to uphold the Constitution and the laws in his capacity as Commander in Chief.

President Abraham Lincoln
Proclamation Calling Forth the Militia
April 15, 1861

Richardson, VII, 3214-15.

Whereas the laws of the United States have been for some time past and now are opposed and the execution thereof obstructed in the States of South Carolina, Georgia, Alabama, Florida, Mississippi, Louisiana, and Texas by combinations too powerful to be suppressed by the ordinary course of judicial proceedings or by the powers vested in the marshals by law:

Now, therefore, I, Abraham Lincoln, President of the United States, in virtue of the power in me vested by the Constitution and the laws, have thought fit to call forth, and hereby do call forth, the militia of the several States of the Union to the aggregate number of 75,000, in order to suppress said combinations and to cause the laws to be duly executed.

The details for this object will be immediately communicated to the State authorities through the War Department.

I appeal to all loyal citizens to favor, facilitate, and aid this effort to maintain the honor, the integrity, and the existence of our National Union and the perpetuity of popular government and to redress wrongs already long enough endured.

I deem it proper to say that the first service assigned to the forces hereby called forth will probably be to repossess the forts, places, and property which have been seized from the Union; and in every event the utmost care will be observed, consistently with the objects aforesaid, to avoid any devastation, any destruction of or interference with property, or any disturbance of peaceful citizens in any part of the country.

And I hereby command the persons composing the combinations aforesaid to disperse and retire peaceably to their respective abodes within twenty days from this date.

Deeming that the present condition of public affairs presents an extraordinary occasion, I do hereby, in virtue of the power in me vested by the Constitution, convene both Houses of Congress. Senators and Representatives are therefore summoned to assemble at their respective chambers at 12 o'clock noon on Thursday, the 4th day of July next, then and there to consider and determine such measures as, in their wisdom, the public safety and interest may seem to demand.

In witness whereof I have hereunto set my hand and caused the seal of the United States to be affixed.

Done at the city of Washington, this 15th day of April, A. D. 1861, and of the Independence of the United States the eighty-fifth.

Abraham Lincoln

By the President:
  William H. Seward, *Secretary of State*

President Abraham Lincoln
Blockade of Southern Ports Proclamation
April 19, 1861

Richardson, VII, 3215-16.

Whereas an insurrection against the Government of the United States has broken out in the States of South Carolina, Georgia, Alabama, Florida, Mississippi, Louisiana, and Texas, and the laws of the United States for the collection of the revenue can not be effectually executed therein conformably to that provision of the Constitution which requires duties to be uniform throughout the United States; and

Whereas a combination of persons engaged in such insurrection have threatened to grant pretended letters of marque to authorize the bearers thereof to commit assaults on the lives, vessels, and property of good citizens of the country lawfully engaged in commerce on the high seas and in waters of the United States; and

Whereas an Executive proclamation has been already issued requiring the persons engaged in these disorderly proceedings to desist therefrom, calling out a militia force for the purpose of repressing the same, and convening Congress in extraordinary session to deliberate and determine thereon:

Now, therefore, I, Abraham Lincoln, President of the United States, with a view to the same purposes before mentioned and to the protection of the public peace and the lives and property of quiet and orderly citizens pursuing their lawful occupations, until Congress shall have assembled and deliberated on the said unlawful proceedings or until the same shall have ceased, have further deemed it advisable to set on foot a blockade of the ports within the States aforesaid, in pursuance of the laws of the United States and of the law of nations in such case provided. For this purpose a competent force will be posted so as to prevent entrance and exit of vessels from the ports aforesaid. If, therefore, with a view to violate such blockade, a vessel shall approach or shall attempt to leave either of the said ports, she will be duly warned by the commander of one of the blockading vessels, who will indorse on her register the fact and date of such warning, and if the same vessel shall again attempt to enter or leave the blockaded port she will be captured and sent to the nearest convenient port for such proceedings against her and her cargo as prize as may be deemed advisable.

And I hereby proclaim and declare that if any person, under the pretended authority of the said States or under any other pretense, shall molest a vessel of the United States or the persons or cargo on board of her, such person will be held amenable to the laws of the United States for the prevention and punishment of piracy.

In witness whereof I have hereunto set my hand and caused the seal of the United States to be affixed.

Done at the city of Washington, this 19th day of April, A. D. 1861, and of the Independence of the United States the eighty-fifth.

Abraham Lincoln

By the President:
　　William H. Seward, *Secretary of State*

President Abraham Lincoln
Proclamation Extending Southern Port Blockade
April 27, 1861

Richardson, VII, 3216.

Whereas, for the reasons assigned in my proclamation of the 19th instant, a blockade of the ports of the States of South Carolina, Georgia, Florida, Alabama, Louisiana, Mississippi, and Texas was ordered to be established; and

Whereas since that date public property of the United States has been seized, the collection of the revenue obstructed, and duly commissioned officers of the United States, while engaged in executing the orders of their superiors, have been arrested and held in custody as prisoners or have been impeded in the discharge of their official duties, without due legal process, by persons claiming to act under authorities of the States of Virginia and North Carolina, an efficient blockade of the ports of those States will also be established.

In witness whereof I have hereunto set my hand and caused the seal of the United States to be affixed.

Done at the city of Washington, this 27th day of April, A. D. 1861, and of the Independence of the United States the eighty-fifth.

Abraham Lincoln

By the President:
　　William H. Seward, *Secretary of State*

President Abraham Lincoln
Proclamation Calling Up Volunteers
May 3, 1861

Richardson, VII, 3216-17.

Whereas existing exigencies demand immediate and adequate measures for the protection of the National Constitution and the preservation of the National Union by the suppression of the insurrectionary combinations now existing in several States for opposing the laws of the Union and obstructing the execution thereof, to which end a military force in addition to that called forth by my proclamation of the 15th day of April in the present year appears to be indispensably necessary:

Now, therefore, I, Abraham Lincoln, President of the United States and Commander in Chief of the Army and Navy thereof and of the militia of the several States when called into actual service, do hereby call into the service of the United States 42,034 volunteers to serve for the period of three years, unless sooner discharged, and to be mustered into service as infantry and cavalry. The proportions of each arm and the details of enrollment and organization will be made known through the Department of War.

And I also direct that the Regular Army of the United States be increased by the addition of eight regiments of infantry, one regiment of cavalry, and one regiment of artillery, making altogether a maximum aggregate increase of 22,714 officers and enlisted men, the details of which increase will also be made known through the Department of War.

And I further direct the enlistment for not less than one or more than three years of 18,000 seamen, in addition to the present force, for the naval service of the United States. The details of the enlistment and organization will be made known through the Department of the Navy.

The call for volunteers hereby made and the direction for the increase of the Regular Army and for the enlistment of seamen hereby given, together with the plan of organization adopted for the volunteer and for the regular forces hereby authorized, will be submitted to Congress as soon as assembled.

In the meantime I earnestly invoke the cooperation of all good citizens in the measures hereby adopted for the effectual suppression of unlawful violence, for the impartial enforcement of constitutional laws, and for the speediest possible restoration of peace and order, and with these of happiness and prosperity, throughout our country.

In testimony whereof I have hereunto set my hand and caused the seal of the United States to be affixed.

Done at the city of Washington, this 3d day of May, A.D. 1861, and of the Independence of the United States the eighty-fifth.

Abraham Lincoln

By the President:
William H. Seward, *Secretary of State*

Lincoln reasoned that the actions of the southern rebels justified his full use of the war powers to suppress their rebellion. There was substantial constitutional theory, if not precedent, to support such a decision, and fortunately his actions were soon challenged in the courts in *The Prize Cases*, [139] so there is on record a Supreme Court decision which weighed the constitutionality of the authority thus claimed to resist the ultimate challenge to the laws of the Union.

Long before the Civil War, in Martin v. Mott (1827), the Court tackled the problem of interpreting the constitutional and statutory power of the President to determine when he was justified in using the militia to preserve the peace when threatened with internal insurrection or foreign invasion. The basis of the reasoning in the decision went back to the section of the Constitution which declared that Congress shall have the power "to provide for calling forth the militia to execute the laws of the Union, suppress insurrections and repel invasions." Congress responded to this grant of power by the act of May 2, 1792, amended in 1795 and 1807, which authorized the President to call out the militia to repel an invasion, or to aid a state in suppressing domestic violence. The question in Martin v. Mott was whether the President had the authority to make that decision when such circumstances existed, or as Justice Story put it:

> Is the President the sole and exclusive judge whether the exigency has arisen? . . . We are all of the opinion that the authority to decide whether the exigency has arisen, belongs exclusively to the President, and that his decision is conclusive upon all other persons. . . . The power itself is to be exercised upon sudden emergencies, upon great occasions of state and under circumstances which may be vital to the existence of the Union. . . . The power itself is confined to the Executive of the Union, to him who is, by the Constitution "the commander in chief of the militia when called into the actual service of the United States" whose duty it is to "take care that the laws be faithfully executed," and whose responsibility for an honest discharge of his official obligations is secured by the highest sanctions. . . . Whenever a statute gives a discretionary power to any person, to be exercised by him upon his own opinion of certain facts, it is a sound rule of construction that the statute constitutes him the sole and exclusive judge of the existence of those facts.[140]

In view of this decision, the challenge to Lincoln in *The Prize Cases* had to be very skillfully drawn. It was initiated by merchants who had suffered losses when their ships and cargoes were confiscated after the President's declaration of a blockade. The plaintiffs did not question the right of the President to act to suppress the rebellion, but they did question the nature of his action, which they alleged could only be executed by the President after a legal war had been declared by Congress. Since in this instance no war had been declared, they charged that the proclamation of a blockade of southern ports and the confiscation of booty in execution of that order were illegal acts.

The Court handed down its decision in 1863, while the war was still being fought, and its endorsement of the "war powers" of the Commander in Chief greatly strengthened the President's prestige and authority to act in emergencies without specific legislative authorization. "If a war be made by invasion of a foreign nation," Justice Grier declared,

> the President is not only authorized but bound to resist force, by force. He does not initiate the war, but is bound to accept the challenge without waiting for any special legislative authority. And whether the hostile party be a foreign invader, or states organized in rebellion, it is none the less a

war, although the declaration of it be unilateral. . . . "He must determine what degree of force the crisis demands."[141]

This decision has stood for more than 100 years without any further serious challenges or modifications by later courts. Mr. Lincoln took his stand, and history passed judgment in the affirmative.

Commander in Chief of the Armed Forces

Polk Sets the Pattern for Dynamic Leadership

The country had to wait until the administration of James K. Polk for a President who would bring both energy and direction to the war powers of the presidency. As Leonard White put It: "He proved that a president could run a war."[142] Before setting out for his inauguration in Washington, Polk told an old friend "that I hoped my friends in Congress and elsewhere would suffer me to conduct the War with Mexico as I thought proper, and not plan the campaign for me & without consulting me."[143] When he became President he saw to it that these expectations were fulfilled. White has written that Polk exercised the responsibility for the conduct of the war "to the limit of his endurance."

> He determined the general strategy of military and naval operations; he chose commanding officers; he gave personal attention to supply problems; he energized so far as he could the General Staff; he controlled the military and naval estimates; and he used the cabinet as a major coordinating agency for the conduct of the campaign. . . . The President was the center on which all else depended; Hamilton's doctrine of the unity of the executive power was seldom more truly exemplified.[144]

Polk's diary reveals how seriously he took all these responsibilities. His confidence in his own judgment remained unruffled in the face of opposition, and, within the limits of the situation and the personnel he inherited, he made the decisions and bore the responsibility for them. The results were not uniformly good, and major errors were made, yet the clear line of responsibility tended at least to clarify the problem and to make corrections much more possible.

Polk was above all a political man, right down to his finger tips—a House of Representatives man at that—and he could sniff out a political maneuver even if it were taking place thousands of miles from the capital. From the beginning he was terribly suspicious of the Commanding General of the Army, Winfield Scott. Scott had covered himself with glory in the War of 1812, when military heroes were at a premium, and, by virtue of both seniority and experience under fire, was the logical candidate to head up the campaign against Mexico. But Polk was extremely wary of Scott's very clear political ambitions, and for that reason he kept this very able general bottled up in Washington during the early part of the war.

Scott was far from blameless, for indeed he did aspire to the nomination for the presidency on the opposition party ticket, and he too was suspicious, oversensitive and quarrelsome with the President and his party. He contributed to his own internment in Washington by writing to the secretary of war explaining his objections to assuming command of the American army on the Mexican frontier. He was so distrustful of the administration that he concluded his letter with the now famous passage:

> My explicit meaning is, that I do not desire to place myself in the most perilous of all positions, a fire upon my rear from Washington and the fire in front from the Mexicans.[145]

Polk commented upon his irritation over Scott's indiscretion in an entry in his diary, dated Saturday, May 23, 1846.

President James K. Polk
Diary Entry Reporting a Cabinet
Discussion of General Winfield
Scott's Political Intransigence
May 23, 1846

Quaife, I, 419-21.

I read to the Cabinet a letter addressed by Gen'l Winfield Scott to the Secretary of War dated 21st Instant, which had been communicated to me by the Secretary on the day it bears date. (See this diary of the 21st & 22nd Instant.) This letter of Gen'l Scott is foolish, & vindictive toward the administration. Without the slightest reason for it Gen'l Scott makes base and false insinuations in reference to the administration, as connected with the command of the army on the Mexican frontier, which I had on the commencement of hostilities requested him to assume. He uses language not only exceptionable but unbecoming an officer. After making false insinuations against the administration, he concludes by using the following language, viz.: "My explicit meaning is, that I do not desire to place myself in the most perilous of all positions, a fire upon my rear from Washington and the fire in front from the Mexicans." I repeat this insinuation is wholly false, and proves, as I think, two things; 1st, that Gen'l Scott seeks a pretext to avoid going to the Del Norte to take command of our army, and 2nd, that his partisan feelings are such that he is unfit to be intrusted with the command. The only reason assigned for making such an insinuation is that in an interview with the Secretary of War a few days ago he had expressed the opinion which he repeats in this letter, that operations on the Del Norte under the late act of Congress authorizing a call for volunteers could not commence before the 1st of September, to which the Secretary had informed him that I wished prompt action, and that the delay proposed was unnecessary. This is what Gen'l Scott calls "a fire upon my rear from Washington." The facts are that war has been declared against Mexico, twenty thousand volunteers have been called out to take the field as soon as possible, I had designated Gen'l Scott solely because he was commander-in-chief of the Army, to take the command; I desired a prompt and energetic movement; whereas Gen'l Scott was in favour of remaining in Washington and not assuming the command before the 1st of September. This as far as I know is the sole cause of his extraordinary & vindictive letter. I submitted to the Cabinet the impropriety, with this letter before us, of continuing him [in] the command. The subject was discussed, the Secretary of the Treasury expressing a decided opinion that he ought not to be intrusted with the command. I expressed the opinion that the administration could not have any confidence in him & that I could not feel safe if he took the command of the army, & said that if I could find any other officer who was qualified, my opinion was that Gen'l Scott should be superseded & such officer assigned to the command.

Polk lost no time in asserting his ideas on the way the war should be fought. Two days after war was officially declared by the Congress, Polk outlined what the immediate strategy of the American army should be. He proposed that they march "a competent force into the northern provinces and seize and hold them until peace was made."[146] He got backing for this plan from the secretary of war and the Commanding General of the Army (Scott) on the spot, and two days later he received the approval of the cabinet. This basic plan was pursued successfully for the remainder of the war, placing the United States in an advantageous position in the peace negotiations, for it already occupied the land it wanted Mexico to cede to it. In his diary Polk recorded these events.

President James K. Polk
Diary Entry Relating his Confrontation
With General Scott on the War
May 14, 1846

Quaife, I, 400-01.

I was exceedingly engaged; members of the Cabinet and members of Congress were calling at short intervals during the whole day. The exciting topic was the War with Mexico, and the raising of troops to prosecute the war.

At 8 O'Clock P.M. the Secretary of War and Gen'l Scott of the U.S. Army called.

I had a long conference with them concerning the plan of conducting the war with Mexico. I gave it as my opinion that the first movement should be to march a competent force into the Northern Provinces and seize and hold them until peace was made. In this they concurred. The whole field of operations was examined with all the information before us, but it would be tedious to detail all the views and the reasons for them which were expressed.

It was agreed to call out immediately for service 20,000 volunteers, and we proceeded to apportion this force among the States of Texas, Arkansas, Illinois, Missouri, Ohio, Indiana, Kentucky, Tennessee, Alabama, Mississippi, & Georgia. After very full examination of the subject the Secretary of War & General Scott retired between 11 & 12 O'Clock P. M. Gen'l Scott did not impress me favourably as a military man. He has had experience in his profession, but I thought was rather scientific and visionary in his views. I did not think that so many as 20,000 volunteers besides the regular army was necessary, but I did not express this opinion, not being willing to take the responsibility of any failure of the campaign by refusing to grant to Gen'l Scott all he asked.

When this plan failed to crush Mexican resistance, Polk developed a further master plan for the war: an attack upon the port of Vera Cruz and a subsequent offensive into the heart of the country to capture the capital, Mexico City. His friend Senator Benton heartily concurred with the plans. After much agonizing debate and hesitation, Polk finally put General Scott in command of the invasion force.

Polk had become disillusioned with his commander in the field, General Zachary Taylor (referred to by his men as "Ole Rough an' Ready," which was an apt description of the old Indian fighter's sloppy attire and the way he slouched in his saddle, as compared to the spit-and-polish West Pointer, Scott, who was called "Old Fuss an' Feathers"). The President thought that Taylor, too, had begun to indicate political aspirations of his own, and he had also crossed swords with Polk on matters of command on several occasions.

Convinced that Taylor was incompetent and utterly incapable of commanding the total operation, and, distrusting Scott, he wanted to make his friend, Senator Benton from Missouri, a lieutenant general who would outrank both Scott and Taylor and could assume overall command of the army. But Polk was a realist, and he knew that neither the Senate nor the army would stand for that. Finally and quite reluctantly he put Scott in full field command of the army, in charge of the attack upon Mexico City via Vera Cruz. Although Polk was not happy with this resolution of the commanding problem, it was the best decision he could have made, while utilizing the considerable military talents of both Scott and Taylor to their best advantage. Again his diary entries reflected the mood and the activity of those times.

President James K. Polk
Diary Entry (Extract) Suggesting
The Invasion of Vera Cruz
August 29, 1846

Quaife, II, 104.

I next brought up the plan of conducting the War, in the event peace should not be made before the setting in of the healthy season (say in November next) and suggested the importance of taking Vera Cruz by a land force to be landed out of reach of the fortress, who could invest the town of Vera Cruz in the rear and by cooperating with the blockading squadron by sea, and submitted whether by these means the Fortress of San juan de Ulloa would not be compelled to surrender for want of supplies in a very few days. I suggested further that if this could be done the fortress after surrendering could be dismantled and blown up, and that our troops on land might then march on the City of Mexico. These suggestions met with a favourable consideration in the Cabinet. The propriety of taking Tampico was also considered, and the impression of all was that it should be done if peace was not made before the healthy season set in.

President James K. Polk
Diary Entries on the High
Politics of Planning a War
November 1846

Quaife, II, 226-32.

Tuesday, November 10, 1846

Before the Cabinet assembled Col. Benton called, as I had requested him to do on yesterday. The subject of the Mexican war was resumed. Col. B. repeated the views which he had before expressed, but more in detail & enforced them. I told him if the movement on the City of Mexico was made, it would be necessary to call out a considerable number of additional troops. I had before informed him of the orders which had been issued for the contemplated expedition against Tampico and possibly Vera Cruz, but a movement on the City of Mexico had not been at present contemplated, nor unless it was ascertained that peace could not be obtained without it. He said that a small force could, he had no doubt, in co-operation with the Navy, starve out or take the town of Vera Cruz, and with it would fall the Castle, but that would not bring peace unless it was followed with a large force on the City of Mexico. I told him I apprehended from all I had learned that Gen'l Taylor would not willingly spare any considerable portion of the force with him at Monterey, & that I apprehended he would not heartily co-operate with the Government in carrying into effect such an expedition unless he commanded it himself, and that I thought Gen'l Taylor a brave officer but not a man of capacity enough for such a command. In this he concurred. I asked who would be the proper officer to command so important an expedition. He did not answer. I spoke of Gen'l Scott. He said he had no confidence in him. Some other officers were named by me. He then said there ought to be a Lieutenant General of the army who should be General in chief. He said it required a man of talents and resources as well as a military man for such a command, & that with a view to obtain peace more depended upon the talents & energy of the officer than upon mere bravery. He then said that if such an office was created by Congress, he would be willing to accept the command himself. I remarked Generally that I would have confidence in him and would be pleased to see him at the head of the army in such an expedition. He alluded to what was apparent to every one, that the Whigs were endeavouring to turn this war to party & political account. He said "I have been looking at events as they have transpired this summer, & left Kentucky where I have spent some weeks and returned to Washington to render you any aid in my power. He said, You know what my position has been (alluding as I inferred to his preference for Mr. Van Buren in the last Presidential election) but let By-gones be by-gones. I quarrelled & fought with Gen'l Jackson; I made friends with him & came to his support, and during the gloomy period of the Bank panic, I have held many consultations with him in this room. Now I will give you any support in this war in my power." I expressed my gratification at hearing these sentiments and said frankly to him that I had never entertained any but the most [cordial] feelings for him.

After much further conversation in relation to the war he left. Shortly afterwards the Cabinet assembled. The chief topic of conversation to-day was the Mexican war and Col. Benton's views of the manner of conducting it, which I communicated to the Cabinet, of course in the confidence which belongs to all Cabinet consultations.

No distinct question was presented for a decision but the views of the different gentlemen were freely expressed. The general impression seemed to be that it would be necessary to call out additional troops with a view to the successful prosecution of the campaign against Vera Cruz, & especially if an expedition against the City of Mexico was resolved upon. No answer had been received from Gen'l Taylor to the despatch of the Secretary of War of the 22nd of September, and it was deemed prudent before any decision was made in regard to the future course of the campaign to await his answer which must undoubtedly be received soon. Mr. Buchanan was in favour of taking Vera Cruz, but disinclined to favour the expedition against the City of Mexico. After much conversation on the subject, & in relation to the state of the finances & the probability of obtaining a loan, the Cabinet adjourned.

This was reception evening. A larger number of persons attended, ladies & gentlemen, than usually do; among them was Col. Benton & his daughter, Mrs. Fremont. The Secretary of War called & informed me that he had received by to-night's [mail] despatches from Gen'l Taylor. Before the company dispersed, I retired to my office with the Secretary of War, and he read the despatches. They were dated from the 6th to the 13th of October inclusive. They contained no satisfactory information upon the points on which Gen'l Taylor had been asked for information in the Secretary's despatch to him of the 22nd of September. The truth is, from my private letters from Gen'l Pillow and from information from other sources, I apprehend that Gen'l Taylor's feelings are anything but friendly to the Executive Government. He is, I fear, disposed to cast all responsibility off himself, and not heartily to co-operate with the Government in prosecuting the war. He has no sympathies for the administration and cares only for himself. This is most reprehensible on his part for I have not only treated [him] with great kindness, but have given him his present promotion. I have known nothing of politics in my treatment of him, but I am forced to believe that he has been recently much influenced by Balie Peyton and other political partisans, and has suffered his bitter political feeling to have much more to do with his conduct that he should have done. I form this conclusion from several sources of information, but refer particularly to my private letters from Mr. Robert B. Reynolds and Gen'l Pillow.

Wednesday, November 11, 1846

. . . Col. Benton called on me to-night at my request. I had a still further conversation with him in relation to the Mexican war. I told him I did not think it probable that Congress would create the office of Lieutenant General which he had suggested on yesterday. He said he thought himself it was doubtful. After speaking about the propriety of calling out an increased force, I told him that in that event I might appoint an additional Maj'r Gen'l. He said that if I did so the General appointed would be the junior officer of his rank, and he would not desire it. I remarked to him that I had supposed he would not desire it, and that in addition to this I had come under some commitment to Gen'l Houston of Texas, if another Maj'r Gen'l was to be appointed. I told him that if the commission to treat for peace, which he had suggested in a former conversation should accompany the army, should be created, it would give me pleasure to place him at the head of that commission. He said if it was settled that a large force was to march from Vera Cruz on the City of Mexico he would accept, for then it would be important & there would be dignity in it. I told him that the inclination of my mind was to call for eight additional Regiments, with a view to the bold movement which he had suggested, & that in the course of to-morrow I would probably decide. I read to him Gen'l Taylor's last despatch & also all the orders & communications which had been sent to him relating to the contemplated expeditions against Tampico & Vera Cruz. He agreed with me that Gen'l Taylor's answer was unsatisfactory & that he was unfit for command. After much further conversation of a free and friendly character he retired.

Saturday, November 14, 1846

. . . The Cabinet fully discussed the conduct of Gen'l Taylor and were agreed that he was unfit for the chief command, that he had not mind enough for the station, that he was a bitter political partisan & had no sympathies with the administration, and that he had been recently controlled, particularly in his expedition to Monterey, by Balie Peyton, Mr. Kendall, Editor of the *Picayune* at New Orleans, and ass't adjutant Gen'l Bliss, who were cunning & shrewd men of more talents than himself, and had controlled him for political purposes. I expressed my deep regret that I was compelled from all the information I had received to come to this conclusion. I stated, what all the Cabinet knew, that I had never suffered politics to mingle with the conduct of this war; that I had promoted Gen'l Taylor & treated him very kindly & given him my confidence as chief in command of the army, but that I was compelled to believe that he had been weak enough to suffer himself to be controlled by political partisans, who had no command in the army, but had attached themselves to it & had attended his camp for political purposes. All were at a loss to designate who should be the chief in command in the expedition against Vera Cruz. I suggested Maj'r Gen'l Butler of the Volunteers, & I think him the best man. Nothing upon this point was decided.

Tuesday, November 17, 1846

Col. Benton called this morning before the meeting of the Cabinet, and held a conversation with me in relation to his plan of the campaign against Mexico, an outline of which he had communicated to me in writing last evening.

The Cabinet met at the usual hour, all the members present. The Mexican war occupied exclusive attention to-day. I read to the Cabinet Col. Benton's plan of the campaign as communicated to me last night. The Secretary of War read a written memorandum from Gen'l Scott giving a statement of the forces now in Mexico, and of the additional forces and preparations which in his opinion would be necessary to make an attack on the City of Vera Cruz and march to the City of Mexico. The force he proposed was about 14,000, and the whole plan was upon a large scale. Much conversation took place on the subject. It had been heretofore resolved to take Vera Cruz if practicable, but it had not been resolved to march from that point on the City of Mexico. In the discussion Mr. Buchanan seemed to consider that such was the determination, and expressed his opinion strongly against it, but remarked that as he was overruled he would have to acquiesce. Mr. Marcy remarked to him that he had not been overruled, for as he understood it no decision had been made by the President and the Cabinet, that he had read Gen'l Scott's plan, but the subject was one for consideration, not yet decided upon. Mr. Buchanan said he was decidedly in favour of taking Vera Cruz but was against marching upon the City of Mexico. Among other reasons which he assigned and he gave them at some length, he remarked that he had not yet seen the budget and did not know where the money was to come from. It being resolved upon to send an expedition to take Verz Cruz, I myself considered it an open question, to be determined according to circumstances hereafter, whether a column should be sent from Vera Cruz against the City of Mexico. If peace should not be made I am decidedly in favour of taking the City of Mexico if we have sufficient force in the field to do it. Great difficulty existed in selecting the commander of the expedition against Vera Cruz. In Gen'l Taylor a want of confidence was expressed in his capacity, while it was known that he had suffered his partisan political feelings to render himself hostile to the administration. His constant effort has been to throw the responsibility of any disaster which might happen on the administration. In this he has been most ungrateful for the kindness which he has received at my hands. All agreed that he was unfit, after what had occurred, for the command of the expedition against Vera Cruz. The difficulty was in selecting a proper officer. Maj'r Gen'l Patterson of the Volunteers, who had been named for the Tampico expedition, it was feared had not sufficient experience. Gen'l Scott it [was known] was hostile to the administration, and it was apprehended would have no sympathy with it in carrying out its plans. After much discussion Mr. Buchanan, Mr. Walker, Mr. Marcy, & Mr. Mason, although all of them had serious objections to him, yet came to the conclusion that as he was the highest officer in command in the army, he should be entrusted with the conduct of this important expedition. Mr. Johnson was opposed to him, and Mr. Clifford was inclined to be so, but expressed no decided opinion. After a long conversation I informed the Cabinet that I would think further on the subject before I decided. I have strong objections to Gen'l Scott, and after his very exceptionable letter in May last nothing but stern necessity and a sense of public duty could induce me to place him at the head of so important expedition. Still I do not well see how it can be avoided. He is the Gen'l-in-chief of the army. If I had the power to select a Gen'l I would select Col. Benton to conduct the expedition. Without coming to any decision the Cabinet adjourned.

Wednesday, November 18, 1846

I sent for the Secretary of War this morning, & held a further conversation with him in regard to the officer to be selected to command the expedition to Vera Cruz. He said he had had great anxiety and trouble about it, but upon full reflection, although he would do so reluctantly, he thought we would be compelled to take Gen'l Scott. After some further conversation I requested him to call on Col. Benton & confer with him confidentially on the subject. He left and returned in the course of an hour & reported that he had seen Col. Benton, who thought as he did, that we would have to use the instruments which the law had given, and under all the circumstances we would, he thought, be compelled to take Gen'l Scott. I was not still [still not] satisfied, & told the Secretary that I would send for Col. Benton & see him on the subject myself. I sent my Private Secretary to invite Col. Benton to see me. Col. B. called, and upon a full view of the whole subject he advised that Gen'l Scott be assigned to the command as the best we could do, although he had no confidence in him. I told Col. Benton I must yield my objections to Gen'l Scott, & would see the Secretary and direct that he be ordered to take the command of the expedition to Vera Cruz. I told Col. Benton that if I could induce Congress to create the officer of Lieut. Gen'l I would appoint him to command the whole forces. He said he would take such a command.

I was busily occupied until night preparing my message. After night upon my invitation the Secretary of the Navy called, & I read to him the part of my message which related to the Mexican war & the tariff. The Secretary of War came in, and I informed him of the result of my interview to-day with Col. Benton. The Secretary of War said that he had thought over the matter in every possible aspect and he was fully satisfied that we would be compelled to take Gen'l Scott for the command against Vera Cruz. The Secretary of the Navy concurred in this opinion. They advised me to send for Gen'l Scott & see him myself in the morning. I requested the Secretary of War to ask him to call on to-morrow at 9 O'Clock A.M. I have no great confidence in Gen'l Scott as a military commander, and after his very exceptionable letter of May last to the Secretary of War, it is with reluctance that I assign him to this important command. If I had the power I would certainly select some other, but I am compelled to use the officers provided by law, and under all the circumstances feel constrained to assign him to this command. He is the highest in command in the regular army and it is his natural position.

Thursday, November 19, 1846

Gen'l Scott called this morning, having been invited by the Secretary of War, as requested by me on yesterday, to do so. I held a long conversation with him as to the plan of prosecuting the Mexican War. I finally said to him that the capture of Vera Cruz was very important to secure peace. To this he assented. I then told him that it was important that the officer entrusted to command that expedition should have confidence in the Government, and that the Government should have confidence in him, and that without a cordial cooperation success could scarcely be expected. To this he agreed. I then intimated to him that if I was satisfied that he had the proper confidence in the administration & would cordially cooperate with it, that I was disposed to assign him to the command. He appeared to be much affected and said at once that he had the utmost confidence in the administration & in myself, and that he would cordially cooperate with me in carrying out my views in the prosecution of the war. He said that he surrendered his whole confidence to me. I then told him that I had at the commencement of the War given him my confidence and had tendered him the command, but that circumstances had occurred to change my determination. I was willing that by-gones should be by-gones & that he should take the command. He expressed himself as being deeply grateful to me & said he would show me his gratitude by his conduct when he got to the field. He was so grateful & so much affected that he almost shed tears. He then said that he would take with him any of the Volunteer Generals whom I might indicate, and asked me to suggest such as I wished to accompany him. I told him that was a delicate matter, and that all I could do was to give him, as it was my duty to do, the character & qualifications of such of them as I knew personally. I told him that the only three of them with whom I was intimately acquainted were Brigadier Gen'ls Pillow, Hamer, & Shields, and I gave him such information as I possessed in regard to each of them. I spoke also of Maj'r Gen'ls Butler & Patterson, whom I knew, but not intimately. I expressed a high opinion of Gen'l Butler. I requested him to prepare a statement of the forces now in Mexico, and inform me what portion of them he would propose to take with him on the Vera Cruz expedition & what corps he would leave under the command of Gen'l Taylor. He said he would do so as soon as he could prepare it. He left, apparently the most delighted man I have seen for a long time, and as he retired expressed his deep gratitude to me.

In addition to his strong control and direction of the military commanders during the entire course of the war, Polk made other important contributions to the role of the President as Commander in Chief. He concerned himself with the everyday details of keeping an army in the field, and consulted frequently with the quartermaster general and others responsible for moving material and men to the front. He constantly rode herd over the army leaders and War Department bureau chiefs, struggling against procrastination and extravagance in their activities. One of his more famous investigations revealed, much to his annoyance, that the army had been purchasing horses and mules in Ohio for use in Mexico at four times the price for which they were available in Mexico.

Of greater lasting importance, however, was Polk's initiative in involving the Chief Executive directly in the military budgeting process. Prior to Polk's administration the President had no responsibility for the budget estimates submitted to Congress by the War Department (or, for that matter, any of the other departments). All of that changed under Polk. Even before the Mexican War he had advised his department heads to examine carefully the various estimates submitted to them by bureau chiefs and to reduce their budget estimates as much as possible. In 1846 the question of department estimates for the 1847 budget came up in a cabinet meeting, and the original estimate submitted by the War Department was considerably revised. In the 1848 War Department budget, Polk discovered that his secretary of war had not even reviewed his bureau chiefs' estimates, as he had been instructed. The President immediately sat down with the paymaster general and commissary general and convinced them that significant reductions could be made. The quartermaster general alone was able to reassure President Polk the following day that he reduced his estimates by almost seven million dollars in a total War Department estimate of some sixty millions. Polk was able to encourage comparable reductions based upon executive review in the Navy Department. It would take another century before these procedures of budgetary review were completely rationalized under executive control, but James Polk was the first President to demonstrate that it not only should, but could, be done.

Despite errors of individual judgment on the part of the Commander in Chief and his subordinates, the war with Mexico was won in a record period of time, thanks to several bold military strokes conceived by the President acting as Commander in Chief and executed brilliantly by his controversial but effective military subordinates. Regardless of judgments of the propriety or justification of the war itself, the United States gained a great deal in the peace treaty with Mexico. All in all, when Polk's wartime experience is compared with that of his only wartime predecessor, James Madison, it is quite obvious that the presidential war powers emerged from his hands greatly enlarged and more clearly defined than ever before.

But lest we assume it was a state of developed coordination and military planning familiar today and quite unknown in that period, Polk records an incident in his diary that ought to quickly disabuse us of that notion. At a cabinet meeting shortly after the landing at Vera Cruz, it was revealed that General Scott's invasion force had received little or no naval support because the secretary of war had failed to inform the secretary of the navy of the time and plans for the invasion. Pearl Harbor was not the first instance in American military and naval history of the total breakdown of communication between the two services.